Human Rights in Iran

Pennsylvania Studies in Human Rights

Bert B. Lockwood, Jr., Series Editor

A complete list of books in the series
is available from the publisher.

Human Rights in Iran

The Abuse of Cultural Relativism

REZA AFSHARI

PENN

University of Pennsylvania Press

Philadelphia

10 9 8 7 6 5 4 3 2 1

Published by
University of Pennsylvania Press
Philadelphia, Pennsylvania 19104-4011

Library of Congress Cataloging-in-Publication Data
Afshari, Reza.
Human rights in Iran : the abuse of cultural relativism /
Reza Afshari.
p. cm.—(Pennsylvania studies in human rights)
Includes bibliographical references and index.
ISBN 0-8122-3605-X (cloth : alk. paper)
1. Human rights—Iran.
I. Title.   II. Series.
JC599.I65 A38   2001
323'.0955 21   2001033037

To the memory of my father Ali Afshari,
secular educator and my first teacher

Contents

A Note on Transliteration   xiii

Preface   xv

Human Rights Discourse   xv
Main Sources Used in This Book   xvii
UN Reports   xvii
Prison Memoirs and Their Significance   xviii
The Structure of the Book   xxi

Chapter 1. Islamic Cultural Relativism in Human Rights Discourse   1

Political Culture: Assuming the Failure of Secularization   1
The Islamic Republic Claims Cultural Exceptionalism   3
The Mirage of Cultural Authenticity   8
The Irrelevance of Cultural Relativism   10

Chapter 2. The Shiite Theocracy   14

Institutionalizing the Shiite Theocracy: *Velayat-e Faqih*   15
Ruling the Contemporary State: The Limits of Islamic Law   19
Islamization of Society   20
Political Context of Human Rights Violations During the 1980s   22
Political Context of Human Rights Violations During the 1990s   23
The Two Faces of the Religious State Under President Rafsanjani   25
Muhammad Khatami's Presidency Since 1997   29

Chapter 3. The Right to Life   33

Through the Prism of Prison Memoirs   33
Monitoring Violations: The International Community During the 1980s   38

Monitoring Violations: The International Community During the
1990s   38
Executions for Drug Trafficking and Moral Crimes   40
Extrajudicial Murders Outside Iran   42

Chapter 4. The Right to Freedom from Torture   46

Through the Prism of Prison Memoirs   46
Monitoring Violations: The International Community During the
1980s   52
Monitoring Violations: The International Community During the
1990s   53

Chapter 5. The Right to Liberty and Security of Person and to Freedom
from Arbitrary Arrest   57

Through the Prism of Prison Memoirs   57
Monitoring Violations: The International Community During the
1980s   61
Monitoring Violations: The International Community During the
1990s   62
Insecurity in Public Spaces and Private Homes   64

Chapter 6. The Right to a Fair Trial   68

Through the Prism of Prison Memoirs   69
Monitoring Violations: The International Community During the
1980s   74
Monitoring Violations: The International Community During the
1990s   75

Chapter 7. The Right to Freedom of Conscience, Thought, and
Religion   83

Political Prisons as the Microcosm of the Ideal Islamic Society   84
The *Tawaban* (Repentant Prisoners)   86
Imposition of the Black Chador   92
A Deluge of Religious Incantations and Rituals   95
Prisoners and Their Islamic Educators   100

Chapter 8. Renounce Your Conscience or Face Death: The Prison
Massacre of 1988   104

The Relative Calm Before the Storm, 1984–88   105
The Summer Massacre   108
A Painful Road to Release   117

Chapter 9. The Right to Freedom of Thought, Conscience, and Religion:
Iranian Religious Minorities   119

Iranians of the Baha'i Faith   119
Killings of Baha'i Leaders   121
Making Allegiance to the Baha'i Faith More Difficult than Ever
Before   123
Sunni Muslim Citizens   128
Citizens of Officially Recognized Religious Minorities   130
The "Protected" Are Unequal   132
Historical Predicament of Being "Protected"   134
Recent Converts to Protestant Denominations   139

Chapter 10. Official Responses to the United Nations: Countering the
Charges of Violations in the 1980s   146

Politicization of the Process   147
Equivalency in Institutional Architecture and Formality of Written
Law   150
Preconditions for Cooperation   152
The Militant Groups   153
Iranian Baha'is   156
Demanding Respect for Islamic *Différance*   158

Chapter 11. Change of Tactics After Ayatollah Khomeini's Death   163

New Diplomatic Initiatives   164
Presenting the Outlawed Political Groups as the Only Human Rights
Violators   167
Creating "Nongovernmental" Delegations and Groups   169

Chapter 12. The Special Representative's Meetings with the Judiciary and
Security Officials   175

UN Visits to Evin Prison   175
Discussions Meetings with the Judiciary Officials   177
The Special Representative Remained Unconvinced   181

Chapter 13. The Right to Freedom of Opinion, Expression, and the
Press   185

Political Context of the Violations   186
Targeting the *Digar Andishan*   188
Resurfacing of Islamic Reformism   189
"We Are Writers"   194

The Chasm Separating Conservative Clerics and Secular
Intellectuals   196
Emerging Pattern of Violations During Rafsanjani's Presidency   200
Khatami's Presidency and the New Political Context   203
Rational Political Discourse De-legitimating *Velayat-e Faqih* and Revealing
Past Violations   205
Renewed Violations   208
The Extrajudicial Killings of the *Digar Andishan*   211
The Wholesale Banning of Reformist Newspapers and Magazines   215

Chapter 14. The Most Revealing Cases of Violations of the Right to
Freedom of Expression and the Press   217

The Death of Sa'idi Sirjani   217
The Case of Faraj Sarkuhi   219
The Cases of Dissident Ayatollahs and Their Associates   224
The Cases of Mohsen Kadivar and Abdollah Nuri   229

Chapter 15. The Rights to Participate in the Political Life of the Country
and to Peaceful Assembly and Association   233

The Extraconstitutional and Constitutional Exclusions   233
The Guardian Council's Abuse of Its Power   236
Open Protests Against Exclusionary Practices   239
Formation of New Political Groups and the Reformists' Electoral
Victories   243

Chapter 16. The Rights of Women   250

Discriminatory Laws and Practices Limiting Human Rights of All
Women   252
Women Fighting Back to Recover Lost Rights   253
The Absence of Secular Voices   260
Cultural Authenticity Reveiling Secular, Emancipated Women   261
Violations of the Rights of Secular Women   268

Chapter 17. UN Monitoring, 1984–2000: Mixed Results   272

The Limitations of the UN Procedure   272
The Embarrassed Cultural Relativists   274
Governmental Human Rights Organizations   278
Enduring Diplomatic Habits of Denials and Misrepresentations   282

Conclusion   288

Respect for Human Rights, a Precondition for Cultural
Discussions   288
The Islamic Republic Violates Rights Like Other States   291
Particular Curses of the Religious State   293
In Defense of State Secularism   297

Notes   303

Selected Bibliography   345

Index   353

Acknowledgments   361

A Note on Transliteration

I have generally followed the guidelines set by the *International Journal of the Middle Eastern Studies*. However, I have not used diacritical marks with the exception of the *ayn* (') and the *hamzah* ('); *ayn* and *hamzah* are also omitted at the beginning or end of words. Well-known Iranian proper names are presented as they usually appear in the press (e.g., Khamenei and Khomeini).

Preface

Human Rights Discourse

Literature on human rights monitoring often focuses on current events, mainly providing information on immediate concerns or responding to urgent appeals. By its own logic, the discourse often lacks the historical dimension that might provide a better understanding of a state, the political culture of its rulers, and the continuity of violations. Commenting on Iran's slight improvement in the treatment of Baha'is in the late 1980s, the UN Special Representative on Iran expressed his desire that the government take further steps to make harassment of Baha'is "a chapter in history."[1] For all human rights monitors, relegating past violations to "history" is understandably accompanied by a sigh of relief. Academics seldom write on the history of human rights violations in a particular state. This creates a problem not only because our knowledge of human rights violations lacks historical depth, but also because the question of a state's political legitimacy might be decided by evaluating its current and recent record, irrespective of its dark history. We need more studies that offer a long-term perspective on the realities of human rights violations in the Middle Eastern states.

The human rights observer in me gravitates toward a different goal. In recent years, spirited debates over Islamic cultural relativism and human rights have attracted scholarly attention. Scores of books and articles have been published and conferences have been held on the theme of human rights and Islam. Even human rights organizations hosted such theoretical conferences and published their proceedings, all in a bewildering search for human rights in Islam. This came at a time when almost all Islamic theorists disagreed as to what Islam might entail for citizens of a contemporary state. The debates, and my own contribution, remained largely theoretical, with only minimal references to actual human rights violations and the socio-political conditions that cause them. I realize that many readers may in fact remain unconvinced as to the validity of various theoretical postulates. Detailed studies are needed of the human rights violations in those particular states for which cultural relativist claims have been made.

Such a study can best examine the relevance of Islamic culture to human rights violations. Ayatollah Khomeini's Iran has presented an almost perfect case. Who is more culturally and religiously authentic than the Ayatollahs? Who is more credible to say what relevance Shiite culture has or does not have for the major issues of our time? The issue is not Islam as a private faith of individuals. It is about what state officials claiming Islamic authority might have to say about the state's treatment of citizens. Islamic cultural relativism in human rights discourse addresses Islamic cultural preferences for the articulation of public policies within the contemporary state. In Iran, liberal Muslims or any other new interpreters of Islam did not come to power. When and if they do, we will have their record to examine. What we have from liberal Muslims today are only ideological claims punctuated by expressed good intentions. A sector of the traditional custodians of religion, the ulema, politicizing Islam did come to power; therefore, it is logical to assume that what we faced in the 1980s and 1990s was the result of Shiite Islam (at least an authentic version of it) injecting itself into the politics of a contemporary state. They created a record of what the "culturally authentic" rulers did. The Western cultural relativists deserve to know the details of that record. It will help them in their theoretical discourses to make better-informed evidential references to the country's human rights practices. Above all, in the long historical evolution of international human rights, Iran's story offers an interesting new chapter.

There is another dimension in this study. The Islamic Republic of Iran has been among the few states for which the UN Commission on Human Rights has appointed Special Representatives. Over years, it has responded to the allegations of abuses. Sometime denunciatory and evasive, often in denial, and seldom helpful in providing accurate information, the government responses were designed to effect the lifting of Iran from UN special procedures of public scrutiny. The government wanted the UN Commission on Human Rights to cancel the mandate of the Special Representative on Iran. The resulting dialogues, falling short of UN expectations, have created extensive records that offer a significant case study for understanding, in detail and over almost two decades, the working of the UN Commission on Human Rights and its special procedures. Thus, this study examines the United Nations enforcement procedures by looking at interactions between the Special Representative on Iran and the regime's high officials and diplomats.

This study remains grounded in human rights discourse. It refrains, with a few exceptions, from diversions to other disciplines like political science and sociology. I do not wish to present the works of the political thinkers of our time (say, Foucault on torture) in order to create an analytical framework for this study. Such a framework, though valuable in general social scientific discourses, diverts attention from the theoretical foundation of human rights. The foundation of contemporary human rights discourse is the

Universal Declaration of Human Rights and its two sister Covenants, which define human rights in international law.

Human rights discourse seeks to marshal increased support for international human rights law. Academic and intellectual acknowledgment of the validity of international human rights law can help its slow process of gaining universal recognition. Human rights scholars hope to create intellectual and academic antidotes to states' arguments rejecting universality of rights and to their denials of violations. State functionaries must realize that their arguments will be dissected, factually analyzed, and evaluated in academic human rights centers and their efforts to rationalize existing violations have no chance in convincing anyone except their own political superiors. Human rights discourse needs detailed academic studies to counter the pernicious power of states to attract international apologists, while they commit human rights violations. Detailed knowledge of events enables us to avoid giving credence to a state's arguments rationalizing human rights violations based on cultural peculiarity. In particular, academics not conferring such credence will help in the development of an international human rights culture. Above all, in the Islamic Republic of Iran's case, those state functionaries who committed human rights violations and the diplomats who offered falsehoods to cover them up must be held accountable in historical memory, if not in an international court of law.

Main Sources Used in This Book

In addition to the Iranian press and official documents, there are three main sources of information: UN reports, especially those written by the Special Representatives appointed by the UN Commission on Human Rights to monitor Iran; reports by the human rights NGOs, especially Amnesty International and Human Rights Watch; and prison memoirs written by those who survived the prisons in the 1980s and left the country in the early 1990s. The NGO monitoring activities and reports are generally familiar to most readers. Thus, I will only make some general remarks about the other two sources.

UN Reports

By the early months of 1980 the international human rights organizations were sufficiently alarmed by the continuous reports of gross violations of human rights. Iran has become one of the few countries that have achieved the dubious distinction of being investigated by UN country rapporteurs under the UN Special Procedures section.[2] In 1984, the Commission appointed a Special Representative on Iran. His mandate was to establish contacts with state officials and to study the human rights "situation" in the Islamic Republic.[3] Three legally qualified men have assumed that position: Andrés Aguilar of Venezuela (1984–86), Reynaldo Galindo Pohl of El Salvador (1986–95), and Maurice Copithorne of Canada (since August 1995).

During his relatively long tenure as the Special Representative, Galindo Pohl's activities revealed all the hopes and frustration, as well as the strength and weaknesses, of the UN human rights regime. Between January 1987 and January 1990, when the government allowed him a visit to Tehran, Galindo Pohl issued six substantive reports that offered a cautious assessment of the human rights situation in Iran. Notwithstanding the shortcomings of the UN process, obstructionist behavior of the government, and the horse-trading attitudes of many members of the Human Rights Commission, Galindo Pohl demonstrated that the monitoring tasks of the Commission are not devoid of value. The government responses to the allegations, although denunciatory and evasive, helped to introduce the concept of human rights in the official discourses of the Islamic Republic.

Although demonstrating gross human rights violations, these reports did not reflect the full scope of what was actually taking place in the country in the 1980s. International human rights NGOs helped to rectify the situation by providing more information and analysis. However, a fuller picture emerges only by examining the prison memoirs that became available in the 1990s.

Prison Memoirs and Their Significance

> In prison, I have always felt that the young women who were carried away to the execution ground had sent their souls back to land on my shoulders. I have felt the weight of those bodies for years, and this is the first time that by writing this memoirs I am trying to free myself from this burden.
>
> —Novelist Shahrnush Parsipur

Human rights scholarship on Iran can now benefit from a number of informative prison memoirs that did not exist in the 1980s, when the UN human rights reports were alleging flagrant violations and government officials and diplomats were adamantly denying their occurrence. They include book-length accounts published by A. Paya, Parvaneh Alizadeh, M. Raha, F. Azad, Hamid Azadi, Nima Parvaresh, Reza Ghaffari, and Shahrnush Parsipur.[4] These particular memoirs follow a chronological order, from arrest to release, describing the harsh and dehumanizing treatments the authors received and events they observed or were told by other inmates. There are other memoirs, often shorter and less useful for substantiating human rights abuses, which only focus on some particularly poignant episodes of life in prison.[5] There are also numerous short prison accounts, written anonymously, that appeared in opposition newspapers belonging to leftist organizations that still show a semblance of life in exile. They are littered with political sloganeering and do not add much to our knowledge of what happened in prison. These I did not use. I have only relied on writers of whose existence and reliability I am reasonably certain. Whatever the forms, the memoirs that I have used are informative, touching, and all equally harrowing. The suffering had aroused in the authors a powerful rage that gave them strength in prison and induced them to write about their experiences after release. They seemed to have felt somewhat unburdened at last by describing their ordeals.

A. Paya (pseudonym for Dr. Parviz Ousiya) was arrested on April 11, 1979, and after more than three months in detention was released on bail, without even being formally informed of his crime. He was a law professor and an accomplished attorney, specializing in international business contracts. He died in London in 1993. Having tacitly supported the revolution and then having been arrested by its zealot functionaries, he faced a situation full of political dilemmas and paradoxes. Prison authorities detained him in a ward packed with high officials of the former regime. Paya's book is a literary tour de force, perhaps the best in the genre of prison writings in the modern history of Iran. For a human rights researcher, however, its value lies in the fact that it describes prison conditions before the militant clerics established their total control over the administration of justice and the prison system.

M. Raha was arrested in the fall of 1981, along with her older brother and his wife. Her real name is Monireh Baradaran. She was a committed revolutionary Marxist and a member of the Organization of Revolutionary Workers, often referred to by the name of its newspaper, *Rah-e Kargar* (Worker's Way). Raha's brother was another Rah-e Kargar activist, who was executed in late 1981. Her prison memoirs, especially the first two volumes, are largely free of irrelevant political commentaries. Following a clear chronology, she supplies the critical dates for important events that shaped her prison ordeal. Her memoirs offer valuable information about female political prisoners.

Alizadeh, Azad, and others were revolutionaries whose thoughts and actions were laden with Marxist convictions and the myths of the Iranian populist movement. Their ideological disposition does not disqualify their reports of personal experiences, unless we believe in a grand conspiracy among ex-prisoners to invent collectively the events they described. The historian may express misgivings concerning the accuracy of what the ex-prisoners—all sworn enemies of the clerical regime—wrote about their experiences in the Ayatollah's prisons. A collaborating testimony by a less ideological prisoner becomes especially valuable.

Parsipur's *Memoirs of Prisons* is such a testimony. Its value lies in the fact that it provides a useful cross-check on the general plausibility of other memoirs written by other ex-prisoners who were more political and less capable as writers. The Revolutionary Guards arrested Shahrnush Parsipur, then a thirty-five-year-old novelist, on a spurious charge. The initial cause of her arrest became irrelevant. What she was, a female novelist with a patently bad (secular) attitude, became the most important reason for her prolonged incarceration, which lasted more than four and a half years. The Revolutionary Guards had also arrested her equally stubborn mother, a believing Muslim for whom Islam had become a personal and private matter. Aware of her own superior social status and relative worth, her mother refused to be reeducated in the proper Islamic conduct by her uncouth interrogators. The authorities set Parsipur free on March 20, 1986. She lives and writes in the United States today.

Parsipur was in the right place at the right time, or more accurately, in the wrong place at the wrong time. Unfortunately for her, this perceptive novelist's witnessing of the Islamic prisons, though life-shattering for her, has given human rights researchers invaluable insights into the workings of "Islamic justice." For the most part, Parsipur was a conscientious writer, cognizant of her intellectual responsibility to her craft and scrupulous in what she chose to describe. She felt that as a writer she was obligated to preserve a certain level of honesty and integrity. "If I transgress that limit, my pen will dry up," she told a confused fellow inmate.[6] No doubt, a careful reader may detect in any prison account cases of faulty memories, exaggerations, face-saving omissions, and misperceptions. However, on the details that concern violations of specific human rights, Parsipur's account depicts a life in prison that is not much different from the one portrayed by M. Raha and other leftist writers.

Despite obvious differences in political views, personal temperaments, and the ways they saw the world, Parsipur, Alizadeh, Raha, Azad, Ghaffari, and others who survived to write about their ordeals offer the reader a picture of prisons that confirms the worst of what human rights monitors imagined during much of the 1980s.

For every category of rights violations that the UN reports examined, I will turn to these personal testimonies. One of the main goals of this study is to show that the prison literature validates what the Special Representatives alleged. In fact, prison memoirs offer descriptions of brutalities seldom discussed in UN reports of the 1980s. Obviously, prison memories could have been presented as a whole in a separate section in the book. However, I have set up the chapter structure in such a way that would allow me to incorporate prison memories into human rights categories presented in the UN reports. I intend to keep this book grounded, as much as possible, in international human rights law. Perhaps another book in the genre of prison literature could use the memories differently. I only hope that I do not diminish their powerful effect.

The Structure of the Book

This is a history of evolving human rights situations for more than two decades. The first period (1979–89) of this study covers the early years of political violence and massive violations of human rights, during which the government adopted a highly obstructionist policy toward the United Nations and the international human rights organizations. This was a phase of noncooperation with the UN Commission on Human Rights and an outright rejection of all allegations of violations compiled by its Special Representatives. After 1989, some significant changes took place both in the nature of human rights violations and the tactics the diplomats used to counter the charges of violations in the UN. These changes have influenced the way I organized the book's chapters. The diplomats adopted a new attitude of apparent cooperation with the Commission, while expressing indignation over the fact that the UN had placed Iran under its special procedure and while doing their best to muster majority votes within the Commission to end the Special Representative's mandate.

Chapter 1 defends the universality of human rights. It also rejects the argument that Islamism offered a viable alternative to the pervasive, practical secularism in a complex state society like Iran. Chapter 2 explains the formation of the Shiite theocracy, *velayat-e faqih*, and the political contexts of human rights violations for the Republic's two periods: the Khomeini decade of the 1980s and the post-Khomeini decade of the 1990s, when a state of normalization was declared by President Hashimi Rafsanjani. The second period witnessed significant changes that eventually led to intensification of factional conflicts within the regime and to Muhammad Khatami's reformist presidency.

Andrés Aguilar, the UN Special Representative on Iran, wrote his preliminary report in 1985 without the benefit of any meaningful response to the inquiries that he had submitted to the regime's diplomats. Aguilar listed five categories of violations:

1. The right to life;
2. The right to freedom from torture or cruel and degrading treatment;
3. The right to liberty and security of person and to freedom from arbitrary arrest or detention;
4. The right to a fair trial; and
5. The right to freedom of thought, conscience, and religion.[7]

Reynaldo Galindo Pohl of El Salvador replaced Aguilar in July 1986. As if taking his cue from his predecessor, Galindo Pohl used the same five categories in writing his substantive reports.

Surely, these five categories fell short of covering the entire scope of violations during the 1980s. Nevertheless, I have found them useful as organizing categories for this study, since they offer an opportunity not only to examine their occurrences but also to present a critical summary of what the UN reports contained in these five major categories. Moreover, the use of these five categories helps to highlight the absence of other significant categories as a major shortcoming in the monitoring process in the 1980s. In this first period, international monitors did not discuss violations of the rights to freedom of opinion, expression, and the press, to participate in the political life of the country, and to peaceful assembly and association. Nor did they deem it necessary to discuss the violations of rights of women. Moreover, the UN reports on Iran paid almost no attention to the violations of the right of secular Iranians to freedom of thought and conscience. The gallows and the images of tortured bodies cast an obscuring shadow over the less bloody violations.

In the second period, Galindo Pohl's reports continued to use the same five categories, to which he now added new ones that reflected the evolving political conditions of the 1990s. I found three of the new categories significant, mainly because they were not ad hoc categories specific to one report or another. They were as follows.

6. The right to freedom of opinion, expression, and the press;
7. The rights to participate in the political life of the country and to peaceful assembly and association;
8. The rights of women.

Thus, this history of human rights violations is organized into these eight categories.

To preserve continuity from the 1980s to the 1990s, I have used the five original categories and discussed, in corresponding chapters, the violations that occurred in the 1980s and then continued into the 1990s. Copithorne replaced Galindo Pohl as the Special Representative in 1995. Disregarding Copithorne's ad hoc categories, I have included his pertinent information and comments in each category.

Chapters 3 to 6 cover the first four categories. Each begins by an analytical presentation of testimonies offered by prison memoirs. Wherever appropriate, I have also included information gleaned from the reports by the international human rights organizations, especially Amnesty International. For the fifth category, I have departed from this procedure by devoting three chapters (7 to 9) to the right to freedom of conscience, thought, and religion, since this particular right assumes a critical importance in a religious state. In Chapter 7, I have relied on the prison memoirs offering a picture of the Islamization process that denied prisoners the right to freedom of conscience. Chapter 8 focuses mainly on the prison massacre of the summer of 1988 that followed the egregious violations of the political prisoners' right to freedom of conscience. Chapter 9 examines the violations of the rights of religious minorities (Baha'is, Sunni Muslims, Jews, Christians, and Zoroastrians).

A major part of the book is given to the government's interactions with the United Nations in which various responses and policies of the Islamic Republic have been examined. In different periods, the officials have reacted differently toward the international human rights community. Chapter 10 analyzes the efforts of the regime to counter the charges of human rights violations in the 1980s. Chapter 11 looks at the regime's changes of tactics, hoping to remove Iran from the UN special procedures. Chapter 12 analyzes Galindo Pohl's discussions with the judiciary and security officials in Tehran.

The three other significant categories of violations that were ignored by the international human rights community in the 1980s are covered. Chapter 13 discusses the right to freedom of opinion, expression, and the press. It also explains that it was during Khatami's reformist presidency that people first read press reports that validated the charges of past human rights violations. Chapter 14 provides the most revealing cases of violations of this right that dominated the human rights discourse in the second half of the 1990s. Chapter 15 deals with the rights to participate in the political life of the country and to peaceful assembly and association. Chapter 16 is written in defense of the human rights of women in general and of secular women in particular. Chapter 17 examines the limitations of the UN special procedures in gaining the cooperation of the regime in clarifying the charges of human rights violations. It also shows the impact that the UN monitoring had on the regime and some of its officials.

Chapter 1

Islamic Cultural Relativism in Human Rights Discourse

The challenge facing human rights advocates has always been formidable: to scale the seemingly insurmountable walls of the sovereign state, to reach into its dark and cloistered domestic domains, and to lend a helping hand to courageous but lonely women and men in the clutches of its security apparatus. When the state is fanatically guided by a sacrosanct ideology, the task becomes infinitely more difficult.

The volcano-like eruption of politicized Islam (Islamism) added a new layer of repression and persecution to the already dense depository of historical injustices. Now the life of the individual could be sacrificed to safeguard not only the state but also "Islam," especially if he or she was secular or a nonbeliever. The debates over Islamization of the state and society (the goal of the Islamist movement) have complicated the task of human rights. As the regime created new patterns of violations, the new rulers, like other ideological suppressors of freedoms, advanced cultural and religious rationalizations to justify human rights abuses. Like other ideological rulers who promised a better world, the Islamists created their own sympathizers in the West.

Political Culture: Assuming the Failure of Secularization

Islamization came over Iran on the trail of a populist revolution that gathered momentum in 1978–79 and overthrew the secular, authoritarian regime of the Shah, Muhammad Reza Pahlavi. To sympathetic scholars the rise of Islamism was indicative of the failure of secularization; that assumed failure lent a new credence to Islamic cultural relativism. We often heard that the *shari'ah* (Islamic law) and its principles provided solidarity and sociopolitical motivation to Muslims who demanded "the immediate application" of the *shari'ah*.[1] Assuming the total failure of modern ideologies in Islamic countries, Muslim thinkers had, in the words of a sympathetic scholar, "advocated a more authentic, Islamic framework for Muslim society."[2] Many

Islamists praised those previously misguided intellectuals who have, thanks to "the insight of the masses, rediscovered the truth of Islam."[3] Some scholars of Islam told us that secularism was "unlikely to receive broad and lasting support in the Muslim world" and that secularism was "receding."[4] Many observers spent the 1980s anticipating a cataclysmic battle between Islamism and secularism, which would lead to a crushing theocratic victory in many Islamic countries. This confrontation has proved much more complex than the singular image of a receding secularism projected by the Islamists and their Western sympathizers.

In 1994, I argued that in the praxis of life in a changing world, we cannot reduce secularization to a cast of mind or a mental trait, nor should we characterize it as a set of abstract principles or an antireligious ethos. The success or failure of Muslims to internalize a secular outlook and values should be determined by what they actually do. Their culture demonstrates internal confusion, and their cultural self-explanations cannot be trusted. If one juxtaposes traditional values with a secular outlook and values, one must note that the weight of tradition is a heavier burden on a Muslim's mind than on his or her actions. The latter are often far more responsive to the practical needs of a changing society than the mind is willing or able to recognize.[5]

"Written and spoken words expressing modernity's sentiments and values unsettle the traditionalist mind," observed Muhammad Mokhtari, the secular intellectual who was killed by security agents in 1999. It fails to locate manifestations of modernity in what people do, imitating Western patterns of city life and architecture and using Western-designed furniture, machines, household items, and everyday appliances. "The traditionalist mind attaches importance to discourses." For this reason, Mokhtari added, the traditionalists who surround themselves with Western artifacts perceive the secular intellectuals' words as the main culprits, the evil transmitters of modernity and agents of undesirable cultural transformation.[6]

Secularism manifests itself abundantly at the level of human conduct in Iran, in the profane and practical attitude toward contemporary life, ultimately rejecting the permanency of anything that claims legitimacy beyond its rendered value. Values converge as people increasingly share in a global commonality of needs, desires, aspirations, and frustrations.

Secular habits have become habitual, and people discover small truths that cumulatively replace the Truth of tradition. Already they have proved more tenacious than the zealotry of the Islamists. As the religiously propelled political storm blew overland, raising a whirlwind of collective hysteria and fear, shrouding women in the dark *hijab* (Islamic covering), and hiding Islamist radicals in the veil of their own fear of modernity, the secular undercurrent continued to flow under the vast swathes of Iranian life. It seeped through cultural fissures, nourishing habits that conform more to the this-worldly and chaotic ethos of contemporary civilization than to the wisdom of tradition or the revealed word of God. Today, life on the streets of Tehran is a bewildering hybrid spectacle. As the dust of the Aya-tollah's Islamization has settled, new habits have taken hold, pragmatically motivating people in their essential socioeconomic actions. With social and economic processes still grounded in an enormous bureaucracy fueled by oil money, all avenues to an individual's "life chance" are as consumption-oriented and money-driven as were the fast tracks under the Shah.

The demise of modern secularism has been greatly exaggerated in Iran. Individualized, atomistic, and competitive, the society that cultural conser-vatives have dreaded has arrived, and religiocultural incantations will not dispel it. Universalized human rights, with their focus on the individual, are not responsible for its arrival; they offer protection for individuals. Assum-ing the total failure of modern secularism in Iran, the Islamists attempted to reconstruct the state to conform with an organicist politics. To justify their actions, they offered cultural relativist arguments that asserted the superi-ority of their "Islamic" model of government.

The Islamic Republic Claims Cultural Exceptionalism

Human rights scholar Rhoda Howard has identified five theoretical chal-lenges in the 1990s to the universality of human rights: radical capitalism, traditionalism, reactionary conservatism, Third World nationalism (left col-lectivism), and status radicalism.[7] The Islamic Republic of Iran has pre-sented perhaps the strongest case of a combination of two of these chal-lenges, that of traditionalism and Third World nationalism.

These challenges have reinvigorated theoretical debates over the rele-vance of culture to human rights. Those engaged in the debate often make evidential references to Iran's assertion of Islamic prerogatives that limit the scope of universal human rights. Cultural relativists advance divergent positions. They all relish the view that human rights do not constitute the cultural ideal adhered to by the world's ethical systems, with the exception of the West. The most uncompromising among them maintain that it is a country's indigenous traditions, and not the UDHR, that should properly determine the scope of rights that are granted to its citizens. They pamper cultural sensitivities especially in areas where human rights challenge patri-archal patterns of authority-subordination.

They often see universal human rights as an expression of the ethical value of Western culture and closely scrutinize any civil and political right whose introduction might require changes in the local cultural tradition. They see their historic responsibility in the preservation of their culture and not in its adaptation to the norms of a universal human rights culture. They assume the existence of many different lifestyles, each underpinning a par-ticular form of governance that would determine the scope of human rights accorded to individuals. They also claim that their Islamic tradition pos-sesses countermodels for every social-legal model that the West can offer.

The officials in Iran used the opportunity created by the debates over universality vs. relativism in human rights to challenge the universal normative consensus that has been formed around the Universal Declaration of Human Rights (UDHR). They challenged the Commission on Human Rights, which expects all states to adhere to international human rights laws.[8] A self-serving fidelity to "Islamic cultural tradition" conveniently cast aside several of the universal human rights. As well understood by human rights scholars, human rights are not only universal but also interdependent and indivisible. One cannot allow derogation in one right without negatively affecting other rights that are left seemingly unchallenged theoretically.

The central challenge that the Islamic Republic presented to the universality of human rights lay in its assertion that religion—namely, Islam—is the supreme cultural principle, more important than any ethical construct that bases its claim to legitimacy on sources other than revelation. The immediate political context was created by the assertion made by Ayatollah Khomeini that the Islamic cultural norms were being corrupted by Western-style freedom, causing immorality in young men and leading young women astray. Questioning the universality of human rights, the regime's ideologues offered their own version of human rights for which they claimed validity, beyond time and space. The claim was grossly misinformed. In the summer of 1995, Ayatollah Ali Khamenei, the Supreme Leader of the Islamic Republic, urged his foreign affairs functionaries to reject "the Western notion of human rights." Referring to the values that the Islamic system was trying to inculcate globally, he asserted, "Today the Islamic system is questioning the identity, goal, and capability of the Western system, and the most superior Western thinkers are gradually realizing the tediousness of the Western system. Thus, the civilization that began with the Renaissance is coming close to its finale. Human beings today are searching for a substitute for the Western system, and the inclination toward Islam in the United States, Europe, and Africa emanates from this situation."[9]

Khamenei was not alone in his misperceptions. President Muhammad Khatami won the presidency on a popular reformist platform in 1997. As the Minister of Culture and Islamic Guidance in 1990, he declared that the decline of the West would herald "Islam's global leadership in the next century." He added that the Islamic Republic must prepare "to be the model for other countries by replacing anti-values with values."[10] Like Khamenei, Khatami was proposing a new doctrine of universalism based on Islam.

The United Nations has formulated human rights standards solely for protecting individuals from abusive states and societies. The clerics politicizing Islam injected a huge dose of metaphysics, from one particular religious tradition, into human rights debates, shifting the theoretical focus of the discourse away from the state's protective responsibilities. For some fifteen years, they envisioned a different kind of task for the state, one that protects the individual, before everything else, from his own probable religious-moral lapses. Considering the term "human rights," the Islamists placed the stress on "human" and not on rights, making sure that they first obtained a "true" human being, mindful of God's presence and fearful of divine injunctions, before considering his rights. The goal was to create the perfect human (*ensan-e kamel*), which stood in "sharp contrast with the goal of Western liberalism, which created normal human (*ensan-e normal*)." [11] This approach justified coercion by claiming to be fulfilling a higher vision of human freedom, one that was achieved by the true discovery of God. Western-inspired liberty was deceptive; true liberty came only when the individual discovered God by freeing himself from all worldly attractions. In this understanding, the focus was on obligation and not right — not the individual's right to freedom of religion and conscience but his obligation to believe in the revealed religion. Commensurately, only the rightly guided opinions that were based on Islamic teachings were worth protecting. [12]

Dr. Hossein Mehrpur was a layperson appointed by the Islamic judiciary to counter charges of human rights violations in the UN in the early 1990s. Following the teachings of Islamist ideologue Ayatollah Morteza Motahhari, Mehrpur asserted that Islam considers the gradual perfection of human beings to be the purpose of the Creation, and they achieve perfection by paying "attention to the Creator of the universe." [13] For Mehrpur, the true worth of human beings manifested itself only in worshipping God and observing religious rules. Thus, the only criterion for judging the superiority of some human beings over others was the degree of their piety and righteousness. "Islamic doctrine does not accept polytheism and blasphemy, and it believes that every effort must be made towards creating the sovereignty of monotheism and God's religion, because a human being without morality and an exalted soul does not possess real human value. To pay attention to this reality was to value human dignity and honor." The state could achieve this goal by preaching, offering guidance, debating, and reasoning.

Mehrpur blamed the United Nations for remaining indifferent to religious values:

> The Commission on Human Rights and other UN organs give no consideration to religious values; it can even be said that there takes place, under various excuses, a kind of struggle against religious values and beliefs. They do not take moral precepts seriously. Nor do they seriously consider the possibility of placing limitations on the individual's liberty for the sake of proper moral necessities that are also considered in the Universal Declaration of Human Rights (Article 29–2). No government would ever be reproached for providing unlimited liberties that are against moral precepts and correct religious values. However, if a government establishes limitations on its citizens for the sake of the protection of public morality, it will be questioned and blamed in UN resolutions. [14]

What Mehrpur and other religious ideologues failed to understand was that those who formulated the universal human rights norms were aware of the danger inherent in a situation where a contemporary state arrogated to itself the power of deciding for citizens what were "correct moral necessities."

What if some individuals offered resistance to this divinely determined human dignity? Then they will be confronted in order to remove this obstacle to human beings' exalted progress. The Islamists used the Qur'anic exhortatory concepts related to struggle against "infidels, polytheists, and corrupters" to facilitate that achievement. Mehrpur asserted that Islam considers the promotion of irreligiosity to be contradictory to the dignity and worth of human beings. It is precisely for the sake of protecting fundamental human rights that Islam forbids "religious and moral carelessness." According to Mehrpur's logic in the early 1990s, Iran could not protect human rights unless a proper religious environment was established.

What the reformist President Khatami entertained for an Islamic civil society was similar to the restrictive views expressed by other clerics who controlled the coercive instruments of state power. Like Mehrpur, Khatami saw the Islamization process as one that inculcated *taqwa* (virtue and piety) before granting liberty to citizens. Again, freedom was depicted as a Western concept, understood by "natural" human faculties, not religiously refined. The Western notion leaves the religiously unsophisticated to judge freedom's scope by his natural impulses for freedom; this could only lead to errors, since he is not guided by the compass of Islamic *taqwa*. *Taqwa* channels the natural, raw instinct for freedom in a religiously virtuous direction. Obviously, citizens with *taqwa* have a higher moral worth than those without. Ayatollah Motahhari, whose influence on men like Mehrpur and Khatami was clear, taught that liberty without *taqwa* would lead human beings astray.[15] Thus, *ensan-e ba-taqwa* (virtuous human) was the same as *ensan-e kamel* (perfect human). Motahhari's view could be a fine sentiment if expressed by a cleric in a state that makes a clear distinction between political power and religious teachings. In a theocracy, however, it immediately provokes a number of troubling questions: How does the state instill *taqwa* in citizens? Who defines *taqwa*? Can one gain *taqwa* without necessarily being loyal to the Ayatollah's rule (*velayat-e faqih*)? Can a teacher or a secular philosopher teach lessons on *taqwa*? What should we do if the official *taqwa* set forth by [state] school propaganda is in conflict with *taqwa* taught in the family? Is it possible for a secular person to live a righteous life?[16]

Of course, this understanding of human rights contradicts the letter and spirit of the UDHR. Mehrpur observed that Article 26 of the UDHR provides for compulsory elementary education, since the international community understood the necessity of basic education for citizens. If education is important enough for the growth of human beings to be made compulsory, "Why cannot the worship of one God and the rejection of atheism be equally compulsory?"[17]

That he posed the point as a question was perhaps indicative of the fact that Dr. Mehrpur, who had served in the Shah's judiciary before the revolution, lacked a strict Islamist turn of mind. A genuine Islamist assertion came from a younger high official in the Foreign Ministry, in a prepared speech to an international audience in Tehran in 1991. Ali Qaderi considered the "limited value" of the UDHR. However, like many other officials at that time, he questioned the legitimacy and continued validity of the universal norms. These officials insisted that "Islamic doctrine had very limited presentation and reception at the time the Declaration and the two Covenants were formulated."[18] Pronouncing the world that was made without them morally and religiously defective, Qaderi demanded, in effect, that the world should pause, acknowledge their arrival, and accede to their demands by reconsidering many of the norms of international human rights laws, so painstakingly put together by the preceding generations.

Taking the UDHR to task, Qaderi asked: Is the Declaration's philosophical foundation rooted in natural law or based on social contract? Is it evolving today? Is it so complete that it has become eternal? Does it contain those common principles that religions share with each other concerning the rights granted to human beings, or is it itself the "mother of religions" to which the state must profess? Has it considered all general human rights? Do human beings possess other rights beyond what occurred to its authors? Can what is essentially the result of the specific experiences of a nation or some nations in a specific geographical location be considered "the epigraph for all locations?"[19] Qaderi was toeing the line of argument advanced by the clerics.[20]

A look at the history of the UDHR will show that its thoughtful and deliberative authors did in fact deal with major issues and questions related to the world's cultural and religious diversities. The human rights scholar Paul Gordon Lauren has observed that some of the drafters were quite familiar with "the pluralistic philosophical and cultural traditions of Europe, the Middle East, and Asia. . . . Indeed, their extraordinary and pioneering efforts to consider a wide range of opinions and values certainly belies later charges that they somehow conspired to 'circumvent fundamental differences' or engaged in 'cultural imperialism.' To help them resolve some of the issues as they prepared a draft international bill of rights, for example, members of the Commission on Human Rights deliberately decided to draw on a number of different sources above and beyond whatever instructions they received from their governments."[21]

Moreover, recognizing the cultural diversity of the world, the authors grappled with the impossibility of ever arriving at a consensus for a universal declaration, if they inserted philosophical or religious precepts into its normative foundation. The representative of the nationalist government of China in the drafting committee bristled at the suggestion of mentioning God, or any notion associated with monotheism, into the document, and if the Catholic delegates wanted to do so, he would suggest equal consideration be given to Confucian ethics. The committee wisely decided to drop the whole thing and reach an agreement that all member states could sign. The result was Article 1, which does not specify by whom all human beings "are endowed with reason and conscience." [22]

Qaderi concluded by inviting the world to reexamine human beings and their rights in "Abrahamic religions." Giving a hint as to what that meant, he made a number of specific assertions, all limiting the scope of human rights: Human beings are not free to eat dirt, nor are they free to make love to another man's wife. Prophets have ordered that human beings do not have the right to doubt the unity of God (*sherk*). Blasphemy and polytheism are strictly forbidden. "Even if it is packaged as the freedom of opinion, the only thing that human beings are given the right to choose is religion. The right to choose is not between religion and irreligion. If they choose wrongly, they will be punished." [23] Punished they were, as is painfully shown by the prison memoirs of the 1980s.

These kinds of assertions in the name of culture and religion negate the foundation upon which the UDHR stands. They present lethal dangers to secular citizens, especially when those who uphold such a binary "Abrahamic" vision are the same people who wield the state's coercive power. The UDHR has aimed at protecting individuals from the power of those who could decide what is proscribed and impose what is prescribed in the name of God, nation, or any other ungodly ideologies. As the details of this study will show, this particular religious state used its (secular) coercive power while remaining largely oblivious to the otherwise familiar religious virtues of compassion and mercy.

The Mirage of Cultural Authenticity

Consciously and deliberately seeking authenticity in one's heritage is itself *inauthentic*, leading to heritagism, an infatuation with one's past that removes Islam from history, superimposes present obsessions on the past and, in doing so, makes the heritage unfathomable. Under the impact of modernity, traditionalism is also pseudomodernized. One cannot protect a tradition if one's discourse is permeated by modern normative concepts. The tradition espoused by today's political-religious activists is itself a badly digested invention of modernity. The ancestors of present Iranians lived the Islamic tradition of the land; Islamist tormentors of Iranian secularists today reconstruct an objectivized past that serves to authenticate a particular political vision of the present.

Authenticity as an intellectual discourse, encompassing a range of ideas, values, and human experiences, should be distinguished from authenticity as a discourse of political legitimation. The latter often subsumes the former; that is to say, if raised outside the domain of private decisions and within the dynamics of the modern nation-state, it subsumes the larger intellectual discourse into a much narrower and more focused issue of political legitimation. It becomes a discourse of hegemonic politics within the confines of the state.

No cultural relativist has called for the dismantling of the modern state that remains, to date, the most spectacular transplanting of an alien cultural structure. By its centralized structures and modern ethos, the state has overwhelmed the old society and rendered the political sphere of the tradition inauthentic. Claiming authenticity in tradition, while struggling to seize the commanding heights of the modern state, is a spectacular political double-cross.

All upholders of consequential ideologies used political categories to declare certain sections of their society as enemies. In the Islamic Republic of Iran, the clerical rulers incorporated their particular view of society into the contemporary state that fell under their control. This binary vision flew out of the ulema's understanding of Islam, whose essence was formed by drawing a sharp line of demarcation between those who submitted (Muslims) and those who refused to believe in the truth of Islam (*koffar*, infidels). Transplanting this vision onto the contemporary state, the clerical rulers targeted the contemporary infidels, the equivalents of the seventh-century *koffar* who had defiled the birthplace of Islam.

Life defeated zealotry and mellowed the revolutionists. In the second decade of their rule, some men in power sought to normalize their state. Out of practical considerations and perhaps under the moderating impact of the human rights language, the clerics reduced the use, at least in public, of the traditional Islamic epithets such as *koffar*. Thus, depending on how specific they needed to be, they began to use less rigid, exclusionary epithets. One that encompassed broad categories of people was the *ghir-e khudi*, outsiders (or the others), in contrast to the *khudi* (insiders). A subgroup of the outsiders was the *digar andishan* (those who think differently), coined to demonize intellectuals. The clerical rulers still employed Qur'anic terms such as *mortadd* (apostate) and *monafeq* (hypocrite) for more specific use. When tacked onto individuals, each epithet was capable of stripping away their human rights. Such individuals were not equal in dignity to "good Muslims," as officially defined. The excluded others, secular men and women, were treated as if they did not truly deserve human rights. As will be discussed in Chapter 13, the Supreme Leader of the Republic considered the *digar andishan* to be outright traitors.

The lay protégés of the powerful clerics, embarrassed by the archaic connotations of Islamic terms like *koffar* (infidels), began to speak of cultural authenticity. Thus, it was against the background of Islamization that the issue of authenticity became a central concern for the religious activists, assuming the character of the headiest intellectual-political dichotomy.

The debate on authenticity turned the critique of secular intellectuals and modern women into demonology. The Islamists denounced secular intellectuals, political activists, and experts not because of their positions on substantive socioeconomic issues or for their advocacy of class interests. Needless to say, in today's world there could be no genuine Islamic authenticity against which to measure the relative inauthenticity of individuals and groups.

The Irrelevance of Cultural Relativism

I defend the position of those human rights scholars who maintain that the universality of human rights is not an abstract philosophical (Western) notion. It is a response to the universality of the modern state as a globally convergent mode of governance. Insisting that the modern state must be the analytical focus, Rhoda Howard has shown that even in emerging Western states human rights concepts were formed despite hostile moral precepts then prevailing in Western culture (Christianity and Judaism). "The society that actively protects rights both in law and in practice is a radical departure for most known human societies."[24] Moreover, Jack Donnelly has noted "The modern economy, with its complex division of labor and extensive role-segmentation, necessarily produces economically and therefore socially distinct individuals. Likewise, modern state bureaucracies are structured to deal (only) with (anonymous or interchangeable) individuals."[25]

The UDHR and other human rights covenants define what is needed to protect a life of dignity and equality in the modern state. Although they originated in the West, their particular substantive foundation belongs to a moral vision that was the result of accumulated experiences in dealing with the abuses of the modern state and market economies. Through human rights standards we scrutinize "a person's or persons' relation to public authority—and indeed to the rest of society."[26] On most pressing issues of rights violations, a syndrome of political, social, and economic factors induces the rulers to violate rights. Violations of this nature are political violations committed by these states. For a Muslim country, as for all complex state societies, the most pressing human rights issue is not local cultural preferences and religious-cultural authenticity; it is the protection of individuals from a state that violates rights, regardless of its cultural-ideological facade. Insistence on the universality of human rights standards is a political demand for the protection of individuals in the contemporary world of modern states and capitalist economies.

In 1979, the revolution brought into power an Islamic government, which, in the view of most politically inclined clerics, set the course for the Islamic development of the country. This study argues that whenever rulers in charge of the coercive instruments of the contemporary state raise the issue of culture, its relevance to human rights discourse suggests itself mainly as a negation, as a barrier prolonging the emergence of a human rights culture. With the exception of this negation, cultural relativism is essentially irrelevant to human rights in contemporary states. More specifically for the main theme of this study, the Islamic Republic of Iran claimed religious-cultural exceptionalism by placing itself above the mundane standards of judgment used by the international human rights community.

First, in this study I hope to show the irrelevance of cultural relativism by showing that despite its metaphysical assertions, piously proclaiming moral superiority, and its cultural claims to exceptionality, the Islamic Republic behaved remarkably similar to other authoritarian states, not only in the use of repressive means to secure the end of state security but also in its rejections and denials of human rights violations. I attempt to show that the tactics the Islamist rulers used to counter the charges of human rights violations were in many respects familiar in the annals of modern authoritarian states, regardless of their cultural traditions.

Second, the unrealized Islamist expectations in Iran indicated the problems of a discourse that assumed cultural primacy as a legal foundation for human rights in a contemporary state. Whatever authentic ethical and legal claims had been offered for an Islamic legal foundation or for the newly created Islamic constitutional rights and obligations of citizens, they were readily amended, violated, or ignored. Why were there so many violations of the regime's own authentic legal edifice? The question brings us back to the dynamics of the state and the same kind of political expediencies that compel other secular, authoritarian regimes to undermine their constitutional and legal structures. The details of this book will show that the Islamists were no more committed to their own religiously based constitution and laws than secular dictators were to theirs.

Adamantia Pollis, a long-time defender of cultural relativism, now argues: "In the light of the absence of an agreed upon concept of human rights a search for a reconstructed universalism is in order. Such a reconstituted human rights theory would facilitate accountability by all States and would enhance the prospects for enforcement since the newly defined standards would embody both Western and non-Western standards." [27] Islamist experiences in the past two decades may indicate the futility of such a search. The details of this study will show that state violations of the universal standards had, in many areas of rights, very little to do with the apparent conflicts between different cultural paradigms. The Islamic rulers enunciated their own standards of rights in a lengthy Constitution and then flouted the law when the interest of the clerical faction in power required it. They facilely prevented any state accountability, even to their own Islamic human rights organizations (see Chapter 17). With such negotiating partners, the search for "the articulation of a new theory" is elusive, and I am not sure that the proponents of Asian culture, particularly in China, present more sincere interlocutors. By presenting the problem as theoretical, the cultural relativist approach may in effect weaken the existing accountability.

Third, the details will show that re-creating a communal society based on "authentic" cultural tradition was a political act that could only be achieved at the most superficial level, using coercion. To a large degree, the social values of personal autonomy and privacy have penetrated Iranian society. This reality has clashed with the policies of the new rulers. All claims to authenticity guiding state policies must be validated by their positive consequences in creating more cultural harmonies and political cohesiveness. In Iran, the reverse took place. As the details of this book will show, the "authentic policies" threw the country into an unprecedented human rights crisis. In the late 1990s, Iran experienced more discord in politics, social relations, and culture. Never before had there been such a high degree of open conflict between the state and its citizens, especially those with higher education and economic means. By 2000, political discord within the Islamic camp was tearing the façade of Islamic unity asunder. In fact, the entire clerical establishment of Shiite Islam was experiencing a major crisis as well.

Fourth, Iran's experience shows the political contingency of the human rights violations. The drive for Islamization of culture became a significant smoke screen for state exclusionary (political and economic) strategy. At the same time, it was a reflection of an intra-elite struggle and a cover for widespread corruption and embezzlements of state resources. Above all, the cultural rationalization, which justified repression, supported regime maintenance. The individual was left unprotected by a state that used contrived, religiously sanctioned political rationales to reincorporate the individual into an imagined communitarian society. Paradoxically, the enormous capacity of the contemporary state's apparatus was used to create a communitarian society, while individuals were left to deal with more of an authoritarian state. Pointing out the roots of autocratic rule in Iran's past history, a young feminist writer in Tehran noted in early 2000 that the Islamic Republic extended such a rule to "personal lives as well." [28]

Finally, notwithstanding these strong affinities of the Islamic Republic with secular authoritarian regimes, there were some major differences. These differences did bring the Islamic Republic closer to the ideological-opportunist dictatorships of the twentieth century. These differences manifested themselves in what I will call the curses of the religious state. The most obvious curses related to the clerical edicts (*fatvas*) declaring any undesirable person as *mortadd* (apostate) or sinful, deserving death. They could also subject such a person to Islamic punishments such as flogging, amputation, and stoning to death. The more enduring ones related to the imposed Islamization that invaded citizens' private lives. In these areas, too, cultural relativist arguments are irrelevant, precisely because such "cultural" practices by the state must be changed for the human rights culture to emerge.

Historical modernization has created a significant social space for the private lives of large numbers of Iranians. Influenced by modern habits and desires, they have accepted the notion of the individual as a private person. The Shah's state, despite its political oppression, protected them from the regressive censures of the religious traditions. The secular state created a relatively safe distance separating the individual from the cultural-religious community whose rituals and norms were set and controlled by the Shiite clerics. Under such protection, the secular individual gradually created a new cultural/social zone within which he was expected to choose his own social associations, occupation, social affiliation, marriage partner, the level and intensity of religious practices, and the consumption of literary and artistic productions. Secular Iranians sought new social rites of civility, separate from the religious rituals. They made private decisions often in conflict with the judgment of the custodians of the tradition. Since the middle of the twentieth century, there has been no shared universe of cultural, legal, and moral discourses between them and the ulema. The religious state invaded this newly formed private space in hope of destroying it. The strongest religious/cultural claims that set the Islamic Republic apart from the rest of the authoritarian states became afflictions on secular and semisecular Iranians. The culture of the rulers must be changed in order for these particular curses to be removed. Cultural relativist arguments cannot justify them; they only add insults to injuries.

The details of the book will explore the familiar territories tramped down by all authoritarian states as well as the unique terrain covered by the Shiite religious state.

Chapter 2

The Shiite Theocracy

The official Sunni Islam, which claims the allegiance of the majority of Muslims in the world, has only the Prophet Muhammad, who is considered to be the last messenger of God on earth. The orthodox Sunnis grapple with complex sets of traditions that his leading followers had developed in his name. In contrast, the Shiite religious landscape in Iran is more imaginitively crowded. The Twelver Shiites have erected a hierarchy of Imams, who as the direct twelve descendants of the Prophet had theoretically inherited a touch of prophetic charisma, if not divine attributes, leaving behind ponderous legacies of sacrosanct words. In theory the clerics consider these twelve superhuman beings as the eternal, rightful leaders, spiritually as well as politically, of the Shiite community. Some three centuries after the death of the Prophet, the Last Imam went into an indefinite period of occultation, to return one day as the Savior. In the past few centuries, an obscure clerical theory maintained that until the return of the Last Imam, the Shiite ulema would be the de facto leaders of the community.

In the recent memory of Iran, however, the Shahs ruled autocratically, allowing the Shiite ulema only as much authority as they needed to manage the religious and personal affairs of his mostly obedient subjects. At the same time, an informal hierarchy of Shiite clerics emerged, at the top of which stood a few senior *mojtaheds* (Islamic jurists). In the twentieth century, they assumed the title Grand Ayatollah. *Mojtahed* is a cleric who, after a lifetime of religious learning, is capable of rendering *ejtehad*, an opinion on Islamic law, based on a set of traditionally recognized sources. Each practicing Shiite is supposed to choose and follow one *mojtahed* as the *marja-e taqlid*, source of emulation. Each *marja-e taqlid* (*marja*, for short) is supposed to be an autonomous authority, whose teachings and judgments are voluntarily accepted by his followers. No more than a few clerics could achieve that august status at any given time. However, from time to time an especially distinguished *mojtahed*, one of the Grand Ayatollahs, received general acceptance by the others as the sole *marja* and his *fatvas* were universally accepted.

The central institution of the Islamic Republic rested on that tradition and distorted it as well.

Institutionalizing the Shiite Theocracy: *Velayat-e Faqih*

Some two decades before the Islamic revolution, in the wilderness of the Iranian political movements against the seemingly all-powerful Shah, several political activists, both clerics and laymen, began reconstructing Shiism politically. They sought to change it from a faith that offers all the ecclesiastical comforts and symbolic references that the Muslim needs to prepare for the Day of Judgment to a revolutionary ideology, Islamism. As such, it would provide assistance to the oppressed in their struggle against the oppressor (the Shah). More specifically, they projected a new image of Hossein, grandson of the Prophet and the martyred Third Imam. Traditionally, the Shiites consider him an ethereal being who is "capable of forgiving sins and granting admission to heaven by virtue of his role as intercessor before God."[1] The new image projected him more as a revolutionary hero, whose martyrdom contemporary Muslims should emulate. Against this background of Islamist activism, Ayatollah Ruhollah Musavi Khomeini emerged as the leader of the Islamist movement and introduced his own version of Islamic rule. This radicalized version of Islam subverted the older version of Islamic reformism that had been gaining currency among liberal Muslims since the turn of the century.

The central institution of the republic was to be *velayat-e faqih* (the vice-regency of the Islamic Jurist). In the absence of the Twelfth Imam, the *faqih* (Islamic Jurist, i.e., a Grand Ayatollah) was supposed to conduct the state's affairs in accordance with God's laws. Khomeini assumed this role and became the Supreme Leader, as Islamic Jurist. *Velayat-e faqih*, as envisaged by Khomeini, was alien to democracy. It was also unfamiliar to the Islamic reformists, who for years desired a place for Islam in the political life of the country. They, too, had to adjust themselves, at least while Khomeini was alive, to the newly politicized Islam, à la Khomeini, which went against the basic liberal tendencies of Islamic reformism. It took people awhile to understand the true meaning and implications of *velayat-e faqih*. Scores of clerical thinkers formulated their own versions of Islamic rule. Some rejected Khomeini's theory that Islamic jurisprudence could possibly justify the *faqih* as the ruler of a contemporary state.[2] Much of the political unrest in Iran in the late 1990s emanated from the fact that, after almost two decades, this institutional keystone failed to gain national acceptance, outside its hard-line supporters.

The politicized clerics wished to base the state on the foundation of Shiite jurisprudence, allowing legislation to take place only in direct correspondence to divine revelations. Implicit in *velayat-e faqih* was a deeply rooted distrust of the people's ability to exercise political sovereignty based on democratic institutions and procedure. Defending *velayat-e faqih*, the influential Ayatollah Muhammad Hossein Beheshti said: "In the present system leadership and legislation cannot be left to the majority at any given moment. This would contradict the ideological character of the Islamic Republic."[3] Because people were capable of committing errors, they needed the *faqih* as the ultimate arbiter of the people's judgment, supervising the legislative body whose laws might reflect the people's errors. *Velayat-e faqih* mirrored the absolute monarchy, hiding in religious-cultural garb the power of one individual over the state affairs.

Before the clerics around Ayatollah Khomeini established total control over the country in 1980, the provisional government under the moderate Prime Minister Mahdi Bazargan appointed four individuals, including the prominent human rights lawyer Abdolkarim Lahiji, to prepare a preliminary draft of the Constitution for the country. The drafters proposed to incorporate the provisions of the UDHR into the Constitution. The clerics in the Assembly of Experts altered this document beyond recognition and submitted for ratification another draft in which all the rights provisions were burdened by Islamic qualifications that purposefully remained undefined. As Shaul Bakhash has aptly observed, the clerics "seemed at once persuaded that Islam provided for basic freedoms and concerned lest these freedoms be used to undermine Islam, create disorder, spread undesirable doctrine, and protect those who deserved punishment."[4] The constitutional provisions for the protection of civil and political rights became limited and conditional. Having carefully studied the Islamist deliberations that transformed the draft constitution, Lahiji has pointed out that the Islamic qualifications were not based on the well-defined *shari'ah* concepts, such as Islamic ordinances (*ahkam*) or Islamic laws (*qavanin*). In all human rights provisions, the clerics stipulated that enjoyment of rights must remain in conformity with Islamic criteria (*m'ayar-ha*), Islamic standards (*mavazin*), Islamic principles (*mabani*), and the foundations (*asas*) of the Islamic Republic. Not only vague, all of these concepts seemed to be interchangeable.[5] Thus, the clerics allowed themselves the leeway to define these unspecified Islamic qualifications according to their own political requirements at any given period. Khomeini and his clerical associates also rejected the term "Democratic" from the original name proposed for the Islamic Republic of Iran.

Ann Elizabeth Mayer also critically evaluated the Constitution and subjected its rights provisions to a comparative analysis with international human rights law. She observed: "As long as an entrenched clerical elite with such adamant hostility to any kind of pluralism fights to defend its increasingly discredited Islamic ideology, Islamic qualifications on rights will assuredly undermine rights." The result was, in Mayer's words, a "remarkable admixture of international human rights principles concerning equality and assertions of the supremacy of Islamic law that directly contravene them."[6]

The admixture can be explained by the fact that the Islamists already had the liberal draft in front of them, to which they added Islamic qualifications.

Khomeini's ideas concerning proper rule under Shiite Islam informed the revision of the original draft. He and his clerical associates were ill prepared to be the authors of an enduring Constitution. They revised it amidst intense political battles, as Khomeini's followers rushed it through a highly politicized ratification process that generated dissension even among Khomeini's more moderate supporters. It coincided with the taking of American hostages. The Constitution, especially its rights provisions, lacked solid, unchanging normative underpinnings. The clerics used the ratification to stifle the vigorous but badly divided secular opposition to the emerging theocracy. The liberal Muslims complained but went along with their radical brethren and voted yes to the Constitution, which imposed vague Islamic qualifications on human rights.

At the end of the last Shah's rule, the Shiite clerics had failed to recognize any *mojtahed* as the sole source of emulation. Using the vacuum that had existed for a number of years, Khomeini's followers began to agitate for his recognition. Then the populist revolution, to the chagrin of many of his equals, catapulted him to a position that was even higher than the sole *marja*. To boast his stature, his zealot followers gave him the title of the Imam. It stuck, despite many humorous illwishers who referred to him as the Thirteenth Imam. Khomeini envisaged *velayat-e faqih* as the rule of the *marja*, and surely he saw himself eminently qualified to assume the position. The Constitution defined the position as befitting the one who possessed all the traditional qualifications and seniority of a Grand Ayatollah plus political and personal leadership abilities. Khomeini's associates had tailored it for him.

Shortly before Khomeini's death, the Constitution was amended, since there was no other person who combined these two sets of qualifications and abilities, in addition to being willing to subject himself to the quagmires of factional politics. Khomeini died before the amendment reached ratification by the Assembly of Leadership Experts (Majlis-e Khobregan-e Rahbari), another constitutional body packed by clerics. The assembly had the responsibility of appointing the Supreme Leader, as Khomeini's successor, and removing him if he failed to perform his duties. Political expediency compelled a few powerful clerics belonging to two competing factions to coalesce against the Montazeri faction and select the former president, Ali Khamenei, not even an Ayatollah at the time, as the next Supreme Leader. A preordained selection by the Assembly of Experts followed. In July 1989, the amended Constitution dropped the required qualification for the Supreme Leader to be a *marja*, further undermining the theoretical rational for *velayat-e faqih*. In the eyes of critics, it became *velayat-e faqih* without the *faqih*. This offered dissident religious figures another reason to renew their objection to the concept of *velayat-e faqih*. A number of Grand Ayatollahs could only view Khomeini's successor with barely disguised disdain, as he was a middle-rank cleric lacking the highest religious credentials. The best that Khamenei's supporters could claim for him was his recognition as one *marja* among others. As will be shown in Chapter 14, the dissident Ayatollahs and their associates who refused to remain silent became victims of human rights violations at the hands of the clerics in power.

Shiite cultural attitudes shaped the contours of this protracted struggle. However, which cultural elements the Islamists in power selected, politicized, and distorted were decided politically, sometimes to the surprise of many traditional clerics. The divinely inspired life of *velayat-e faqih* has been bedeviled by contentions and rejections, casting a long shadow over Islamists' claim to cultural authenticity and causing many human rights violations.

The populist revolution that preceded the Islamic Republic was itself nourished by a multifaceted tradition. Significantly, the concept of *velayat-e faqih* was absent from the opposition political discourses that had evolved since the first Iranian revolution in 1905–11. That tradition was largely shaped by the Western secular concepts that had gradually seeped into the Iranian national consciousness. The Islamic Republic could not simply free itself from this modern (non-Islamic) tradition. The very notion of a constitution is an example of an idea that was Western and modern, and yet the first thing the Ayatollah felt compelled to do was to write a constitution. Other non-Islamic notions are "parliament," "nation," "republic," "elections," "popular sovereignty," and the three branches—legislature, judiciary, and executive—of the state. These and many other essential concepts formed the institutional backbone of the Islamic Republic. Reflecting this long-standing influence, article 6 of the Constitution provided that "the administration of the country's affairs will be regulated by the will of the people." The Constitution also provided for periodic elections for the president and the members of the Majlis.

Thus, the absolute rule of the *faqih* (the Supreme Leader) coexisted in a contradictory way with the reality of popular sovereignty. The contradiction was enshrined in the Constitution, which provides for elected assemblies, while granting ultimate power to the *faqih*. The dual attribution of sovereignty did not appear problematic to the drafters of the Constitution, who assumed that the overwhelming majority of the people would continue supporting the Leader-Jurist unconditionally. Therefore, devoid of major political disagreements, the entire system would be free of all political or constitutional contradictions. Khomeini constantly emphasized unity around the banner of Islam, which would make the Godly Republic different from all other republics. The mundane social practices, intense personal conflicts within the ruling groups, and feverish jockeying for official positions and wealth proved much stronger than his ideological presupposition of an Islamic unity devoid of political conflicts. The human rights consequences of that contradictory political arrangement will be examined in Chapter 15, dealing with the right to political participation.

At the level of bureaucratic institutions, economic life, and state affairs, Islamization has proven problematic, creating unexpected twists and surprising shifts and generating heated disagreements within the clerical caste. The management of the modern state in a complex society proved far more complicated than the task of imposing Islamic morality on the public space, superficially altering the attitudes of city dwellers, and forcing secular women to don the chador.

Ruling the Contemporary State: The Limits of Islamic Law

Like a protective shield forged by immutable Islamic ordinances, the *shari'ah* was supposed to cast a wide net covering the entire length and breadth of the modern state. Ironically, however, the rule of the clerics has helped to underline its woeful limitations. The net is full of holes, through which flow all sorts of modern institutions and Western habits, making the Islamic state a bewildering hybrid, confusing the clerics more than the secularists. In a detailed study of the Constitution of the Islamic Republic, Asghar Schirazi, an Iranian-born scholar in Berlin, has convincingly demonstrated the inherently limited capacity of the *shari'ah* in providing the legal foundation for the contemporary state. Schirazi has shown that once the first Majlis met, it became apparent to its members that they could not solidly ground their legislation on what the mullahs call the *shari'ah*'s primarily ordinances: Due to its antiquity, the *shari'ah* "does not provide *ahkam* [ordinances] for regulating most problems which arise in governing a modern state."[7]

The political clerics created the Guardian Council, a twelve-member constitutional body, to oversee the Islamic validity of the legislative process. It could reject parliamentary bills that it deemed contradictory to the *shari'ah*. Six of its clerical jurists were appointed by the Leader, and six lay jurists were nominated by the Head of the Judiciary, himself an appointee of the Leader. A majority of the six clerical jurists, that is, four men, could block any legislation passed by the Majlis. From the beginning, the Council became more conservative than many of the Majlis deputies. The activist Majlis and the conservative custodians of the *shari'ah* in the Council were stuck in a legislative impasse over such major initiatives as laws governing land distribution, commerce, and banking. In that situation, Khomeini felt compelled to intervene. For him, the survival of the Islamic regime was the only issue. Sweeping aside the legislative impasse, he issued the infamous *fatva* (religious edict) that must have shocked the less political Ayatollahs: the existence of the Islamic state superseded all Islamic ordinances. The inherent inadequacy of the *shari'ah* appeared ominous for the survival of the Islamic Republic: "In the relevant decree issued on 7 January 1988, Khomeini announced that government rule was 'derived from the absolute dominion of the Prophet of God.' This was 'the most important of God's ordinances (*ahkam-e elahi*)' and stood above 'all ordinances that were derived or directly commanded by Allah.' If a measure was in the interest of the state and Islam, it could annul all other Islamic ordinances, even prayer, fasting and the pilgrimage to Mecca."[8]

Khomeini created the new "Council for Assessing What Is in the Interest of the Order" in February 1988. The Assessment Council (also referred to as the Expediency Council), whose members Khomeini appointed, was given the final authority in deciding legislative disputes between the Majlis and the Guardian Council. The amended Constitution accommodated the new arrangements. A nonelected body, the Assessment Council became the highest legislative authority and one of the most powerful centers of decision making in the Islamic Republic. The next Supreme Leader, Ali Khamenei, appointed the former president, Hashimi Rafsanjani, as the chief of the Assessment Council in 1997.

Schirazi does not assume that changes the clerics introduced into Iran's legal system were insignificant. Yet these changes, though considerable, did not amount to the full Islamization envisaged by the clerics. To show the inadequacy of the main corpus of the *shari'ah* public laws, Schirazi has discussed the instances where the clerics tried to bring laws into strict Islamic conformity but "came up against difficulties."[9] Forced to accept the reality, they adopted laws whose origins can hardly be traced back to the *shari'ah*: "A cursory glance at the history of the Islamic Republic makes it clear that the basis for most fundamental decisions throughout all phases of the state's development and on all levels of government was the interest of the ruling system—or more correctly, the interest of those persons, groups and camps who participated in power."[10]

This should not surprise the students of contemporary authoritarian states. The clerical rulers and their lay associates retained or brought back many of the previous regime's laws. They felt compelled "to accept laws which were to a certain extent the result of Western-influenced change in Iranian society over a period of several decades."[11]

Islamization of Society

It has become apparent that forced re-Islamization of Iranian society failed. However, the society paid a heavy price. From the beginning, the clerics' revolution was fiercely verbal. The craftsmen of holy words used language to disorient and intimidate secular Iranians in general and leftist activists in particular. They believed in the power of the Qur'anic language and its once extraordinary effect on the minds of the faithful. Unfortunately for the clerics—and even more so for secular Iranians—the world that had spun that particular language had been altered and could not be remade by injecting a new vigor into the old incantations. In 1979, the political clerics were unsure of their ability to rule alone and held back in their skill at unleashing a torrent of Islamic oratory and political rhetoric that demonized secular political groups and intellectuals. In 1981, however, they put all restraints aside.

State legitimacy was sought in a rhetoric that infused a dazzling dose of Shiism, with its historical love affair with martyrdom and lamentation, into a radical version of Third Worldism, which was then uttering its last gasp elsewhere in the post-Nasser Middle East. By mid-1980, there was no escaping the barrage of the religious verbiage, creating a new rhetorical frame of discourse and affecting the citizens' relationship to political narrative and to the previously existing national symbols and images. This was the time when the clerically dominated state had established a total monopoly over press and airwaves, parading scores of Islamist ideologues on radio and television. They purported to show the fallacies of Marxism, nationalism, liberalism, or any other modern, ungodly ideologies that have made an impact on modern Iranian thought. The official media was full of hectoring, denunciations, and ill-informed assertions. The clerics veiled in religious symbols their insatiable thirst for total political power.

They also used the language to instill guilt, especially in women, for succumbing to the imperialist plots and temptations that had reduced them to "consumer robots." The propagandist language disparaged modern women for "painting" their faces with cosmetics that the West sold them. Newspapers, magazines, radio, and television referred to them as Western dolls, and the less literate and more raucous *hezbollahis* in the streets of Tehran screamed "Whores" in their faces. Their language differed from other authoritarian discourses only in its intense use of religious rhetoric. Otherwise, it shared a common universe with all such discourses in its obsession with the enemy, its triumphant oratory, its lack of a sense of humor, and its monopoly over "truth." Compelling submission to the politicized Islam of the Ayatollah, the language constructed a new line of authority replacing the Shah. Mirroring the exaggerated titles the last Shah's courtiers invented for him to affect the relationship between authority and subordination, Khomeini's seminarians began to refer to him as the Imam, the Great Leader of the Islamic Revolution, and the Leader of the Oppressed Peoples. The dimensions of these titles were supposed to be global.

The missions of moral cleansing, which violated the right to freedom of conscience of secular Iranians, gave birth to a new profession, which soon proliferated into a score of organizations and groups, engaged in such tasks as "propagation of virtue." Their task was to purify the society from all the sinful habits of urban life. From the perspective of the Shiite mullahs, life in Tehran was deeply demonic, steaming with the debauchery of modernity. Islamization was in full swing. Brandishing Western-made guns, young men with stern faces and frustrated desires became the scourges of urban centers. They descended on social gatherings where women mingled freely with men and clamped down on sinful polluters of the environment, in particular those who dared to entertain any thought of popular music and dance. They also forced the emancipated women to don the Islamic headscarves. Color in clothing was banned, rouge was outlawed, cheers were silenced, and fun was exiled, all giving cause to the celebrated secular poet Ahmad Shamlu to lament the revisitation of the Middle Ages. Entertainment was emptied of its modern content. The urban landscape of public entertainment had already shrunk, as nightclubs and bars were burned down at the instigation of lower-rank clerics. Alcohol, music cassettes, videos, gambling, and prostitution were driven into a thriving underground, profitable for both those who offered the vices and those who policed them. The latter quickly learned to cash in on the lucrative business to be found in the shadowy alleyways of urban life. Secular teachers were simply dismissed, and the Islamic Cultural Revolution closed the universities to thousands of qualified professors. The purge extended to many important offices in the large bureaucracies of the Shah's regime, and every vacated chair of a purged bureaucrat became a lucrative seat for a newly empowered supporter of Khomeini. The purges did not stop at those who were still alive. The Islamist ideologues purged the history of modern Iran of scores of secular, nationalist, and leftist characters. New books extolled the political virtues of those who had carried the banner of Islam in political movements since the turn of the century.[12]

Political Context of Human Rights Violations During the 1980s

The large number of executions of military officers and high-ranking civil servants in the early days of the revolution revealed the politicized clerics' vengeful temperament in that particular time. They also established the arbitrary and hectic pace that characterized the subsequent treatments of the much younger participants in the revolution. The Shiite clerics in power also believed they had finally received the God-given chance to rid Iran of the "depraved Baha'i sect," or force them back into the Shiite fold. Politically, the highly repressive character of the regime emerged during the process by which the clerics severely restricted the basic freedoms and rights of political activists. They achieved their goal by forcibly removing all secular, leftist, and liberal political forces and individuals from the wide and unwieldy array of political activities that the revolution had opened up in 1979. The clerical success dislodged some four million Iranians and sent them to all parts of the world, especially to the United States, which had educated many of them or their sons and daughters. Paradoxically, the presence of so many Iranians in the United State has strengthened, in the long run, the links between the two nations.

In 1980–81, the violent closing of the revolutionary political space left behind a trail of blood, both inside and outside of prisons. Witnessing the prison cruelties, the novelist Shahrnush Parsipur called the period an "intersection of blood, slime, and stupidity."[13] After June 21, 1981, the revolution ravaged its more secular youths, piling up death, maimed bodies, and shattered souls.

As the politicized clerics began establishing the absolute rule of the Islamic Jurist (*velayat-e faqih*), all the secular and leftist organizations faced certain political annihilation. So did the members of the Organization of Mojahedin-e Khalq (the Mojahedin, a radical Muslim group, whose remnants eventually established a base in Iraq).[14] With their backs against the wall on June 20–21, 1981, the Mojahedin ordered its mostly young and inexperienced members to resist the emerging theocracy. Sporadic attacks against the Revolutionary Guards failed miserably. The Mojahedin bombed official buildings, killing scores of influential clerics and laymen. As discussed in the next chapter, the Mojahedin youngsters received the full brunt of the Ayatollah's rage. The face of death smiled at those young men and women as clerical judges declared them to have engaged in a "war against God." Firing squads kept reloading their American-made guns, perforating the bodies of the proponents of the "American Islam," as the clerics referred to the Mojahedin's version of "revolutionary Islam."

It is not accurate to attribute the use of brutal force to suppress radical opponents to the clerics' fear for the security of their regime. If anything, the Ayatollah and his men were overconfident about their ability to retain their hold on the reins of state. Any observer who watched the events of that fateful summer in Tehran's streets, as this writer did, would have been struck by how unequal the fight was. There could have been no doubt about the outcome of the armed confrontations in which Revolutionary Guards crushed the Mojahedin and other leftist groups. The clerics and their security agents depicted the opposition as the fifth column of the imperialist powers, and they gained political mileage among their own followers by that misleading depiction. They were, however, confident that all of the leading members of the opposition groups would be captured or killed, their "safe houses" dismantled, and their printing presses halted. The clerics suppressed the resistance, and the fear it evoked continued to keep everyone silent until well into the 1990s.

Political Context of Human Rights Violations During the 1990s

By the mid-1990s it was increasingly apparent that the once ferocious script of the Islamist Revolution—that peculiar mixture of anachronism and an outdated Third World radicalism—was left with only aging actors and a declining audience. Many aspects of the state bureaucracy and economy had been discreetly reverting to their pre-1979 characteristics. The revolution was powerful enough to wreak havoc but not powerful enough to change the nature of the contemporary state or the secular habits of middle-class

Iranians. The Shah's state had reasserted itself, bulky and corrupt, with its bureaucratic practices and its technocratic agenda and objectives. A new generation of technobureaucrats also appeared, desiring to placate secular, middle-class Iranians and to make the Islamic Republic more amenable to the West.

Khomeini's death in June 1989 removed an obstinate and xenophobic obstacle to more cooperative relations with European countries and the United Nations. The more opportunist and less traditional cleric Ali Akbar Hashemi Rafsanjani became president in August 1989. By this time, many high officials within the regime recognized that the rigid, ideological recourse to Shiite symbolism, though still somewhat effective, was losing its once powerful legitimizing and mobilizing appeal. With the destructive war with Iraq ended, the semiofficial press began, under President Rafsanjani, to create a different kind of imagery projected to validate legitimacy: the cleric-president, posing for "photo ops" in the Shah's style, surrounded by Islamic technobureaucrats in double-breasted suits but without neckties, explaining their latest showcase projects. The goal, however, remained the same: reinforcement of state legitimacy and justification for those who controlled its policies.

Many people had already begun reverting to the everyday Islam they knew best. Islamic technobureaucrats, appointed by Rafsanjani, began articulating yet another new version of Islam, one that can be safely housed in state bureaucracies, that is devoid of the zealotry of the revolutionary version, yet is capable of sustaining the Islamic legitimacy of the authoritarian regime. Rafsanjani's version of politicized Islam announced itself in a semisecular discourse that stressed cultural authenticity, economic development, and national self-determination, as practiced within the predictable confines of the religious state, guided by the benevolent, authoritarian Supreme Leader. As will be discussed in Chapter 13, this opened an opportunity for other Islamic activists to free themselves from Khomeini's version of Islamist rule (*velayat-e faqih*) and revert to the older Islamic reformism that was far more attuned to the liberalism of the twentieth century.

The Islamic Revolution had failed to deliver on its promises, and many Iranians were tired of the ideological fire and brimstone of clerical rulers who—themselves in the grip of internal confusion—issued contradictory statements about their intentions and politics. The zealotry of radical Islamism had become routine; meanwhile, there appeared a strong desire for normalcy, compromise, and ideological surrender. Instead of the Shiite ideologues Islamizing the state and society, the technobureaucrats were transmuting the Ayatollah's vision of a God-fearing Shiite Iran.

The mercurial President Rafsanjani tried to boost his legitimacy among the middle class by showing that he was capable of ruling the country rationally and effectively. For this purpose he depended on technobureaucrats he gathered around his cabinet. The official claims invested a great deal of

hope in the future of Iran as an advanced, prosperous society with a materi-
ally strong state. Thus, the state propaganda projected a new catchphrase:
"Stability in Iran's affairs."[15] Technobureaucrats sought legitimacy not so
much in Islam but in managerial process. In the words of an influential member of the Majlis (parliament): "Today our biggest struggle [jihad] is to make
the Islamic government efficient. If the government is inefficient, the legitimacy of the system is questioned."[16]

Under Rafsanjani, the ideological commissars continued to display their
forbidding faces, but a new breed of Iranian technobureaucrats strengthened its positions as the second stratum of power, just below the politically dominant theocrats.[17] Although coming from a more modest social
class than the Shah's technobureaucrats, they exhibited the same traditional
habits, especially in their ability to adjust to a subservient position and to
flow with the political currents. They were the clients of the clerics to whom
they owed their positions in the state administration.

The Two Faces of the Religious State Under President Rafsanjani

Transcending the Islamist challenge, the Iranian state has remained pivotal
in the distribution of power, wealth, and status. Two interrelated tendencies became apparent in the early 1990s. First, some educated Iranians have
always been susceptible to the attraction of power. A strong disposition to
conformity was induced by their upbringing in an educational system that
was one of the main institutions of the twentieth century's (Foucauldian)
disciplinary state, which survived any postrevolutionary shock. The Muslim technobureaucrats had situated themselves within that tradition, where
their accommodationist orientation legitimated the hegemony of dominant
discourse in the state.

Second, the technobureaucrats tried to repress any consciousness of the
human rights violations of the regime they served, denied their occurrence,
or accepted them as normal events well into the late 1990s. The Iranian-
born scholar Rejali has pointed out the tendency on the part of the Shah's
technobureaucrats to consider torture as an integral or routine part of the
contemporary state, thus ignoring evil as if it were normal. Rejali asserted
that torture was intrinsically linked to modern politics, while arguing that
it was important that "the specific linkage be interrupted."[18]

As during the Shah's regime, the technobureaucrats sometimes tried to
distance themselves from the "system," while continuing to partake of the
benefits the state offered. Seemingly unaware that they might in fact be
masking the repressive nature of the regime by their smoke screens of technical expertise, they wanted no political, or nontechnical, responsibility for
the repressive apparatus of the state. At times, they seemed embarrassed
about the backward outlook of their clerical patrons. In his last interview
with a European journalist, the late Mahdi Bazargan, the first Prime Min-

ister of the Islamic Republic, who was pushed aside and taunted by radical Islamists, described how some of the technobureaucrats behaved even
apologetically toward him.[19] In public, however, they were mostly careful to
comport themselves in ways that respected the ideological dictates of the
clerics; they also observed the etiquette of social interactions imposed by
the clerics. They played that game until 1997, when the regime faced its most
serious challenge since the fall of its first president in 1981.

Clearly, these laypersons yearned to be recognized by the outside world
as modern experts dedicated to progress in their respective fields. Outside
recognition would serve as an ethical justification for their service as political appointees in a repressive clerical regime. This desire may explain a penchant for holding seminars on every conceivable topic to which outside academic participants, including American apologists, were invited.[20]

Concerning human rights violations, the Iranian state reemerged during
Rafsanjani's presidency with its two familiar faces: the visible and the invisible. Technobureaucrats who were publicly visible rendered themselves
unaccountable for the human rights abuses that were taking place. Those
who were hidden beyond the walls of the security apparatus remained out
of reach.

Kept hidden from the bureaucratic side of the state, a fearsome security
apparatus was erected connecting the Intelligence Ministry's officials to the
security services of the Revolutionary Guards, the *basiji* paramilitary forces,
and the national police force, all linked with a caste of interchangeable characters with the Revolutionary Courts. In the mid-1980s, the urgent need for
a centralized intelligence organization overcame Khomeini's initial reluctance to agree to anything that would resemble the Shah's security apparatus, the SAVAK. With his approval, the Majlis passed the bill setting up
the Intelligence Ministry, and the ruthless and well-connected Muhammad
Muhammadi Reyshahri, the former clerical judge of the military tribunal,
assumed the post in 1986. All his successors were clerics. An informal procedure removed the selection of the Intelligence Minister from the president's discretion and made it a prerogative of the Leader. Reyshahri selected
a number of clerical deputies who controlled the regime's security web for
the next fifteen years. Men like Fallahian, Mir-Hejazi, Muhammadi Golpaye-
gani, and Pur-Muhammadi served in various security-related posts inside or
outside of the Ministry. The end of the war with Iraq brought hundreds of
zealots from war management to the security services. The bureaucratic side
of the state had very little knowledge of their mostly illegal activities. All indications are that the terrorist network that assassinated hundreds of Iranians was set up under Reyshahri's henchman and successor, Ali Fallahian.
The Ministry even created an extensive money-generating apparatus ("business enterprises") to finance its activities outside the governmental budget.
It paid for its secret operations without the knowledge of the bureaucratic
side.

In 1992, the Partisans of the Party of God (Ansar-e Hezbollah, or *hezbol-lahis* for short) were reorganized and became in effect the semiofficial instrument of the security apparatus. A mistaken impression had been created that the *hezbollahis* were merely spontaneously formed crowds. The new circumstantial evidences divulged by the reformist press in 1999–2000 indicated otherwise. In this new form, the *hezbollahi* leaders were recruited from the war-hardened *basijis* (irregular, militia-type force) and other drifting veterans who had become nostalgic about the revolutionary ethos of 1978–80 and ill at ease with the mild manifestations of bureaucratic normalcy. The regime had originally formed the *basijis* during the Iran-Iraq war for mobilizing volunteers, especially among underclass youths. The *basijis* constituted a different, less militarized version of the Islamic Revolutionary Guards Corps, who had been the scourge of the anticlerical activists in the early 1980s.

The leaders of the *hezbollahis* were closely associated with the controlling faction in the Intelligence Ministry and certain commanders of the Revolutionary Guards. They also received support from the office of the Supreme Leader and coordinated their activities with the Association of Combatant Clerics (Jame'eh-ye Ruhaniyyat-e Mobarez), the dominant clerical faction in the 1990s. The Leader was perhaps beholden to this powerful cabal that prepared the way for him to assume Khomeini's position. The *basijis* general Hossein Allah-Karam was recognized as the head of the *hezbollahis*. They created their own publications and received critical support from the well-founded semiofficial daily *Kayhan*, which was under the control of Hossein Shari'atmadari, a former Deputy Intelligence Minister under Reyshahri. Therefore, the violent *hezbollahis* were an integral part of the security network that had been created by the first Intelligence Minister and his associates. They could not to be presented, as the diplomats tried to do in the second half of the 1990s, as a nongovernmental organization working to preserve Islamic values.

Ali Fallahian, the young, black-bearded mullah, became the Intelligence Minister in 1988, replacing Reyshahri, who moved to another critical task of supervising the prosecution of the clerics who challenged the new Supreme Leader. In the last years of Rafsanjani's presidency, observers often discussed domestic policies in terms of the conflict between "moderates" and "hard-liners," a portrayal that did not help in understanding human rights abuses. In fact, the "pragmatic faction" that advocated a moderate approach to the West represented none other than one faction (the technobureaucratic one) within the visible face of the regime, masquerading the repressive face of the mullah power holders in the security apparatus.

In 1996, Mohsen Reza'i, then the radical commander of the Revolutionary Guards, pointed out the availability of different forces to preserve the clerical regime. Reza'i distinguished between the threats emanating from armed organizations (e.g., the exiled Mojahedin) and political threats originating from "antirevolutionary political currents that are unarmed." In the Islamist lexicon, the latter included all those Iranians who oppose clerical dominance in Iran, especially secular cultural producers and intellectuals. For the first threat, he said, the regime had the armed forces, including his own Revolutionary Guards; on the other hand, to deal with the "political currents," the regime possessed "an abundance of mobilized and popular forces [*basiji* and *hezbollahi*] who would diligently and timely perform their role." He further explained what was needed in the face of nonviolent political threats: "Under those conditions, there is no need for the use of weapons or violence, nor is there a need for the involvement of the Revolutionary Guards. In those conditions, the use of violence is absolutely not expedient, and the enormous forces of the *hizbollahi* and *basiji* would adequately deal with the threatening political currents against the revolution. This would be accomplished without the Revolutionary Guards making any moves. It has always been that way."[21]

In late 1999, when the internal conflicts had further intensified, the new commander of the Islamic Revolutionary Guards, Yahya Rahim Safa'i, reminded the reformers of the "*basiji* volunteer forces." He stated that their current number of five million would be increased to ten million by the end of the Third Five-Year Development Plan in 2004. Their goal would remain the same: to confront "domestic and foreign conspiracies."[22]

Thus, the institutionalization of the Islamic revolution also created a division of responsibility for the state security apparatus, a division that resulted partly in privatization of the means of repression and violence. This arrangement worked, more or less effectively, until the end of the Rafsanjani presidency in 1997. As a cleric with close ties to other political clerics and as the President, Rafsanjani was capable of maintaining a delicate balance between the two sides of the state. He did not allow himself or his (nonsecurity) ministers to pry deeply into the affairs of the secret side, often defending both the security apparatus and the judicial system that were together the main violators of human rights. He also kept the Ministry of Culture and Islamic Guidance in check, never permitting it to unduly arouse the anger of the hard-line clerics, who easily took umbrage at signs of cultural and artistic permissiveness. Tensions grew gradually between the dominant Islamist discourse of intellectual austerity and worship of martyrdom and the more permissive discourses that called for a return to normalcy in all affairs of public life. Rafsanjani never allowed these tensions to get out of hand, as evidenced by the resignation in 1992 of Muhammad Khatami, then the Minister of Culture, who felt that it was time for a slight reduction of intellectual and cultural controls.

Reflecting these broader trends, the Foreign Ministry changed its denunciatory policy toward the United Nations in the fall of 1989 and began a concerted effort to remove Iran from the UN special procedures of public scrutiny. Iran's isolation in the 1980s had begun to disturb the technobureaucrats. In February 1996, Foreign Minister Ali Akbar Velayati expressed his frustration in an interview against those who had opposed any dialogue with the United Nations over human rights. "Ambassadors of foreign countries come to us and raise these issues on behalf of their governments and want answers. With great difficulty, we have to find out these issues one by one and we must reply through our diplomatic correspondence. We go to a country to buy goods; they tell us straighten up our human rights. We want to meet with someone, they make the same condition for us." He added that if he did not respond to the international concerns, the country would suffer economically.[23]

By the end of the 1980s, the organizational abilities of opposition groups, especially the radical Mojahedin, were crushed by the execution of hundreds of members and the cowing of others who were left alone to ruminate about their bitter feelings of defeat and disappointment. The repression swept Iranian politics clean of all overt opposition to the theocracy. A manageable state of normalcy, free from the sight of bodies hanging from cranes, could be maintained; it allowed a more credible domestic background to emerge, one that was more supportive of the official denials of human rights violations. The regime's diplomats increased their contacts with the UN Special Representative, "frequently by telephone." [24]

The bureaucratic, visible side of the state sought normalcy and responded to international concerns. In the meantime, the Intelligence Ministry, the Revolutionary Guards, and the Judiciary in charge of the Revolutionary Courts made sure that the political power of the clerics remained unchallenged. They also used unofficial groups and paramilitary organizations (*hezbollahis* and *basijis*) to carry on vigilante actions.

At any event, the closure of the first period (1979–89) set the conditions for the second phase of hidden human rights violations, when relatively fewer Iranians dared to challenge openly the clerical rule or to claim their human rights. The diligent presence of the *hezbollahi* gangs proved sufficiently intimidating. Prisons were largely emptied of political prisoners, and the cracking of bullets became less frequent. Free from the daily executions of political opponents, the Islamic Republic of Iran was in a position to issue an invitation to the Special Representative of the Commission on Human Rights for a visit to Iran in January 1990.[25] Chapter 11 will examine the change of tactics aimed at removing Iran from the UN special procedures of public scrutiny.

Muhammad Khatami's Presidency Since 1997

Given the controlling nature of *velayat-e faqih*, the widespread desire for lifting the burden of Islamization could find no open and independent manifestation outside officially recognized political space and tolerated political groups. In one way or another, individuals and groups within the regime began discreetly to express political views that reflected that fundamental desire; the interests and demands of people of means and education began to be voiced by former Islamists who belonged to the regime but were pushed out of positions of influence. This development will be further explained in Chapters 13 and 14. It appeared that *velayat-e faqih* might in fact be subverted from within.

In the second half of the 1990s, President Rafsanjani began to use his considerable political skill and energy outside the clerical establishment by expanding the controlled network of technobureaucrats, who themselves had become—in the absence of any alternative political forums—tribunes for the aggrieved middle classes. His ties to the clerical (political) establishment always prevented him from upsetting that delicate balance which he had created between the two sides of the state or from allowing his administration to be the willing conduit for widespread discontent among the youth and women.

However, the Islamic Republic's institutional framework, which was supposed to effectively mediate between the institution of *velayat-e faqih* and popular sovereignty, did not perform as effectively as expected. One fundamental contradiction existed between the attempt at ideological reconstruction of the state and society and the acceptance of a formal electoral process. The Islamic Constitution provided that the president and representatives of the Majlis be elected by popular vote. By allowing popular elections, the desire of the people of means and education found an avenue of expression within the system, leading to Khatami's election.

Hojjat al-Islam Muhammad Khatami had served as the Minister of Culture and Islamic Guidance for a few years in Rafsanjani's cabinet, until his resignation in 1992. Hojjat al-Islam (proof of Islam) is the title of a middle-rank cleric. As an established cleric and a son of a well-known provincial Ayatollah, Khatami had all the credentials of an insider, and his younger brother had married Ayatollah Khomeini's granddaughter. Yet, during his youthful journey through the Shah's educational system, he had tasted the forbidden fruits of Western-style modernity and secularism. Before permanently donning the clerical cloak, he was adorned in the smart uniform of a junior officer in the Shah's army, serving the mandatory military term for university graduates.

After his resignation as a minister in Rafsanjani's first presidency, he received the post of director of the National Library, which allowed him to keep his contacts with Islamic intellectuals. Perhaps he had somehow managed to create in his own mind an amalgam of Islamic norms and behaviors with modern secular thoughts and habits—the balance always tilting, to the chagrin of secularists, in favor of the former. Hoping to bridge the vast ideological divisions, he apparently assumed that all young Iranians, if allowed, would willingly create such a balance in their own minds, allowing them to remain deeply committed to Islam, while becoming tolerant of some of the cultural manifestations of modernity. He has been thrust into an almost impossible position, playing the role of a compassionate pragmatist who would preserve the Islamic regime and satisfy the secular youth yearning to join the global culture.

In the exciting presidential election of May 1997, the women and youth of Iran discovered the candidate Khatami. His victory surprised the powerful clerics in control of the Guardian Council, who could never guess that Khatami would trample their official candidate, Ali Akbar Nateq-Nuri, at the polls. Many secularists and liberal Muslims, weary of conservative Islamic restrictions, perceived Khatami's election as a popular rejection of the hard-line Islamists and the Supreme Leader, Ayatollah Ali Khamenei, who had left very little doubt about his own preference for the hard-line cleric Nateq-Nuri. The close identification of Nateq-Nuri with the dominant political faction and the perceived closed association of the Leader with the same faction seemed to have been a significant reason for millions of Iranians not to vote for him. Khatami benefited enormously from this negative vote.

A significant development for human rights violations took place after Khatami became president. The delicate balance between the bureaucratic administration and the security-judicial apparatus was disturbed. This undermined the relative independence of the Intelligence Ministry, which had acted with impunity and without accountability. It also opened the Judiciary to criticism by the technobureaucrats.

The hard-line clerics and the Leader understood that the institution of *velayat-e faqih* had come under attack, and they were characteristically determined to defend it at any cost. *Velayat-e faqih* had created a vast system of clientelism, in which influential clerics and lay *hezbollahis* were linked through a web of political and financial interests throughout the country. The young men on whom the clerics bestowed machine guns would fight to preserve the only institution that offered them legitimacy. The powerful cliques of lumpen managers in charge of state-owned enterprises and foundations—all operating under the Leader's protective umbrella—would not peaceably fold their lucrative tents and return to private sectors. Aware that their political existence was irrevocably tied to *velayat-e faqih*, they began the process of frustrating the newly elected President, in particular trying to defeat his agenda for more tolerance and openness.

Defending *velayat-e faqih*, the daily *Resalat* declared ominously: "In the Islamic system, the legitimacy of all posts and organizations is derived from and depends on *velayat-e faqih*."[26] And the equally hard-line Ayatollah Muhammad Yazdi, Head of the Judiciary, defended *velayat-e faqih* against "poisonous pens" who conspired beyond closed doors but dared not express their points of views in major newspapers. "Those who do not understand Islam do not have the right to express an opinion about Islam."[27] Even the former president, Rafsanjani, rushed to defend *velayat-e faqih*. In an interesting twist, he linked *velayat-e faqih* to the well-established sense of Iranian nationalism that the clerics had despised two decades earlier. He portrayed it as the only guarantor of the unity and integrity of Iran,[28] in the same way that the last Shah maintained that without the institution of monarchy the country would disintegrate. From the opposite side, the ousted Ayatollah Hossein Ali Montazeri, the elderly warrior of the clerical revolution of the 1970s, entered the fray by throwing his weight behind the critics of *velayat-e faqih*. Closely watched by security agents since his removal from power in 1989, Montazeri questioned the legitimacy of the exclusive clerical rule. In response, the Leader invited the judicial officials to bring Montazeri to trial for treason against Islam and the people. The future of both *velayat-e faqih* and the Iranian people's relations with their Shiite clerics remained uncertain. Chapters 13 and 14 will examine the consequences of the intraclerical factionalism not only for the violations that took place during Khatami's presidency but also for validating the violations that had taken place before 1997.

The following chapters do not attempt to provide an exhaustive account of every and all violation that took place; however, they provide enough examples to enable the reader to make an informed judgment on the issue of cultural relativism in human rights discourse. Vociferous claims to Islamic laws and culture helped to hide the state practices behind a thick veil, in the same way that Marxist claims in the Soviet Union had to be peeled off to reveal the brutalities of the Stalinist rule. The makeup behind the veil betrayed the high moral plateau erected by the Islamist ideologues. The devil is in the details of the state practices, to which I now turn, beginning with the first five categories of human rights violations. Again, in each category, I will first rely on the prison memoirs; then I will turn to international human rights reports for the 1980 and finally to the situation in the 1990s, relying on all sources.

Chapter 3

The Right to Life

> The international community considered the taking of life by summary
> or arbitrary execution, whether or not justified to combat insurgency or
> terror, an assault upon a fundamental right.
>
> —William Korey

The Shiite ulema's understanding of the medieval Islamic laws meshed with
the overreaching power of the contemporary state, determining the applicability of the death penalty, its frequency of use, and the methods of executions. In 1979, many of the Shah's generals and high civil servants (and later
radical participants in the revolution) heard for the first time in their lives
the deadly concepts of the Ayatollah's justice. As capital crimes, the *mofsed fel
arz* (one who sows corruption on earth) and *mohareb* (warring against God)
called for divine retribution, now meted out by the authoritarian modern
state. The clerics used frightening, unfamiliar terms—in Arabic largely un-
intelligible to the Persian-speaking Iranians—to signify the advent of the
Islamic justice system. The *mofsed fel arz*, even the very sound of it, struck fear
in the hearts of prisoners. The Islamists emptied the term of its traditional
Islamic notions related to sins and imbued it with new shades of meaning,
derived from the experiences of nation-states in the twentieth century. An
Islamic judge explained the novel meaning of "sowing corruption on earth"
for a helpless defendant, facing certain death. It means spreading wretchedness, depriving people of their rights and freedoms, and undermining the
independence, security, and well-being of the country.[1] The contemporary
jargons of the nation-state would have confounded the medieval jurists who
had formulated the *shari'ah*.

Through the Prism of Prison Memoirs

Paya's *Prison of Monotheism* is valuable because it offers a prison description
before the hard-line Islamists had established their total control. In this par-

ticular right, however, he could offer only a glimpse of the executions the clerics carried out during the first months of the revolutionary regime, when it hastily killed many of the highest officials and military chiefs. It did so in the most haphazard way and outside the established prison system. Scores of them were hastily judged as *mofsed fel arz* and executed on the rooftop of the school in which Khomeini had set up his headquarters after his return from exile. Some were taken to prisons, and Paya noted a number of executions during his detention in Qasr prison.[2]

Those earlier executions were only a dress rehearsal. For the much younger and far more radical prisoners who were captured in 1981, death came swiftly and without much ado. A political scientist observed: "The list of those who were executed, arrested or in hiding read like the Who's Who of the original revolutionary coalition that opposed the Shah."[3] Almost all of our writers passed through Evin's infamous death-evoking corridor in ward 209. Perhaps more by its chaotic and fearsome appearance than by any prior planning, the setting struck terror into the hearts of the blindfolded prisoners. The right to life did not exist in the mullahs' prisons. The militant members of the Islamic Revolutionary Guards Corps, which was formed to protect the revolution, arrested the doomed Marxists and the Mojahedin. They placed them in a cell for a short stay, then escorted them out to an interrogation room for tortured confessions, then a few doors away to the clerical court of summary justice, and finally to the prison yard for execution. At every turn, they reinforced, by their hateful words, the prisoners' feeling of inexorable doom.

As the inmate population of political prisoners increased during the winter of 1980 and the spring of 1981, the radical activists, motivated by the ideology of resistance, continued their struggle inside prisons. The defiant spirit of many prisoners had yet to be subdued. Gaining strength outside prisons, the clerical repression was about to crush its young victims, even before they would clearly realize what had transpired. In the meantime, the radical prisoners continued singing their revolutionary songs and shouting their slogans in support of their own competing ideologies.

The memoirs show that the prisons had become the madhouses of the revolution, reflecting many of the contradictory impulses of the populist movement in modern Iranian history. Ideologically imprisoned in their own minds, the politicized youth found themselves on the opposite sides of the enormous political chasm the revolution had opened. Before the clerics imposed a deadly silence, the confines of the prison wards witnessed a mixture of ideological certitude, unbending personalities, and conflicting traditions of political struggles. Upheld by prisoners and guards alike, these conflicting impulses were about to devour the revolution's best children. In the suffocating air of prisons, the images of the Prophet and his Imams raising their sword against the infidels collided with the images of the bearded Karl Marx and his Russian and Chinese apostles holding up the Communist Manifesto.

In fact, all the political symbols of Iranian populist movements clashed. The guards obsessively shouted "*Allah oh Akbar*" (God is great); the young activists responded "Death to the Reactionaries," meaning the mullahs. Moreover, dragging the drama into the gutter were the Revolutionary Guards, who brought with them the thuggery of urban squalor. No one was able to step back, see the brink, and stop the insanity that was enveloping both the victors and the victims. The young victims died in front of the firing squads; soon their equally young executioners perished in the bloody battlegrounds of the Iran-Iraq War. The clerics' binary vision had already envisioned a place in the inferno for the former and a promised spot in paradise for the latter.

Tragically, the Supreme Leader fit into this caste of shortsighted, if not paranoiac, followers. Ayatollah Khomeini lacked a balanced judgment, one befitting the national leader of a complex polity during a critical transitional period. Bellicose and irritable, he was incapable of placing the entire national experience in a proper historical perspective. Despite his appearance, he lacked the temperament and wisdom of a national sage. Many of those young men and women whom he executed would have been passing through the normal course of their lives, doing what youngsters do everywhere, if it were not for the suddenly opened political arena. The revolutionary opening was so breathtaking that very few politically inclined young men and women could step aside and deliberately consider the irrevocable course of action on which they were about to embark. Khomeini was incapable of seeing them as the victims of circumstances he himself had helped to create. His binary Islamic frame of reference, seeing the world in terms of believers and nonbelievers, and his vengeful personality made it impossible for him to accept the fact that the educated youth of Iran would not blindly follow him as the *vali-e faqih*, replacing the authoritarian Shah they helped to overthrow. The other middle-rank clerics around him were hardly any better. They displayed a zealous determination to hold power regardless of cost. Lacking historical foresight, the new national leaders in turbans were only the nemeses of the young, inexperienced groups whom they destroyed.

As the prison memoirs show, the young revolutionaries were ill-prepared for the ferocious assault. They still perceived their security in the light of their own experiences in the Shah's prisons or what they had heard from the tales of the previous generations who passed through the previous regime's security apparatus. The Shah's repression offered no realistic measure of what was to come.

The revolutionary interregnum was ending, as the clerics began to institutionalize their political order. The novelist Parsipur described the day the Revolutionary Guards invaded the prison, beat up everyone, and executed a young woman, Farideh Shamshiri, who was carried away by her own revolutionary sloganeering.[4] After the crackdown, the leftist revolutionary posturing ended and the prisons ceased to be an arena of political struggle against the mullahs, as if they were a continuum of the streets of Tehran during the revolutionary heydays. At last, the prisoners comprehended the peril they faced.

When the guards took two young women out to be executed, Parsipur agonized over her own place in that historic derangement. "The girls left and my nerves twitched beyond my control. Desperately upset, I sought refuge at the corner of the cell. Evaluating the event in my mind, I began to see that a traditionalist father [Khomeini] has suddenly decided to punish his non-traditionalist children, and both are now battering each other to death. In the middle of this, a door was opened and a hand dragged me inside this house to witness this deadly fight."[5] The father, the nontraditionalist youth, and the defiant writer are familiar figures in the drama of modern Iranian history. This offers a picture far more complex than the confining vision of cultural relativism.

Even those who survived saw the face of death in the Ayatollah's prison. For Alizadeh it came when she was blindfolded and taken to the prison yard. She described what must have been the most horrifying prison experience for her, an episode from which she drew the title of her book, *Look Carefully, It Is Real.* The guards ordered the prisoners to remove their blindfolds. They instantly saw a young man, hanging by his neck from a tree. Alizadeh described the dead man's skinny face and tortured body. Then she described the man in charge of the deadly exhibition. "Standing on the top of a table next to the corpse, was a man in the Revolutionary Guard uniform, holding a stick in his hand. Twenty-five or thirty, chubby, of medium height, the Revolutionary Guard displayed an empty look in his eyes, empty of all expressions—no pride, no embarrassment, no mischievousness, no pity. As if offering a sheep's corpse for sale, he was turning the hanging body around by using the stick in his hand; with a coarse and indifferent voice he kept repeating: 'Look carefully, it is real.' On a piece of cardboard attached to the body's chest was scribbled, Habibollah Islami."[6] That was his name, a true Islamic name. Other memoirs described the same or similar encounters.[7]

Assadollah Lajvardi, the vengeful Revolutionary Prosecutor in charge of Evin prison, arranged other gory episodes and televised them to the nation. In one of them, he displayed the bodies of murdered Mojahedin leaders, with a banner hoisted atop the piles. It was the Persian translation of the Qur'anic verse that encourages the killing of those who conspire against God.[8] Modernist interpretations of Islam had yet to succeed in making such verses inoperative in the late twentieth century. To the degree that a culture harbors that kind of brutality, we must demand changes. Cultural relativism cannot explain it away. These events defy rational, historical explanations, as do men like Lajvardi.

Political prisoners looked into the face of death on those nights when prison guards snatched away some of the inmates. Those who remained behind searched anxiously through the newspapers for the names of those who were executed. Almost all prison memoirs described the nighttime executions. Parsipur, for example, described the horror of a night when the Revolutionary Guards executed scores of prisoners within the confines of Evin prison. She, Raha, and Azadi vividly remembered the horrendous sound that reverberated inside the prison walls, like the sound of steel girders being unloaded from trucks and falling to the ground.[9] Roger Cooper, who spent the second half of the 1980s in Evin on the accusation of being a British spy, was quite disturbed by the "knowledge that only some twenty yards away . . . one or even a whole group of political prisoners had just been executed."[10] Those nightly executions would plunge the ward into deep grief; the following morning was a drizzly day of mourning, particularly in the women's wards from which the prisoners were taken out.[11] The inmates engaged in collective mourning familiar to people who grew up under the shadow of the ever-present Shiite lamentation. In an especially painful night, Raha and her sister-in-law knew that their brother and husband was among those marked for execution that evening. Every year thereafter in prison, Raha commemorated the anniversary of that night with a silent and loving dedication to the memory of her fallen brother.

The prison eventually formed a cloistered mental world, linking the politically diverse prisoners with each other and their prison guards. The executed became heroes and heroines to those prisoners who remained defiant.[12] On the other hand, to those who had already submitted to Islamist authorities and repented, the executed prisoners appeared as deadly evidence of the futility of the past struggle and the stupidity of continuing it in prison. Still for others who had regained their individuality and reverted to their former apolitical state of mind, the entire episode was one of waste. As movingly depicted by Raha's first volume, the first two groups were locked together in anguish, constantly tormenting each other by their mere presence. The third group chose the path of least resistance, marked their time, and tried to avoid frictions with other prisoners and authorities.

By early 1983, when the Revolutionary Guards arrested Parvaresh, the waves of mass execution in Evin had subsided. However, executions did not stop once the period of perceived immanent danger to Khomeini's rule ended in 1982. One cannot assume that the executions were due to the state of siege created by the armed encounters with the Mojahedin. Executions continued during and after 1983, when clerical rule was securely established.[13] The clerics continued executing members of the leftist groups or the Mojahedin. They executed even the leading leftists who had been forced to offer their public repentance, broadcast nationally. The clerics showed no mercy when they could easily afford to be magnanimous toward their captives. Above all, the Islamic Revolution, despite the clerics' strident claims to religious and moral superiority, acted no differently from other twentieth-century revolutions in the treatment of real or potential political opponents.

Monitoring Violations: The International Community During the 1980s

The UN Special Representative, Galindo Pohl, paid considerable attention to violations of the right to life, without benefit of the details that prison memoirs offered later. For the period 1979–85, he estimated that the regime executed some 7,000 men and women. Abrahamian provided the figure of 12,500 executions to June 1985.[14] The sense of urgency that Amnesty International's reports conveyed for both the large number of executions and the methods of execution was largely absent from the UN reports.[15]

In the early 1980s Amnesty International gathered detailed information about mass executions and recorded a number of cases in which minors were executed in the Islamic Republic of Iran for political offences. Among the many former prisoners interviewed by the organization's representatives outside Iran was a young man who had himself been sentenced to death when aged 16 in a town in northern Iran, and had managed to escape from prison. In this case, Amnesty International was able to verify the details of his testimony by interviewing another prisoner, a member of a different political group, who had been imprisoned with him. Neither was aware of Amnesty International's interview with the other. Amnesty International has also received reports of the execution of juveniles, some as young as 11, in 1981 and 1982.[16]

The flurry of revolutionary executions diminished after 1983. The decline in the number of executions reflected the fact that by the mid-1980s the regime had crushed all the revolutionary and secular groups, with the exception of national minorities, and terrified the middle class and modern women into passive resistance. In 1987, Galindo Pohl noted "a certain evolution in the situation of human rights away from the state of affairs in earlier years." The number of executions for 1984 and 1985 reached 500 and 470, respectively. Galindo Pohl observed that the trend seemed to have continued for 1986.[17] An abrupt rush of executions bloodied political prisons again in 1988. It was, as will be discussed in Chapter 8, the infamous summer massacre of political prisoners.[18] Whatever the cause, the 1988 massacre was another indication that whenever political interests demanded it, the new rulers put aside the niceties of their own Islamic constitutional provisions. The massacre was coldly calculated and planned, and it should have preoccupied Galindo Pohl for some time. The full extent of the tragedy became apparent in the following year, as Amnesty International sounded the alarm. Yet Galindo Pohl failed to discuss the massacre with Iranian authorities when he visited Tehran in January 1990.

Monitoring Violations: The International Community During the 1990s

In the second decade of the Islamic Republic, executions for political offenses declined but did not cease. Amnesty International's summary report for 1994 stated: "Political prisoners continued to be sentenced to death by Islamic Revolutionary Courts using procedures that fell short of international standards for fair trial."[19] Many of these executions took place in the border areas populated largely by national minorities, where during most of the 1990s the regime faced some not-too-threatening armed oppositions. In Iranian Kurdestan, organizations like the Democratic Party of Iranian Kurdestan (KDPI) continued their precarious existence. Seeking Kurdish regional autonomy, it engaged in armed resistance against the Islamic Republic. The KDPI had managed to survive the brutal repression of the 1980s, by using whatever assistance it could receive from the Iraqi government during the war years. Amnesty International noted: "As the war drew to a close the leadership of the KDPI appeared willing to negotiate a truce with the Iranian Government. However, the assassination of Dr. Abdul Rahman Ghassemlou, the leader of the KDPI, on 13 July 1989, which evidence suggests was carried out by agents of the Iranian Government, was followed by a resurgence in the fighting in Kurdustan. The KDPI, and the Marxist Komala movement, have suffered the same fate as other political opposition movements in Iran. Hundreds of their members, supporters and sympathizers have been imprisoned and many executed in secret after unfair trials."[20]

The Arab minority in Khuzestan and the ethnic Baluchis in Sistan-Baluchestan also engaged in armed oppositions. The government's activities in these regions often included harsh punitive military actions, resulting in the loss of lives. Therefore, most of the victims of political executions belonged to national minorities, particularly Kurds and Baluchis.[21] Human Rights Watch observed: "In the course of combating armed opposition groups, the Iranian military has reportedly destroyed villages, expelled village populations, and mined broad areas." The number of Kurdish villages destroyed in the armed conflicts reached 271 between 1980 and 1992.[22]

One side effect of the reduction of political executions was that the international community began to pay attention to executions of relatively large numbers of common criminals, drug traffickers, and those who were charged with "moral" crimes. There was no accurate way of separating the numbers of executions for political offenses from other categories of capital crimes. Galindo Pohl observed again in 1992 that the government had ordered the Iranian press not to report on all executions.[23] Despite official concealment, Galindo Pohl and his successor Maurice Copithorne, as well as international human rights organizations, listed the known executions for each year of the 1990s. Including all categories, the numbers ranged from the relatively high number of seven hundred executions in 1990 to the low of fifty in 1995.[24] In his February 1994 report, Galindo Pohl concluded that "the use of the death penalty has not diminished radically, as the Special Representative requested in 1991 . . . and the authorities have not taken the necessary steps for it to do so."[25]

The regime hanged the convicts in public or in prisons; some were stoned to death. Amnesty International asserted: "It is outrageous that recorded executions in Iran should have more than doubled in 1996 at a time when the worldwide trend is to abolish the death penalty."[26] Copithorne concluded in 1997: "It is clear that the present situation with regard to the death penalty is not in accord with international norms in this regard. The Special Representative is concerned that on this subject it does not appear that progress is being made towards recognizing in full measure the right to life." He also noted that the death penalty was imposed for ambiguous offenses. Copithorne objected in particular to public hanging.[27]

Copithorne continued to express concerns about the large number of executions in 1998 and 1999. By following the press reports, he determined that the regime executed more than 155 individuals in 1998, many of them in public, and 138 individuals in the first half of 1999. He believed that these numbers were not accurate, since "it is widely assumed that many executions are not reported in the media." He noted that the state officials had agreed to provide him with an accurate number of executions. He received none.[28]

The International Covenant on Civil and Political Rights allows only for "the most serious crimes." Galindo Pohl suggested that the Islamic Penal Code needed a lot of fine-tuning to recognize gradations from "crimes" to "serious crimes" and "most serious crimes." He suggested that the law of Islamic punishment (*hodud*) lacked "any gradation of penalty to accord with different degrees of participation in the offense." This resulted in very unfair trials, especially for individuals charged with political crimes.[29] His statements carried an implicit assumption that trials under different laws would have resulted in different verdicts. This assumption ignored the utterly political procedure that governed the behavior of judicial authorities in political cases.

Executions for Drug Trafficking and Moral Crimes

From early 1989, the international monitors noted a sharp increase in the number of executions for nonpolitical offenses, especially after the government turned its anti-drug-trafficking activities into a political campaign. "Many executions were carried out in public with victims being hanged from cranes in public squares or from a gibbet mounted on the back of a lorry which could then be driven through the streets with the bodies still dangling."[30]

Galindo Pohl observed that the numbers were increasing. Amnesty International stated that the regime executed some 1,100 people for drug trafficking between January 1989 and July 1990. The regime enacted a law in January 1989 that "imposed the death penalty as sole and mandatory punishment for individuals in possession of more than 5 kilograms of hashish or opium, or more than 30 grams of heroin, codeine, methadone or morphine." The regime intended to capture the drug traffickers and execute them immediately, oblivious of the time requirements of due process of law. Turning justice into a political campaign, other authoritarian regimes also shortened the time span between commission of a crime and execution. They often arranged well-publicized spectacles for collective public executions within a few days of the announcement of the crimes.[31] In his report dated November 2, 1989, Galindo Pohl raised serious reservations about the campaign. He questioned the procedure in the emergency courts where an intelligence officer, and not the judge, prevailed in deciding the outcome of the case. He commented that the odious nature of the crime should not excuse the government from adhering to the due process of law. He further expressed his displeasure at the procedure that ensures the closure of cases "in three, four or five days."[32] Here, too, the executions had no visible redeeming qualities. Politicizing a critical social problem may have diverted serious attention to the problem of addiction engulfing the young population. After two decades of Islamic rule, the reformist government of President Khatami acknowledged for the first time the alarming number, according to official estimates, of at least two million addicts in the country, some 100,000 of them in prison.[33]

In the mid-1990s the Iranian press briefs often referred to those who were killed as *ashrar* (evildoers), an old epithet that was also used by the Shah's regime for both political opponents and common criminals in the countryside. The term *ashrar* deliberately made it impossible to determine from the press accounts to which of the two categories the killed individuals belonged.[34] The government never gave a detailed account of any trial held for the *ashrar* or even what happened to them if arrested alive.

In addition to the speedy execution of drug traffickers, the Islamic courts meted out death sentences to individuals accused of specific violations against Islamic prohibitions. Early in the revolution, the clerics declared a war on prostitution. On one occasion when placed in a solitary section of Qasr prison, Paya noticed the presence of a few women in a cell at the end of the ward. He learned that they were prostitutes, and one day he could clearly see them washing clothes. Paya commented that those women made history, since they were among the first group of women who were executed for prostitution in the modern history of Iran.[35] History would remember it as a tragic loss of lives with no redemptive qualities; two decades later a reformist official looked behind the veil and acknowledged the widespread presence of prostitutes who had become increasingly younger due to economic hardship.[36]

The new Islamic Codes stipulated in 1982 the death penalty not only for premeditated murder but also for rape and other "moral offenses" such as adultery, sodomy, and habitual drinking of alcohol. The law failed to conform to international standards, stipulating that states should not resort to the death penalty, except as "a quite exceptional measure." For the first time in Iran's history, the state's legal codes specified the exact nature of the macabre practice of stoning. As if borrowing a passage from Salman Rushdie's novels, the law states: "In the punishment of stoning to death, the stones should not be so large that the person dies on being hit by one or two of them; nor should they be so small that they could not be defined as stones."

In April 1989, the riffraff were collected in a soccer field to participate in the stoning of twelve women and three men. Galindo Pohl repeated reports by Iranian state television concerning the proper size of the stones.[37] Stoning continued into the second half of the 1990s.[38] In one grotesque example in 1997, a woman who was charged with having sexual relations outside marriage survived the stoning and was found breathing in the hospital.[39] Apparently, the village inhabitants were horrified by the stoning and forced the authorities to stop it.[40] On November 21, 1997, *Salam* reported the stoning of three men and three women in the city of Sari. The reformist President Khatami did not call publicly for an end to this savage punishment, although the embarrassed technobureaucrats seemed to have succeeded in reducing its occurrence.

Extrajudicial Murders Outside Iran

Since 1987, Amnesty International has reported on the extrajudicial executions of a number of Iranians, mostly opponents of the regime who paid with their lives for continuing their political activities abroad. Among the most prominent Iranians assassinated during the second period were Dr. Shahpur Bakhtiar, a nationalist leader and former prime minister; Dr. Abdolrahman Qassemlu, the genuinely democratic Kurdish leader, and Dr. Kazem Rajavi, brother of the Mojahedin leader.[41] Relying on "the judicial, political or administrative authorities in the countries" in which the assassinations took place, Galindo Pohl reported in 1994 on fifty-nine assassination attempts on Iranian opposition leaders in exile.[42] A report published by Britain's Parliamentary Human Rights Group counted 150 attempts in the first seventeen years of the Islamic Republic. Each attempt caused the murder of one or more individuals, resulting in 350 deaths.[43]

Assassinations, whether inside the country or outside, present international human rights monitors with the most intractable violations of the right to life. They may occur as the result of an automobile accident or a direct armed assault, where the perpetrators have many opportunities to prepare their escape route carefully. Even if they are caught at the crime scene, which is not often the case, connections with the government are hard to prove conclusively. It was almost certain that Iranian security officials had set up an assassinating apparatus abroad in the late 1980s. However, too many attempts caused mistakes and eventually left evidence that enabled the police in several European countries to trace the assassins to the Iranian embassies. One major complication was that many states, most significantly the European ones, did not wish to endanger their trade relations with Iran over the assassinations of a few Iranians on their soil. Even if there was some clear evidence, the political decision makers could prevail over judicial authorities not to pursue the case vigorously. In some cases the accused or convicted prisoners were hurried out of Europe in exchange for some unspecified favors from the Islamic Republic.

The assassination of Shahpur Bakhtiar in August 1991 prompted an extensive probing by the French investigative judge Jean-Louis Bruguiere. A detailed judicial report asserted that "Iranian intelligence services effectively took part in carrying out this criminal conspiracy."[44]

The Islamist diplomats would denounce any evidence, short of a smoking gun in the hands of an assassin carrying an identification card of the regime's Intelligence Ministry. On December 3, 1993, a diplomat complained about Galindo Pohl's reports on assassinations, accusing him of ignoring that all such allegations had been "categorically rejected by the Islamic Republic of Iran" and that they had never been proved. He pointed out "the absence of conclusive data," adding that despite these facts, the Special Representative discussed the cases in detail in his reports. "Still worse, the report's conclusions are framed in such a way as to impart to the reader the impression that they were based on facts and conclusive data, which simply is not the case."[45]

There were just too many assassinations of Iranian opposition figures, and the accumulated evidence influenced the judgments of the international human rights monitors, pointing the finger of blame toward Tehran.[46]

Galindo Pohl responded to the denial of the Islamist diplomats: "It is not the Special Representative's intention to give his readers impressions that might lead them to erroneous conclusions. The Special Representative cannot, however, but mention cases in which there are statements by judicial, political or administrative authorities containing specific indications of the involvement of Iranian agents, on the assumption that the authorities are well aware of what took place and have taken into account the consequences for international relations of their statements."[47]

Galindo Pohl's successor, Copithorne, came to the same conclusion in his report of October 15, 1997. He also acknowledged the government's denials of involvement in the assassination plots, but pointed out that some legal proceedings in courts of different countries found "a strong connection" to the regime.[48]

The regime's assassination machine made a major blunder on September 17, 1992, in the murders in the Mykonos restaurant owned by an Iranian expatriate in Berlin. Three leaders of the Democratic Party of Iranian Kurdistan and their political confidants had gathered for dinner and informal talks. Kazem Darabi, the Iranian agent, and four Lebanese hired guns walked in, guns drawn, yelling obscenities and firing bullets. Party leader Sadeq Sharafkandi and three other men died that night. Convicting the four assassins on April 10, 1997, the German court found that the order for the killing had originated from Tehran's top leadership, including the Supreme Leader. Galindo Pohl noted in 1995 that Klaus Gruenewald, director of the Federal Constitutional Protection Office, had succeeded in linking the organizer of the assassination, Kazem Darabi, to the security agencies in Iran.[49] "To the Special Representative's knowledge, the Berlin verdict is the first occasion in which a foreign court has clearly attributed responsibility for the assassination of Iranian opposition figures abroad."[50] The unrelenting German prosecutor in charge of the case had managed to overcome German diplomatic hesitations. The evidence was strong, and the court's verdict struck a severe blow to the clerical regime. Amnesty International welcomed "the fact that four people have been brought to justice for these killings." It observed that "for years, Iranian dissidents have been dying in circumstances suggesting that they were killed by Iranian Government agents. This trial has shed some further light on the mechanisms by which such killings occur."[51]

In March 1996, a federal court in Germany had already issued a warrant for the arrest of Ali Fallahian, Intelligence Minister in Rafsanjani's cabinet, concerning the Mykonos restaurant murders.[52] Fallahian had publicly acknowledged his involvement with the regime's actions abroad against political opponents. In an interview with the government television in Tehran, the minister bragged about his Ministry's pursuit of the exiled opposition groups. "We keep them under surveillance, and we have penetrated their main organization. We have complete information about their activities. We have been able to strike vital blows to them."[53] After being indicted by the Berlin court, Fallahian called the Berlin trial a political soap opera.[54]

The official reactions in Tehran were revealing. On Tuesday, November 12, 1996, the German federal prosecutor, Bruno Jost, read the indictment in which he accused the top leaders in Tehran of being involved in the murders. The Iranian semiofficial press remained silent until the day after the Head of the Judiciary, Ayatollah Yazdi, denounced the indictment in his Friday sermon. Then a torrent of abusive statements directed against Germany hit the semiofficial press on November 16–19. Some editorials were a sad commentary on the clerical mind-set that ruled Iran; some were outright pathetic; a few were amusing. Ayatollah Yazdi, whose judiciary has often acted as an instrument of repression in Iran, lectured that "the judicial system should be independent in every country and the judicial procedures free of political pressures from the other organs." He added that "reliance on foreign power will be the most dangerous phenomenon threatening a country's judicial system." Perhaps more out of ignorance than malice, the Ayatollah assumed that "American power" had corrupted the German judiciary. The Assembly of Experts, one of the highest constitutional bodies, declared that the German judicial officials had forgotten their own crimes during World War I and World War II.[55] The cleric Abu-Torabi, the Leader's representative in Tehran University, did not see the Germans as having been criminals in those wars. Like many other clerics who expressed the same view, he discovered a conspiracy against Germany: "The German government must become aware that International Zionism will trap the Germans, the same way it has reduced the United States of America to an abject and weakened position. Its real goal is to indirectly show the weakness of the German nation, who had stood up against Zionism in World War II."[56]

In assassinating its political opponents, the Islamic Republic was in the company of several authoritarian regimes, only a bit more relentless. Like them, only its self-interests following the Berlin debacle compelled the regime to curtail drastically its assassination plots in Western Europe. The officials' responses to the news of the indictment and orchestrated protest rallies bore all the trademarks of contemporary authoritarian regimes, revealing not only the character of the regime but also the working of the semiofficial press on critical issues.

Chapter 4

The Right to Freedom from Torture

> If the freedom-lovers and phony supporters of human rights realize
> the implications of what they are saying, they would see that their words
> object to God; it is because in the Day of Judgement, God would burn
> the skins of those who are condemned to Hell and would make them
> grow new skins. Thus, it suits them to address their speeches and inter-
> views, with bold headlines, against God and to issue statements against
> the Exalted Greater asking why God tortures in the Day of Judgement.
>   —Ayatollah Yusof San'ei, appointed by
>   Ayatollah Khomeini to the Guardian Council

Article 38 of the Constitution proudly prohibited torture in the Islamic
Republic of Iran, but the regime's interrogators cavalierly resorted to the
most familiar forms of torture, mainly for the purpose of extracting confessions. Prison wardens also continued inflicting pain on the captives for
disciplinary punishment—or just out of sadism. Islamic punishments like
flogging and amputation of limbs and fingers revived ancient forms of torture and gave them judicial standings within the nation-state.

Through the Prism of Prison Memoirs

Paya's memoirs enable us to see a distinction between the early period when
he was in prison and a later period when the clerics established their total
control over the country and its prisons. Paya could only testify that torture
was present in the background, but its signs were not readily visible. After
the Islamists began to eliminate all other political groups, torture became
a routine practice. Paya was not tortured, nor did he himself witness a tortured body. During the early days of the revolution, prisoners felt offended
by the verbal abuse of interrogators and guards. They also complained about
the restrictions imposed on visitation rights and the failure of prison guards
to inform prisoners whether they had visitors on the specified days. Paya
considered such practices to be a "psychological annoyance."[1] In a not-too-

distant future, the young prisoners who were brought into prisons and who endured the brutal routine of daily tortures would have considered such infractions on their rights as negligible inconveniences.

Later, torture was as common for the young revolutionaries in Evin prison as the unpalatable food or the cold water in the shower stalls. All the memoirs provided multiple images of torture, collapse of will, confession, and repentance—or those of torture, resistance, and death.[2] Alizadeh wrote: "Around me and across the corridors there were prisoners, many of whom had their [flogged] feet wrapped in bandages. Some were lying down with their blankets pulled over their heads."[3] The ex-prisoners remembered the infamous Evin corridors where prisoners waited in front of interrogation rooms for unforgettable shrieks of pain and moans of agony.

Inflicting torture and extracting confessions were irrevocably linked together. As if demonstrating the Islamic respect for written words, the interrogator gave the victims paper and pencil before commencing the beating.[4] The interrogators sought sensational stories of crimes and confessions and fumed with anger when a prisoner produced only a few innocuous lines. Like many other prison practices, there was an absurd surrealism in the entire sequence, especially for those who refused to confess and repent. Concentration seemed to have been impossible in such a delirious condition, in which the tortured person could not even hold a pen in her hand. One ex-prisoner said that sometimes after torture she had no awareness of what she was writing. She said that only in the next interrogation sessions could she guess what she might have divulged before.[5]

The primary method of torture was lashing, mostly on the prisoners' backs and on the soles of their feet. Every prison account provided descriptions of torn-up flesh and infected soles. The novelist Parsipur was in prison several months before she was physically tortured. In 1981, she noted that women prisoners in Evin walked back from their interrogation sessions wearing very large slippers, which gave their flogged, swollen soles a slight measure of comfort. Parsipur described the swelling as the size of an orange. She saw tortured bodies all around her.[6] Alizadeh witnessed the same.[7] The extent of Raha's back injuries horrified her cellmates when she took her first painful shower. She described other bathers who wrapped their legs in plastic bags so that water would not penetrate under the bandage to the wounds.[8]

Lashing had been a familiar method of torture during the Shah's regime. But the new regime's interrogators injected a dose of Islamization. Azad described how the guards tied her to a metal bed frame. The man who administered the lashes was a Revolutionary Guard. He performed the Islamic ritual of ablution, then picked up a whip, explaining piously that whipping was a religious duty (*farizeh*). Standing over Azad, he said that she was in the first room of the process, behind which there were other rooms. Anyone who did not come to her senses (*adam nashod*) would be taken to the second room, and then the next until she reached the cemetery. He did not explain whether the same religious duty had also prescribed those deadly threats. Azad remembered the excruciating pain and passed out.[9] Hours after his arrest, Parvaresh was taken to the same basement where he received a severe beating from the Revolutionary Guards and his interrogator. They then forced him down on his stomach on a metal bed frame and tied him up. Shouting *Allah oh Akbar* (God is great), a guard began lashing the soles of his feet with a cable.[10]

The new regime's torturers added at least two new methods to the country's ingenious collection in the twentieth century. The first was the twisting of arms into an excruciating position known as the *qapan* (steelyard). One arm would be extended over the shoulder to reach the other arm, stretched from the side toward the back. The guards would pull the hands to meet behind the back to be handcuffed. "Soon the pain would extend from the arms to the entire body." They placed Raha in the *qapan* position. She wrote that the guard kept "slightly striking" her hands, which despite its mildness delivered a blow to her entire nervous system.[11] Parvaresh and Ghaffari both observed that among the male survivors of the *qapan*, many suffered from displacement of the shoulder joints and deformed wrists.[12]

The second new method of torture seems to have been an invention of Hajji Rahmani, the infamous warden of Qezel Hesar. Having been interrogated and in some cases sentenced, many prisoners were sent from Evin to other prisons for long terms. Therefore, the clerical courts had already processed, with or without sentencing, most of the political prisoners in Qezel Hesar. Beatings, sleep deprivation, and other physical abuses continued, less to extract confessions than to turn them into repentant prisoners, the *tawaban*. Sometimes torture was administered as punishment. Those who showed no inclination "to return to Islam" were called Intransigents (*sar-e mowza'-ye*, literally, those who remain in their positions). For this reason, the warden readily subjected them to torture as punishment for any insubordination or infraction of rules.[13]

Hajji Rahmani's instrument of torture was the so-called *dastgah* (literally, apparatus). On the edges of a room close to the walls, guards erected wooden partitions that separated each prisoner from the next in such a confined space that they were unable to move. They kept the prisoners in that position day and night, only allowing them to go to the lavatory once a day. All the women who were placed there suffered drastic weight loss. Parsipur referred to the *dastgah* as a *qabr*, a burial vault.[14] Parvaresh also described the *dastgah* for the male prisoners.[15] Calling it Doomsday, Ghaffari wrote that at night the guards ordered prisoners to lie down at eleven and return to the crossed leg sitting position at six the following morning. "Days rolled into weeks, and so into months. Some inmates capitulated." They asked for paper, telling Hajji Rahmani that they would write anything he wanted.[16] Raha wrote that in the early days she wondered "how many more days we would have to sit like statues, not knowing that it would last not for days but months. This savage torture continued for exactly ten months, and what happened to us during this time was a catastrophe, a very painful one."[17] None of these details could appear in the reports issued by the international human rights organizations or by the UN Special Representative. These methods of torture could have no cultural rationale, Islamic or otherwise, and most definitely no redeeming qualities.

After the initial confusion of the early 1980s, prison authorities learned the value of Islamic justification and began to present torture as the Islamic *ta'zir* (Islamic discretionary punishment). In the Law of *Ta'zir* that the First Majlis (parliament) passed, insulting government officials and lying to authorities were considered offenses deserving seventy-four lashes to be repeated until the truth was told. The interrogators could technically declare a prisoner's answers to be lies, punishable by lashing. By convincing themselves that they were applying Islamic law, the interrogators rationalized torture. The prison memoirs, however, revealed the arbitrariness of judgments reached under a highly questionable notion of due process of law. When lashing the prisoners, the guards told them they would continue until they agreed to give the required videotaped interview. Only in our electronic age and according to a bizarre interpretation of the *shari'ah* law could one link the medieval concept of *ta'zir* to the camcorder. Traditionalist rulers are capable of giving an enormous elasticity to their culture, making it difficult for cultural relativists who take the first step with them to decide where to stop along the way.

Prison memoirs are full of stories of punishments that could not be justified by the Islamic *ta'zir* and were not authorized by a qualified cleric, as they must. Hamid Azadi described severe beatings without the guards even bothering to seek the formalistic injunction by a mullah. One instance took place late in the evening and continued until the following morning, when the guards dragged the prisoner back to his cell.[18] The reign of terror Hajji Rahmani had imposed on his prison was sustained largely by indiscriminate beatings of prisoners that bore no resemblance to *ta'zir* punishments. Ghaffari described one of the numerous episodes when the Hajji's men rampaged through the ward, indiscriminately attacking prisoners.[19]

Alizadeh described what took place in Evin prison the day after a powerful bomb leveled the headquarters of the ruling Islamic Republic Party, killing at least seventy-two of Khomeini's closest allies, including the influential Ayatollah Beheshti, on June 28, 1981. The reactions by the Islamic Republic authorities set a pattern. A terrorist attack on the rulers outside the prisons would trigger instantaneous retaliation against political prisoners who had no hand in planning the attack. This was truly a mockery of any kind of justice, including Islamic. In the words of one author: "One Hojjat al-Islam would be assassinated, and another Hojjat al-Islam would threaten the entire world with revenge."[20] (Hojjat al-Islam is a title, below Ayatollah.) The

Islamic Revolutionary Guards arrived, machine guns in hand, and brought down a torrent of hysterical yells, slaps, and kicking. They rushed the blind-folded prisoners to the yard, beating them and firing their guns in the air. Alizadeh heard a guard yelling, "This is the day when we will have collective executions," a derisive jab at the leftists' love of collectivism. The episode came to an unexpected end through the action of a guard who was most likely a mole with the Mojahedin, the main anticlerical Islamic group. Shout-ing political slogans, he opened fire, killing the warden and then jumping to his death from the rooftop.[21]

Detention of mothers with their babies was an act of cruelty against both. Children suffered under prison conditions that lacked basic facilities even for the adults. Early in Raha's detention, her ward held a one-year-old boy, humorously referred to as the only man in the neighborhood. Raha saw many other children in prison. Some were there because the mothers had no one to care for their children outside of prison.[22] Azad wrote that dur-ing her early months in Evin, she saw some twenty children, ranging from infancy to five years old. In her ward, there were ten to twelve children, in-cluding her own daughter. Mothers were allowed a longer stay in the prison yard to avail themselves and their children of the fresh air. They were also assigned a separate washbasin for the children's clothes. In the first year of her incarceration, Azad's baby, Sahar, came down with bronchitis. The per-son in charge of her cell refused to grant a visit to the prison physician until the baby developed a very high fever. But once taken to the dispensary, she received the treatment available in the prison. She felt lucky because the female Revolutionary Guard who was the nurse on duty was both kind and conscientious. The mother and daughter remained in the dispensary for five days before being returned to the ward.[23]

Azad considered the presence of children to be an added burden on the mothers, especially women whose investigations continued without pro-ducing the required confession/repentance. The injured feet and soles of a mother caused a great deal of anguish for her child. Children learned to play doctor by bandaging each other's feet, as they watched adults doing every day. After spending one year in Evin prison, Azad's daughter learned to walk and talk. She used words specific to prison life.[24]

The prosecutor Assadollah Lajvardi, who became Evin's warden, had ar-gued that according to Islam the place of a very young child was with her mother, thus offering an Islamic requirement for keeping babies in prison. As often in such situations, however, he eventually discarded the "Islamic" requirement. All children were removed from the prison in the summer of 1984, most likely because of international attention to their presence.[25]

The authorities punished noncompliance with cruel and degrading treat-ment. Compliance meant wearing the black chador, performing daily pray-ers, writing a letter of repentance, giving interviews in front of other pris-oners, and denouncing previous political affiliations.[26] In essence, it meant renouncing one's conscience. This extrajudicial punishment had nothing to do with the original sentences that the prisoners had received. In one year, the Hajji subjected the inmates in the punishment ward to endless periods of sleep deprivation by lining them up in the walkways and forcing them to stand all night.[27]

Unparalleled in the history of modern prisons, one traditional cultural practice became an official policy, compounding the problem of the over-crowded prisons and creating a novel punishment for prisoners. The traditional Shiite Muslims always considered a non-Muslim to be *najes* (physically and spiritually unclean, polluting). In prisons, the category of the untouchables covered the entire leftist population. Of course, the Baha'is were the *najes* people par excellence. In the 1970s, when the Islamists were themselves prisoners of the Shah's regime, they insisted that their infidel inmates (the Marxists) should not "touch their things."[28] In the 1980s, when they became prison officials they imposed the cultural-religious proscription as a prison rule. As shown in other instances, the Islamic Republic and ancient prejudices fed on each other. Such a practice underscores the relevance of a traditional culture as mainly a negation of the notion of equal concern and respect for all human beings.

The repentant prisoners (*tawaban*), taking their cues from the zealot guards, particularly objected to being placed in the proximity of the *najes* leftists. The Islamists forbade the *najes* prisoners to touch anything that was moist or wet, like a teacup, since the traditional Shiite Muslims considered water to be the main conduit of *nejasat* (impurity). In 1984 Raha was transferred to Evin's ward 4, where the mainly leftist inmates, with a few Baha'i women clustered in a corner, lived in rooms 4 and 6. According to Raha, the female leftists' relationships with the Baha'is in the ward appeared normal, even cordial, and in Raha's case very friendly. Together they constituted the *najes* population of the ward. They were painfully reminded of their humiliating status during those designated nights when the showers had water. They were always the last group to use the showers, since good Muslims refused to follow the *najes* individuals in an area tainted by impurity. A Baha'i woman in room 6 had a beautiful three-year-old daughter. She was also a petite *najes*, not allowed to stroll into other rooms or even play with a Muslim child in the ward.[29] Azad's description of prison in the provincial city of Shiraz showed that the problems created for the *najes* prisoners were even more egregious than those experienced in Tehran's prisons.[30] Azadi saw the humiliating epithet of *najes* "was used as a psychological torture."[31] It caused, in Raha's words "daily torment and pain."[32]

For being a secular woman and for refusing to become the woman she was not, the Islamists punished Parsipur. Early in 1984, they placed the novelist, whom they already considered a nonbeliever, in the *dastgah*, where she suffered greatly. They pronounced her *najes*, since she did not perform her daily prayers. They prohibited her from touching anything other prisoners could possibly use and asked her to eat her meal alone, away from the common eating arrangement in the cell.[33] By then, she had spent more than three years in prison, still in legal limbo without being charged or tried.

Monitoring Violations: The International Community During the 1980s

Galindo Pohl's reports described most of the basic violations, but he could not portray the full horrors that political prisoners experienced in the first postrevolution period. Amnesty International's reports came closer to capturing the full story of the Ayatollah's torture chambers.[34] Only prison memoirs showed that by 1981 political prisoners in the Islamic Republic of Iran were terrified.

When informed of cases of prisoners having been tortured, Galindo Pohl brought them to the attention of the regime's diplomats, citing many of them in his biannual reports. He noted that it appeared the guards inflicted torture mostly during interrogations, with the goal of extracting confessions about the prisoners' activities and political association before their arrest.[35] However, those who testified before Galindo Pohl informed him that the torture continued beyond the interrogation phase, often extending into the period after conviction.[36] In fact, Galindo Pohl rightly assumed that prison authorities often used torture as an instrument of chastisement. The punishment of the accused began at the time of his/her arrest, as the arrest itself was an indication, if not proof, of guilt.

Ex-prisoners who managed to escape to Europe spoke to Galindo Pohl about the lingering pains, both physical and psychological, resulting from prolonged torture.[37] Galindo Pohl received testimonies very similar to what the prison memoirs offered.[38] Learning from practice, torturers improved their craft after 1987, reducing the significant traces of physical marks on the bodies of their victims. "New sorts of cable were being used for flogging and tortured prisoners were being separated from the others and kept elsewhere, until they showed no trace of torture."[39] They also began to appreciate the value of psychological torture, which was now preferred to "physical torture, with the aim of avoiding visible marks."[40]

Some ex-prisoners told Galindo Pohl of a new policy that in effect diffused and privatized the torture of political prisoners by mixing them with "brutal common criminals." They alleged that political prisoners were tortured and raped by their sadistic inmates.[41] However, none of the more credible memoirs referred to such mistreatment and rape at the hands of common criminals. It is conceivable that such practices took place in the provincial prisons. Amnesty International "received reports of various kinds of sexual abuse of both male and female prisoners, including rape."[42]

The fear of sexual abuse is understandable; however, the prison memoirs revealed very little about physical sexual abuse in Tehran's prisons. There was some verbal sexual harassment. Parsipur suggested that one reason there were few credible stories about sexual abuse is that the offenders, so rumor had it, targeted only women who faced immediate execution. Since "none of the dead has returned," no one could substantiate the rumors.[43] At any event, references to sexual assaults were sporadic and often nothing more than rumors.

During his first visit to Evin prison in 1990, Galindo Pohl had a moving encounter with Nureddin Kianuri. He was the former secretary-general of the Tudeh Party, the leftist organization formed in the late 1940s. The elderly Marxist leader appeared "genuinely distressed" and complained strongly about conditions in prison. With prison officials watching, the old man told the Special Representative that he had been tortured; he spoke of beatings and other humiliations, and held up as evidence his partly paralyzed hands and crushed fingers.[44] He was the head of a pro-Soviet party that gave its full support, until it was banned, to Khomeini because of his anti-Imperialism.

Another political prisoner who had never committed a violent or radical act was Muhammad Tavassoli, a former mayor of Tehran from the early months of the revolution and a member of Premier Bazargan's group. Like Abbas Amir-Entezam, he had conducted some discussions with American diplomats in Tehran on Bazargan's behalf. He told the Special Representative that during his nine-month detention "he was beaten, insulted, intimidated and forced to remain in cold cells or seated on the same chair for long hours. The purpose of such practices was to make him confess things he had never done."[45]

Ibrahim Yazdi, another early associate of Khomeini, had not been in prison, but he also testified about prison conditions and torture. Yazdi sounded credible when he spoke of the ordeal of his nephew, Hasan Zadiri, who had been arrested instead of Hasan's brother. Then prison authorities informed his parents that he had committed suicide.

Monitoring Violations: The International
Community During the 1990s

The cases that Galindo Pohl included in his reports were brought to his attention between 1992 and 1994, although it appeared that some of the witnesses described the torture they had experienced during the 1980s.[46] It is certain that the number of victims of torture in the mid-1990s were far fewer than those who suffered in the 1980s.[47]

Nevertheless, news of torture continued to reach the outside world in the second half of the 1990s. Amnesty International was able to gather reports about the torture of relatives and associates of Grand Ayatollah Sayyid Muhammad Shirazi (see Chapter 14).[48] The main method of torture continued to be the flogging of feet and backs, although Amnesty received reports indicating the use of prolonged standing, detention in confined spaces, and sleep deprivation.[49] Referring to another dissident cleric, Amnesty reported: "Sheikh Ali Ma'ash is said to have required medical treatment after his release for the effects of torture, including for a toe on his right foot which was broken and left untreated."[50]

In the late 1990s, when the intra-regime conflict intensified to such a degree that security officials even tortured several technocrats working for the greater Tehran municipality, the reformist press published the news, causing a journalistic uproar (see Chapter 13). However, the most graphic testimony of the period was offered by Ahmed Batebi, a university student whose photo in demonstration was carelessly published on the cover of the London *Economist* of July 13, 1999. Capturing an attractive young man with a Che Guevara-type posture, the photo could easily create the mistaken impression that he played a major role in the bloody riots that followed student demonstrations. His arrest without warrant, prolonged interrogations accompanied by lashing, severe beatings that left him with broken jaw and teeth, sleep deprivation, and other familiar forms of torture were all reminiscent of what political prisoners experienced in the 1980s. The interrogators wanted a public confession that would make him a leader in a plot causing unrest in the country. "During the interrogations, they threatened several times to execute me and to torture and rape my family members." He had to sign a confession, "fearing that they would carry out their threats."[51] The accounts given by another student spoke of similar agonies.[52] Notwithstanding the often-discussed reforms in the Khatami administration since 1997, the interrogation methods applied to nonreligious political prisoners had changed little since the 1980s.

Increasingly in the 1990s, the international human rights organizations exposed Islamic punishments as torture. The Special Representative often used semiofficial Iranian press reports to document cases of "corporal punishment" of persons convicted of various Islamic infractions and crimes.[53] Noting a UN resolution that prohibited amputation of limbs, Galindo Pohl declared it incompatible with international standards. He said that it would not be easy to reconcile certain Islamic laws with the international instruments related to human rights. Moreover, in 1986 the Human Rights Committee interpreted the International Covenant on Civil and Political Rights (Article 7) as prohibiting, inter alia, "corporal punishment, including excessive chastisement as an educational or disciplinary measure."[54]

Amnesty's monitors were also disturbed by the amputation of limbs and fingers and flogging. "The reports of flogging received by Amnesty International have not mentioned any medical examination either before or after the infliction of the prescribed number of lashes, and it has received reports of women who, having been flogged when pregnant, have subsequently had miscarriages."[55]

The imagery created by the clash between those ancient practices of amputation and flogging and our modern expectations and sensitivities (medical examination) is striking. An American journalist observed that the Islamists have become "more high-tech when it comes to Islamic amputations," building electric guillotines that can do the task in seconds.[56]

Reports of judicial amputation of limbs and the Islamic lashing continued into the 1990s.[57] Galindo Pohl reported many of the cases.[58] A few examples will suffice to show the severity of the problem. In late 1992, the fingers of five individuals charged with thievery were amputated in public in the city of Sari. "Judges, administrative officials and hundreds of onlookers" watched the gory spectacle.[59] Galindo Pohl quoted a news item, dated October 17, 1993, on the amputation of the hand of a man charged with robbery and selling of narcotics in the city of Mashhad. "It was also reported that four fingers of the right hands of 14 persons were chopped off in August 1993 by orders of the Islamic Revolutionary Courts for disturbing public order."[60] Galindo Pohl noted a news item in the daily *Salam*, March 14, 1994, indicating that in the city of Qom, two men lost four fingers each from their right hands. They "were chopped off in plain view of other prisoners." Another major newspaper reported on November 7, 1994, that the same thing happened to two men in another city.[61]

Amnesty International's summary accounts for 1994 observed: "Flogging and amputation as judicial punishments remained in force," and in the second half of the 1990s, the Iranian press periodically reported the cases of amputation.[62] In November 1995, a court in Isfahan convicted a sixteen-year-old girl who was an accomplice to a triple murder, imposing penalties that included gouging out her eyes.[63] On September 2, 1997, *Salam* reported that a thief who had broken into a store and stolen twenty-eight cameras was sentenced by a court in Tehran to amputation of four fingers from his right hand. Copithorne continued condemning the amputation of limbs, recommending that the government abolish this punishment.[64]

Islamic punishments of flogging, amputation, and in particular stoning to death truly disturbed the international monitors. Amnesty International strongly objected to stoning to death. In 1990, it wrote: "Flogging, knifing or other forms of corporal punishment prior to execution, including being struck by stone which do not immediately result in death, clearly constitute torture and as such are expressly prohibited by the ICCPR."[65] In the 1990s, Galindo Pohl strongly condemned the Islamic practice of stoning, particularly to punish moral crimes.[66] The stoning of a woman to death in Isfahan on November 1, 1992, prompted him to write that such an act was considered torture and "inadmissible under the international standards."[67] Copithorne also called stoning the most abhorrent of inhuman punishments. He urged the government to remove the pertinent article from the Islamic Penal Code and to make sure that stoning would not be carried out throughout the country.[68] He observed that all cases of stoning were officially sanctioned by the Supreme Court and were not therefore "random acts of excess."[69]

The Right to Liberty and Security of Person and to Freedom from Arbitrary Arrest

> Everyone has the right to liberty and security of person. No one shall be subjected to arbitrary arrest or detention.
>
> Anyone who is arrested shall be informed, at the time of arrest, of the reasons for his arrest and shall be promptly informed of any charges against him.
>
> —International Covenant on Civil and Political Rights

Forced Islamization was a main cause of violations of the right to liberty and security of person. Over the years, the Islamists formed a host of official and semiofficial groups, hoping to impose strict Islamic morality on the reluctant middle class. The end proved illusive, but the means generated considerable insecurity in everyday lives of many Iranians.

Through the Prism of Prison Memoirs

Again, I begin with Paya. The most difficult thing for Paya to accept was how this unfortunate turn of events happened so soon after the revolution in which he placed some hope. Taken blindfolded into the prison walkway, he murmured to himself, "Islamic justice?" He wondered why the Revolutionary Guards left a group of helpless prisoners blindfolded in a prison room, a security threat to no one. In fact, the blindfold has become a trademark of authoritarian states regardless of culture. He saw blindfolding as a deliberate humiliation of prisoners.[1]

With regard to the right to security of person, the value of the memoirs lay in their depictions of the characters and personalities of the Revolutionary Guards who arrested the authors and jailers who controlled their lives in prison. In their hands, the security of person ceased to exist.

In the early days of the revolution, Paya agonized over the character of his jailers. He was heartened by rare encounters with the few prison authorities who paid attention to human rights and due process of law. He saw that a "fundamentalist group" was succeeding in gaining control over the prison system, the Islamic Prosecutor's Office, and the courts. That group considered every prisoner to be a convict until proven otherwise. Its members had no hesitation in placing, to various degrees and of their own volition, restrictions on the daily lives of the prisoners, "unbecoming to the revolution's prison, which was supposedly Islamic." He was intrigued by those few prison officials and guards who showed sensitivity to any reference to the emerging resemblance between the prison system under the Ayatollah and that under the secular Shah.[2]

However, Paya's overall impression of the guards was negative. He saw them as mostly illiterate ruffians, transplanted from the rough alleyways of traditional neighborhoods to the prison wards of the revolution. He thought that they used their newly acquired power in the same way that neighborhood bullies handled theirs, without the opportunity to engage in direct blackmail in prison. They lacked the necessary "revolutionary behavior," which should have distinguished them from their predecessors in the old regime. Paya remarked sarcastically that the revolution did not replace bourgeois with proletarian values. The guards lived in a lumpen world that often existed wherever education and formal cultural exposure did not.[3] Thus, Paya was premonitory about the plight that the much younger prisoners faced from 1981 to 1988: "Ignorance in itself is not a fault, since it reflects lack of education, itself indicative of the social system's failure. However, placing power without accountability in the hands of ignoramuses is dangerous. They consider themselves important, and they compensate for their own sense of inferiority by suppressing others who are otherwise their cultural superiors. They exercise power. Their conduct may appear ignoble or even ridiculous. In practice, for those over whom they exercise power, it is not a trivial matter. Not only their freedom but also their reputation and even their lives are endangered in the hands of these little dictators."[4] This was a befitting description of all prisons kept by the petty dictators who took power in the Middle East in the second half of the twentieth century.

The situation changed radically in 1981, and Islamization of the prison system purged the guards Paya found more agreeable. Whether making arrests, dispatching victims from cells to interrogation rooms, or administering lashes, the guards remained totally impervious to the pain and suffering that engulfed the prisons. Their cruelty was more capricious than institutionalized. Perhaps they were capable of feeling the pain of others. However, like most egregious human rights violators, they divided the world in terms of the "Self" and the "Other," according to the Islamic binary vision of the believers and the infidels (*koffar*). The prison wardens and the revolutionary prosecutors were incapable of seeing their captives as human beings, utterly vulnerable and in pain.

The interrogators saw their captives primarily through their group identities, as Mojahedin, Fadai'i, Paykari, Royalists, and so on, and sometimes housed them in separate cells. Parsipur mentioned that there was also a room for the "ambiguous and uncertain," those who could not be easily categorized. The prisoners also took notice of each other through these largely dehumanizing categories. One way that the warden in Qezel Hesar punished an individual prisoner, say, a royalist, was to send her into "exile" to a room populated by radical Fadai'ian or Mojahedin.[5]

The Revolutionary Guards' stinging remarks, inflicting mental anguish on the captives, gave a clue to the mentality of the functionaries of the budding security apparatus. Driving Alizadeh to prison, one of the guards asked disdainfully about her occupation. "A teacher," she replied. He asked, "Do you teach Marx and Lenin to the kids in class?" He continued taunting. Alizadeh maintained her composure and remained silent. While waiting inside the prison, another guard approached her, asking why she had been arrested. She repeated what the guards had told her: "To answer some questions." The young man replied, "At first everyone comes in for some questions, but once they feel the strokes of the whips, then the hidden places of weapons and safe houses would be revealed. Then a few more questions for which there would be only one answer: hanging." Another Revolutionary Guard disparagingly reminded her of those hypothetical days "when you engaged in political debate with hundreds of strange men," implying that such encounters were a blight on a woman's Islamic honor.[6]

Dr. Ghaffari believed that the most sadistic guards were those who, before being assigned to prisons, had participated in the Iran-Iraq War, carrying its deep scars. Political prisoners became the targets of their frustration and anger. They were already brainwashed, believing that while they were sacrificing their lives for Islam and the Islamic revolution, the infidel prisoners were conspiring to overthrow the Islamic system. The clerics told them that the prisoners had revolted against God, the Qur'an, and Imam Khomeini and that they were "domestic enemies more dangerous than Saddam."[7]

Throughout the years of incarceration, prisoners encountered and described many characters. A few of them will be presented here to show that there was almost nothing unique about them and that they, like other prison guards of ideological regimes, were mostly uneducated, rough simpletons whose zealotry reflected the revolutionary regime's propaganda. Alizadeh and Parsipur, for example, each described Tayebeh, a female Revolutionary Guard, who worked in their ward in Qezel Hesar prison. Alizadeh portrayed Tayebeh as a brute, behaving hatefully toward all prisoners and becoming ecstatic when someone in authority assigned her the task of beating a prisoner. At one point she told the prisoners in an overcrowded room that if she were the head of the Revolutionary Court, the prison "would have been less crowded," meaning that she would have executed all of them.

Parsipur gave a more nuanced portrayal. As a curious and probing author, she showed interest in everyone around her, including those whose ignorance and violent temperament often infuriated her. Thus Parsipur searched for hidden layers of human experience behind the official face that Tayebeh and other women like her presented to their socially superior but captive audience. Parsipur saw Tayebeh as a harsh, ill-tempered young woman, but with a strong character hidden beneath the apparent brutality.[8]

Another guard, Farzaneh, was a young woman who, Alizadeh wrote, "from time to time would, by her own estimation, express pity on us and would say there is always a possibility for repenting and turning away from the misguided path." Nevertheless, Farzaneh followed the warden's orders, never hesitating to torment the prisoners.[9] Parsipur probed deeper and discovered that Farzaneh, who had a beautiful face, had earned her living in a decidedly un-Islamic profession as a dancer and singer before the revolution.[10]

Both Raha and Azadi wrote about a fearful figure in Evin prison they only called by his first name, Mojtaba. He was Mojtaba Halva'i. Azadi first met him when he was a guard who verbally abused and physically mistreated the political prisoners. He was eventually promoted to deputy warden for security in Evin prison. Azadi wrote that Mojtaba dressed in the "style of American commandos and wore a pair of Ray-Ban glasses."[11] The male dress code for all security functionaries of the contemporary states has become universal. The Western-style state has been borrowed, the whole kit and caboodle, but the required safeguards that should come with it offend cultural sensitivities. Since 1979, the wardens were replaced a few times, but pretentiously Islamist Mojtaba stayed on, often making himself available for punishments, especially lashing. Clad in the olive uniform of the Revolutionary Guard, with his trousers tucked inside his military boots, the infamous jailer greeted Raha and other prisoners upon their return to Evin in the spring of 1986. Mojtaba's bulky figure, disheveled beard, and frowning expression made a frightening impression on Raha. He thundered his welcome to the newly transferred female prisoners: "This is not Qezel Hesar. Listen carefully, this is Evin! The time for giggling is over. This is the end of talking back and wagging tongues."[12] There was nothing culturally Islamic about his words, actions, or even appearance that deserved to be invoked by the world's cultural relativists. His stereotyping expressions toward women could be found in the annals of all misogynist cultures.

Like Mojtaba, many of the prison wardens and the Revolutionary Guards who proved to be a menace to security of prisoners grew up in the rough and tumble of city culture that nourished urban hooliganism. Many of the interrogators were tough young men who had left their rural backgrounds for the less desolate religious seminaries. Some had become clerics; some were still students when revolution catapulted them to positions of power beyond their dreams; and a few had passed through university courses and become familiar with revolutionary Islamism on the Shah's campuses. They had hardly heard of the Universal Declaration of Human Rights. Nor were they cognizant of the fact that their government was a signatory to the International Covenant on Civil and Political Rights. They lived a universe apart from the human rights notion that everyone is entitled to equal concern and respect.

Monitoring Violations: The International Community During the 1980s

Galindo Pohl observed that the Republic's constitutional safeguards of this particular right appeared not to conflict with the pertinent articles of customary international law. In practice, however, the Revolutionary Guards and other self-appointed guardians of Islam made a mockery of their own constitutional provisions. They did not bother with the nicety of a warrant for making an arrest, nor did they feel obligated to divulge the reason for detention. The Special Representative observed that in some cases formal charges came months after the arrest. They kept political prisoners incommunicado for long periods.[13]

No one with any kind of political activity in his/her past felt secure. Amnesty International observed: "Often an individual is arrested at home, being informed that he or she has to answer some questions, which may require absence for some hours, a period which in practice may extend to many months or even years in detention."[14]

Amnesty International identified the Islamic Revolutionary Guards Corps and Islamic Revolutionary Committee as the two major organizations responsible for the lawlessness that prevailed in the process of arbitrary arrests and detentions. Their arrests without written authorization often involved "acts of brutality towards the person being detained and his or her relatives, accompanied by insults and threats, and frequently followed by systematic physical and/or psychological torture."[15]

Galindo Pohl stated that the government also resorted to the collective punishment of the families of those suspected of armed political activities. The prosecutors detained family members in order to obtain information on the whereabouts of their relatives who had gone into hiding. In such cases, there were no formal charges, nor were there any trials; the detention could last for a long time. A news item revealed on August 4, 1987, "that 36 parents had been arrested because their sons had not reported for military service."[16]

From time to time, citizens of another country would be trapped in the system. In the 1980s, the best-known case belonged to Roger Cooper, a British citizen with long personal connections to Iran, including a daughter by an Iranian former wife. Security agents arrested him in Tehran in December 1985 on the fabricated charge of being a British spy.[17] In the late 1990s, Helmut Hofer was sentenced to death for having sexual relations with an Iranian Muslim woman.[18] The same charge was also added to Cooper's crimes.

Having served the hard-liners' political purpose of countering the German government, Hofer paid a large fine and was released two years later.

It is rather surprising that in the 1980s Galindo Pohl had very little to report on the forcible imposition of the Islamic dress code on modern Iranian women. As will be discussed in Chapter 16, it was a violation of freedom of conscience as well as of the security of the person. Nor was there any meaningful reference to the insecurity of individuals whose un-Islamic behavior in public incurred the wrath of the morality police. In this period, it may have been a reflection of his reluctance to comment on what appeared to be Islamic cultural practices.

Monitoring Violations: The International Community During the 1990s

In the early 1990s, Galindo Pohl continued to report cases of arbitrary arrest and detention.[19] The Islamist leaders imagined an anticlerical conspiracy in every public expression of discontent. Galindo Pohl was aware of the fact that arbitrary arrests in such a climate of official hysteria would invariably lead to trials without "internationally recognized standards of fairness."[20]

In the spring and summer of 1992, demonstrations against the regime took place in economically depressed urban neighborhoods; they turned violent for several reasons, including police provocations. Security forces opened fire, killing or wounding scores of demonstrators. The regime resorted to arbitrary arrests of many young men from lower-class backgrounds. Some were charged with creating terror and destroying public property; four were executed in the city of Mashhad. One man was charged with burning the Qur'an because he reportedly led an attack on the office of the Islamic Propagation Organization and torched the building, which housed, among other books, copies of the Qur'an. Demonstrations and riots in Shiraz took place in May, and in early June the officials announced that four people had been hanged. Amnesty International indicated that the numbers of executions were higher than the official counts. "Others were sentenced to long-term prison terms and floggings following unfair trials."[21]

Unrest, arbitrary arrests, and executions continued in 1993.[22] Then on April 2, 1995, an angry demonstration turned into a riot in Islamabad, a shantytown outside Tehran. Security forces opened fire, killing an indeterminate number. They also arrested many of the rioters. A short ride could have taken Tehran's semiofficial reporters to the scene of the riot, yet it took three days for the press to report the bloody event, a testimony to the nature of the press control at the time. The Islamic Revolutionary Guards sealed off the community. Reuters reported helicopters firing teargas to control the crowd.[23] The authorities and the controlled press acknowledged the unavailability of water and increased bus fares as the main hardships causing demonstrations and riots.[24]

Arbitrariness characterized the regime's response. It described every event as a political conspiracy hatched by enemies of the state. The world is all too familiar with the actions of poor people seeking amelioration for their problems and letting their frustrations flare up in an uncontrollable rage. The Islamist rulers knew that any collective expression of discontent had to be nipped in the bud, lest it spawn a general political uprising. They also remembered how during the Shah's regime they themselves made political hay out of such spontaneous bursts of anger in Tehran's shanty-towns, depicting the rioters as the oppressed Muslim masses. Now the champions of the oppressed had a hard time reporting on the demonstrations of the oppressed against them.

It is interesting to note that the moderate newspaper *Salam* and the hard-liner *Resalat* denounced the rioters with the same ferocity. After the crackdown came official counterdemonstrations, where the official crowd condemned the "opportunists and the *ashrar* [evildoers]" and shouted, "Death to the American Hirelings." [25] The official demonstrators listened first to the Interior Minister and then to the shantytown's official cleric. To counter the mainly economic slogans of the rioters, the official crowds chanted: "Long live Khamenei and Rafsanjani! Death to America! Death to England! Death to Israel!" A senior security official told the press that people had returned to their daily lives. He added that "during the last two days they have repeatedly come to the security personnel to thank them for their decisive action in the arrest of the perpetrators of the event and demanded their punishment." [26] Some twenty years earlier, one could hear almost the same words from the mouths of the crowd-control commanders of the Shah's regime in another shantytown outside Tehran. Authoritarian scripts seldom change in essence, despite changes in idiomatic expressions.

The urban disturbances in the summer of 1992 provided an excuse to regroup and prepare the fearsome *basijis* (an irregular militia-type force) for street actions in major cities. Thus, they became the main threat to the security of persons in the 1990s. As mentioned in Chapter 2, a less militarized version of the *basijis* are the Partisans of the Party of God (Ansar-e Hezbollah, or *hezbollahis*), the unofficial vigilantes, who also engage in street patrols and violent attacks on the dissidents.

The full impact of the *basijis* and the *hezbollah* vigilantes was felt by the intellectuals, journalists, and university students throughout the 1990s, leading to the assaults on Tehran's university students on July 13, 1999, during the most intense street actions that the clerics witnessed since they came to power in 1979. Mohsen Reza'i, the former commander of the Revolutionary Guards, was accurate when in 1996 he described the division of responsibilities among the regime's different forces (see Chapter 2). Elaine Sciolino of the *New York Times* explained their actions in 1999: "When thousands of people refused tonight to leave Enghelab Square, one of Tehran's largest intersections, hundreds of baton-wielding vigilantes, many riding in twos on motorcycles, swooped down, witnesses said. The vigilantes indiscriminately arrested, threatened and beat people in the crowd, following them as they ran through the streets in search of refuge. Uniformed security officials stood by and watched, blocking off large areas so the vigilantes could roam freely."[27]

There was nothing unique in the formation of the *basijis* and the *hezbollah* vigilantes, since other authoritarian rulers have also created paramilitary groups to protect themselves from their citizens' wrath. The curse of the religious state became more apparent when these groups routinely harassed secular Iranians throughout the 1980s and 1990s. Chapter 16 will examine the insecurity that the Islamists created for secular women. In the early 1990s, the secular dissidents and liberal Muslim intellectuals cautiously began to raise their disjointed voices of discontent. Many of the violations of the right to liberty and security of the person took place because of the efforts to suppress these voices. I will examine their cases in Chapters 13 and 14.

Insecurity in Public Spaces and Private Homes

What needs to be emphasized here is that the regime continuously violated the right to liberty and security of secular Iranians in public spaces and private homes. It was only in the 1990s that Galindo Pohl began reporting on the pervasive human rights violations of those whose appearance and attitudes did not fit the official Islamic model. Like the violations of the right to freedom of religion, thought, and conscience, this category of violations was ignored in previous reports. The reason for the neglect could not have been the dearth of pertinent information. The international press often reported on the harassment of young men and women in public. Amnesty International reported many such violations. For example, an Iranian man wrote to Amnesty International: "In the summer of 1987 I went with a girl from Tehran to visit my aunt in the north of the country near the Caspian Sea. We were travelling by car and at 11 P.M. were stopped by Islamic Revolutionary Committee personnel in Ramsar. They asked us to show our identity papers. These showed that we were not married, or related in any way, and the Committee officers accused us of involvement in immoral acts. I was separated from the girl at the Committee headquarters. They tied me up with one arm twisted behind my back and the other arm across my chest. I was then suspended by my wrists from a tree in the courtyard and left hanging for about five hours." The hapless man endured one hundred lashes in the full view of the public in the middle of the town.[28]

According to an official account covering the period between March 1989 and April 1990, some 5,200 men and 3,500 women were arrested in Tehran. Their crimes included "illicit relations between boys and girls and married women and men." The official statement expressed regret that "the majority of cases involved married women, many of whom with proper husbands." Life went on behind the Islamic trappings and despite the theocracy. The second larger category covered "women who exhibited corruption on the streets [a reference to wearing makeup or sunglasses] and appeared without proper Islamic *hijab* [*bad-hijabi*]." It added that the majority of women who were detained for *bad-hijabi* "agreed that proper Islamic *hijab* is a principle and value and its absence is an anti-value." [29] The statement did not say what intimidation produced such an agreement.

In 1994, Galindo Pohl began to report on the harassment and arrest of individuals in public spaces and private homes. He mentioned the irregular *basijis*, who were from time to time brought into the streets to cleanse the public of anti-Islamic vices. The insufficiently Islamic youngsters in middle-class neighborhoods became their new preoccupation. They set up checkpoints "and stopped cars to sniff their occupants' breath for alcohol and check for women wearing make-up or traveling with a man not their close relative or husband." They repeatedly attempted to rule the streets, since the newly enacted regulations left the mostly secular victims helpless against arbitrary detention. [30]

The regime's diplomats simply "denied the allegation" and insisted that the *basijis* did not arrest on the streets, as Galindo Pohl had alleged. [31] In the report that covered the second half of 1994, he stated that "nine women were arrested in a private home . . . for playing cards." [32] Home invasions continued. The morality police arrested twenty-eight young men and women between the ages of seventeen and twenty at a private evening party. During the search, the police found evidence of corruption—a cassette-player, music cassettes, and videocassettes of "repulsive films," a reference to the run-of-the-mill Hollywood movies. The authorities sentenced the youths to fines and ten lashes each and imposed additional prison terms on three of them. They also fined the parent hosts. [33] The middle-class families have also learned that before holding noisy parties they must "see" the local authorities in charge of the moral purity of the neighborhood. Bribery became a thriving source of income for the regime's moral patrols enforcing Islamic norms. [34]

"The bribe is the cheapest part of our parties," a Tehrani confided to the experienced American journalist Judith Miller, who added, "Wealthy Teheranis paid Revolutionary Guards between 100,000 and 500,000 rials— or between $30 and $156—to ignore loud Western music and the consumption of alcohol at weddings and other celebrations." [35]

Islamists attempted to impose sexual segregation even within private gatherings—or at least benefit financially from such attempts. The law prohibits mixed-sex wedding parties. A police regulation in 1995 restated that bands would not be allowed to perform at such parties. It demanded "that brides remain fully covered throughout." In 1995, in the city of Mashhad, 127 of 128 guests at a ceremony were sentenced to be flogged or fined. The bride's sentence was 85 lashes. "The only wedding guest acquitted was a youngster. The groom's father was the only one sentenced to a jail term— 8 months—plus a fine of $16,700 and seizure of some of his property." [36] Iranians experienced such humiliations during the 1980s and much of the 1990s.

Among the most tragic examples of the violation of the right to security of person was the one that resulted in the death of Ali Reza Farzaneh-Far, a man in his early twenties. From a well-to-do religious family, he nevertheless had adopted a Western lifestyle of fun and entertainment. On April 11, 1996, he was in the thick of a party with men and women of his age when the morality police showed up at the door of the apartment on the eighteenth floor in an upper-middle-class complex. It appears that it was a typical "wild" party, where young women wore modern, fashionable dresses—in the eyes of the Islamist no better than being naked. The guests drank alcoholic beverages and some perhaps smoked "joints." There was a great deal of confusion as to how Ali Reza fell from the eighteenth floor to his death. The official story had it that, drunk and under the influence of narcotics, he attempted to escape by descending from the balcony to the floor below and fell. A rumor spread across northern Tehran that the police threw him out the window. As in other authoritarian states, people believed rumors more than official explanations, compelling the chief of police to deny them officially. The authorities and the semiofficial press diverted the focus of the tragedy from the death of a man in a private home to the lifestyle of the people at the party. They depicted a scene of downright debauchery,[37] in effect saying that Ali Reza deserved death because of his un-Islamic habits. To open the doors of private homes in unending and futile efforts to safeguard society's Islamic morality became a distinctive curse of the religious state.

Fearing persecution, far too few women have written about their encounters, in a way similar to what the prison memoirs presented for those who bore the brunt of clerical morality in the 1980s. Cherry Mosteshar was an Iranian journalist who returned to Tehran after the revolution and filed news and feature articles for the London press. Her identity crisis as a Persian woman in the West and her journalistic quest brought her back to Iran in the early 1990's. She witnessed many of those "little" harassments in the daily lives of Iranians. She wrote about a few of her own experiences. "It amazes me that the debate over human rights violations is often restricted to how many people are kept in prison or physically tortured, while many states administer a more subtle torture, the denial of identity and power over one's life." [38]

After two decades of the clerical rule, the youth were no longer as docile as they appeared in the 1980s. Even in Tehran's lower-middle-class and working-class neighborhoods, the bitterly disappointed Islamists saw young men and women engaging in "anti-Islamic" activities such as being attracted to the opposite sex or playing "decadent" music. In late 1999, one young man told a reporter that they were no longer afraid of the morals patrols. The reporter added that "such remarks are not just bravado." In December when a young man in defiance of the Islamist rule was confronted by another "young man with links to the morals police," a bitter argument ensued, at the end of which the enforcer of Islamic morality "lay dead with multiple stab wounds." In an insecure environment that was further aggravated by unemployment and disillusionment, an act of defiance turned into a murder for which the young man was sentenced to death.[39]

Chapter 6

The Right to a Fair Trial

In this prison, the prisoner is considered first a criminal, then an accused, and last, sometimes, a human being.
—Parviz Ousiya (A. Paya)

The guard's reply—one I was to hear again and again in the course of the next five years—sent a shiver down my spine: "You wouldn't have been brought here if you were innocent."
—Roger Cooper

Under the rubric of the right to a fair trial, the UN Special Representative Galindo Pohl often, and appropriately, discussed "the administration of justice" in the Islamic Republic. Following his lead, this chapter will examine the lack of due process of law by looking at a few judicial cases that revealed many of the peculiarities of the Islamic court system.

In 1979, the clerics whom Khomeini appointed as Islamic judges conducted "Islamic revolutionary trials" in a rather haphazard way in applying what they understood to be Shiite penal law. In 1982, the Majlis (parliament) inserted the ancient judicial concepts in the general Islamic Penal Codes and codified the four Shiite judicial categories into state laws for a provisional period of five years.

The *hodud* category defined punishment for crimes against divine will, such as rebellion against the Islamic state, apostasy, various sexual crimes, and the consumption of alcohol. The next was the *qesas* laws (retribution). Until 1991, when the clerics bowed to the reality of the contemporary state and modified the *qesas* laws, they in effect privatized punishments, by allowing the victim or his/her family the prerogative of deciding the punishment for homicide and aggravated assault. Based on *lex talionis*, private parties could demand punishment equal to the harm the victim had suffered. In a homicide, the victim's family could demand the death penalty or accept financial compensation based on a specific "Islamic" formula, *diyat*, according to which the worth of a male or female Muslim was determined. This privatization of punishment created uncertainties and miscarriages of justice, especially in cases where crimes had taken place within a family, where the members proved reluctant to exact punishment on one of their own. In 1991, a modification of the *qesas* laws stipulated prison terms when the private plaintiffs chose to forgive.

The third category of *ta'zir* laws (discretionary punishments) covered crimes not included in the first two categories, and their punishments were left to the discretion of clerical judges. As it turned out, this category covered many of "minor" crimes that are commonly committed in urban societies. The fourth category of the *diyat* laws provided a rather primitive chart for compensation to victims of homicide, assault, and battery.

The clerics sacrificed the lives of hundreds of young men and women to the imperatives of the Islamic judicial concepts of *hodud* and *qesas*. They also introduced the practices of stoning to death (*rajm*) and cross amputation (*salb*). These menacing concepts became common judicial categories for the authoritarian state. Here the curses of the religious state hit early and hard.

Through the Prism of Prison Memoirs

I will start with Paya's memoirs, covering the early days of the revolution. The clerics held trials and ordered the summary executions of hundreds of high officials and military men of the Shah's regime. For them and hundreds others who remained in prison, the most obvious predicament was the absence of due process of law. The Islamists took Paya to a prison ward full of men whose cases were all pending, some waiting in vain for weeks.[1] After the initial rush of executions, the new regime experienced a crippling shortage of prosecutors and judges, for which the detainees suffered greatly. According to one account, "over 7,200 cases were pending, while revolutionary tribunals were handling over 20 cases a day."[2]

Paya had been in prison for a short while when a middle-rank cleric who introduced himself as Khomeini's representative visited the prisoners and inquired about their condition. He requested that the prisoners write their demands and forward them to him. With the help of a few other political prisoners, Paya provided a list that they all felt included the main requests of all prisoners in the ward. It is significant for this study to note that most of the eleven demands addressed the absence of due process of law. They included the right to a fair trial in a competent court, the right to a defense attorney, and a speedy investigation after the arrest. The prisoners also demanded to know the charges against them.[3]

True, Paya (Dr. Ousiya) was an attorney familiar with the modern concepts of rights and due process of law. Yet it is accurate to assume that such a list of demands would have emerged from any prison ward in Tehran. This point is pertinent to the debate about cultural relativism. In a prison ward in

Iran in the midst of the revolution, political prisoners articulated demands that were in accordance with international human rights law. Whatever the origin of international human rights standards and regardless of their philosophical underpinnings, these demands reflected not philosophical musings but vital needs of prisoners who had found themselves thrown into the state prison without the required safeguards.

Paya rejected the argument presented to him by some of the guards that the nearly undesirable conditions in prison were due to the "revolutionary conditions" or "revolutionary excess."[4] Against the background of the "general expectations of the revolution," the prevailing injustice compelled him to engage in a one-man hunger strike that soon landed him in solitary confinement. He continued to demand that the authorities respect his right to due process of law.

Because he had landed in prison shortly after the victory of the revolution, Paya hoped that the revolutionaries would be able to set up a justice system that was much better than what existed before. The sad reality, however, was that outside the prisons all the main participants in the revolution, with the notable exception of Prime Minister Bazargan and his associates, sought a different kind of retribution. They called for severe punishment for those who had previously denied justice to the people under the Shah's regime. Revenge, and not due process of law, ruled the unforgiving sentiments in the streets of revolutionary Iran. A typical editorial commentary by a nonclerical activist encouraged responsible officials to be more vigilant in dealing with "criminals" who had succeeded in eluding the hands of the revolution. The frequently expressed revolutionary sentiment demanded harsh treatment for "the household slaves of the Shah."[5]

As days passed, Paya felt even more despondent facing the "wall of silence."[6] He was imprisoned with no one feeling responsible either to bring him to a court of law or set him free. Hundreds of other prisoners shared his fate, but they suffered much longer. Paya had committed no offenses. Perhaps the absurdity of his arrest, or some influential outside connections, secured his conditional release.

For the members of leftist groups who crowded the prisons from late 1980, the judiciary was characterized by the absence of justice, in any sense of the term, Islamic or otherwise. Almost all writers of prison memoirs attested to the fact that the clerics conducted prison trials in courts, which consisted of a judge and a male secretary. Alizadeh was brought to the court blindfolded, and when she received permission to remove her blindfold, she saw two men sitting behind tables. One was a young mullah who played the role of the Islamic judge, and the "other was a thirty-something man with a frowning face." In front of him the prisoner saw a tray, a sugar holder, a teapot, and cups. He served tea to the judge and himself.[7] Other prisoners also mentioned the revolutionary secretary in charge of the teapot.

It is useful to look briefly at the experiences shared by Parsipur, Parvaresh, and particularly Raha in facing their Islamist prosecutors and judges. Parsipur's trial also took place in prison, and the procedure appeared farcical. The cleric-judge sat next to the male secretary, neither of whom was particularly attentive to the file in front of them. Knowing that Parsipur was a novelist, the cleric showed more interest in discussing social issues with her than in examining the charges against her. At the time, many mullahs shared this inclination, perhaps wishing to impress the secular intellectuals who possessed a superior education.[8] The judge ended the session without making any decision on her case.

A total lack of due process of law characterized the state of siege of 1981–82. The situation failed to improve in 1983–84, when a much calmer political climate prevailed and the regime's survival no longer seemed threatened. Parvaresh wrote that his presence before the mullah-judge in the summer of 1983 took not more than ten minutes, although by then he had already been in prison for five months. What followed typified many of the political trials. The judge read the indictment. Parvaresh did not elaborate on the indictment other than mentioning an accusation that he had not revealed the truth of his activities during his interrogations. He was then asked if he was a Muslim. Parvaresh gave an answer that would have infuriated any mullah. "I did not select Islam myself, which makes it impossible for me to put it aside. If I am called a Muslim, it is only because I was born to a Muslim father and mother, otherwise I had no choice in the selection." The judge retorted by asking if he had therefore selected Marxism. Feigning, Parvaresh replied that his inadequate knowledge of Marxism made such a selection improper. The judge then asked if he was willing to do a taped interview denouncing his organization. His negative answer ended the session. The clerics sentenced him to seven years, although it took awhile before they informed him of the sentence.[9] As described in Chapter 8, he faced the same kind of inquisition later in the more deadly climate of prison massacre.

Sometime during the summer of 1982, the interrogators finally took Raha (Monireh Baradaran) to see the judge who read the indictment: "Tendency towards Marxist thoughts, reading the leftist press, and participating in their demonstration." Raha objected that the demonstration took place legally in front of the U.S. Embassy. The religious judge interrupted her by asking if she would give a taped interview. "Why interview? I was nobody," she responded, ending the court session. Three years in prison was the verdict.[10] A few months later, the authorities transferred her and her sister-in-law to Qezel Hesar prison, where she met the novelist Parsipur.

The circumstances that surrounded Raha's second trial in 1984 also revealed the lack of due process of law and the absence of fair trial. The militant political fervor of the earlier years had greatly subsided; nevertheless, arbitrariness in judicial process continued unabated. The fact that some of her former comrades revealed new information about her affiliation with the leftist group Rah-e Kargar brought about the new phase of interrogation and trial. A young prosecutor told her that whatever information she possessed was no longer important. "Thus, there is no need for whipping. If it were two years ago, your death under flogging would have been certain."[11]

Raha had endured two years of physical hardship and psychological turmoil that took a heavy toll on her body. "I wanted to die, but without committing suicide. In other words, I wanted to be relieved." She had stopped eating and ended up in the prison infirmary; it was not a hunger strike, she added.[12] The prosecutor was sometimes polite. At one point, he even allowed her to make a telephone call to her family. "It was months that they had no news from me."[13] This was the spring of 1984, exactly at the time when across the world, and unbeknown to Raha, the Commission on Human Rights decided, amid Iranian diplomats' denunciations, to appoint a Special Representative to monitor Iran. Obviously, the Commission members were unaware of this young woman's valiant struggle to endure the Ayatollah's prison without compromising her intellectual integrity and secular conscience.

On a suffocatingly hot summer day in 1984, the guards dispatched Raha for her second trial in front of the same judge who had sentenced her to three years in 1982. She now realized that the new indictment against her included detailed accounts of her behavior and nonconformity in prison. They even added the prison "hunger strike" to the list of her offenses. Again, the judge asked her if she felt repentant. Feeling what she described as a bitter pain in her heart, she answered affirmatively. She had come a long way and had endured considerable suffering and lost a dear brother to execution; she knew that she was also facing a death sentence. She had to wait another six months to be told of her new sentence: ten years from the time of the second trial, so that the more than two years she had already spent in prison were not counted.[14]

During the relative improvement in prison conditions in 1985 (see Chapter 8), an unexpected opportunity presented itself to Raha. A cleric who visited the prison as a member of the "amnesty commission" placed a piece of paper before her to sign. It was her amnesty paper, providing that she would express repentance in front of other prisoners. She was quite surprised that at a time when other prisoners waited by the door for hours to gain access to the commission, the cleric was giving her that opportunity. Soon she realized that traditional habit of finding family connections with influential men was responsible for the favor. The cleric told her that he knew her family and was indebted to her father for his service to him and to Islam. He said that he was ashamed to examine the file of the daughter of such a devout Muslim father. The stories of devout fathers and leftist sons and daughters were familiar during the 1960s and 1970s, adding complexities to the country's political tapestry. The connection worked; despite

Raha's refusal to denounce her past political affiliation, the cleric changed her sentence to three years.[15]

Thus, in 1985 Raha began serving a new three-year term. While not overly optimistic about her release on conclusion of her sentence, in the summer of 1987 she was taken for yet another interview with a prosecutor. He asked if she was willing to denounce the organization she belonged to during the revolution of 1979. Raha's answer was again negative. The official simply retorted that until she satisfied that condition she would remain in prison. Shortly after that interview, her sentence was increased to ten years in prison. In the Ayatollah's justice system, an act of reprisal was as arbitrary as an act of kindness. By then, she had spent six years in Tehran's three main prisons. According to the new term, she had to serve another seven years, although at no time did she receive any sentence longer than ten years.[16]

Raha's case belonged to those who experienced the clerical court. There were others who languished in legal limbo. The prosecutors lacked enough information on some prisoners, whom they referred to as *mashkuk* (under suspicion), and postponed their court appearances indefinitely until the prisoners could be "discovered." They had been arrested because of associations with other activists or because they fell under suspicion by the burgeoning Islamist groups. Once inside prison, it was almost impossible for any prisoner to set himself or herself free. The revolutionary prosecutors believed that if the young prisoners were truly innocent they could not have been in prison in the first place. Now that they were there, the interrogators had to prove them guilty. A person whose identity was not fully "discovered" would be exposed to everyone inside a prison until identified. The guard would take the person to the meeting hall (the *hosseiniyyeh* in Evin), where they would announce her or his name. They would also broadcast the name to all prison wards, hoping for discovery by repentant prisoners.[17] In Azad's case, it did not take long for someone to identify her.[18]

The prisoners welcomed any sentence other than death. However, the sentencing did not signify the end of a process whereby the prisoners expected to settle into prison routine, waiting to complete their sentences. As examined in Chapter 7, for Raha and many others, the postconviction ordeal began in the hands of prison wardens.

Regardless of the original sentence, there would be no release without the formal taped repentance, *towbeh*, which was an extrajudicial concept. Never charged or sentenced, Parsipur stayed in prison for as long as she did because she was unwilling for a long time to offer anything that would smack of repentance. Raha wrote that no one could get out of prison without the infamous finale, the taped interview, which would have to be given in front of prisoners and shown on closed-circuit television. Azad also wrote about prisoners who had served their time but who refused to submit to the final interviews.[19] The absurd process did not necessary end once the prisoner submitted. In many cases, it appeared that prisoners endured an open-ended process of trial and conviction, with intermittent new interrogations, physical punishments, and reversed sentences.

Monitoring Violations: The International Community During the 1980s

The international human rights community noted not only the trials and executions of the "enemies" of the Islamic revolution but also the grossly unfair trials held for those who participated in the revolution as Khomeini's allies. In this category, one of the most discussed cases of miscarriage of justice belonged to Abbas Amir-Entezam, whom Galindo Pohl visited in Evin prison in December 1991. He was Prime Minister Bazargan's deputy in the provisional government in 1979 and unjustly accused of being a spy for the United States.[20] His case revealed the Islamists' bizarre understanding of the legal indictments that tragically ruined many lives in the 1980s. The seizure of the American Embassy led to Bazargan's resignation and the eventual arrest of Amir-Entezam in December 1979. The Islamic Revolutionary Court charged Amir-Entezam with espionage and convicted him for treason, based on his contacts with American diplomats in Tehran. The absurdity of the charges has since become clear.[21] An equally revealing part of the indictment accused him of committing crimes merely by entertaining political views other than those Khomeini advocated at the time. The court sentenced him to death, and only the timely intervention of Bazargan reduced the sentence to life in prison.

Overall, Galindo Pohl concerned himself ardently with violations of the right to a fair trial, hoping for concrete progress in judicial practice toward a modicum of respect for due process of law. The detailed attention to this particular right, both in his reports and in his discussions with judicial authorities, was due to the fact that it lent itself more easily to formal discussion than other rights whose violations were more hidden. As will be shown in Chapter 12, textual and legalistic discussion often ensued whenever he brought up the right to a fair trial. Violations of the right to security of person, on the other hand, remained hidden behind the veil of official denial and rejection, and the practice of torture followed no set of published rules and regulations that could be formally discussed and criticized. Anyone could analyze the inadequacies of laws covering trials without reference to actual practice. Observers could refer to the published text of the Islamic Penal Codes and point out conflicts with international human rights law. As for actual practice, state documents and reports revealed its shortcomings.

For example, they showed the inability of individuals accused of political crimes to avail themselves of legal counsel. Having endured the bloody rituals of torture and written confessions in prison, prisoners stood alone and utterly defenseless. They faced a clerical prosecutor-judge with conspiratorial mind-set, an unyielding determination, and a vengeful temperament, all unbecoming to the judicial bench. This much Galindo Pohl's reports revealed.[22] Galindo Pohl understood the disastrous consequences for justice in a state whose officials were either unfamiliar with or negligent of due process of law.

Amnesty International offered similar but more forthcoming observations for the same period, consistently pointing out that under no circumstances did the detainees benefit from attorneys' service. It portrayed "an almost entirely arbitrary system for the administration of justice with widely disparate sentences being passed in different parts of the country for the same offences, and with a system offering little or no possibility of redressing the many wrongs that inevitably resulted."[23] Amnesty International further observed:

Individual judges would appear to have had unbridled powers, local officials have used their position to achieve personal gain or to conduct vendettas, and law enforcement authorities have abused their authority by, for instance, inflicting torture on prisoners in their custody. The lack of centralized authority has been conducive to widespread arbitrary arrest and detention, torture and executions, while at the same time denying victims of human rights violations recourse to impartial tribunals whereby they could challenge their detention and present a defence in the course of a fair and public trial. All too often, following summary trials, death sentences have been imposed and swiftly carried out.[24]

Monitoring Violations: The International Community During the 1990s

By the early 1990s, Galindo Pohl felt increasingly pessimistic about any meaningful reform in the judicial process. He was troubled by the gruesome sentences issued by the judiciary. For example, an official announcement of sentences on February 14, 1990, had a macabre ring to it: "Gholamhossein Golzar, 27 years old, discharged employee of the Agricultural Bank of Hamadan: 74 lashes for committing robbery; 92 lashes for participation in a forbidden act, and decapitation by the just sword of the Imam Ali; Gholamhassan Golzar, aged 28, discharged employee of the Hamadan Municipality: 74 lashes for committing robbery; 74 lashes for participation in a forbidden act, and decapitation by the just sword of Imam Ali; Reza Khanian, 23 years old, fruit and vegetable centre clerk: 74 lashes for committing robbery; 50 lashes for participation in a forbidden act; amputation of hand for committing assault and battery, and hanging by scaffold."[25] These sentences fell into the category of Islamic punishments that Galindo Pohl's diplomatic interlocutors had asked to be excluded from international scrutiny (Chapters 10 and 11).

In his February 1994 report, Galindo Pohl again raised the issue of public repentance as a practice contrary to due process of law. He provided three specific cases that took place in 1993, two involving members of the Kurdish resistance active in Iranian Kurdestan.[26] In the third case the prosecutors arrested Ali Mozaffarian in late 1991, charged him with espionage for foreign countries, and broadcast his "confession" in the province of Fars. Galindo Pohl suspected that the confession was "obtained as a result of physical or psychological pressure." A leader of the Sunni Muslims in Fars, Mozaffarian was a surgeon and an outspoken critic of the government's policies toward the local Sunni community. As usual, the clerics spiced up the indictment by adding the sexual crimes of adultery and sodomy.[27]

In his 1993–95 reports, Galindo Pohl took a broader vision, often commenting on the entire system of the "administration of justice." [28] He noted "that there have been some reforms of the law, particularly on penal justice, concerning appeals against decisions and sentences and the presence of a defence lawyer." [29] However, he found the reforms falling short of creating proper due process in accord with international human rights law. The reforms, unsatisfactory as they were, excluded the political trials before Islamic Revolutionary Courts, whose summary proceedings were still shrouded in secrecy.[30] The most significant shortcomings of the reforms emanated from their being more grounded in what Ayatollah Yazdi considered to be Islamic principles. He rejected the court proceedings that existed under the Shah as being based on the French system. In his new Islamic General Courts, a cleric controlled the entire proceeding, acting both as the public prosecutor and the presiding judge, delivering the verdict. Amnesty International had already seen the problem in 1990.[31]

Galindo Pohl was also concerned about "the lack of transparency and predictability in the application of Iranian law." He quoted Ayatollah Yazdi as saying on June 26, 1992, that the laws in the Islamic Republic of Iran were derived from different Islamic treatises (*resalat*). One important treatise, the *Tahrir al-Vasila*, belonged to Khomeini. The fact that the Islamic treatises might not be in agreement on the important issues of crime and punishment, Galindo Pohl concluded, has caused uncertainty in legislating legal codes in the Islamic Republic of Iran. He was also informed that *fatvas*, religious edicts written by different Ayatollahs, "had played a major role in court decisions." Galindo Pohl observed that the issuing of such *fatvas* "had undermined the principle of equality before the law and contributed to the issuing of confusing and often inconsistent judgments by Iranian courts." A court's verdict might be influenced by a *fatva* issued by a cleric, and since *fatvas* sometimes differed on similar cases, no equitable application of the law was obtained. Judges in civil matters used *fatvas* to make decisions. They were also used in numerous instances of seizing property.[32] "The new Islamic Penalties Act, which replaces the 1982 Penal Code, follows the basic layout of the old law; it has not introduced the technical reforms that would make the punishment fit the offender's particular circumstances, adjusting criminal responsibility to match the degree of involvement in the offence." [33]

In his 1995 report, Galindo Pohl seemed to have lost his considerable patience with the regime over reform of the judicial system for which he had previously expressed some hope. He "noted that there has been no known reform of Iranian criminal law designed to bring it into line with international standards, nor do efficient measures appear to have been taken to guarantee due process of law."[34]

During the 1990s, many of those who faced Islamic courts were individuals whose identity and affiliation international observers knew well. This period created its own mode of political activism that increasingly involved Islamic liberal groups and moderate secular individuals. During the first period of overt suppression, the leftist and radical secular dissidents were defeated, executed, driven into exile, or frightened into silent inaction. Their political dormancy created a new opportunity for liberal Muslims to renew cautiously their political activities. As mentioned above, the institutionalization of the revolution, the reemergence of the bureaucratic state, Khomeini's death, and the desire of President Rafsanjani to offer the world a regime with a slightly different face all contributed to the creation of a new political dynamic. As will be fully discussed in Chapter 13, Islamic reformers began to sense a respite in relations with the dominant clerical power. They had originally felt a certain affinity with the Islamic revolution but were later pushed aside by the politicized clerics. To test the limit of the regime's tolerance, they began expressing their opinions. The 1990s witnessed open letter writing by certain personalities well known in politics, arts, and literature. Thus, many of the violations of the right to fair trial evolved from the suppression of freedom of expression. Moderate Muslim dissidents became targets of judicial prosecution.

I will only focus on two judicial cases to highlight the peculiarities of the Islamist justice system in dealing with political offenses during most of the 1990s. One of the trial cases that Galindo Pohl followed in the summer of 1990 involved a group of liberal Muslims who had signed a critical open letter drafted by the ex-premier, Mehdi Bazargan, a veteran Islamic activist, and addressed to President Rafsanjani.[35] The letter—signed by ninety individuals, twenty-three of whom were arrested—reminded President Rafsanjani of grievous situations prevailing in the country and called for the restoration of basic rights. Presenting the arrests in their proper political context, Human Rights Watch stated that these liberals "represented the principal window of protest against arbitrary government action." In June 1990, the Islamic Revolutionary Prosecutor accused the letter's signatories of acting as a fifth column, "in the interests of the enemies of Islamic Revolution and the Iranian people."[36] More specifically, he charged some of them with espionage. On June 27, 1990, Galindo Pohl expressed his concerns for fair, public trials for the detainees.[37]

Well covered in the press in the United States and Europe, the letter became a thorn in the side of officials in the Foreign Ministry and the Judiciary. The Revolutionary Court could not denounce the signatories as terrorists, nor could it credibly accuse them of anti-Islamic activities. The letter confirmed some of the allegations in Galindo Pohl's reports. Specifically, it showed that there was no agreed upon, internal judgment on the cultural validity of those laws and practices that the government upheld as Islamic. Thus, it effectively undermined the veracity of official claims that domestic laws and practices were based on indigenous Islamic cultural norms and as such should not be subject to external (Western) judgment. The former premier and his associates, each with a career of Islamic political activism, announced publicly that certain practices of the Islamic Republic of Iran violated international human rights law.

Farhad Behbahani, one of the signatories, offered his forced repentance in a televised interview. During Galindo Pohl's second visit to Iran in October 1990, Behbahani said "that the authorities had resented that the open letter had reached foreign media." The government maintained that the United States and its direct and indirect agents concocted all allegations of human rights violations. Therefore, anyone who spoke of human rights violations was taking a position "in conformity with the policy of a foreign Power."[38] The timing of the letter, as much as its content, caused the arrest of the signatories. Indicative of the inherent shortcoming of the international monitoring process, Behbahani, who had suffered brutal beatings for two months, could not speak to Galindo Pohl about his torture-induced repentance. A decade later he revealed how his interrogators chained him to a wooden bed and flogged his feet beyond human endurance.[39]

Expressing his concern about the news of Behbahani's broadcast repentance, Galindo Pohl stated again that such an extrajudicial act violated due process of law.[40] After his second visit to Iran, Galindo Pohl observed: "Televised confessions have aroused considerable skepticism and they are seen as lacking spontaneity and authenticity. In view of this situation, the practice does not contribute to the proper administration of justice. Rather, it undermines and obscures the administration of justice for purposes alien to it, particularly when the practice takes place in the course of the investigation."[41]

Significantly, Galindo Pohl expressed his anticipation concerning the trial of the letter's signatories, clearly intending to make it a test of the much-promised improvement in the conduct of trials.[42] In the following year, Foreign Ministry officials informed him that on December 10, 1990, some of the signatories had been released from prison. They added that the Special Representative would be informed about the rest of them "as soon as the judicial proceedings are concluded." They never informed him. In fact, all the accused spent between six months and three years in prison for writing the letter. There was no mention as to what happened to the charge of espionage that was leveled against some of the signatories, nor was there any indication that they had been brought to trial before being released. Most likely, the government's responses reinforced Galindo Pohl's opinion concerning the absence of due process of law. People were arrested whenever the Judiciary in conjunction with the intelligence officials decided on the arrest, and they were released whenever the same authorities decided on the release, a remarkably normal behavior of all authoritarian states. After his third and final visit to Iran in 1992, Galindo Pohl observed that the government had failed in this case which he had presented "as a test case for the effectiveness of due process of law." [43]

Another revealing example of grossly unfair trials involved the "Zendehdel network." The Special Representative Copithorne's visit in February 1996 coincided with one of the sessions of the show trial of six individuals who were "the ringleaders of a conspiratorial group" of some 150 people.[44] The six were brought to trial seven years after their arrest. It was a strangely motley assortment whose members included, by the prosecutor's account, royalists as well as radicals belonging to organizations like the Mojahedin and the Kurdish Marxist group Kumaleh.

The trial took place following Ayatollah Yazdi's Islamic reorganization, making the court the sole domain of one cleric who would act as both the prosecutor and the judge—in this case, the cleric G. H. Rahbarpur, the Head of the Revolutionary Courts in Tehran. The charges were also bewilderingly multifaceted. In the opening session of the court, Rahbarpur stated that the mission of the Zendehdel network was to create economic crisis. It wanted to create corruption, propagate obscenity, cause confusion in the system, and invalidate moral and revolutionary values, all leading to the overthrow of the system of the Islamic Republic.[45] Perhaps with the exception of sexual charges, this kind of multifaceted charges was in character with other authoritarian regimes.[46]

The indictment against H. Zendehdel asserted that he and the group had been in contact with Admiral Madani, an exiled figure with a nationalist political affiliation. The indictment charged that the group used "prostitutes, female singers and dancers, and loose women" to recruit new members. They also used drugs and alcoholic drinks.[47] Moreover, Zendehdel was made to denounce all of his business activities during the Shah's regime as crimes, for which he was also being prosecuted. That was not all. Zendehdel confessed to "setting up a gang for spreading financial corruption, facilitating the illegal departure of 17 individuals and helping them getting asylum in the United States." He also confessed to "creating a house of pleasure, contaminating women with moral corruption, sexual relations with a lot of women, pimping (qawadi), gambling, transferring classified military information to foreigners, creating corruption by bribing hundreds of government officials."[48] His speech sounded like the typical tortured confession to an incredible assortment of crimes, which, if true, would have made him the greatest criminal of all time.

Reminiscent of the Stalinist show trials, Zendehdel continued his confession by pondering the punishment that he richly deserved. "I am a traitor and *mofsed fel arz* [one who sows corruption on earth], and a hundred hangings are not enough of a punishment for me. Other corrupters on earth must realize that the outcome of any struggle against the Islamic system is only disgrace and humiliation."[49] There was another strange twist in this grotesque trial. Zendehdel told the court: "I was Jewish, and in the year 1985 converted to Islam to protect my economic benefits."[50] And the ugly head of anti-Semitism raised its head when a major conservative newspaper with close clerical connections thundered that Zendehdel was "a symbol of the continued disgrace of the homeless Jews."[51]

The court convicted Zendehdel and A. Majd-Abkahi of the crime of "corruption on earth" in July 1996 and hanged them. They also executed A. Yazdanshenas, a former air force officer. The other three men received prison sentences of seven to twenty-three years and between 110 and 200 lashes. The court also sentenced to death the wife of one of the accused. Amnesty International seriously doubted the fairness of the trial. It also received reports that the prisoners were subjected to torture.[52]

The Special Representative Copithorne was in Tehran at that time but failed to arrange a private meeting with Zendehdel in prison.[53] He attended the trial for forty-five minutes. His report of the trial did not indicate that the bizarre assortment of charges had alarmed him. The only observation he made was that "the judge played a much more active role and the lawyers a more passive role than in any trial the Special Representative has attended elsewhere. Indeed, the Special Representative was left with the impression that the judge was clearly not a neutral third party between the prosecution and the defence."[54]

Again, the fact was that the prosecutor was also the judge. The Islamists of different stripes within the regime had remained oblivious to this peculiar Islamic arrangement until one of them, Gholam Hossein Karbaschi, the Mayor of Tehran, was caught in its tentacles. In the thick of a cabalistic maneuvering, Ayatollah Yazdi arrested the Mayor in April 1998 and placed him on trial for embezzlement and abuse of power. The trial became a revelation for many. Ayatollah Yazdi had often bragged about the superiority of the Islamic justice system compared with what other civilizations could offer; for that reason, he asserted, it was necessary for the world to become "more familiar with the Islamic judicial system."[55] Throughout Karbaschi's trial, the judge acted as a vigorous prosecutor to prove the criminality of the accused, and at the end he sat back as a judge to decide his guilt or innocence and impose the prison term.[56]

For most of the 1990s, Ayatollah Yazdi can be characterized as the main director of the show trials, whose leading stage actor was Rahbarpur. Underlining the point, I will return to Amir-Entezam, who was by 1995 the longest held political prisoner in the country. This will further shed light on Rahbarpur's judicial style. Amir-Entezam suffered in the Islamist prisons in the 1980s. By the time the judicial authorities were willing to set him free in late

1995, he rejected the offer of clemency and renewed his demand that he should be given a chance to prove his innocence and clear his name in an open court, held according to international norms.[57]

Rahbarpur, the Head of the Revolutionary Courts in Tehran, responded. Amir-Entezam's letter from prison, which stated his case and was published in Europe, captured the attention of the international media. Abdolkarim Lahiji, a prominent Iranian-born attorney in Paris and Deputy President of the International Federation of Human Rights Leagues, helped to publicize the injustice done to Amir-Entezam. The clerics became furious. Rahbarpur denounced everyone in a press conference: "This letter is a fabrication and is prepared and distributed by the runaway enemies of the Islamic Revolution outside the country, with the purpose of striking a blow at the prestige of the Islamic system." He reiterated the old, trumped-up charges, including spying for the CIA. He reminded everyone that Amir-Entezam had been sentenced to life. He added, "With regard to what is found in his file indicating heavy crimes, if the case is re-tried, he will most likely get the death penalty." He went on to charge and convict the attorney Lahiji in the same press conference. "As an unfit element, a Freemason, and a runaway spy, Lahiji is under indictment by the Revolutionary Court." Misleading or exaggerating as usual, he added that Lahiji and his associates were responsible for most of the negative propaganda directed against the Islamic Republic of Iran from Europe and that the letter attributed to Amir-Entezam was "also prepared by Lahiji and other anti-revolutionary runaways, under the guidance of their masters (America and Israel)."[58]

Dr. Lahiji was lucky not to fall into the hands of the prosecutor/judge. Zendehdel had no such luck. The judge's idle talk against the first man renders the accusations against the second incredible.

Until the state of acute crisis that the regime experienced at the end of the 1990s, the clerics in charge of the security and judicial apparatus of the contemporary state were still more preoccupied with the task of eliminating or neutralizing the real or imagined enemies of the revolution. Thus, trial proceedings for political opponents and critics of the regime remained constant since the early 1980s. However, the accused individuals in the 1990s were far less radical than the prisoners in the first period, and their treatments were correspondingly less harsh—except for those charged with espionage or street disturbances. As will be shown in Chapter 14, the judicial crisis of the late 1990s (especially the farce trials of the two well-known reformist clerics) revealed the depth of judicial maladies in the Islamic Republic. The crisis led to the "retirement" of the Head of the Judiciary, Ayatollah Yazdi. Even then, the regime's diplomats repeated at the United Nations the charades about the independence of the Islamic Judiciary.

Despite Galindo Pohl's mostly negative judgment, his successor began with a somewhat different understanding and with a more conciliatory approach to the clerics in charge of the Judiciary. Copithorne concluded: "The

Special Representative nevertheless believes he detected an atmosphere for change. One of his Iranian interlocutors preferred the term *maturation*. He noted that norms were now being more clearly articulated and suggested that that was because of a clear need for a more uniform application of the law. The sense of arbitrariness that the Special Representative felt he detected was not a reflection of a concern over the security situation but of the strongly held view that Islamic theory required a highly independent judiciary."[59]

The last remark appears curious, since an "independent judiciary" is a distinctly modern notion. Moreover, Copithorne's comments misrepresented the Judiciary under Ayatollah Yazdi's control. It remained, in critical political conflicts, a potent instrument for safeguarding the clerics' hold on state power. Yazdi's pretentious "independent judiciary" was a convenient ploy, hiding the fact that the Judiciary remained impervious to any constitutional provision. It functioned as the most potent instrument for preserving the political power of the clerics who served the Supreme Leader. It must be remembered that the Head of the Judiciary was appointed by the Supreme Leader, the most politically significant figure in the Islamic Republic.

When Copithorne wrote his report expressing understanding for judicial independence, international human rights organizations had noticed the implementation of the judicial reform law that the Majlis had passed in August 1994. As Human Rights Watch observed, the new law of the General Courts (Dadgaha-ye Am) worked "against the independence of the judiciary, and to the detriment of the rule of law."[60] The law reflected Ayatollah Yazdi's efforts to Islamize the Judiciary completely.

In the late 1990s the 'independent' Islamic Judiciary had become a curse of the state, and the Islamic reformers expressed deep frustrations about their inability to change it. Akbar Ganji asked: "If people view the judicial system to be political and dependent on one faction, how are they to express this view? If people disapprove of the men in charge of the system and their policies, in what legal way can they act to remove them?"[61] In a sarcastic remark, the weekly *Rah-e Now* observed that Yazdi often used his sermons at Friday prayers in Tehran to issue judicial verdicts against those he considered enemies of the state.[62] By 1999, Copithorne also acquired a better understanding of the regime and seemed to agree that Iran needed a legal system "that is less arbitrary, less driven by ideology, less cruel towards its dissidents and criminals; in short a system based on the rule of law built around respect for the personal dignity of all individuals."[63]

Chapter 7

The Right to Freedom of Conscience, Thought, and Religion

> Everyone shall have the right to hold opinions without interference.
> —Article 19 of the ICCPR

> In fact, in its general comment 22 (48) of 20 July 1993, the Human Rights Committee observed that the freedom to "have or to adopt" a religion or belief necessarily entailed the freedom to choose a religion or belief, including the right to replace one's current religion or belief with another or to adopt atheistic views, as well as the right to retain one's religion or belief. Article 18, paragraph 2, of the International Covenant on Civil and Political Rights bars coercion that would impair the right to have or adopt a religion or belief, including the use of threat of physical force or penal sanctions to compel believers or non-believers to adhere to religious beliefs and congregations, to recant their religion or belief or to convert.
> —UN Thematic Special Rapporteur Abdelfattah Amor, 1996

The architects of the Islamic Republic were the first religious-political activists to take over a Western-style authoritarian state and transform it into a theocracy. Once in control of the state's coercive apparatus, they introduced an all-encompassing project to re-Islamicize the society. Inflicting a particular curse of the religious state, the Islamic Republic parted ways here with other authoritarian states. Persuasion, education, propaganda, intimidation, arrest, torture, and execution were the means to achieve the goals of re-Islamization. This chapter uses the information contained in prison memoirs to illustrate how the new rulers carried out Islamization in prisons with the intent of rehabilitating the incarcerated dissidents, violating their right to freedom of conscience, or physically eliminating them. The relative calm before the storm and the prison massacre of 1988 will be discussed in Chapter 8, which is an extension of this discussion on the right to freedom of conscience.

The first UN Special Representative, Andrés Aguilar, upheld the notion of international human rights law.[1] So did Galindo Pohl. Notwithstanding their clear theoretical stand on the normative universality of human rights, in practice the international monitors had trouble responding to practices that the rulers claimed could not be considered violations, since they emanated from Islamic laws, norms, and practices. The details indicate that in the important area of the right to freedom of thought, conscience, and religion, the international community, while upholding the universality of rights, made implicit concessions to the new rulers who claimed that the religious and cultural norms of their country determined the state's policies and practices. In the 1980s, Aguilar's successor, Galindo Pohl, hardly mentioned in his reports the plight of secular Muslims or nonreligious Iranians whose right to freedom of thought, conscience, and religion was violated by the state-imposed Islamization process. This was perhaps due to misplaced deference to Islamic sensitivities of the men in power. More alarmingly, it may also be indicative of the impact that the regime's aggressive cultural relativist claims, and the support they received from sympathetic observers, have had on the discourse and practice of human rights.

It appeared that the international monitors had tacitly accepted, at least in the 1980s, the rulers' image of their revolution and state, one that involved millions of devout Muslims who supported the Islamic state. If a minority of nonconformists were forced to respect the religious values of the majority and to accept restrictions on their private and public lives, there was very little that the international human rights organizations could do in terms of exposure or condemnation. Out of consideration for people's "Islamic sensitivities," some even shied away from mentioning assaults on the lifestyles and conscience of secular Iranians, especially women. It appeared culturally "natural" that women in the Islamic Republic should observe the Islamic dress codes; that men and women should not mix together in public spaces or at parties, even in private houses; and that every citizen used Islamic expressions in public discourses. A former professor recalled: "I and thousands of others had to decide each day how we would begin our lectures at the university. The new Islamic masters ordained that all lectures begin with an Arabic prayer for the Lord. Because I refused to do this, I began every class session with a great deal of anxiety." [2]

There was no grand cultural consensus on these practices, and there was nothing "natural" about these restrictions that violated the right to freedom of thought, conscience, and religion.

Political Prisons as the Microcosm of the Ideal Islamic Society

Prisons mirrored the Islamization project that was discussed in Chapter 2. The fact that I want to emphasize in this chapter is that during the 1980s the political prisons in the Islamic Republic of Iran were microcosms of the larger society. While widespread, the violations of the right to freedom of thought and conscience took place in the streets, at work, and even in private homes; these violations were mostly diffused in the larger society. By contrast, the prisoners provided captive subjects for reconversion in the Islamization program.

It is in regard to the right to freedom of thought, conscience, and religion that prison memoirs enable the reader to understand the relevance of culture and irrelevance of cultural relativism to human rights. They provide the details that are often absent in theoretical debates about the relationship between culture and human rights. The memoirs reveal the fact that, aside from the brutal suppression of the Baha'is, the regime's chronic, significant violations targeted the rights of secular citizens and nonreligious Iranians. Imposed Islamization was the primary cause of the violations of the right to freedom of conscience. Again, Islamization of prisons reflected the parallel attempt to impose Islamization on the larger society.

In the early months of the revolution, before the establishment of authoritarian clerical control, political prisoners were largely free from vigorous and ruthless Islamization. Paya's memoirs offered invaluable insights into this early period. The prison population consisted of mostly middle-aged and elderly officials, civilian and military. The young revolutionaries were still free for a few more months, the Marxists earnestly pursuing the mirage of a socialist Iran and the Mojahedin chasing the "classless Islamic society."

Paya's inmates, men of higher education and upper-class background, showed a particular form of religiosity and intellectual disposition. Among those who escaped immediate execution, few were tortured. All were verbally abused, but no one's right to freedom of thought, conscience, and religion was egregiously violated. No one sought to force them to accept a new definition of Islam. Faced with a critical predicament, they sought refuge in their old faith, a privatized and personalized Islam with a much calmer and meditative disposition than the politicized Islam that moved the Ayatollah's throngs to frenzy. The prisoners dusted off the once glittering modernism that the late Shah had heaped upon them from the faith of their childhood and the memories of their fathers' devotion. In the concrete corner of a desolate cell, in the cold winter of 1979, the old faith offered a cushion of psychological comfort, if not a miracle of freedom.

Paya's vivid sketches humanize some of the Shah's generals whom the revolutionary media routinely demonized. For a short time, he shared an isolated cell with a senior general who had educational and technological responsibilities in the Shah's armed forces. Not exactly a man of the sword, the general passed his days in prison by reading, mostly the Qur'an, and uttering the Shiite du'a (prayer), impressing the discerning Paya as "a symbol of love and an expression of faith."[3]

On some Thursday nights (Friday being the Sabbath), prisoners gathered in a large room that served as a kind of "neighborhood takiya" for religious prayers and chanting. They would replace the regular electric bulbs with blue ones, creating a contemplative atmosphere. The space resembled, in Paya's words, "an intersection between legerdemain and an evening party in Fellini's films." In that particularly dreary and anxious period of captivity, they sought solace in the traditional religious practices they grew up with. They endured their unbearable lives by resorting to prayers and invocations of divine names in the traditional Islamic *monajat* (whispering hymns, praising God). They melodiously recited the well-known verses of the *du'a* (prayer). They also collectively engaged in *dhekr*, the rhythmically verbal ritual of invoking God's name. Paya noted derisively that they did so with an unstated hope that "the curtains of evil and wickedness would be punctured and relief (*farraji*) be materialized."[4] To be rescued from their imperilment, they kept pleading to the same Shiite Imams whose names Ayatollah Khomeini invoked to sanction their demise. Such was the paradox of the revolution, mixing politics with Islam. Concerning the right to freedom of thought and conscience, it is significant to note that the zealot prison guards played no role in these nightly sessions. They did not put an end to them, nor did they try to steer these particular expressions of faith toward their own fundamentalist religious practices. Politicized Islam, à la Khomeini, had no place among prisoners—yet.

Paya would have been shocked to see the drastic deterioration of prison conditions in the next phase of arrests and executions, which began in late 1980, after he had been released. Outside the prison walls, the mullahs had already begun realizing a new definition of Islam for a society that has been, in its own way, devoutly Muslim for centuries.

The *Tawaban* (Repentant Prisoners)

Once the clerics monopolized power, the force used to impose Islamization in prisons was decisive and brutal, free of those intermediary social processes that tended to mitigate the impact of such force in a large city like Tehran. The treatment of political prisoners showed the true nature of the rulers' political culture. Perhaps at a time of national crisis, prisons often display more clearly the rough temperament of an illiberal political culture, destroying life, inflicting torture, and remaining impervious to the pain and suffering of its victims. An ominous process in the prison aimed to remold the prisoners' thought and conscience, using a crude combination of physical torture, psychological pressure, Islamic "teachings," and public confession. It was in the prisons that the politicized clerics' true intentions, as well as their vision for the larger society, were clearly revealed.

Thereby, the Islamic Republic added a new term to Iran's prison lexicon: *tawaban* (singular *tawab*, with a clear religious undertone), and herein lies an egregious violation of the right to freedom of thought, conscience, and religion. In fact, they wished to turn the entire secular population of the country into the *tawaban*. From a few prisoners in 1981, the *tawaban* numbers grew in 1983.[5] Neither the human rights organizations nor the Special Representative could examine, in any meaningful way, the process by which the *tawaban* were made. Galindo Pohl had almost nothing to say about the phenomenon. Amnesty's comments were short and general; moreover, it discussed the process in the context of torture.[6] In fact, torture was one of the means used in the process. The result was a severe violation of the right of political prisoners to freedom of thought, conscience, and religion, as well as the freedom to hold opinions without interference.

Tawaban were prisoners who had recanted. In extracting formal recantations, the clerics intended to show that they were the masters of history, with the constant support of the entire Islamic nation. God was on their side, and history, with its teleological direction and ultimate destiny, had vindicated them. For the political clerics, it was not enough that they write their own version of divinely inspired history and celebrate their monopolistic claims. The captives were forced to engage in a verbal self-mutilation of their own past. By their confession and recantation, the prisoners were required to deliver a version of history that rendered them, prior to their repentance and return to Islam, as the essence of all evils, ancient and modern.[7]

What the prisoners said in their recantations is a significant chapter in modern Iranian history. Ervand Abrahamian has fully discussed the incredible texts of repentance, comparing them with the ones extracted under the Pahlavi Shahs.[8] The process that created the *tawaban* is most relevant to the human rights discourse. It also makes clear the irrelevance of cultural relativism to human right discourse. The phenomenon grew out of the process by which politicized Islam was placed at the ideological command of the contemporary state. It resulted from imposition of clerical control over those Iranians who had broken away, emotionally and intellectually, from the traditional culture of their country.

The phenomenon of repentant prisoners, though primarily political in impetus elsewhere, appeared religiously induced in the Islamic Republic of Iran. In the minds of the Shiite clerics, repentance and recantation were associated with heretical views. They were required to undo apostasy and bring the misguided back to the religious fold. The entire *tawab* phenomenon is better understood in light of the rulers' attempt to empty the process of its political significance and imbue it with religious symbolism. Repentance was, in a sense, a second conversion to Islam, as understood by the Islamists. In the eyes of clerical rulers, these young men and women were imprisoned not because they had made a political mistake and supported the wrong political groups but because they had succumbed to carnal desires and committed sins.

Assadollah Lajvardi in Evin and Hajji Rahmani in Qezel Hesar were the chief agents of the Islamization process. As the Revolutionary Prosecutor in Tehran, Lajvardi had become a permanent fixture at Evin prison. After the assassination of Evin's warden, he assumed his office as well. Prisoners believed that he never left the prison; they also saw his wife attending many of the show confessions he staged at Evin. A shopkeeper before the revolution, Lajvardi had spent a few years in Evin as prisoner of the previous regime. Professor Abbas Milani, a former inmate in the Shah's prison, recalled: "He was awful to look at, his face ravaged by a pitiless disease, probably small pox. Perhaps his soul, too, was devastated by the tortures he suffered in prison and the humiliation he must have felt in a world that seemed to become more and more hostile to his beliefs."[9] Now in charge of the same prison, he seemed to have been determined to make it an Islamic prison. Ghaffari wrote that he was "the epitome of a spiteful, inadequate nonentity, given power over life and death."[10] Energetic and omnipresent, boastful and shifty-eyed, coarse in speech and manner, Lajvardi had a voracious appetite for theatrics in the prison. He brought shame, self-hatred, and suffering on all those who were subjected to his abusive shows of forced confessions and recantations. He was a true persona of the new regime in the prison system, the personification of a curse of this particular religious state.[11]

Hajji Rahmani (the Hajji), another merchant-tuned-revolutionary whom all prisoners loathed, was the warden of Qezel Hesar prison. The Hajji was illiterate and rough-edged, a blacksmith before the revolution, who owned his own shop in a middle-class neighborhood in Tehran. Raha portrayed him as both ridiculous and ruthless. He was a bulky man, marching back and forth in front of his captives and dragging his feet in heavy boots. He wore a military jacket and trousers that made him look like "a caricature of the corporals at the service of Latin American military dictators."[12] Ghaffari completed the unflattering profile: "Our rotund governor was enthusiastic about his job, and would do the rounds of the prison blocks, flanked on either side by his guards, intermittently stopping to cuff an unfortunate prisoner or send another flying by buffeting him with his stomach"[13] The Hajji had also served time in Qezel Hesar prison during the Shah's rule.

The Hajji housed the defiant prisoners who refused to renounce their secular conscience in ward 8, marked for punishment. After passing through the torturous process controlled by the interrogators and prosecutors and receiving their sentences, the defiant prisoners would have to retell their "stories" to the Hajji. Moreover, he demanded that prisoners write letters to him, confessing past sins and professing their reconversion to the righteous path of Islam.

The Hajji forced the prisoners to acknowledge their own "intrinsic weakness of soul in the face of temptation."[14] Raha observed that "Lajvardi and other prison authorities always impressed on political prisoners that they were sinful human beings who had confronted the God-supporting nation [*umat-e hezbollah*]."[15] Roger Cooper noted that the authorities considered the inmates to be mentally defective for turning their backs on Islam; they were forced to undergo "intensive religious instruction."[16] The religious state authorities were unable to admit that young people were attracted to secular political ideologies for rational political reasons. How could that attraction be possible at a time when political Islam was alive, marching to the divinely inspired tones of Imam Khomeini? A diabolical force must have possessed anyone who was not a Khomeini supporter.

The *tawaban* could not quietly await their redemption, patiently marking the days until they were set free. Their redemption would come, or so they hoped, only if they took on all the Islamic habits, public appearance, and rough attributes of their tormentors. Showing exaggerated gratitude to the men in power, some of the *tawaban* ingratiated themselves with prison officials.[17] Prisoners had to submit to the required confession, denunciation, and repentance and pass the Islamic benchmarks set for them. Then, the *tawaban* would have to prove their sincerity by participating in violating the right to liberty and security of other prisoners who refused to repent.

The overtly active *tawaban* attended interrogations of other prisoners and assisted by finding contradictions in the prisoners' answers.[18] Raha wrote about one *tawab* who prepared other prisoners for their execution by writing their names on their legs with a marking pen for positive identification after execution.[19] The activities of two young women, one eighteen and the other nineteen, fascinated and repulsed Parsipur. Paralyzed by fear, they were capable of doing anything to save their lives. One of them had already participated in an execution, firing the last shot into the head of a prisoner who appeared to have been only fourteen.[20] Lajvardi seemed to have believed that participating in the execution of one's own comrade was a sure sign of sincerity of repentance and conversion.

Revolutionary guards took the willing *tawaban* along on their daily patrols in order to identify leftist or Mojahid activists among people in the streets.[21] Hardly an Islamic cultural novelty, they were the equivalents of the "markers" the Argentinean junta used to hunt down the "subversives" during the Dirty War of 1976–83.[22] The *tawaban* meddled in every aspect of the personal lives of their cellmates, reporting on their conversations, attitudes toward religious classes, and performance of religious obligations.[23] With their faces totally covered up to conceal their identity, they made "discovery" visits to prison cells for the purpose of identifying anyone who had refused to divulge previous association with the revolutionary groups. The practice was often repeated, and the female prisoners humorously referred to the masked visitors in search of unidentified activists as "suitors."[24] The male prisoners referred to the hooded men in discovery missions as the Ku Kluxes.[25]

As previously discussed, repentance was an extrajudicial measure that was imposed on even those political prisoners who had served their sentences. A prisoner who wished to be set free would be brought to a large gathering of prisoners, where he/she was expected not only to denounce all previous political associations but also to beg for forgiveness. This was just the beginning of the farcical session. The *tawaban* who were present and knew the helpless prisoner would stand up and denounce him/her for insincerity. They might accuse the prisoner of still "remaining" on his/her political positions and supporting his/her organization, or of not being sufficiently sincere or enthusiastic when participating in the ward's religious ceremonies.[26]

For unrepentant leftists, one of the most agonizing experiences was seeing leading comrades at the confession and repentance tables, denouncing their former thought and embracing Islam. The real demoralization sank in when Lajvardi displayed the leaders of various organizations to the captive audience in Evin's main hall, the *hosseiniyyeh*. Raha described an uproarious gathering in April 1982, when Lajvardi presented one of his stars, Hossein Ahmadi Ruhani, a leader of the organization Paykar Dar Rah-e Azadi Tabaqeh Kargar (Struggle for the Liberation of the Working Class). He had belonged to the Islmaic Mojahedin before 1975, when he declared himself a Marxist. The prison episode that Raha described revealed the agonizing dilemma the repenters faced. With a political background that appeared as convoluted as the contour of Iranian radical ideologies of the 1970s, Ruhani voiced his regrets for becoming a Marxist and opposing the clerical regime and repeated the version of history that the Islamists had concocted for him: The Mojahedin abused Islam by mixing it with Marxism and deceived everyone by pretending that they were revolutionary Muslims.

Having heard Ruhani's repentance, the prisoners were jolted by a desperate and daring female prisoner, Manizheh Hoda'i, who introduced herself as a member of Ruhani's organization. She was the wife of another Paykar leader. Perhaps sensing that his show was becoming more dramatic, Lajvardi allowed her to speak. She did so by directly addressing Ruhani and telling him that he had "never understood what he wanted, either at the time when he was an Islamist activist or when he said he had become a Marxist. And even now he did not understand why he once again chose Islam and the Islamic Republic."[27] The painful irony of her denunciation was revealed when she cryptically acknowledged that, a few days before that infamous session, she had also given a taped interview. She criticized the Paykar organization and declared her new conviction that the Islamic Republic was an "anti-imperialist" regime. The show became even more bizarre when she proceeded, in front of the stunned prisoners, to criticize her own previously taped interview, which had not yet been broadcast. The conflict between what Lajvardi demanded of her to save her life and the agony of preserving her conscience was crushing her. She was executed before the spring of 1982 ended. She was the second member of the family to be executed; her brother, Bizhan Hoda'i, was executed in Evin prison. As for Ruhani, he regularly appeared on the *hosseiniyyeh*'s stage, and the prisoners referred to it as the Ruhani show. He was executed in the summer of 1984.

As will be shown later, this was at a time when the regime's diplomats heatedly denied that any human rights violations were taking place in Iran. They also denounced the UN's decision to appoint a Special Representative as an expression of Western hostility to the Islamic revolution.

The presence of the *tawaban* in 1982 and 1983 put pressure on all inmates to conform, leading many to pretend that they had become the characters that the authorities wanted.[28] Pretending seemed to be much easier for many of those prisoners who had been monetarily converted to the revolutionary ideologies that loudly announced themselves in 1978–79 and then reverted to their former nonideological existence. They were neither dogmatic Marxists nor devout Muslims, the two categories that suffered most in the reconversion drive. Some were educated, nationalist liberals who were caught in the tentacles of the revolution. Ideologically and religiously noncommittal, these prisoners cared very little about Islam and the battles between its different versions. As one former prisoner said: "They didn't believe in the notion of sin; therefore the corollary notion of repentance (*towbeh*) had no meaning. Since neither had any emotional, ideological hold over their imaginations, they could easily pretend, if it meant reducing restrictions and mitigating the regime's atrocities inside prison."[29] Ideological indifference was a blessing.

For the committed intellectual Muslims and some of the Mojahedin sympathizers who took the religious notion of sin and *towbeh* seriously, the trauma of forced repentance was doubly painful. Unfortunately, we do not have credible memoirs written by such individuals. The accounts given in the exiled Mojahedin publications are too general in nature and often littered with uninformative diatribes. For devout prisoners who were against the Islamic regime, the notion that in opposing Ayatollah Khomeini they had somehow committed sin was repulsive. For what sins should they repent? Moreover, they were asked to "convert" to something that they considered archaic in rituals, reactionary in politics, and in no way in accord with their progressive understanding of Islam. This made it more difficult for them to submit to pressures to repent.

The committed Marxist prisoners remained contemptuous. Raha, Ghaffari, and Azad divided the prison population into two categories, separating the heroes who resisted from the villains who capitulated. In this convoluted world, torture—and not an independent act of bravery or a prolonged service to the revolutionary causes—was the arbiter of who would rise as a hero and who would fall as a turncoat. Raha and Azad had little patience for the *tawaban*, considering them scum who betrayed their comrades and even their own spouses. Raha observed that the prison "was a paradox, where the most sublime resistance and epochal endurance existed alongside the most despicable wickedness." Years later, when Raha was reflecting on the forced confessions and repentance, she could not allow herself the magnanimity of forgiving the "fallen" comrades belonging to different organizations. She considered repentance a disgrace (*kheffat*), a breech of faith with the cherished values and principles of Iran's secular, revolutionary tradition, which had strongly influenced the life experiences of her generation. Since the turn of the century, a few generations of young Iranians had participated in making that tradition, leaving behind a trail of death and a legacy of shattered dreams and blemished lives. Watching the confession and repentance of her fellow radicals, she felt she was partaking in the ignominy that was debasing the ideology's past heroes. It appeared as if the repentant Marxists had become an open wound implanted on the bodies and souls of their resisting comrades. Raha wrote: "I did not sit behind a microphone for an interview, but those who did were a part of my past and my life's attachments."[30] They fell, and as they did, a part of her collapsed, too.

Azad was also unforgiving of the revolutionaries who forfeited their chance to become martyrs and thus real heroes. If for Raha the symbol of betrayal was Ruhani, for Azad the infamy belonged to Vahid Sari'ol-Qalam from another leftist organization. It was interesting that the wives of Ruhani and Sari'ol-Qalam were among the most forceful *tawaban*.[31] Azad was particularly bitter about the educated leftists who offered their expertise to prison authorities. For example, Sari'ol-Qalam, who had studied computer science in the United States, was chosen by prison authorities to computerize information in Evin prison. He helped to create "charts" for all leftist organizations, graphically depicting their hierarchy of leadership and the position of each individual in it. When in the fall of 1984 it was the turn of the Rah-e Kargar, Azad's group, she was taken to the "chart room" and questioned by Sari'ol-Qalam and other ex-leftists. Azad found a way to express her contempt, and Sari'ol-Qalam responded by a dejected silence.[32]

Not even his computer skills could save Vahid Sari'ol-Qalam's life. He was executed, it was said, in front of the families of Revolutionary Guards who were killed in an armed confrontation in the Caspian Sea littoral, initiated by the remaining members of the organization to which Vahid previously belonged. Again, the Islamic judges imposed the death penalty on a man for planning and executing a crime in which he played no role. According to Azad, the news of his execution reached Qezel Hesar prison in the fall of 1985. Azad described the fear and indignation that the news created among the prisoners. Especially fearful were the *tawaban*, whose tenuous hope for security of life dimmed in light of the well-known fact that Vahid had cooperated diligently with prison authorities. The authorities executed a living proof of the success of the Islamization process.[33]

Imposition of the Black Chador

In prisons, as in society, the linchpin of the Islamization drive was women's appearance in proper Islamic *hijab*. From time to time, prison authorities waged what can be called the war of the black chador. The Hajji in Qezel Hesar demanded, as did officials in other prisons, that women wear the black chador, covering all except the eyes. The authorities desired to make the prison a microcosm of the perfectly integrated Islamic community that was somehow eluding them in the larger society. They refused to accept the more casual chador, usually a mixture of white, gray, and black, worn by many traditional women. It was not a sufficiently strong testimony to one's religious commitment. The emblem of politicized Islam was the black chador, which was, moreover, a political symbol of clerical dominance as enforced by the *hezbollahis*. The all-black chador prison was the surest sign of the success of the Islamization process of "reeducation." The clerics demanded it in cities but failed to enforce a universal compliance outside the prisons, where their success offered the authorities at least a partial consolation.

Yet some women, including Parsipur, resisted and endured, as long as they could, the harsh punishment for noncompliance. Intelligent and articulate, Parsipur managed to preserve her graceful posture for most of her time in prison. However, her discreet gestures of independence and defiance eventually infuriated the guards, who probably saw that her noncompliance was setting a bad example for the younger prisoners. The black chador was one of the most difficult things for Parsipur to accept. She displayed a remarkable spirit of resistance that would have made previous generations of emancipated women proud. She dragged her feet and complained in whatever way she could, always expressing her dislike for the fact that the Ayatollah had succeeded again in covering the Iranian women in *hijab*. As discussed in Chapter 16, this was the same kind of struggle that thousands of women waged outside, in whatever way possible, against the violation of their basic human right to freedom of conscience, a violation that was barely mentioned in the UN reports.

The prison authorities' preoccupation with proper female garb was a corollary to their obsession with sex. Roger Cooper, who spoke Persian and was retained for five years in Evin, developed a good understanding of prison guards. "Politics, religion and sex," Cooper observed, "seem to be the only subjects that interest young fundamentalist Muslims." He further observed that their education was very limited; even on religious matters, they were "quite ill-informed."[34] He could have said the same thing about sexual matters. Other prisoners also noticed the preoccupation with sexuality. Parsipur wrote that in her trial session during which the mullah-judge started a general discussion with her, he asked "a psychological question concerning the sexual relations of father with daughter." Her cellmates were not surprised when she later mentioned the judge's question with an overt sexual overtone. One told of a case in which court officials grilled a "retired prostitute" about her various sexual escapades. "The behavior of the trial officials was so insulting that the poor woman had never felt so humiliated in her entire life of active prostitution." Parsipur was beginning to learn about traditional men's fascination with sexual topics.[35]

During her second arrest in 1990, when Parsipur was held in prison among petty criminals and drug abusers, she noticed a young woman who constantly attracted the attention of the revolutionary guards. "She was a young woman, very beautiful, with a tall stature, to some extent plump. For this reason, the Revolutionary Guards constantly paid attention to her. For all kind of reasons they would call her into the yard." [36]

Ghaffari observed that some interrogators were often interested in "discovering" hidden histories of illicit sexual activities in a prisoner's past. During his own interrogation, Ghaffari noticed that the interrogator wanted to link his political past with illicit sexual activities, adding to his crimes. Ghaffari added that it was not important whether the prisoner was a professor like him or a common worker. The interrogators interjected questions about the prisoners' sexual habits. The mullah-interrogators were especially delighted to discover a weakness related to carnal desires. [37]

In Qezel Hesar prison, the warden took a keen interest in women's appearance. Perhaps he derived a perverted enjoyment in personally harassing, and sometimes teasing, modern middle-class women. He enjoyed exercising authority over them, something that he could not do as a blacksmith before the revolution. He would enter a ward or cell without warning, and all women had to be properly covered. As the prisoners scrambled for their scarves or chadors, he would yell and sometimes strike any woman within reach. [38] Thinking about those occasions when the Hajji hit the female prisoners, Parsipur wrote: "And we were all slowly diminishing in our humanity. All the theories about inherent human dignity and worth were receding on the face of this practice that sought to induce a slavish obedience." [39] The prisoners' appearance at all times triggered a barrage of verbal attacks: "You filth, why don't you have proper stockings; stupid, why does your hair show." Parsipur observed that the purpose of this abusive language was to bring "the soul of the individual down to an abyss." [40] The secular women in the streets of Tehran had the distinct displeasure of hearing the same verbal abuses.

It seemed that the Hajji suffered from an inner contradiction that manifested itself among some traditional Muslim men who face the sociocultural expressions of modernity, especially as displayed by women, with profound moral ambiguity or perhaps a split personality. It might indeed have been the case that modern secular women—outwardly self-assured, poised, and attractive—evoked in traditional men like the Hajji a sense of dismay mixed with an ineradicable allure. The inner desire remained hidden, and the sense of revulsion was openly expressed. Ghaffari considered the Hajji a brutal, dirty old man. He satisfied his libidinous fantasies by forcing female prisoners to invent sexual escapades during the revolutionary period, when they were, the Hajji assumed, residing with male comrades in the "safe houses." The women had to describe their sexual activities in front of the video camera. [41] The Hajji was living proof that in a regressive culture sexual repression leads to perversion, which the religious rhetoric conveniently masked.

Parsipur described one session when the Hajji demanded the presence of all inmates. Walking into the hall, the Hajji faced the women who were squatting on the floor with the black chadors pulled tightly around their figures.[42] He silently stared at "that anonymous blackness,"[43] and then barked at them indignantly: "Black Crows [*Kalagh Sia-ha*]!" This contemptuous utterance startled the novelist, who wrote: "The human-beings-turned-crows looked at the Hajji in silence." Parsipur observed that the women had painfully learned that they must don the black chador if they ever hoped to be released from prison. Now it appeared certain that the same ugly appearance that was imposed on them "has become another pretext used for their further humiliation."[44] The modern middle-class women found themselves caught in the perverted clutches of the traditional Muslim men. They were as contemptuous as they were helpless.

A Deluge of Religious Incantations and Rituals

As the routines of torture and execution devoured the young victims, the prisons' loudspeakers became shriller, endlessly blasting the sound of prayers, sermons, Qur'anic recitations and the *du'a komeil* (long, melodious verses recited on Thursday nights).[45] In larger society, many of the modern middle-class Iranians endured the agony of being bombarded by the lamenting sounds of Shiism, and no one dared in the 1980s to speak about the unpleasant experience. A decade later, when some Western reporters could go to Tehran, they often heard complaints about the overabundance of broadcasts of "ritualized sorrow" by Iran's two-station television.[46]

To secular prisoners, the radio churned out nothing but primitive propaganda, offending their conscience. Reflecting on an agonizing moment inside the ward in the fall of 1981, Hasan Darvish wrote: "That wooden box attached to a corner of the ceiling was a source of our sufferings. It would call to prayer, admonish, melodiously recite lamentations (*nowheh*), and tell moral anecdotes."[47] Parvaresh recalled that every morning the loudspeakers would broadcast Qur'anic recitations. "They would not leave us alone for even a moment. It appeared that death or madness would be the best outcome for us."[48]

Particularly infuriating to Raha in 1984 was the endless singing over the loudspeakers of the *nowheh*, whose semiliterate verses mourn for all kinds of martyrs. The list of Shiite martyrs is a long one, from those who fell in the battlefield of Karbala in the seventh century to those slaughtered in the frontlines of the recent Iran-Iraq War. For Raha, as for all secular Iranians, the *nowheh* was the sound of death, invoking a sense of estrangement toward everything in this world.[49] For some prisoners, especially those from a modern middle-class background, the experience of being in a confined space and exposed to such overwhelming doses of Islamization was traumatic. Azad wrote: "From my childhood I associated the sound of the *adhan* (the call to prayer) and the Qur'an with dead bodies and burial ground, and it created fear in me."[50] Parvaresh found the climate of political religiosity quite suffocating in Qezel Hesar prison in the fall of 1983.[51] This ferocious exhibition of politicized Islam was a far cry from the subdued expression of religiosity that Paya witnessed among prisoners in the first months of the revolution.

Prison authorities now forbade any independent expression of religious devotion, understood as an oppositional political activity. The most ironic aspect of the violation of the right to freedom of thought, conscience, and religion manifested itself in those confrontations where both the guards and the inmates were devout Muslims. Each upheld a particular image of "true Islam." One reason that compelled young men and women to join the Mojahedin organization was their traditional fidelity to Islam; otherwise, the socialist organizations had a more glamorous past and a more articulate leadership. One day a group of Muslim prisoners held a group prayer in the walkways of Qezel Hesar prison. At the end they recited a "unity prayer." The angry warden put an end to the practice.[52] The clerics and their henchmen constantly badgered the Mojahedin captives for their misbegotten version of Islam. They maintained that no true Muslim could refuse, in sound mind, to submit to the power of the clerical rulers.

Alizadeh described an altercation between a middle-aged female prisoner and a guard. Badmouthing the guard, the woman demanded that he return to her the Qur'an that she had brought to prison. Using foul language, the guard retorted that the prisoner was forbidden to have a copy of the Qur'an with the Persian translation. "You would abuse it and mislead the other prisoners," the guard told her. What the guard meant was that the prisoner would be able to quote the Qur'an in Persian and impart a misleading meaning to the original Arabic verses. In a highly politicized climate and in the view of that guard, a nonconforming Muslim could not be trusted with a version of the Qur'an in the language she understood! Alizadeh later heard that the same woman, whom the young inmates affectionately called "Mother," was tortured and executed.[53] Parsipur recalled numerous incidents, almost all comic-tragic, that took place during the prayer sessions. In one episode, a young female guard's admonishment concerning the proper procedure for the afternoon prayers offended some older prisoners. They angrily retorted: "Dear daughter, we have been praying all our lives; now you want to teach us how to pray?"[54]

Tragically, the politicization of Islam and its mixing with the state's repressive apparatus meant that some Muslims could no longer be considered Muslim. By committing political offenses, they forfeited their right to be Muslim. Their families did, too. In some cases, the prosecutors informed the families of an execution only after expiration of the Islamic forty-day period of mourning. They would not allow the family members to engage in Islamic rituals, including wailing on the graves of executed prisoners. The police dispersed mothers who gathered at the gravesites of their executed sons and daughters.[55]

From Evin, the Islamization fervor spread to other prisons. Parsipur described an episode in Qezel Hesar prison during a tearful night of commemoration of Imam Hossein's martyrdom (Hossein, grandson of Prophet Muhammad, the third Shiite Imam, killed in Karbala in 680). It is worth translating and quoting at some length. The guards were preparing the prisoners for the evening lamentation, and Parsipur noticed that the leftist inmates were also joining the ranks of the mourners of Imam Hossein. "The atmosphere had suddenly changed. Only during my childhood once or twice I attended ceremonies like that. Since I could not comprehend the reason for crying and weeping, I did not attempt to participate in them. In prison too I had no intention of participating in the commemoration."[56] However, the leftist inmates' intention to attend the gathering worried her. Not wanting to stand out, she blended in with the crowd. The Mojahedin sat, cross-legged and chador-cladded, on the floor at the center of the hall.

Parsipur heard the sounds of mourning coming from the adjacent ward. Those who were to conduct the commemoration entered the hall, and the drama began. The organizers included Farzaneh, the ex-dancer-singer-turned-revolutionary-guard, and two repentant prisoners, an ex-Mojahed and an ex-Paykari. These three women had covered themselves from head to toe in black chadors. At the entrance of the section, the trio faced the crowd. Farzaneh noticed the presence of the novelist in the captive audience. Ignoring her, she instead fixed her gaze on a leftist prisoner who was sitting, a scarf covering her head, in front of the door. The ex-dancer began to display her flair for theatrics. Raising her right arm and thrusting it toward the young woman in front of her, she shouted: "What happened to Hossein?" Not understanding the meaning of the question, the leftist woman hesitated for a second before realizing that Farzaneh expected her to participate in the mourning of the Shiite Third Imam. She replied: "Was killed!"

With visibly contrived anger, Farzaneh shouted back, correcting her: "Shahid Shod!" (Was martyred!) Understanding her own indiscretion, the young leftist repeated, "Shahid Shod!" The captive audience was about to witness a surrealistic transfiguration of the traditional Shiite commemorative practice. Lamentation for Imam Hossein for the sake of seeking salvation in the next life became a rally of political sloganeering, mourning the "martyrs" of the Islamic revolution. The sacred history of Shiism converged into the propaganda of the Islamic revolution. The secular prisoners who were mostly indifferent to the former and intensely hostile to the latter were playacting. Farzaneh shouted, "Kalantari?" Prisoners immediately noticed that Kalantari was a man among the Islamic Republic's leaders killed in the devastating bombing of the clerical party headquarters, widely attributed to the Mojahedin. Realizing what was taking place, the young leftist woman answered, "Shahid Shod!"

Eventually all inmates realized that they must repeat that catch phrase, and disjointed voices were heard from around the room, until all prisoners began to answer Farzaneh in unison: "Shahid Shod!" Farzaneh's voice surged up toward hysteria as she shouted one by one the names of almost all "martyrs" of the bombing explosion at party headquarters. After each name, the crowd shouted back, "Shahid Shod," while raising their voices to a higher pitch for the next name. The anguished sound of wailing augmented these rhythmic questions and collective responses. Having sufficiently whipped up the crowd, Farzanah was ready for the famous martyrs of the 1979–80 revolution, like Bahonar, Raja'i, and Ayatollah Beheshti, the influential cleric close to Khomeini.[57] Reaching the climax of her own frenzy and beating her chest in hypnotic thuddling rhythm, Farzaneh screamed: "What happened to my Beheshti?! What happened?! What happened?!"[58] The crowd shouted back: "Shahid Shod!" In the meantime, the grandson of the Prophet was somehow forgotten, and the evening, at least in these melodramatic moments, became more a commemoration for Ayatollah Beheshti, one of the celebrated martyrs of the revolution.

Lights were turned off, and candlesticks were lit around the hall. A mixture of modern revolutionary politics and the traditional Shiite practices, this farcical commemoration proceeded in earnest, roaring into the depth of night. The other two women joined Farzaneh, each taking her turn in leading this wary and strange chorus of the mostly radical activists, many of whom were supposedly agnostic, if not atheist.

Adding humor to her description, Parsipur wrote that a leftist young woman, a Zoroastrian in religion, was sitting next to Parsipur's mother. Like everyone else, she was beating her chest. Parsipur's mother perhaps realized how hard it must have been for a person in another religion to take part in such a masquerade of Shiite lamentation. She recalled the old legend that Imam Hossein's wife was Zoroastrian in origin, the daughter of the last Persian king before the Arab invasion of Iran. She turned to the Zoroastrian woman and consoled her: "My daughter, never mind; after all Imam Hossein was your son-in-law." The young woman, continuing to beat her chest, answered back: "Very well, Imam Hossein was our son-in-law, but what about Beheshti? What relation does he have with us?" The tearful spectacle ended shortly before five in the morning.[59]

It became apparent to Parsipur that the young prisoners were mourning not so much for Imam Hossein—and certainly not for the hated Ayatollah Beheshti—but for themselves. They needed it for the predicament they faced in the dreary outcome of the revolution they helped to foster. There was nothing in their past Marxist or nationalist ideological education that could have prepared them for this outcome. However, they were familiar with the consoling practice of lamentation in the Shiite culture of Iran; they understood it almost instinctively and made the best of it. Having lost close relatives and comrades during the clerical crackdown, the prisoners were themselves in mourning. However, under the watchful eyes of the *tawaban*, they "dared not cry" in their cells. They could not show tearfulness while undergoing reconversion. Taking advantage of the "opportunity," they were weeping with all their inner pains and anxieties.[60]

The formal religious ceremonies were irritants to the secular conscience; nevertheless, they were also occasions that broke the monotonous prison life for many bored prisoners. In contrast, the imposition of formal daily prayers was an assault on their conscience; they had no entertaining or consoling qualities.

Parsipur, considering herself Muslim, agonized over her predicament: "I was born in a Muslim family, my father always performed his daily prayers, and my mother has prayed for years. I never harbored any opposition to religion. Of course, I did not perform the obligatory duties, but I never lost my respect for the religion. In prison, I found myself in the middle of a torrent of religious affairs. However, these affairs have no resemblance to what I understood of Islam."[61]

Defending her right to freedom of thought, conscience, and religion, Parsipur refused to perform the daily prayers and was ready, or so she thought, to pay the price. In one encounter with an interrogator, Parsipur demanded to know the reason for her continuous incarceration for four years, without being formally charged with any crime. After listening politely, the man replied by asking her why she did not perform her daily prayers (*namaz*), thus not so discreetly pointing out the reason for her prolonged detention.[62] Raha wrote that at the height of the Hajji's draconian Islamic rule in Qezel Hesar prison, performance of daily prayers was mandatory. When Azad was transferred to Shiraz, she learned that the punishment for not performing the obligatory daily prayers was much harsher in a provincial prison. Her cellmate told her that as early as 1982 the nonconforming prisoners were lashed five times every twenty-four hours in place of the required five sessions of daily prayers.[63] Azad was so horrified by the stifling conditions in the Adel Abad prison in Shiraz that she wished to be returned to Tehran's Evin.

In 1984, when Raha faced the possibility of a death sentence, her interrogators made it clear to her the conditions that might save her life. "After a period of hesitation and internal struggle, one day I began performing the *namaz*." She added that in Qezel Hesar prison, it was a rule. In her new condition in Evin prison, it was "a choice between life and death." To escape death she ostensibly threw her conscience overboard. "Death was constantly in my nightmare, but in reality I ran away from it [by becoming compliant]. This was at the time when I felt a profound sense of estrangement with my life. In escaping death, I felt dejected, especially every time I bent over in prayer."[64] That year she fasted during the month of Ramadan. "That was the only year that I fasted or pretended that I was fasting and suffered a tremendous psychological torment. Even today, after the passage of many years, the agonies of those days are often repeated in my dreams and nightmares." [65] Ghaffari wrote that after the prison massacre of 1988 prisoners were brutally forced to pray; each day at prayer, instead of the prescribed verses, the leftist prisoners mumbled profanities, directed against Khomeini, the Islamic Republic, and Islam. [66]

Underlining the relevance of culture to human rights discourse, the culture of one group of citizens had become the source of anguish of conscience for another group, only because the authoritarian state has become the cultural meddler. This reality leaves cultural relativists with no credible argument. Prison authorities understood and demanded only one particular conscience, whose one-dimensional existence manifested itself solely in prayers, fasting, rituals of commemoration, and outward loyalty to the Ayatollah, expressed in laudatory language. In such a mono-conscience world, why would anyone need the right to freedom of conscience? The leftist prisoners especially felt the enormity of the pressure. "And now it was the moment that they all had to resemble their guards," Parsipur observed. She noted that the Islamization drive systematically altered the prisoners' characters. She noticed that "their natural and happy expression was changing, partly because of executions and torture and partly because of the pressure inside the prison." She added that in that fearful climate of the early 1980s, many prisoners began to seek shelter behind the official "concept of Islam." She felt that the burden imposed by "this concept of Islam was becoming heavier from one moment to the next." [67]

Prisoners and Their Islamic Educators

The writers of prison memoirs frequently expressed their contempt toward the pretentious jailers. For example, Parsipur observed, "Individuals who have attached themselves to an old religion and attempted to impose it perforce on other people think that they and that religion are synonymous. The instrument of force they wield fell into their hands suddenly and of course temporarily. However, the reality is that they are incapable of truly changing anyone's thought. In all the prison years one point was clear, and that was the fact that the [intellectual] stature of prison guards was overall less than that of the prisoners. In fact, this caused the death of many of the prisoners, since all of them were unable to deny their own superior stature — even at that moment [of their severest predicament]." [68]

For every pain they inflicted on prisoners' bodies, the authorities came up with a *shari'ah* law or a Shiite tradition. They capped their designs by resorting to the notion of Islamic guidance and reeducation (*ershad*). The formal instrument of *ershad* was the prison closed-circuit television program that often ran daily from early morning to early afternoon. In one prison the programs that prisoners had to watch covered such topics as philosophy designed to show the fallacy of historical materialism compared with Islamic ideology and to explain human nature from the Islamic point of view. The future foreign minister, Ali Akbar Velayati, who was a physician by training, offered distorted lessons about recent history. Hadad Adel, another future high official, explained Islam's view on man and his destiny. One prisoner reported that on the days when philosophy was the subject under discussion the atmosphere in the room where prisoners viewed the program was particularly tense. The *tawaban* pretentiously wrote down whatever the "professor" was saying. "The other prisoners were forced to sit under visible tension and listen to a discourse that they considered absolutely worthless in terms of science and culture." The prisons in the provincial cities were probably worse than that in Tehran. One prisoner expressed his extreme contempt for the Islamic *ershad* he witnessed in Adel Abad prison in Shiraz.[69]

The other instrument of the *ershad* was a series of formal classes on different Islamic topics held in Evin's new building—the Amuzeshgah (training institute). In their propaganda, the authorities described the Amuzeshgah as an example of an Islamic prison where clerics shepherd prisoners from irreligion to the true Islamic path. The regime's diplomats presented the same picture to the international human rights community. They also claimed that prisoners were being trained in useful crafts, for example, in workshops full of sewing machines.[70] Every attempt at education in the Amuzeshgah provoked scorn in secular prisoners like Azadi, who hardly saw the mullahs worthy of respect or emulation.

The leftist prisoners despised both the messages and the messengers. Azadi described a Revolutionary Guard who was in charge of bringing books to prisoners. Although the man imagined his responsibility to be "important and sensitive," Azadi wrote that his "backward views," appearance, and behavior amused prisoners, especially when he mimicked the gesticulations and verbal expressions that prisoners associated with the mullahs. Ayatollah Morteza Motahhari, the assassinated ideologue close to Khomeini, authored most of the books that he brought to prisoners. Azadi wondered what prison authorities would have done without Motahhari. "Despite the high-sounding claims about philosophy, sociology, and ethics, the regime was deprived of modern texts to defend its ideology. For the regime, Motahhari's books had the distinction of depicting Islamic trifles that belonged to the Stone Age in a language that appeared contemporary and modern." In addition to Motahhari's book, there were texts by Ayatollah Khomeini and Ayatollah Abdolhossein Dastghaib, as well as the Qur'an and the collection of the Second Imam Ali's Sayings (*Nahj al Balagheh*). He added that the prisoners read these books for entertainment.[71] Otherwise, the Islamic education in the prison clearly existed only on sufferance.

Other programs and activities also provoked contemptuous laughter. For example, in the Amuzeshgah, the *tawaban* formed a chorus, daily practicing the Islamic revolutionary songs that the national radio constantly played. Azadi wrote that a repentant prisoner led the chorus.[72] This seems to be the chorus that serenaded the UN Special Representative upon his first visit to Evin's gate in 1990.

Azadi witnessed the earliest attempts to hold formal classes on Islamic topics and believed that Ayatollah Hossein Ali Montazeri, who was still Khomeini's designated successor, appointed the clerics who succeeded each other as Islamic teachers in Evin. To Azadi, who saw the mullah instructors as uneducated and ignorant creatures from bygone eras, the entire reeducational effort seemed crude. The mullahs who came to the prison from Qom were outsiders, not directly associated with the men in charge of security and prosecution in prison. Their captive students, especially those with university education, made things difficult for them. From the very beginning, the better educated prisoners presented the cleric teachers with a problem they could not logically address. It was obvious that the appointed instructors from Qom wished to create a respectable learning environment, one befitting their own self-image as molded in the religious seminaries. However, in the eyes of the students, the Islamic instruction lacked logic and intellectual soundness. Moreover, the clerics' higher moral and intellectual claims sounded hollow amid the miserable conditions of captivity, regardless of what the better educated prisoners thought of the rustic professors with turbans. When speaking of superior Islamic values against other worldly ideologies like Marxism, the instructors wished to create and maintain a proper environment of Islamic learning. Prisoners were quick to point out the obvious incongruity between that high moral ground and the harsh reality of captivity. The clerics from Qom probably realized that prison authorities could compel prisoners to gather in the auditorium and sit through ideological and political tirades. However, they could not make them participate willingly in a meaningful reeducational effort in a classroom environment.

Azadi provided many examples of prisoners' efforts to subvert the clerics' indoctrination. At the end of each session when a few minutes were given to questions and answers, prisoners often shifted the focus from the abstract, ideological discussions about Islam to the intolerable prison conditions, including torture. In one class on Islamic ethics, a prisoner who was in the last year of medical school before the revolution injected a question. "While prisoners are enduring daily hunger, allowed only two minutes to go to the lavatory, and suffering from intestinal diseases, how can one speak of ethics?" In another session, a young man who belonged to the Mojahedin became very emotional. He lifted his arms in front of the cleric, showing both of his wrists, around which blackened circles of dead tissue had congealed. "Is this not a crime that they hung me for hours by my wrists that created these slavery rings around them. This is torture; if it is not, give us evidence that the Qur'an and other religious books say that this act is Islamic." Becoming visibly upset, the cleric could only offer an excuse: "If there was no act of terrorism, no one would have dared to do these terrible things to another person." [73]

Another revealing encounter involved Dr. Muhammad Ali Maleki, a former president of Tehran University during the early months of the revolution. A moderate Muslim, he was imprisoned for supporting the Mojahedin. Azadi met him in the Amuzeshgah. Ghaffari wrote that Maleki was cautious in prison, wanting to give no excuse for his execution. Prison authorities asked Maleki to attend ideological classes taught by young clerics. Yet Ghaffari commented that the teachers should in fact have been his students, since his knowledge of Islamic subjects and Iranian politics was far superior to theirs.[74] Azadi saw Maleki in a class taught by a young cleric named Beheshti, who boasted of the ideological superiority of Islam, particularly that of Shiism. In the course of his discussion, the mullah contemptuously rejected Darwin's theory of evolution. Maleki, who was patiently listening to the cleric's ramblings, could no longer maintain his silence and politely admonished the young mullah for rejecting achievements that were the result of years of scientific research and experimentation. The session ended with other prisoners objecting to the mullah, who never showed up again.[75]

The memoirs showed that without the use of force, the clerics had very little chance of changing the views of their young captives or affecting their secular conscience. The better educated prisoners could perhaps understand ignorance, but they could not accept its glorification, even less so its right to rule the country. The use of force and the threat of death better explained the phenomenon of confession and repentance. The point worth mentioning here is that the officials presented this kind of activities "in university-like conditions" to the outside world as examples of the program that was changing the character of prisoners and reeducating them in proper Islamic values. They "had the right to read, they were treated with kindness and respect. . . . The results of that treatment were evident in the voluntary public confession made by many detainees."[76] In reality, they violated the right to freedom of thought.

Chapter 8

Renounce Your Conscience or Face Death

The Prison Massacre of 1988

Between 1984 and the prison massacre of 1988, there was a period of relative improvement in prison conditions. The significance of that period—which prisoners called the "intermission"—lies in the fact that some prisoners used the opportunity to try to reassert their secular identity and regain a measure of respect for their freedom of conscience. It needs to be emphasized that in the massacre, the violation of the right to life was a consequence of the egregious violation of the right to freedom of thought and conscience. For this reason I discuss the massacre in this category and not in the category of the right to life.

By 1984, the regime seemed to have sifted through the population of political prisoners. Those who survived and accepted the consequences of their intransigence appeared to have settled in for a long haul.[1] Outside, almost all the leftist groups had vanished. So had the main source of moral, political, and organizational support for the political prisoners. Prisoners who escaped execution found themselves extremely vulnerable, a situation not unexpected in a postrevolutionary period in a country like Iran. The leftist political movement had failed to take root among the populace, leaving the youths it mobilized during the revolution at the mercy of its ruthless enemy, the political clerics. Outside of prisons, the captives had no constituencies to support them, no statesmen to inquire openly about their fates, and no journalists to investigate their cases. The rapidly depoliticized society disowned them, with the exception of their mothers and elder family members. Despite the frightening atmosphere of harassment and intimidation, the mothers kept forming queues wherever the possibility of inquiring into the fates of their loved ones presented itself.

Inside prison walls, the small clusters of hunkered-down comrades relied on their own inner strength, now more mindful of their own personal dignity than their allegiance to a failed revolutionary ideology. Prisoners like Raha often lamented the fact that members of each group coalesced, placing a chasm between themselves and other prisoners. It was perhaps an indication of the sectarianism that often plagued the Iranian left. Amidst a total collapse of all formal political standards and in an environment of profound insecurity, it was also perhaps a protective tactic the suspicious prisoners employed for emotional survival.

The Relative Calm Before the Storm, 1984–88

Hardened by the suffering they had endured, political prisoners were pleasantly surprised to see that, beginning with the summer of 1984, prison authorities reduced the hardships of everyday life. Many prisoners believed that the changes were attributable to the influence exerted by Grand Ayatollah Hossein Ali Montazeri, who had taken an active interest in prison conditions.[2] At the time, he was still Khomeini's designated successor. Montazeri's faction within the regime seemed to have succeeded in removing Lajvardi and his clique from the prison system. The same clique returned to control the system in late 1987. In a letter that Khomeini sent to Montazeri in October 1986, when the two men were beginning to draw apart, he clearly blamed the improvement in prison conditions on Montazeri's associates, if not himself. Khomeini referred to what he believed was Montazeri's "unfortunate inclination to be influenced" by negative things he read or heard. He accused Montazeri of reacting to bad news and discussing it publicly. He noted that the delegates Montazeri sent to prison showed faintheartedness by improperly ordering the release of a few hundred of the Mojahedin, which resulted in the subsequent increase in "explosions, terrors, and thefts."[3] The charge was unfounded.

In any event, some of the new wardens were clerical associates of Montazeri.[4] The warden who replaced the infamous Hajji Rahmani referred to his predecessor as "truly crazy."[5] The "boxes" of the *dastgah* were photographed and dismantled. One survivor of the Hajji's torture informed Raha that the new managing team even acknowledged in front of prisoners that placing them in the "boxes" amounted to torture.[6] This was the first time after the fall of President Bani Sadr that intensification of factional conflicts within the regime led to an acknowledgment of torture. However, it did not reach the press. As discussed in Chapter 13, the conflicts leading to the election of President Khatami in 1997 provided another rare opportunity for the reformers to discuss torture. Internal rivalries in authoritarian regimes are sometimes helpful to human rights documentation.

At various times during the years of the intermission, political prisoners were generally left alone to spend their time as they pleased. From time to time, some endured punishments, but the environment became less foreboding.[7] During the summer and fall of 1984, authorities reviewed the files of some prisoners. Several of them made their way through an easier repentance procedure to freedom. In a Qezel Hesar ward, where Parvaresh was detained, the prisoners were finally allowed to openly celebrate the (non-Islamic) Persian new year, the first day of spring, 1985.[8] In the women's wards, the rule of all-black chador slacked off, and some prisoners appeared with the less formal, colored chador. The exception seemed to have been the Islamic Mojahedin, who continued wearing the black chadors that secular women abhorred.[9]

Parsipur's mother was freed in the fall of 1984, after the mullahs made her sign a paper acknowledging that she had been arrested because of "her connection to political groupings," something she never had.[10] The person responsible for Parsipur's cell informed everyone that an inquiry was made, "asking the clerics whether a Muslim who does not perform the daily prayer was a physically and spiritually polluting (*najes*) person or not." The answer was negative, and she told Parsipur that she was "no longer *najes*." Not feeling particularly grateful, Parsipur refused to be anything but *najes*. The novelist recalled the young woman saying, "Look, things have changed. Conditions are not as they were in the past." Parsipur retorted, "Look, my dear, conditions have changed and now the new group in charge of prisons say that I am not *najes*. However, conditions can change for a second time; then I will be considered *najes* again. Therefore, now that I am *najes*, let me remain *najes*."[11]

Conditions did indeed change again in the summer of 1988, but in March 1985 Parsipur went home. She still did not know for what crime she had spent four years, seven months, and seven days in the prisons of the Islamic Republic of Iran, time that left an enduring mark on her health.[12]

The relative absence of systemic brutality reinvigorated prisoners' spirit of defiance. Raha noted that the prisoners began to speak of "my rights" and "our rights" as prisoners.[13] The significance of this period lies in the fact that the unrepentant secular prisoners used the opportunity to renew their struggle to reassert their right to freedom of thought and conscience. Obviously, many felt defeated, and shattered dreams littered the prisons. However, despite years of violent attempts to remold their conscience, a minority of prisoners continued to struggle to preserve their identity.

The highly exaggerated news about the Mojahedin's "military camps" beyond the Iranian border in Iraq may have reached inside the prisons, giving false hope to the Mojahedin prisoners. They were as much victims of the Islamic Republic as helpless captives of the propaganda of their own irresponsible leadership. A false hope again seemed to have boosted their morale. Parvaresh noted that in 1986 the Mojahedin refused to refer to themselves in front of prison authorities as *monafeqin* (hypocrites), the Islamically pejorative term the clerics used for them.[14]

The Islamic chador, obligatory prayers, and fasting were still part of the daily struggle. This indicated that the leftist prisoners still resented the Islamization process that sought to alter their secular thought and conscience. With improving conditions in Qezel Hesar in the middle of 1985, Raha regained enough of her self-confidence and stopped performing her daily prayers.[15] In 1986, the issue of the black chador reappeared at Qezel Hesar. Prison authorities demanded that any woman who walked out of the ward for any reason must cover herself with the black chador. Most prisoners in ward seven, where Raha lived, refused to obey. They were forbidden to leave the ward, even if they needed medical help. The guards subjected a number of nonconformist prisoners to the Islamic punishment of flogging. At the end of the summer of 1986, all those who rejected the black chador were transferred to Evin prison, to be subjected to further punishment.[16]

During the intermission, it became clear that the authorities were willing to free some political prisoners, sometimes with a minimum formality of repentance. It was also a time of widespread political apathy in the larger society. In a way, the collapse of the leftist movement removed the shadow of shame that hovered over the prisoners who ostensibly submitted to the authorities. They were now left to deal with their own specific situation and their own conscience, without being greatly concerned about the "revolutionary movement" passing a negative judgment on them. Thus, Raha's reflections on the preconditions for freedom had become more agonizing because freedom under such conditions had become more tempting. The argument for a formal expression of submission appeared increasingly more forceful, if not convincing. "Why not denounce, in one simple sentence, past political associations and get out of this living hell?" The advice from the prisoners' families was to put aside stupidity and childish obstinacy. "By uttering one sentence your thought will not be altered. Everybody knows that this is just for appearance. You must be *zerang* [clever, cunning] and recognize the situation accurately." The notion of "*zerangi*" has a convoluted cultural connotation that far exceeds the straightforward meaning of "cleverness." It implies the presence of a special, desirable intelligence that takes advantage of an immediate situation, with no regard for larger societal considerations, personal convictions, or moral scruples. To use "*zerangi*" appeared unacceptable to Raha at that moment. Years later, in a thought that may reflect a new maturity she gained when she moved to Europe, she reflected on the question. "In a society that has not experienced democracy and liberty, to pretend compliance to the ruling thought, to remain silent and to feign acquiescence are considered politic; they mean '*zerangi*.' Truth and liberty are sacrificed to hypocrisy and submission."[17]

In the spring and summer of 1986, it appeared to Raha, who was then in Evin prison, that the authorities were emptying Qezel Hesar prison of political prisoners. They were transferring the men to Gohar Dasht and the women to Evin.[18] Parvaresh made the same observation, adding that in Gohar Dasht there were no *tawaban* left in the male wards. They had been sent to Evin or set free.[19]

The Summer Massacre

The prison memoirs seem to indicate that Ayatollah Montazeri's moderating influence on the prison system caused the relative relaxation in the policy of forced Islamization and the concomitant slacking off of punishments. Thus, the advent of an open attack on his associates, leading to his downfall, signaled the beginning of a reversal of that trend in the prison system. Political prisoners were to pay for his "undue" interference.

Montazeri's opponents among the powerful clique around Khomeini fired their opening salvo against his political faction in May 1986. They arrested Mahdi Hashimi, a cleric and the leader of the World Organization of the Islamic Movement, who was also the brother of Montazeri's son-in-law; the clerics knew well Hashimi's close family relation to Montazeri. In November 1986, a Lebanese newspaper revealed the secret U.S.-Iran dealings known as the Iran-Contra affair. Hashimi was the source of the leak. The powerful Speaker of the Majlis, Rafsanjani, was in charge of this opportunistic, short-term rapprochement with the United States. The unraveling affair brought Rafsanjani into a major confrontation with Montazeri. Khomeini entrusted Hashimi's case to Hojjat al-Islam Reyshahri, the newly appointed Intelligence Minister. Reyshahri held grudges against Montazeri for intervening in, among other security issues, the prison system Reyshahri had helped to create. In a televised show, he made Hashimi confess to a number of crimes, including murder and kidnapping. Reyshahri's brutal style of torturing was the catalyst in breaking the radical Islamist.[20] Reyshahri also charged him with the crime of sabotaging foreign relations, a reference to the news leak. In what seemed to have been the first act of the Special Court for Clergy in August 1987, Hashimi was sentenced to death; he was executed on September 28. Raha felt that the arrest would weaken Montazeri's position, and by doing so, it would have a negative impact on prison conditions.[21]

According to Raha, within the next few months, Evin's new deputy warden, Hossein-Zadeh, conducted short interviews in which he asked each prisoner about her/his views. The inquiry concerned the Islamic Republic, religion, and Marxism. In response to the prisoners' short answers, which he disliked, he mumbled threatening comments to the effect that they would pay a heavy price for their intransigence in protecting their conscience. Raha added, in hindsight, that the prisoners did not take his threats very seriously, or at least their frightening dimensions escaped them.[22]

Parvaresh noted that similar inquiries took place in the male sections of Gohar Dasht prison in late January or early February 1988. With the benefit of hindsight, he also saw the inquiry as a preliminary part of a plan that had been in the works for weeks before the advent of the summer massacre. Whereas the leftists were questioned about their continued allegiance to Marxism, the Muslim Mojahedin were asked about their loyalty to the Mojahedin organization. The male prisoners of Gohar Dasht faced a more threatening procedure. According to Parvaresh, some of the militant Mojahedin did not return to their wards after the inquiry; they spent the rest of the winter and spring in solitary cells before their execution in the summer.[23]

Parvaresh noted the prison rearrangement in Gohar Dasht. He also noted that in March and April 1988 the warden began separating the Mojahedin prisoners from the leftists. Furthermore, they categorized and housed the prisoners according to the years in their sentences. Accepting the count of prisoners that Parvaresh provided, I can conclude that at that time there were no more than six hundred leftist prisoners in Gohar Dasht, which housed most of the male political prisoners in greater Tehran. There is no estimate as to how many Mojahedin were imprisoned at that time.[24]

Raha began her discussion of the bloody summer events with the surprising July 18 announcement that Khomeini had accepted the UN Security Council's Resolution 598 calling for a cease-fire in the Iran-Iraq War. Three days after the peace announcement, Mojahedin forces launched an incursion into western Iran, crossing the border from a base in Iraq, taking the border town of Mehran. Within a few days, the authorities in Tehran cut off the prisoners' contacts with the outside world, canceling visits by family members, preventing the delivery of newspapers, and removing the television sets. Not even the sick prisoners were allowed to go to the central infirmary at Evin. Ominous news and rumors circulated inside the male wards in Gohar Dasht prison. Parvaresh could offer no firsthand observations until he faced the inquisition. But he heard that on July 27, only a week after the end of the war, an ad hoc commission was set up for Evin and Gohar Dasht prisons. Ayatollah Morteza Eshraqi and Hojjat al-Islam Ja'far Nayeri were the two clerics who sat in judgment.[25]

As sounds of anguish reverberated inside the wards, the regime's propaganda broadcasts in the state-controlled media celebrated the total annihilation of the Mojahedin's July incursion. Raha heard over the state radio that during the Friday sermons, Ayatollah Musavi Ardabili had whipped the crowds into a frenzy as they chanted, "Death, death, death to the *Monafeqin*." [26]

All indications were that the summer massacre began with the hanging of the long detained Mojahedin prisoners, who had nothing to do with the military activities in western Iran. The prisoners faced the commission, which had no proper judicial task other than inquiring about their thoughts on *velayat-e faqih*, the Islamic Republic, and the Mojahedin organization. No consideration was given to the prisoners' alleged crimes or to the sentences under which they had served since the early 1980s.[27]

In Gohar Dasht prison, the one-cleric commission asked each prisoner whether he would still associate himself with the Mojahedin organization or would agree to denounce the group's military operation. Some answered truthfully, displeasing the cleric, who ordered them hung inside Gohar

Dasht's amphitheater. Here Parvaresh saw a direct link between the prison massacre and the Mojahedin's failed incursion into western Iran.[28]

The ghastly affair assumed all the characteristics of a typical campaign in which the authorities could easily whip themselves into a generalized frenzy. In the prisons, the revolutionary guards again assumed the menacing posture of the early years of the Islamic revolution. In the middle of the night, Raha heard them stamping their feet rhythmically and shouting, "Death to the *Monafeqin*" and "Death to the Infidels," creating a state of siege.[29] It is not difficult to imagine that in such an environment, regardless of Khomeini's original intentions, it was only a matter of time before the action became a generalized inquisition that would devour leftist prisoners with seemingly effortless momentum. "At the end of August 1988 the 'Death Commission' turned its attention to the prisoners from leftist groups held in Gohar Dasht Prison."[30]

It is illustrative to follow the event from the vantage point of one prisoner. On August 27, 1988, the guards brought a group of leftist prisoners from Parvaresh's ward to the Ayatollah Inquisitor, who had to judge their apostasy. Parvaresh wrote that he could not be sure about the exact details of what happened in other wards. He could state accurately that the guards removed between fifty and sixty prisoners from his ward on August 27. One or two survived; the rest were hung the same day. Parvaresh named six whom he knew personally. When his turn came, the guards took him to a queue of a large group of prisoners from different wards. On that day, the questioning proceeded in two stages. D. Lashgari, a deputy warden, asked each prisoner whether he was a Muslim and performed his daily prayers.[31]

Parvaresh waited in the queue and anxiously watched everything around him, and the long wait gave him a chance to ponder his own answers to the deadly questions. Should he renounce his conscience and live? Years later he wrote about his predicament at that critical moment of his encounter with Ayatollah Eshraqi: "During all those years in prison, all of my efforts and those of many other fellow prisoners were intended to concede to them as few points as possible. We wanted to prove to them our ideological and personal resoluteness. But now, were we not losing our identity by accepting what was offered to us?"[32] Parvaresh entered the room without yet clearly knowing what answers he would give to the Inquisitor. "Sitting behind a desk in front of me was Ayatollah Eshraqi, in his clerical attire, his bulky trunk covering the entire chair." The angry and agitated warden, Nasserian, whose real name was Shaikh Muhammad Moghiseh-ye, stood by Ayatollah Eshraqi. At that moment, Parvaresh had no doubt about the deadliness of the Ayatollah's intention. "All those individuals present in that room were busily killing the prisoners during the past two months, and it seemed that their appetite was insatiable." Parvaresh chose life. "If it is the case that you are going to hang me, then I am a Muslim," he answered the Inquisitor's seminal question. The reader may recall that in 1983 his answer to the same question put to him by another cleric was somewhat different. "Eshraqi asked if I had ever prayed. I answered yes, when I was a child. He asked if I had ever gone to a mosque. I answered yes. He asked if I prayed while in prison. No, up to now I have not prayed. At this point Nasserian entered the conversation and with an angry and hateful tone in his voice asked: 'What then, are you a Muslim or not?' I answered again: If the threat of hanging wants to make me a Muslim, I am a Muslim." [33]

The interview ended with Nasserian kicking him out of the room. For whatever reasons, Ayatollah Eshraqi decided not to dispatch him to the prison's amphitheater where gallows had been set up. In a convoluted way, he had pronounced, "I am a Muslim," and perhaps that appeared acceptable enough to the Shiite cleric. In the absence of the rule of law, even the slightest personal inclination of liking or disliking could decide the life or death of a helpless prisoner. The Ayatollahs were creating havoc in the functioning of the contemporary state.

Raha agonized over the same question Parvaresh had faced. Guards took away the female Mojahedin prisoners en masse for execution, as they did with their male counterparts. The female leftists, however, fared better. Raha wrote that a number of times judicial authorities visited the ward and demanded only yes or no answers to questions like "Do you perform your daily prayers?" and "Are you willing to give an interview denouncing your past association?" [34]

Those who were waiting for the inquisition to receive them spent their days in agonizing anticipation. At least among those who were around Raha, no one seemed to be willing to renounce her conscience without offering some degree of resistance. Sometimes they found solace for their wretchedness from their own sense of humor, contemptuously targeting the macabre Islamic penalty of daily lashes and the antiquated judicial tentacles that had fatally caught up with them in the late twentieth century. The leftist women were aware that the clerics considered only renegade females of Muslim parentage to be apostates, punishable by daily whipping. One woman said that she would first tell the judge that her parents were Marxists. Noticing the concern of others for her parents, she added that the mullahs could not lash them, since they had died years ago. When another inmate retorted that the mullahs might "begin inquiring into the thought of our ancestors," her fellow inmate responded by saying that she would say that her grandparents were Utopian Socialists! [35]

In Gohar Dasht prison, the prosecutors asked those who had confirmed their faith in Islam to prove it by performing the required daily prayers. If they refused, they would receive twenty lashes for each of the daily five sets of prayers, one hundred lashes every twenty-four hours. [36] Similarly, the female leftist prisoners who escaped death suffered under the daily regimen of lashes. A judge told the prisoners that the punishment of a female infidel was death under prolonged whipping. In fact, the clerics treated women differently from men. Men were considered responsible for their apostasy and had to meet their death. But because women were not totally responsible for such a momentous act, the clerics would punish them with imprisonment until they saw the light and repented. This one misogynist rule saved some lives! The leftists' option was to repent and begin performing their prayers. They executed the female Mojahedin not for apostasy but for continuing to support their organization.

Raha recalled the spectacles of lashing in the five sessions, from before dawn to just before midnight. Each time the guards took one prisoner at a time to the walkway and tied her to a metal bed, while her inmates inside the cells heard whips whistling through the air. Under the dehumanizing regime of five whipping sessions a day, many prisoners began to pray, but felt ashamed for doing so. Raha saw an increase in the number of attempted suicides.[37]

Each day at prayer times, Ghaffari watched the compelled prisoners "going through the charade." He wrote, "We were forced to take part in this empty pantomime five times a day. Each day we would witness comrades being lashed, or hear others scream from other blocks. This went on for months, well into 1990."[38] Otherwise, the prisoners' intense speculations about the daily events were heart-wrenching, again placing the human rights situation into a clear relief. Their conversations revealed that none of them could say what was taking place and why. Certainly, their families had no knowledge of what was taking place inside the prisons. The prisoners were puzzled by the fact that one group was taken, without any apparent reason, to meet the inquisitor before another group. They were mystified by the fact that a woman who was taken away on an earlier day was returned to the ward long enough to tell her friends what was happening. Then they took her away and executed her.[39] They clearly associated the killing of female Mojahedin prisoners with the Mojahedin's activities in Iraq and their ill-fated incursion into western Iran. However, they did not know why female members of the Tudeh Party and the Fadai'ian-e Khalq (Majority Faction), both pro-Soviet Marxist, were the first prisoners to be taken out and whipped in lieu of the daily prayers. It seemed that after the years of intermission, the prisons reverted to the clerical arbitrariness that characterized the years 1981–83.

How many prisoners had the Ayatollah sacrificed? "Amnesty International has recorded the names of over 2,000 prisoners reported to have been the victims of a wave of secret political executions between July 1988 and January 1989. Amnesty International has no way of knowing the full extent of the massacre. . . . However, the organization has interviewed dozens of Iranians whose imprisoned relatives were killed at that time and has received written information about hundreds of other prisoners who were among the victims."[40]

Two sets of figures provided by Raha and Parvaresh indicate that Amnesty's estimate for Tehran was low, but not much off the mark. Parvaresh's own best estimate was more than 2,500 prisoners killed in the Gohar Dasht and Evin prisons during the summer of 1988. His estimate for the entire country was 4,500 to 5,000. One can doubt the figure of 10,000 to 12,000 (Ghaffari's estimate) for the entire country. In contrast to the first years of the revolution, in 1988 the executioners did not publish body counts for their daily activities. An official veil of secrecy shrouded the massacre; the rulers have since continued to deny that a mass killing took place inside their prisons. Mojahedin publications abroad threw around the figure of 30,000 for the entire country, which is clearly a habitual exaggeration, although it has published the names, ages, birthplaces, and the time of execution of 3,210 Mojahedin members who had been executed in that summer.[41]

A short profile of a prisoner will offer a glimpse of the tragic end to a troubled life. Amin (a pseudonym) was a junior in the National University in Tehran at the time of the revolution. He married a fellow student and became a member of the Marxist Fadai'ian-e Khalq (Majority Faction). Until his arrest in the spring of 1982 when the organization was banned, Amin felt that he was participating in the political activities of a legal group. Refusing to give the mandatory repentance, he remained in prison for six years. The Islamic judges had never had any reason to sentence him to more than two years in prison. His senseless and utterly unjust execution came on September 1, 1988. His wife was informed four months later.[42]

What were the reasons for the massacre? We may have to wait a long time, perhaps after the opening of prison documents, for a satisfactory answer. Unable to comprehend the reasons for the policy that physically eliminated many of them, the surviving prisoners linked the massacre with two events that preceded it: the end of the war with Iraq on July 18, 1988, and the Mojahedin's armed incursion into western Iran a few days later. However, as indicated above, some prisoners saw, retrospectively, in officials' inquiries into their thoughts an element of planning that was in the works months before those two major events. There seemed to have been plans to reinstate the harsh treatments that had previously been accorded the unrepentant Mojahedin and the leftists who refused to return to Islam's fold.

The renewed harsh treatment in political prisons appeared to have targeted Ayatollah Montazeri, as a kind of revenge against his previous interventions to secure prisoners' release and improve conditions for infidels and the hated Mojahedin. The men he removed from positions of authority— even Lajvardi—returned just before the planning of the massacre.[43] Perhaps they were planning, with Khomeini's approval, to deliver an insulting blow to the meddling Montazeri, who already had fallen afoul of Khomeini. Intelligence Minister Muhammad Reyshahri, who was in charge of the overall policy of the inquisition and massacre,[44] had developed an intense enmity toward Montazeri. He was also instrumental in the execution of Mahdi Hashimi, a close relative and associate of Montazeri. The end of the war with Iraq and the Mojahedin incursion might, in fact, have provided a sudden acceleration of the process. They infused it with the desire for a bloodier revenge. Revanchism has always been a major part of the clerical concept of justice.

The disgraced Ayatollah Montazeri saw the execution of the prisoners as a personal attack on him and on the role he had played in making the prison system less harsh. He was dismissed as the anointed successor to Khomeini in March 1989, but conflicts between him and Khomeini had been growing throughout 1988. Three of the private letters that Montazeri wrote in July and August 1988 have since been published. The first letter was dated July 31, 1988, only a few days after formation of the "Death Commission" in Evin and Gohar Dasht prisons. The letter shows that the massacre was not yet in full swing.

Montazeri seemed to have been well informed. He began his letter by referring to Khomeini's order concerning the execution of the Mojahedin, an indication that the order had come from Khomeini himself. Montazeri saw no apparent "negative consequence" in executing those Mojahedin who participated in the armed incursion into western Iran. However, he did object to the execution of those who had been held in prison for years and had no hand in planning Mojahedin activities abroad. "Their unexpected execution, without their involvement in any new activities, inappropriately countermand all the Islamic judicial standards and the prior rulings of Islamic judges." His second letter left no doubt that he considered his main foe, Reyshahri, responsible for "miscarrying" Khomeini's order, one that he considered unjust and un-Islamic in the first place. He wrote that in every prison the Intelligence Ministry played the main role. The third letter was addressed to three men who were in charge of the daily operations of the massacre, including Ayatollah Eshraqi. Ayatollah Montazeri warned that the killing of prisoners would remain a blight on the Islamic Republic of Iran.[45] Years later, in August 1999, his son, Ahmad Montazeri, issued a statement to the reformist press making the same points. He associated his father's fall from grace with his objection to the execution of prisoners "for crimes committed by others."[46]

The regime was experiencing a period of self-created political commotion reminiscent of the early 1980s. Khomeini's about-face in accepting the end of war with Iraq was a nerve-racking decision, since for eight years he had closely identified himself with the goal of a definite victory over Iraq achievable by the use of his martyrdom paradigm. His acceptance of the cease-fire signaled the collapse of that paradigm. He sought to protect himself by warning the nation not to listen to those who might logically suggest that a similar peace option was available much earlier and with far less cost. After the cease-fire announcement, a flare-up of military activities by the Iraqis in the south end of the front and the simultaneous incursion of a few thousand Mojahedin fighters in the West added intensity to the tremor. In response, the regime launched another of its mass-mobilization drives to defend the Islamic Republic.[47] The regime organized a huge demonstration in Tehran on August 3, and the front pages of the semiofficial dailies were emblazoned with "Renewing Allegiance with the Imam."[48]

The agitated political climate on the streets of Tehran had always characteristically made a negative impact on the clerics' understanding of justice for political prisoners. The military incursion into western Iran may have removed all the lingering inhibitions that had kept Khomeini from carrying out what he thought was a proper Islamic verdict for the Mojahedin. He already had declared them, collectively, to be the *mofsedin fel arz* (those who sow corruption on earth) at war against God. Evidence of this fact came in 1990, when Ayatollah Yazdi, the powerful Head of the Judiciary, explained that in the Islamic Republic one category of Islamic judicial punishment, apart from those specified by law codes, was Khomeini's personal verdicts, an example of which was the death penalty he issued for Salman Rushdie. Yazdi clarified that what Khomeini had rendered was not a mere *fatva*, a religious pronouncement on an issue, but "a verdict to kill." Coming to his main point, Yazdi asserted that because Khomeini's judicial verdict on the Mojahedin condemned *all* its members to death, those responsible for carrying out the verdict were not to be burdened by "doubt and hesitation" (*tardid*) as to whether each individual member fit into the deadly categories of *mofsed* and *mohareb*. Thus, they need not examine the guilt or innocence of each member separately.[49]

By the end of the year, the news of the killings had created such a negative public impression that Ayatollah Khamenei felt compelled to offer a justification for it. In December 1988, he spoke of "those who have links from inside prison with the hypocrites [Mojahedin] who mounted an armed attack inside the territory of the Islamic Republic."[50] He failed to explain how such links could be possible. Other leaders also continued referring to those who attacked from Iraq and those who had "joined them," never explaining the nature of that joining, especially for those who were in prison at the time.[51]

As mentioned before, Galindo Pohl failed to discuss the issue of the massacre during his visit to Tehran. However, in his report he mentioned the regime's hysterical attitude by quoting the Chief of Justice, Ayatollah Musavi Ardabili, telling the press that he was under pressure "from public opinion" clamoring for the execution of all the Mojahedin who were captured during their 1988 military incursions into western Iran. The cleric expressed satisfaction that during the military operation the regime's armed forces had killed many of the Mojahedin intruders, saving him the effort of preparing "files to have them executed."[52]

Other officials denied that the massacre had occurred. The families of the executed prisoners were still searching the unmarked graves for the bodies of their loved ones, when in November 1988, Muhammad Ja'far Mahallati, the regime's Permanent Representative to the United Nations in New York, "denied the allegations." He repeated the official line that "many killings" took place "on the battlefield" following the Mojahedin incursion into western Iran.[53] In another response, Mahallati resorted to diplomatic clichés about "sovereignty and territorial integrity," while defending the hanging of captured Mojahedin members on the steel foundation of a construction site in the middle of a city. The government only applied "the national laws on the punishment of war crimes, spies and agents of the army of aggression."[54] The Interior Minister Abdollah Nuri, who became a celebrated reformist in the late 1990s, told Galindo Pohl that "a campaign had been organized abroad alleging that invaders captured on the battlefield had been executed en masse, together with imprisoned members of the same group."[55]

Galindo Pohl concluded that "among those executed were prisoners who were serving sentences, including some whose sentences were about to be concluded in a few days and others who had been recaptured. The international media and organizations that monitor human rights agreed that those executions were the culmination of very summary judicial proceedings, where there had been any, and that they lacked the procedural guarantees instituted in the International Covenant on Civil and Political Rights."[56]

This much we know now. We can also ask a couple of plausible questions. Was it possible for Khomeini and his close associates to consider with premeditation and carry out with deliberation a plan whose aim was to empty the prisons of political prisoners? They may have thought that it would put an end to the domestically and internationally irritating problem of keeping a large number of political prisoners. Killing the most intransigent prisoners could intimidate others to bend and more readily accept the conditions of their release. One fact supports this view. The massacre ended just before the tenth anniversary of the Islamic revolution in February 1989. The clerics used the occasion to issue an amnesty for those whose lives were spared, many of whom had already repented. The amnesty, of course, was conditional on signing the required repentance and, in some cases, paying a large sum of money. Political prisoners were then released. Parvaresh noted that late in 1989 the state media announced, with great fanfare, an amnesty for political prisoners. "Reyshahri, the Intelligence Minister, claimed that it covered all political prisoners except 900 prisoners whose release was dangerous." Raha noted the same fact. The diplomats informed Galindo Pohl of an amnesty of the same number of prisoners.[57]

Whatever set of circumstances caused the summer massacre and whatever its human toll, the issue of human rights violations is painfully clear.[58] In the case of those who were executed, their right to freedom of thought, conscience, and religion was trampled. Their right to life was then washed away in the bloody streams of Islamic reconversion. As for the secular nonbelievers who survived, the clerics forced them to renounce their conscience to save their lives. Then the prophets of cultural authenticity left them with two equally unpalatable choices between the physical pain of the Islamic lashes and the psychological agony of Islamic prayers.

A Painful Road to Release

The prisoners, especially the men, were totally demoralized. "They saw everything was finished. Their group and their past friends, these hopes and movements, were all buried."[59] All those past attempts to maintain group solidarity and uphold the tradition of resistance had become meaningless; the reality of the destruction of all leftist organizations had sunk in. No longer under the enormous shadow of past myths of the leftist movement, they also realized that they must make their own personal decisions. In doing so, they were no longer under the watchful eyes of a few comrades, real or imagined, who would pass judgment on those who relented. Raha had to travel the road alone and make her own decisions.

Let me end with Monireh Baradaran (Raha), who agonized over her possible release. Her writing revealed that at this highly demoralizing period she was hoping, perhaps subconsciously, that somehow she would be released without submitting to conditions that would violate her conscience. She was aware of the fact that other prisoners with a long history of credible resistance and defiance were going home.[60] A visit by her sister increased Raha's dilemma. Her sister was apprehensive and whispered to her that it was an extremely dangerous time, implying that she should perhaps consider signing what the authority in charge of her case demanded. That official had just ended her six-month solitary confinement and returned her to a common ward.

In the early summer of 1990, the new warden again interviewed the female prisoners, pressuring them to take advantage of what seemed to Raha a further slackening of the conditions of release. He was even prepared to grant the willing prisoners a renewable leave of absence to go home for a specific period.[61]

Raha was left with only one rationale for refusing to submit. She thought "the minimum that I should expect from myself is not to repeat and sign the words that are dictated to me."[62] The women inmates, including those whom she respected, were signing and getting out. By early fall 1990, authorities seemed to have adopted the policy of dissolving the category of political prisoners by bringing into their ward a large group of common criminals. She was undergoing the last agony of her nine-year incarceration in the Ayatollah's prisons:

I felt that I too had to go. I had not made a decision about what to do. However, for the first time I was thinking about life outside prison. I walked all day thinking. . . . Should I continue the resistance? I had always stated that as long as the decision to stay and resist was a group effort, I would stick with it. In my view, it was an action, no matter how limited, against official inquiry into people's minds. Did I want to be among the last, among the longest held prisoners? . . . But how could I simply say that I accept the condition of release after nine years of imprisonment? Solely for that reason I stayed in prison during the last few years and endured months of solitary confinement.[63]

In the fall of 1990, she told the warden that she would accept the conditions. The warden was in a hurry and demanded only her signature on the form for a leave of absence. He seemed to have wanted the ward emptied that same evening. "It was an autumn night, around 10 o'clock. I had signed the paper and was traveling, along with my family, the empty streets toward home."[64] Thus ends this remarkable woman's memoirs, *A Simple Truth*, a credit to all secular women of modern Iran.

The Right to Freedom of Thought, Conscience, and Religion

Iranian Religious Minorities

For most of the 1980s, the Special Representative's attention remained focused on the plight of Baha'is, who suffered more than any other community during the period under consideration. There was no discussion of other religious minorities, as the official discrimination against them was overshadowed, in international human rights reports, by the regime's brutality toward Baha'is. Only in the early 1990s did the international human rights community begin to pay attention to the situation of other religious minorities.

Iranians of the Baha'i Faith

The change of regime in 1979 introduced new patterns of violations, creating new victims and adding new rationalizations in a constant attempt to deny and counter the charges of human rights violations. In both regimes, violations occurred mainly because of the rulers' understanding of state security. Some recognizable groups of victims changed in the new regime, but Baha'is have remained a permanent fixture in the country's fertile landscape of human rights abuses. They may constitute the largest non-Muslim minority. Since they do not exist officially, it is hard to determine how many thousands of them live across Iran; estimates vary from 150,000 to 500,000. The Baha'i faith has never achieved official recognition in Iran, its troubled birthplace. Islam asserts that the Prophet Muhammad was the "the seal of prophesy," after whom there would be no divine revelation. The Baha'i Faith, which originated in the 1840s, challenges that assertion. In its birthplace city of Shiraz, the Islamic zealots destroyed the Baha'i shrine, the House of the Bab, that was associated with the founder of the faith, and the city's three Ayatollahs witnessed and sometimes urged the persecutions and murders of the city's Baha'is.[1] Since they were assumed to have been Muslims before accepting this "false" revelation, the Iranian Baha'is are considered to be apostates, especially by the Shiite ulema. Moreover, the Baha'i World Centre in Haifa offers an excuse to the hard-liners to depict Baha'is as "Zionist agents."[2] The clerics always magnified the conspiratorial prism through which other Iranians perceived this faith, depicting it as nothing more than an illegitimate creation of some often unnamed foreign enemies of Islam. Galindo Pohl observed that Baha'is have "no status, rights or protection under the law."[3] Even under the last Shah, these prejudices remained unexamined and unchallenged.

Baha'is in Iran have tried to keep their co-religionists in the West informed on specific cases of arrest, prosecution, torture, and execution that have taken place since 1979. And in contrast to opposition groups like the Mojahedin, who often exaggerated the cases by inflating the numbers of victims, Baha'is have provided more accurate information to the United Nations Commission on Human Rights.

We can better understand the human rights situation in the Islamic Republic by considering the identities of its main victims. As for Baha'is, political considerations cannot fully explain the violent suppressions of their human rights. It seems that motivations for anti-Baha'i policies and actions originate in the clerics' blind hatreds, whose roots lie in a pre-modern religious prejudice, not directly linked with the self-protective polities of an authoritarian state. The prejudice against the Baha'i citizens issues from the clerics' elemental anxiety of facing a homegrown religious faith that has challenged Shiism. This anomaly, separating the Islamic Republic from other authoritarian states, is another curse of the religious state.

The clerics have continued to present the faith as a political sect engaging in counter-revolutionary and espionage activities for foreign enemies, especially Israel. This channeling of religious enmity to a political cause, expressed in a language that resembles the discourses of the Third World's nation-states, took place in the clerical anti-Baha'i activities during the 1960s.[4] They have constructed the anti-Baha'i rhetoric in political, conspiratorial terms in order to prevent any discussion taking place in religious terms, which would give recognition to the Baha'i faith.

In May 1996, the Head of the Judiciary called it "an organized espionage ring."[5] Sometimes the newspaper announcements, as well as official pronouncements, gave the lie to the official claim that the Baha'i faith is not a religion. If it is not a religion, why have the clerics taken such pains to show that it is a misguided challenge to Islam? If Baha'is were prosecuted for their espionage activities and not for their faith, then why do the regime's internal documents proudly display such a religious zeal in attacking them?[6] The anti-Baha'i rhetoric is often constructed within the duality of good and evil, always referring to the Baha'i faith as a wayward sect (*ferqeh-ye zaleh*), in contrast to the *din-e mobin-e Islam* (the sublime religion of Islam).[7]

The value of Olya Roohizadegan's eyewitness account of the tragic destruction of a score of female Bahai's prisoners in Shiraz in 1982–83 lies in the details of the encounters between the prisoners and the Islamic inter- rogators and judges. The latter's efforts were intended to make the prisoners recant and return to Islam, not to force them to confess to political activities or espionage. In the middle of a heated exchange about God and spiritu- ality, an agitated Islamic prosecutor asked the youngest woman in the group: "What harm did you find in Islam that made you turn to the Baha'i faith?" [8] It was clear that all the women who were hanged during the summer of 1983 could have saved their lives if they had agreed to the prosecutors' demand: "I ask you to recant and come back to Islam. If you do, I will let you go." [9] Many Baha'is told the Special Representative that "it had constantly been made clear to them that, if they recanted their faith, all measures against them would cease and they could regain their posts and studies." [10] The Baha'i International Community has accurately placed this fact "among the stron- gest proofs that the persecutions were based solely on religious beliefs." [11]

In the 1990s, officials and the conservative press have continued to deny the fact that Baha'is are under pressure because of their religion. Yet, al- most in the same breath, they show their contempt not so much for the "illicit political activities" that often remain vague and without substance but for the faith. After asserting the falsehood of Galindo Pohl's assertions concerning human rights violations of Baha'is, the semi-official daily *Resalat* asked: "Really, why do Galindo Pohl and the West show so much sensitivity toward Baha'ism and Iran's Baha'is and express affection for them?! Should not the formation of this unknown and phony faith called Baha'ism, which has aroused the hatred of the world's Shiites and caused enormous blood- shed, be condemned?" [12] During his interviews with officials, the UN Special Rapporteur on Religious Intolerance, Abdelfattah Amor, often witnessed "an almost instinctive rejection" of Baha'is.[13]

It is in cases like Iran's Baha'is and other religions whose revelations are considered "false" by the intolerant majority that the significance of the UN provisions to protect the right to freedom of thought, conscience, and reli- gion becomes apparent. Herein the irrelevance of cultural relativism is self- evident.

Killings of Baha'i Leaders

Seven Baha'is were killed in mob actions during the upheaval of 1978. To in- capacitate a community of faith, the clerics directed their wrath toward the recognized leadership of Baha'i administrative institutions, at both national and local levels. They arrested the leaders and processed them in summary trials. In the summer of 1980, all nine members of the national Spiritual Assembly were abducted and executed without their families being able to recover their bodies. They "disappeared." Other leaders, as Galindo Pohl observed, were "ill-treated, tortured to death or executed." The charges against them often included almost everything that the clerics held in their conspiratorial phantasm, including espionage for the Great Satan, cooperation with the Shah's regime, and assistance to Israel.[14] In addition to systematic persecution, harassment, and discrimination, more than two hundred Baha'is, mostly in positions of leadership, have been killed since 1979. An additional fifteen Baha'is "have disappeared and are presumed dead."[15]

As was the case with the executions of political opponents, the intensity of the killing of Baha'is tapered off. Once the formal Baha'i administrative ability was crushed by eliminating its leading members, the community obviously became less willing to continue openly reproducing new leaders. They no longer formed a national Spiritual Assembly. By the late 1980's some Iranian government officials became aware of the negative press that this persecution and harassment was receiving in Europe and the United States. To the extent possible, they began a policy of concealment.

Executions continued sporadically on a diminishing scale. In November 1989, Galindo Pohl listed the names of two men. One had remained in prison from November 1983 until December 1988, when his family received the news of his execution; the other was arrested in 1986, and his family learned about his execution in November 1988.[16] The same report cited the international press about two military generals who were executed early in January 1989. The generals, who were charged with being Baha'is, were already in prison serving seven-year terms.

A three-and-a-half year halt in the execution of Baha'is ended when the regime executed Bahman Samandari, a businessman from a prominent Baha'i family, on March 18, 1992. In his report, Galindo Pohl stated that the Islamic prosecutors charged him with the crime of espionage but gave no evidence to prove his guilt.[17]

In the next several years the international monitors became familiar with the tragic stories of Hasan Mahbubi, Behnam Mithaqi, Kayvan Khalajabadi, Bakhshollah Mithaqi, Ali Zolfaqari, Zabihollah Mahrami, Musa Talebi, Mashallah Enayati, and Ruhollah Ruhani.[18] Some were executed; some were still in prison in 1999.[19] Among them, I will mention the hanging in July 1998 of Ruhollah Ruhani, fifty-two, a medical supplies salesman and father of four, since it occurred during the reformist Khatami administration. Authorities in Mashhad had charged him with the crime of converting a Muslim to the Baha'i faith. Ruhani was denied due process of law and the service of an attorney, and his family remained unaware of the death sentence until after the execution. "The woman whom he was accused of converting to the Baha'i faith refuted the accusation stating that she had been raised as a Baha'i."[20]

Another case that deserves a brief examination belonged to Zabihollah Mahrami. Charges against him kept changing, as different levels of the Islamic Judiciary became involved. Mahrami was a Baha'i who felt compelled in 1985 to sign an official form stating that he was a Muslim, most likely in order to keep his job in the city's Department of Agriculture. Like other Baha'is who had signed a similar form, he never converted officially to Islam. For seven years he went about his life as if he were a Muslim. In the 1990s, the always intrusive local authorities became aware of his continued allegiance to the Baha'i faith. Assuming that he had reconverted, they charged him with the crime of apostasy. To the Shiite mullahs, religious conversion is a one-way street, always toward Islam; once in it, there would be no point of return. Copithorne noted that there was "no provision in codified Iranian law making apostasy a crime."[21] Nevertheless, the absence of formal law did not prevent clerics from making reference to Islamic edicts concerning apostasy. The revolutionary court in the city of Yazd convicted Mahrami on January 2, 1995. The capital punishment had to be approved by the Supreme Court in Tehran.

In cases like this we get a better understanding of the working of the justice system in the Islamic Republic of Iran. It is also revealing of the dynamics of the human rights discourse.

Human Rights Watch explained:

The Supreme Court, ruling at a time when the country was under scrutiny at the UN Commission on Human Rights following visits to the country by two special rapporteurs of the Commission and the special representative on Iran, referred the case back to a civil court. The Supreme Court ruled that the Revolutionary Court was not the appropriate tribunal to address a case of this nature.

But the authorities did not comply with the Supreme Court ruling. Instead, they introduced new charges of espionage and brought Mahrami for trial before a revolutionary court again, and in February 1997, the head of the Revolutionary Court announced that Mahrami had been sentenced to death on charges of espionage for Israel.[22]

In 1997 the Supreme Court confirmed the death sentences imposed for apostasy against Mahrami and Talebi, another Baha'i man with a similar case.[23]

Making Allegiance to the Baha'i Faith More Difficult than Ever Before

Based on the information received, you are a Baha'i and therefore not entitled to a pension payment. However, should you convert to Islam and demonstrate remorse for having been a Baha'i and further provide this office with proof that you have embraced Islam, steps will be taken to restore pension payments to you.
—From an official letter sent to a Baha'i

Baha'is had a clear understanding of their predicament. The goal of the harassment and persecution was to secure "their conversion to Islam by depriving them of freedom, of the means of subsistence, of their personal property, and of the possibility of studying at universities."[24]

The clerics' intention was to destroy the conditions needed for their survival as a community with a distinct religious identity. They attacked Baha'is on all possible grounds and in all spheres of public life, from elementary education to professional occupations, from marriage ceremonies to cemeteries. In 1987, Galindo Pohl wrote that persecution included "torture, arbitrary imprisonment, denial of education and employment, arbitrary seizure of homes and possessions, confiscation of community assets, and seizure, desecration and destruction of holy places."[25] They could not manifest their faith, hold public meetings, maintain places of worship, teach their faith to their children in their own schools, or disseminate their literature.[26]

The clerics destroyed the beautifully maintained Baha'i cemetery in eastern Tehran. Baha'i cemeteries remained closed, making it difficult for Baha'i families to bury their dead properly.[27] In his 1995 report, Galindo Pohl wrote: "It is said that the Baha'is must bury their dead on waste land specified by the Government and that they are not entitled to identify the graves of their loved ones."[28]

While the policy toward the leadership threatened the Baha'i community's organizational existence as a faith, the individual Baha'i was subjected to harassment, making the adherence to the faith costly. In his report of January 26, 1989, Galindo Pohl cited a news item published in a daily newspaper on October 12, 1988. The government announced that it had confiscated the property of fifty Baha'is and "invited the legal Muslim relatives of these Baha'is to contact the authorities."[29] It was impossible for Baha'is to seek redress through the courts, since they had already been declared ineligible, as "unprotected infidels," for a recourse to law.[30] On September 21, 1993, the court in the city of Shahr-e Rey failed to impose a just penalty on two killers because the murdered man was, in the language of the verdict, "a member of the misled and misleading sect of Baha'ism."[31] There were many similar cases throughout Iran. Even the Baha'i victims of automobile accidents had to forgo any restitution of damages. For example, when the "driver of the car was found guilty of involuntary manslaughter, the relatives of the victim were not entitled to receive compensation because the victim was a Baha'i. Instead, the defendant was sentenced to make a payment to a government fund."[32]

The Islamic Republic continued to block their employment in the public sector and to deny them pensions, as well as access to higher education. A typical notice issued by the General Employment Office in December 1987 listed thirteen individuals whose bank jobs were terminated because they belonged to "the depraved Baha'i sect."[33] The conditions for their survival in the private sector were also made extremely difficult, with the government still confiscating Baha'i-owned businesses and properties.[34] "A person who had been involved in scientific research for many years related how she had been ousted from Tehran University, together with other Baha'i profes-sors who were now trying to survive as truck drivers or flower salesmen." [35] If a known Baha'i government employee wished to retain her post, she would have to undergo the humiliation of public recantation.

The Iranian-born scholar Abbas Milani has written: "I knew a single mother of two teenage daughters who, after agonizing soul-searching, sub-mitted to have her picture published in the newspaper in Islamic dress, with a note declaring her unflinching commitment to Islam and Shiism. . . . I saw her wilt away with every passing day." [36]

Galindo Pohl's reports also offered information on other kinds of ghastly discriminations. One described the tragic fate of Fereydun Shomali, who was burned in a fire that was deliberately started in a factory where thirty Baha'is worked. Suffering a severe injury in one eye and undergoing hospi-talization and surgeries, he required a cornea transplant. The local Islamic Committee that had to authorize the operation refused to do so on the grounds that the eye of a Muslim "could not be given to a Baha'i." The man had to find a Baha'i cornea. The Baha'is who offered this information to Galindo Pohl in Geneva gave him a copy of the forbidding letter. It reads in part that "since Mr. Fereydun Shomali has personally confessed his connec-tion with the Zionist Baha'i faction, the cornea graft is not to be performed for religious reasons." [37] No verses of the Qur'an or passages of the tradition of the Prophet and the Imams were presented to explicate "the religious rea-sons" for the denial of the cornea transplant. Of course, "the religious rea-sons" could possibly be applicable only to an apostate who had challenged Islam and converted to another religion, and not to a "spy" in a nation-state. The motivations for mistreatment and persecution were patently religious.

As will be discussed in Chapter 11, the reversal of policy in 1989 some-what eased the pressure on the Baha'i community. Galindo Pohl's overly optimistic impression in 1990 was that the status of this religious minority was "moving towards quite broad *de facto* tolerance." [38] In the first half of the 1990s, the violations against Baha'is continued to take up most of the space in Galindo Pohl's reporting on religious minorities. [39] In 1996, Galindo Pohl's successor Copithorne expressed his concern and reiterated "his view that the situation for the Baha'is in the Islamic Republic can improve only if there is a significant change in attitude towards them on the part of the Iranian authorities." [40]

Between 1996 and 1998 "more then two hundred Baha'is were arrested and detained for periods ranging from two days to six months." [41] In 1999, at least six Baha'is were on death row and seventeen in prison with or without formal sentences. [42] Limitations on travel abroad were still in place, although some Baha'is succeeded in receiving limited exit permits. The problems faced by Baha'i physicians and lawyers continued unabated. No bank credit was made available to Baha'i applicants. Baha'i marriages and divorces were not legally recognized, nor was a right to inheritance, a situation Ann Mayer has aptly described as "civil death."[43] The properties of a deceased Baha'i would go to the state if there were no Muslims in the family. The regime continued denying the Baha'is retirement pensions.[44] As late as October 1998, Baha'is were arrested for burying their dead without government authorization,[45] which could not be granted if the deceased's faith was truthfully stated.

Thus, it was positive news when a "partial lifting of the ban on meetings allow[ed] a maximum of 15 Baha'is to attend their 19-day feast." No restriction was imposed on the number of persons attending a funeral ceremony. "Finally, the restrictions affecting married conscripts were now also being applied to Baha'is."[46]

Baha'is had to be extremely daring to attempt circulating among themselves any books pertaining to their faith. Obviously no open classes could be held for educating children in Baha'i spiritual and moral values.[47] Baha'is understand the significance of education for a persecuted religious minority. Although the regime readmitted students from Baha'i families to the elementary and secondary schools, it continued to deny them higher education.[48]

It is worth quoting a passage from an excellent report that the UN Special Rapporteur Abdelfattah Amor wrote in 1996. The Deputy Minister of Education denied to him that there existed a prohibition against university acceptance of Baha'is. "He indicated that access by the Baha'is to higher education should not pose a problem provided that the Baha'is did not flaunt their beliefs in educational institutions." Again, as far as the regime's technobureaucrats were concerned, Baha'is should not tell the truth. Not believing this assertion, the Special Rapporteur observed:

Erosion of the standard of education was seriously affecting the Baha'i community. The directives of the Supreme Cultural Council of the Revolution concerning the level of education were quoted: "They can enroll in schools provided that they do not declare their Baha'i identity. Preferably, they should enroll in schools with a strong and impressive [Islamic] religious ideology. They should be expelled from the universities . . . as soon as it becomes apparent that they are Baha'is." The Baha'i representatives indicated that . . . they did not engage in proselytism, but, if questioned, would acknowledge their religious affiliation and could give explanations concerning their faith.[49]

The meaning of the 1991 memorandum issued by the Supreme Cultural Council and approved by the Supreme Leader was unambiguous, demanding in effect that Baha'is forfeit their faith socially, so that it might slip away into oblivion to the satisfaction of the Shiite ulema. It called on the government to deal with the Baha'is "in such a way that their progress and development are blocked."[50]

During Copithorne's visit to Tehran in early 1996, the officials blamed their own victims by complaining that Baha'is had been trying to establish for themselves de facto recognition as a religious minority. They had done so by not accepting what was expected of them, that is, to avoid all circumstances which would indicate that they were Baha'is. As an example, the officials referred to instances when Baha'is completed the section on various government forms, like passport applications, where the religion of the applicant was asked. "It was suggested that to respond to such a question with the name of an unrecognized religion was attempting to obtain constitutional recognition for that religion."[51] Thus, the officials complained that the Baha'is wrote the truth, instead of assuming a false Islamic identity. To protect partially the rights of gays in the U.S. military, the Clinton administration adopted a policy of "don't ask, don't tell." To deny the rights of Iranian Baha'is, the regime has adopted a policy of what I call "we ask, you lie."

It is a testimony to human perseverance that, despite this egregious institutional denial, Baha'is made an extraordinary effort to offer some degree of higher education to their youth. In a climate of intimidation and fear, they managed, beginning in 1987, to establish classes and laboratories in their private homes and offices for some one thousand students, studying through correspondence and in classroom sessions.

On September 29, 1998, the government security forces raided some five hundred private homes and offices, putting an end to these remarkable educational efforts, and arrested at least thirty-six teachers and administrators.[52] No matter from what political or religious angle one looks at this, the picture appears quite pathetic in that the security agents went on a rampage, confiscating textbooks and laboratory equipment and arresting academic lecturers and instructors. Almost at the same time, President Khatami was on an official visit to the United Nations in New York, where he once more emphasized the importance of an intercivilizational dialogue. The picture back home presented an inauspicious backdrop for any kind of dialogue to ensue.

Gradually, all those who were arrested following the raids were freed. The exceptions were four faculty members, sentenced to prison terms ranging from three to ten years, who remained in detention in Isfahan. The court cited Article 498 of the Islamic Penal Code, which stipulates prison terms for anyone organizing an association that the clerics consider detrimental to the internal or external security of the country. This was quite typical of the way the officials perceived security threats, a perception that has produced numerous human rights violations since 1980.

Iranian society has created, with state support and encouragement, "nongovernmental organizations" for the sole purpose of harassing the Baha'i citizens. The citizens' spontaneous and semispontaneous acts of violence have been reported, both under the Shah and more so under the Ayatollah. The case of Iran's Baha'is clearly demonstrates that human rights are legitimate claims to be addressed not only to the state but also to the society. The latter can, if not legally restrained, engage in serious violations of the human rights of minorities. This has direct bearing on the current discussion in Iran concerning the notion of civil society, as advocated by President Khatami.[53] The Shiite Muslims have a long way to go in accepting the right of Baha'is to assert their claim to a universal religion that, in their belief, transcends Islam. This blind spot in the Iranian consciousness, even among most iconoclastic intellectuals, has been an unexamined aspect of modern Iranian society. Although secular Iranians have provided employment opportunities in professional companies for a number of Baha'is, there has been no civil association formed by liberal Muslims to defend Baha'is or other religious minorities. Secular Iranian writers are legendary in expressing poetic solidarity with all the oppressed peoples of the world. Sadly, they remained wordless, during both the monarchy and the theocracy, on the Baha'i sufferings. It is only in recent years and in the exile literature that this author is aware of one moving poem by Morteza Rezvan, expressing sorrow for the treatment of his Jewish and Baha'i countrymen and the shame of Iranian poets who had remained silent for too long.[54]

President Khatami and other Islamic reformers were indifferent to the continuous discrimination and harassment of Iranian Baha'is. Facing questions in a press conference in Paris on October 29, 1999, Khatami denied human rights violations and attributed the reports to "the Baha'i organizations' propaganda outside Iran."[55] The Baha'i International Community properly asserted: "It is, therefore, not the actions of the Baha'is but the circumstances of Iranian history that have conspired to make the 'Baha'i case' a litmus test of sincerity for Iranian public figures who represent themselves as voices of reform and progress."[56]

Sunni Muslim Citizens

It was in the 1990s that Galindo Pohl first described violations other than those committed against the Baha'i religious minority. The Constitution envisions a religious state and recognizes Shiite Islam as the official religion. It accords "full respect" to five other Islamic jurisprudencial schools, covering the affairs of the Sunni Muslims of Iran. The respect is intended for religious education and matters of personal status (marriage, divorce, inheritance, and bequests). According to Article 4 of the Constitution, "All civil, criminal, financial, economic, administrative, cultural, military, political, and other laws and regulations must be based on Islamic criteria. This principle applies generally to all articles of the Constitution, as well as to the other laws and regulations, and the *foqaha* [Shiite jurists] of the Guardian Council take decisions in this regard." The Constitution remains silent as to the "Islamic criteria," leaving their definition to the whims of the highly politicized legislators and other supervisory bodies in their legislation or rulings.

Sunnis are a large minority in Iran, perhaps some 20 percent of the entire population. What is politically significant is that almost all of them belong to non-Persian-speaking national groups, such as the Kurds, Baluchis, and Turkamans. The Kurds, having long suffered from the frustration of their national aspiration for independence or autonomy, have now experienced religious discrimination by the Shiite state, which in attempting to forestall Kurdish demands for autonomy has also curtailed the Sunni religious prerogatives. This double jeopardy was the curse of the religious state, separating it from other authoritarian states. For much of the 1980s and 1990s, the central authorities exercised a measure of control over Sunni religious institutions, even appointing politically agreeable Sunni clerics to head the Sunni mosques. The regime has also placed limitations on the expansion of Sunni mosques, and where mosques were attacked by Shiite mobs, the local security authorities took no actions. "Despite the fact that more than one million Sunnis live in Tehran, many of them Kurds, no Sunni mosque exists to serve their religious needs."[57]

Sunni activists testified that they, along with other religious minorities, were denied by law or practice access to such government positions as cabinet minister, ambassador, provincial governor, and mayor. They alleged imprisonment, execution, and assassination of Sunni leaders. Copithorne observed that although some of the information he received was difficult to confirm, he was "left with the clear impression that the right of freedom of religion is not being respected with regard to the Sunni minority."[58]

State-sponsored ethnic and religious repression often spurred a social atmosphere of incitement and suspicion, provoking regressive social elements in conjunction with security officials. In the absence of official clarity and accountability, every event became suspect, engendering an often bloody chain reaction. For example, when a Kurdish cleric in western Iran died, his Sunni followers suspected foul play. The mysteries that surrounded his death inevitably congealed into beliefs, causing street protests that led to more bloodshed in the city of Kermanshah. The arrests that followed further poisoned the atmosphere.[59]

Predominantly Sunni Muslim, the Baluchis live in the southeastern province of Baluchestan, adjacent to Pakistan. Since the revolution, the Sunni Baluchis have expressed their frustration and resentment toward the Shiite regime in a variety of ways, including street demonstrations in the city of Zahedan. The regime has often responded by arresting Sunni religious leaders.[60] Baluchi activists have died or disappeared.[61] Some leading figures have fled the country to avoid imprisonment. They have then been the targets of fatal attacks in which the Iranian government was suspected of involvement.[62]

Disturbing circumstances surrounded the deaths of three Baluchi Sunni leaders. The first was Haji Muhammad Zia'i.[63] His death took place on July 20, 1994, five days after security officials had last interrogated him in the city of Lar on the Persian Gulf. His mutilated body was discovered beside a road, the victim of a car accident, as the official tales spun. The government's contradictory accounts, however, contained many discrepancies, causing human rights organizations to doubt their accuracy.[64] Then came the death of Molavi Ahmad Sayyid. He had been sentenced to five years in prison, without being charged, following his return in 1990 from studying in Saudi Arabia, when he had opened a school for Sunni Muslims in Baluchestan. His body was found outside the Persian Gulf city of Bandar Abbas on February 2, 1996, "five days after being arrested at the airport as he returned from a six-week trip to the United Arab Emirates."[65] The regime spun no new tale and remained silent about his death. Human Rights Watch observed that since he "was last seen alive in the custody of the authorities, suspicion falls heavily on the government as his killer."[66] The third Baluchi religious figure, Abdolaziz Kazemi Vajd, was found dead outside Zahedan on November 5, 1996.

In the second half of the 1999s, the Baluchi region became an active conduit for narcotics coming from Afghanistan or Pakistan, with Iranian Baluchis carrying the illegal cargo through the desolate borderland.[67] The regime's accounts of military activities in Baluchestan failed to distinguish between those who were killed in the anti-narcotic activities and those who were the victims of human rights violations.

The relative press freedom in the late 1990s allowed some Sunni intellectuals to refer discreetly to past violations. Sa'id Towfiq observed that past violations created a high degree of distrust in the Sunni communities in general and among the Sunni ulema in particular, making it difficult for them to take the promised reform seriously. He called on them to move alongside the Shiite reformers and claim their rights openly. He was not asking to forget the fact that the Sunni ulema were the victims of extrajudicial killings and that many Sunnis were repeatedly subjected to harassment, imprisonment, and interrogations. He wanted them to remember that "at the same time many of the dissident Shiite clerics, as well as religious and nonreligious intellectuals, also fell victim to these kinds of calamities and injustices." Calling for cooperation to build a new civil society, he added: "While we have different beliefs and opinions, we have endured similar pains."[68] As will be further explained in Chapter 13, the reformist climate of the late 1990s allowed references to be made to the two decades of violations that the regime's diplomats denied vociferously.

Citizens of Officially Recognized Religious Minorities

Iran's Islamic tradition recognizes followers of three monotheistic religions, Zoroastrianism, Judaism, and Christianity (Armenians, Assyrians, and Chaldeans), as people of the book (*ahl-e ketab*).[69] Reflecting this premodern tradition and the inherent inequality therein, the Constitution recognizes them as "the only religious minorities who, within the limits of the law, are free to perform their religious rites and ceremonies and to act according to their own canon in matters of personal affairs and religious education." The caveat "within the limits of law" in Article 13 subjects the rights that the Constitution grants them, like the rest of the population, to the qualifications based on Islamic criteria. To put it differently, they are free to perform their religious rites and ceremonies within the limits of Islamic *shari'ah*. With the exception of fewer than 200,000 Armenians, the majority of whom belong to the Armenian Church, other recognized communities each have well under 50,000 members, the numbers estimated for the Zoroastrians. The Iranian Jewish community is one of the oldest in the world, numbering probably not more than 30,000, down from some 100,000 before the Islamic revolution. The Jews, as well as the ethnic Christians, have admirably retained their diminished presence in the country, despite the fact that in the entire modern period no meaningful official recognition has been given to their presence, nor has there been any real appreciation of their achievements.

According to Article 64 of the Constitution, the recognized religious minorities had five deputies in the Majlis, elected separately by their own communities. The Armenians have two deputies. The members of the recognized minorities participated in presidential elections, but only a Shiite Muslim could be elected president of the republic. Article 144 practically bared members of religious minorities from joining the professional armed forces of the republic, as it stipulated that the armed forces must remain Islamic and "committed to Islamic ideology."

The recognized religious minorities were somewhat free to practice their religion and raise their children according to their religious instructions. But the necessary interactions with the authorities were never free of tensions. Their freedom of expression in their places of worship or other public gatherings was subject to monitoring by the Ministry of Culture and Islamic Guidance. Of course, they were forbidden to proselytize. There were strict rules to keep Muslims out of public gatherings of religious minorities. Periodically, the authorities in the state educational system placed restrictions on Armenian language instructions in Armenian schools. They forced all minority schools to accept religious instructions from Muslim teachers, appointed by the Ministry of Education. Apart from the absurdity of such an arrangement, religious instructions were to be conducted in Persian. Restrictive practice varied at different periods and in different provinces, but they created both anxieties and frictions with authorities. The minorities had to grapple with the ubiquitous applications that citizens had to complete for almost everything, and almost invariably they included the question about the applicant's religion. The answer could have a significant impact on the outcome, for example, reducing the prospect of a public sector employment.

The "Protected" Are Unequal

Rhoda Howard's generalization describes well Iran's particularity: "In traditional societies principles of social justice are based not on equal human rights but on unequal social statutes and on the intermixture of privilege and responsibility."[70] The status of "protected religious minority" stood in opposition to equality of status protected by the UN Covenant on Civil and Political Rights.

Islamic groups and leading personalities entertained different views concerning minorities; nevertheless, they all shared in the belief of Islam's unquestioned superiority over other religions that they condescendingly "respected."[71] The Shiite clerics perceived the notion of "protected minority" (*dhimmis*) as an achievement for Islam, and their lay associates in the UN often referred to the concept with pride. However, the notion subverted the concept of human rights because it was derived from the clerics' ancient understanding of the country as a sacralized land with an eternal religious (Islamic) essence, the abode of Islam. The drafters of the Islamic Constitution saw the Christians, Jews, and Zoroastrians in those terms. At that time, the fear of the state persecutions had not yet silenced all the protests, and the representatives of the religious minorities objected to the constitutional provisions that defined them as the *dhimmis* and set them apart as "minorities." The Zoroastrian representative, among others, bitterly objected to the status and reminded everyone that during the revolution the Ayatollahs had promised more freedoms to the religious minorities. "Zoroastrians who are indigenous to this land and have no country other than Iran are only recognized as second-class citizens and have no right to participate in politics, law, or the military."[72] The *dhimmis* perspective implied that the non-Muslims just happened to be there, more or less as "guests." They occupied a precarious social position somewhere between citizens and subjects, and their well-being depended on the Islamic compassion of higher authorities who, it was hoped, would make decisions not too detrimental to their lives. As anthropologists Fischer and Abedi observed, they were protected only as long as they played by the *dhimmis* rule and were "content to be subordinate, nonpolitical elements within a Muslim polity."[73] The hard-liners within the regime continued casting aspersions on their loyalties and portraying them as conduits for Western cultural corruption.[74] In fact, the Islamic Cultural Propagation Organization used the term "protected minorities" only for outside consumption, since the hard-liners in charge of this well-founded state organization had no qualms about referring to them as the *koffar* (infidels).[75]

The leaders of protected minorities often protested against the bigoted misrepresentations of their communities by the hard-line Islamists. However, they were unable to overcome the curse of being the *dhimmis,* and their language of protest had to remain within that "protected" confine, reaffirming their discriminatory status. Unable to draw on the international human rights law, as secular (Muslim) dissidents often did in the 1990s, they could only remind the zealots of the Islamic "protective" pronouncements, expressed on their behalf by Ayatollah Khomeini and other more benevolent Ayatollahs, such as Montazeri and Taleqani. They defended their "rights" in accordance with the "Islamic principles." One remarkable exception was the courageous human rights appeals made by Bishop Haik Hovsepian Mehr, a leader of the much less "protected" converts to Protestant denominations, discussed below.

One way to understand the meaning of "protected minority" was to look at what the Shiite clerics required of Muslims in relations with the Jews and Christians. The Islamic state actively proselytized through its educational system, which also covered the minority children. If a Muslim converted to a "protected" religion, he/she could be punished by death; conversely, an occasional conversion to Islam was celebrated, but not when the convert was a man intending to marry a Muslim woman. In that case, even an ex-Jew or ex-Christian would offend the "honor" of Muslim men by engaging in sexual intercourse, even in marriage, with a woman born in Islam. If she married a Jew or Christian, she committed adultery, subject to severe punishment. The Islamic law of inheritance was shaped by the concept of the *dhimmis*. A religious minority could not inherent from a Muslim. If a member of a religious minority family converted to Islam, he would be the sole inheritor of the family's assets and properties. The law rewarded opportunism. The humiliation that came with the notion of a protected minority, coupled with the Muslims' condescending attitudes or disdain, was truly intolerable.

Even their right to political representation in the Majlis that was based on religious denomination set the religious community apart from the rest of the nation, as though Jews, Christians, and Zoroastrians had no national political concern beyond their own religious communities. This constitutional arrangement, which encourages each individual to vote for a nominee of his/her own faith, created a religious apartheid that consigned the individual, in the words of one human rights group, "to electoral ghettos."[76] According to the committee that gave official approval to political parties, non-Muslims could not be members of a nationwide political party formed by Muslims.

Official discrimination was reflected in the Islamic Penal Code, which was finally ratified in 1991. Iranian lawyer Shirin Ebadi has documented the different and discriminatory treatments that the Penal Code accorded to protected religious minorities. For example, a Muslim convicted of the murder of a religious minority would not be subjected to *qesas*, the Islamic retribution that included the death penalty. The Penal Code remained silent as to what should be the legally required punishment, leaving it to the discretion of the Islamic religious judge. "Unfortunately, our Penal Code, by being silent with regard to the kind of punishment of such a murderer, creates the impression that the murder of a non-Muslim in Iran carries no punishment."[77] Ebadi repeatedly pointed out that the Penal Code set the *diyat* (compensation or blood money for murder or injury) for a protected religious minority at half of what it accorded to a Muslim. In one interview Ebadi offered an hypothetical example of two children, a Muslim and a Zoroastrian, being hit by a car driven by a negligent Muslim driver; the blood money given to the Muslim family would be twice as much as that given to the Zoroastrian family.[78] Writing in Persian in Tehran and examining the conflicts between the Islamic Penal Code and international human rights law, Ebadi had to choose her words carefully. She observed that the law implicitly granted more value to the life of a Muslim than to the life of a protected minority, and she entertained a hope that the judicial authorities might change the law. Numerous other cases of discrimination in Islamic Penal Code could be cited.[79]

Historical Predicament of Being "Protected"

Once again in Iran, the recognized religious minorities found themselves in precarious positions; their long-term well-being often depended on their ability to stay on the good side of the Shiite clerics, who had transmogrified themselves to the state rulers. This had been a logical consequence of being "protected" religious minorities. Historically, their leaders had often discreetly opted for a correct, cooperative posture toward the existing power, hoping to reduce harassment and mistreatment. During the monarchy, they relied on the Shah's "enlightened" authoritarianism against the Shiite extremists, although the Shah's regime could occasionally allow abuses to mollify the clerics. To buy protection, the minority leaders heaped adulation on the Shahs.

In certain periods of political upheaval, they often found themselves in a political crossfire, in the midst of battling (Muslim) factions, each expecting to receive the overt support of the recognized religious minorities. Especially precarious were the times when they could not be sure of the outcome of the political conflicts among Muslim factions. Self-preservation demanded that they make no enemies among the competing factions. For example, the historian Janet Afary explained that during the constitutional revolution early in the twentieth century, when the constitutionalists were fighting with the conservatives about establishing the first Majlis, the Jewish leaders in Tehran were not sure how to react. When conservative clerics put pressure on them to denounce the Majlis, or else face destruction of their neighborhood, the vulnerable Jews, whose sympathies lay with the constitutionalists, consulted with the Majlis deputies and devised their own slogan to be used in an anticonstitutionalist rally: "Speaking for the Muslims, we want no constitutionalism."[80]

The populist revolution of 1979 offered a passing opportunity to young secular Jews, Armenians, Assyrians, and Zoroastrians to overcome the old *dhimmis* distinction, to break away politically from their own communal constraints and conservative religious leaders, and to form minority groups in association with the larger national, mostly leftist, organizations. Desiring integrative politics, they supported non-clerical Muslim revolutionaries, not under Khomeini's control. They would have considered the concept of *dhimmis* offensive. They were defeated, as were their progressive Muslim allies. When Khomeini replaced the Shah as the supreme political authority in 1979–80, the traditional leaders of recognized religious minorities had no option but to make the Ayatollah the target of their adulation. Throughout the early 1980s, as the institutionalization of the Islamic Republic proceeded amid general repression, the leaders of the religious minorities and their deputies in the Majlis felt compelled to strike correct relationships with the new rulers, some of whom could hardly hide their disdain for them.

It was also in character with the traditional practice of scapegoating religious minorities at the time of factional conflicts for political ascendancy that thirteen Jews were imprisoned in the provincial city of Shiraz on charges of espionage in March 1999. "The spying charges bear every earmark of a trumped-up case," observed John Burns of the *New York Times*.[81] Manuchehr Eliassi, a member of Parliament representing Iranian Jews, smiled "at the notion that Israel would recruit more than a dozen spies from the outlying city like Shiraz, hundreds of miles from the capital, better known as the birthplace of mystic poets than a center of state secrets."[82] He could have added that among the "spies" were a rabbi, a sixteen-year-old student, and a butcher who sold Kosher meat. Many observers believed that it was a ploy on the part of hard-liners to create an intractable political problem for President Khatami, heighten conflicts with the United States, and undermine the policy of opening to the West.[83] "Jewish groups outside Iran noted that the March arrest of the 13 Jewish individuals coincided with an increase in anti-Semitic propaganda in newspapers and journals associated with hard-line elements of the Government."[84] Again, the Jewish leaders tried to stay clear of the conflicts between the conservative forces that caused the arrest and the Islamic reformers who were the real targets of the conservative machinations.

In the Islamic Republic of Iran, non-Muslims became religious minorities in a religious state. Moreover, dangerously looming in the society's alleyways were the politically aroused zealots, always ready to support their religious state in their own unsavory ways. These were hardly spontaneous actions by the ignoramuses. From time to time, especially in the early years of the republic, certain factions competing for power proved their zealotry by attacking religious minorities.

The Shiite bestowal of official recognition always came with strings attached. In the nineteenth century, the corrupt mullahs demanded money for protection. After 1979, however, the clerics became the rulers of the state, demanding political paybacks in return for proper observance of "recognition."

Again, the minority leaders reacted, almost intuitively, with the long-term prospect of survival of their communities in mind. Self-preservation in a political environment that could turn hostile was their main consideration. From the beginning of the Islamic Republic in 1979, the key to understanding their public words and gestures must be found in their effort not to be perceived as hostile to the dominant Islamic political forces in the country, however constituted. In the early years of the Islamic Republic, a pestering issue was the emigration of many members of religious minorities. As anti-Semitism found official expression for the first time in Iran's modern history and the anti-Israeli state propaganda became shriller, Iranian Jews felt quite uncertain about their future under the theocracy. Early in 1979, the execution of Habib Elqaniyan, a wealthy, self-made businessman, a symbol of success for many Iranian Jews, hastened emigration.[85] The departure of the chief rabbi for Europe in the summer of 1980 underlined the fact that the hardships that awaited the remaining Jewish Iranians would far surpass those of other protected minorities.

The remaining leaders of the Jewish community, as well as those of the Armenian, Assyro-Chaldean, and Zoroastrian communities, were careful not to present emigration as a negative commentary on the Islamic Republic. They learned quickly from the official political discourse that the safest explanation was the one that pointed the finger of blame at the West. Unable to deny the link between the departure of their coreligionists and the Islamic revolution, they prudently stressed that the regime exerted no direct pressure on those who left. Certain unnamed countries that "perceived the revolution negatively" had urged them to leave. They told the UN Special Rapporteur on Religious Intolerance, Abdelfattah Amor, that they "were not subjected to any interference by the authorities in their internal religious activities, which could be exercised freely, particularly with regard to worship and religious traditions and management of their affairs and religious institutions."[86]

The leaders of "tolerated minorities" were always communicative about what was allowed to them and reticent about what was forbidden. They had to maintain a correct relationship with authorities and to endure silently the Islamic restrictions imposed on all Muslim Iranians, including the Islamic dress code,[87] the separation of the sexes in public, the prohibition of many books, films, and musical compositions, and the prohibition of alcoholic beverages in restaurants. They had to tolerate the indignities of being forced to post signs in their shop windows, indicating ownership by a non-Muslim, so that the Muslim customers might avoid coming into contact with the impurity emitting from the *najes* (impure) operator. As Sorour Soroudi, an Iranian-born Israeli scholar, observed, the old Shiite tradition created elaborate regulations, linking non-Muslims' spiritual impurity with their physical impurity. They aimed to minimize contacts between Muslims and non-Muslims and to restrict "the social and occupational freedom of the *dhimmi* communities."[88] In the Islamic Republic, the issue raised its dirty head wherever non-Muslims owned and operated a business or manufacturing establishment that created points of contacts with Muslims, either during the course of operation or in the "polluted" products reaching the market.

UN Special Rapporteur Amor, whose Islamic background seemed to have prepared him better to withstand cultural grandstanding and intimidation, was less impressed with the cultural arguments of the men in power. He understood the problem and recommended that the Islamic Republic not apply the Islamic rules to non-Muslims. He emphasized that the existing communities' traditions concerning dress should be respected; he believed "that dress should not be turned into a political instrument and that flexible and tolerant attitudes should be shown so that the richness and variety of Iranian dress can be maintained without coercion."[89]

The leaders had also faced a host of less taxing problems with reference to their ability to have more control over their own schools, such as observing Sabbath in Jewish schools. They wished to maintain their ability to communicate directly with authorities about resolving these practical problems. They wanted to reach "short-term, medium-term and long-term agreements, compromises and solutions."[90] Whenever they felt it was necessary to take a public position on certain critical issues, they did so in total accord with the official party line. They told the Special Rapporteur that they were trying to avoid the situation where their problems were "manipulated by other countries" that followed their own political agendas against the Islamic Republic of Iran.[91] Galindo Pohl noted a predicament shared by religious communities. He learned that "Zoroastrians in Iran were afraid that any information about their problems and alleged restrictions would produce more hardship and that the authorities would consider that they were creating adverse publicity."[92]

The leaders of the officially tolerated religious minorities understood well what the Shiite religious authorities who controlled the state expected of them, and they mostly obliged. They realized that they should, regularly and publicly, express thanks for the "protections and privileges" that the new system had accorded them. They also understood that the clerical rulers used these expressions as political capital for legitimating the existing state power. Ayatollah Yazdi, the intrusive Head of the Judiciary for most of the 1990s, often made good use of that political capital. Denouncing Galindo Pohl's reports concerning restrictions on the religious minorities, he pointed out "that the leaders of the religious minorities have acknowledged the existence of their own places of worship, schools and other organizations, and they have repeatedly expressed their gratitude and thanks for these things."[93]

From time to time, and often in unison, as if in a coordinated campaign, the leaders of different religious minorities expressed political opinions that defied logic. They could only make sense in light of their predicament as recognized religious minorities. The Jewish leaders had to go so far as to openly denounce the policies of the state of Israel. It was disquieting to read a news item that reported the Jewish representative in the Majlis criticizing, in carefully chosen words, certain anti-Palestinian violent actions of his co-religionists in Israel, especially when upon the conclusion of his remarks the other (Shiite) deputies burst into the chant "Death to Israel!" The contemporary state violating the human rights of its citizens left behind a trail of pathological behaviors.[94]

The leaders' responses to the UN reports on human rights violations in the Islamic Republic followed the same predictable pattern. Within two weeks after the release of Galindo Pohl's report in the winter of 1993, almost all major leaders of the recognized religious minorities—Armenian, Assyro-Chaldean, Jewish, Zoroastrian—issued statements. All followed the official script, denouncing the Islamic Republic's enemies who hoisted the banner of human rights to weaken the regime and harm the nation. "We the Assyrian religious and social leaders consider this kind of unfounded propaganda to be a tool used to put pressure on the Islamic Republic of Iran."[95]

One Armenian association forwarded a letter to the UN office in Tehran, denying Galindo Pohl's "irresponsible allegations of the violations of the rights of religious minorities in the Islamic Republic of Iran" and suggesting that "Khomeini's *fatva* for the killing of Salman Rushdie, like his other *fatvas*, must be carried out."[96] It was hardly coincidental that at least seven of these different announcements were issued within days of each other. In late 1995, the regime even managed to take a senior Armenian priest to Geneva to testify in front of the UN Commission on Human Rights about the "equal rights" that Christians enjoyed in Iran.[97]

Equally baffling, if not placed against the Jewish community's predicament, was the statement by the Jewish leaders concerning the arrests of thirteen Jews charged with espionage for Israel in June 1999. "The Islamic Republic of Iran has demonstrated to the world that it has treated the Jewish community and other religious minorities well; the Iranian Jewish community has enjoyed constitutional rights of citizenship, and the arrest and charges against a number of Iranian Jews has nothing to do with their religion." The bureaucratic side of the state needed such a statement, and the Jewish leaders in Tehran had no choice but to oblige. It was issued on June 13, and the following day the Iranian diplomats in New York extensively quoted from it to show "the fallacy of reactions" to the arrests. The statement continued: "We are confident that the Judiciary of the Islamic Republic of Iran will adjudicate this case in justice and with fairness, and after according the accused the right to defend themselves, will issue the verdict."[98] This "confidence" in the Islamic Judiciary was obviously disingenuous because the Islamic reformers who were being prosecuted by the same Judiciary were raising serious questions about the legality of its many actions (see Chapters 13 and 14).

Overall, what the leaders of religious minorities felt compelled to say reflected negatively not on them but on the regime that created such an intense sense of insecurity. However, some of the leaders of the "protected minorities" were themselves representatives of their own religion's fundamentalist trend. Hardly champions of international human rights for the individual members of their own flocks, they sought to preserve their own sectarian strength by encouraging adherence to traditional values and practices. The late Archbishop Ardak Manukian, leader of Tehran's Armenians, believed that the restrictions "were minor ones that simply helped to accentuate the faith."[99] The Society for Iranian Jews expressed its appreciation of "the auspicious victory of the Islamic revolution in Iran. Because of it the Jews of Iran pay closer attention to their own religious affairs." Moreover, "the synagogues and the shrines of Iranian Jews have flourished by the increased attendance of the devout and committed Jews."[100]

The UN human rights provisions are designed to prevent these kinds of abuses, which are very common around the world and which can be rationalized by recourse to the cultural peculiarities of many countries. It is intolerable to live under a government that denies equal dignity to the "protected" religious minorities. Equally intolerable are political conditions under which their concerns for long-term survivability compel them to engage in such disingenuous attestations as described above. Only those who have migrated to the West feel less constrained to express, in private conversations, their deep resentment at being told by the Islamists how to live their lives.

Recent Converts to Protestant Denominations

The coming of Western Protestant missionaries further enhanced Iran's historical religious diversity. Their efforts at evangelism and conversion have, over more than a century, created a small but visible community. They belonged to the Anglican Episcopal Church, the different Protestant denominations, and the nonethnic Catholic Church. When Galindo Pohl began to pay attention to religious minorities other than the Baha'is, he noted that the recognition granted to the old Armenian and Assyro-Chaldean communities was withheld to the new Christian community of Muslim converts. Conversion took place among Muslims as well as among the recognized minorities with ethnic identities. Their survival and growth depended on their proselytizing works, unnerving the Shiite clerics. Galindo Pohl noted that the "prohibitions against conversion from Islam create an environment of religious intolerance."[101] Official recognition of ex-Muslim Protestants would have decriminalized apostasy.[102] Government officials insisted that under the existing laws, "conversion was not a crime and that no one had been punished for converting." [103] The Islamic Civil Code was silent on apostasy, but the Judiciary provided legal space for the clerical judges to apply traditional Islamic law, not codified in state laws. The only reference to apostasy was made in Article 26 of the Press Law, which forbade the press to insult Islam and what it holds sacred. The crime was punishable by fines, lashing, and prison terms, but "if the degree of profanity reaches the level of apostasy, the sentence for apostasy shall be rendered and executed." The law did not identify the punishment for apostasy, leaving it to the Islamic judges to impose the death penalty if they desired.

The persecution of Protestant clergy began in earnest shortly after the establishment of the Islamic Republic. "The largest Protestant denomination, the Episcopalians, were forced to cease their activities after the confiscation of church properties, the arrest of several pastors, and physical attacks on church leaders and their families." [104] Between 10,000 and 15,000 Iranians adhered to the Protestant churches. From 1988, the hard-liners in charge of the Intelligence Ministry began to pay closer attention to the recent Iranian (Muslim) converts. They closed down the Garden of Evangelism in July 1989 and the Bible Society of Iran in February 1990. This was at the time when the Intelligence Minister, Ali Fallahian, was expanding the reaches of his security apparatus. The sale of the Bible in Persian translation was prohibited, and on at least one occasion authorities confiscated 20,000 copies of the New Testament in Persian translation. They also closed down a number of Protestant churches in the provinces. [105] The authorities harassed the congregations, placing them under surveillance with the goal of forcing them to forgo their religious activities. They put Protestant ministers under pressure not to conduct services in Persian. [106] The recognized Christian groups each had a particular ethnic-national identity, and they conducted religious services in its own vernacular. The Muslim converts to Christianity spoke Persian. The Shiite clerics experienced a kind of cultural shock upon hearing that Protestants recite their liturgy in Persian, as if the language, with its rich depository of lamenting vernaculars, were monopolistically entrusted to the mullahs.

Hossein Sudmand was the first Christian pastor whose name appeared in the UN reports. The regime charged him with apostasy and executed him on December 3, 1990. Some two years before his arrest, he had become a minister in the Church of the Assembly of God in the city of Mashhad. But it was the convoluted case of Mahdi Dibaj that focused the attention of the international human rights community on the plight of the Christians. [107] A leader of the fledgling Christian community, his conversion to Christianity went back to 1948, when evangelicalism shaped his sense of mission. By the time he came to the attention of the Special Representative, Dibaj had endured a long and painful incarceration without even the formality of a trial. The prison interrogators hoped that it would induce this remarkably principled pastor to renounce Christianity and re-embrace Islam.[108] The Islamic revolutionary court in the city of Sari sentenced him to death on charges of apostasy on December 3, 1993. Galindo Pohl made a direct appeal to the government to grant clemency to the pastor.[109]

But persecutions of Muslim converts to Christianity continued, as security agents made discordant efforts to close their churches.[110] Dibaj's ordeal soon involved Bishop Hovsepian Mehr, the head of the Council of Protestant Churches and one of the most senior priests among the Iranian clergy. An Armenian by ethnicity and a Protestant in faith, he was already the target of harassment and interrogations. Distraught at having to witness the senseless persecution of his colleagues, the Bishop committed the ultimate political crime by issuing a poignant public statement that caused his death. He explained the plight of the members of the Protestant Assemblies and called upon the UN Special Representative to investigate the violations of their right to freedom of religion. In response, the regime increased the pressure and predictably demanded from all Christian denominations a public expression of satisfaction for the good treatment they had received in the Islamic Republic.[111] Bishop Hovsepian Mehr had already refused to sign a similar statement declaring that religious minorities enjoyed all the possible rights and denouncing the Special Representative's allegations of human rights violations. At the time of real crisis, these leaders received threatening messages from the hard-liners in Tehran.[112]

It did not take long before the lives of both Dibaj and Hovsepian Mehr reached their tragic ends. The history of the two clergymen's confrontations with the regime, their violent deaths and the torturous paths that the officials took in explaining the murders revealed volumes about the workings of a religious state. The decisive international response to the news concerning Dibaj's death sentence included a direct appeal from the Vatican. Unexpectedly, the security authorities freed Dibaj on January 16, 1994. From the outset, this appeared suspicious, since the always defiant regime never overtly submitted to such international appeals. Three days after Dibaj's release, the body of his main defender, Bishop Hovsepian Mehr, was found in a street in south Tehran. Then, on June 20, 1994, Dibaj disappeared. The police reported the discovery of his body in a wooded area west of Tehran.

In a kind of denunciation that often preceded bloody actions by vigilantes or security agents, the hard-liners in the semiofficial press vehemently objected to the decision freeing Dibaj. The writers of *Jomhuri-ye Islami* thundered that, according to the Islamic Republic's regulations and the *fatvas* of all Islamic jurists, a man who converted from Islam to Christianity was an apostate (*mortadd*) for whom there could be no punishment but death. Moreover, they accused Dibaj of insulting "the Prophet of Islam and all that is sacred in Islam."[113] These were identical charges to those behind the death *fatva* against Salman Rushdie. This incendiary language has often proven ominous in the Islamic Republic of Iran. The history of the two men's confrontations with the regime, as well as the aftereffects of their murders, strongly suggest that security agencies had a hand in their tragic ends. As discussed in Chapter 13, the infamous Sa'id Imami, Deputy Intelligence Minister, was in charge of the operation.

Next, the Rev. Tataous Mikhaelian, the new President of the Council of Evangelical Ministers, disappeared on June 29, 1994; his body appeared in Tehran's morgue a few days later. During his visit to Iran in December 1995, the Special Rapporteur Amor noted the traumas experienced by Iranian Protestants as the result of the murder of the three clergymen.[114]

At first, the regime's often vociferous spokesmen remained silent about the murders. Then they denounced the victims as political activists with agendas above and beyond their church activities. In a press report dated August 1, 1994, Muhammad Javad Zarif, the Deputy Foreign Minister, denounced the Protestant churches as political organizations.[115] He is the same official who high-mindedly claimed, at the 1993 UN Conference on Human Rights in Vienna, that the superior Islamic principles would enrich the concept of human rights. Finally the directors of the Intelligence Ministry unfolded their master plan of diversion, muddying the field of investigation in such a way that no clear picture could be obtained. They blamed the People's Mojahedin Organization, presenting the murders as "a carefully planned conspiracy against the Iranian State and an attempt to stir up discord and antagonism between the ethnic and religious communities." The regime's diplomats, in particular, hoped that the international human rights community would not hold the state responsible for the murders.[116] A bomb blast in the mosque of Imam Reza, a holy Shiite shrine in Iran, killed twenty-six people on June 20, 1994. The regime blamed the Mojahedin for the attack and tied all the cases into one knotty story.

This official tale simply ignored the immediate background of the regime's persecution of the victims. Shortly before his murder, Bishop Hovsepian Mehr wrote that "converts have been beaten and hanged upside down for many hours and beaten with thick wires for hours."[117] Thus, the regime's brutal hostility toward the ex-Muslim converts to Christianity was well known, raising "questions about the government's involvement in the murders."[118] On the other hand, there has never been any indication of the Mojahedin's malice towards Iran's religious minorities. Why would an opposition organization take such a senseless risk of murdering Christian ministers? Only to discredit a regime that has no credibility in protecting human rights? Fewer than a handful of states have ever achieved the dubious distinction of having a Special Representative appointed to monitor their human rights violations.

The judicial theatrics that followed increased suspicions of the international human rights monitors. The government presented a young woman by the name of Farahnaz Anami, who was arrested, according to official press reports, on July 6, 1994.[119] In a typical televised confession, she declared herself the killer of Reverend Mikhaelian. The authorities also presented Batul Vaferi and Maryam Shahbazpur as accomplices in the crime. The two women, the government maintained, were arrested when they were trying to place explosives in a holy shrine and in Khomeini's mausoleum, both in south Tehran.[120] This left the killers of the other two ministers unidentified. However, the three women repeated a version of the story to the Special Rapporteur Amor, to the effect that "the murders of pastors Dibaj and Hovsepian had been committed by another unit of the Mojahedin organization."[121] They told the Human Rights Watch monitor that another Mojahedin member killed Dibaj and fled the country.[122]

In a sharp departure from past practices, the regime held an open, televised trial in Tehran's Revolutionary Court, even allowing observers from the Western embassies to attend. The accused persons were provided with defense attorneys. The regime's security agents based the entire case on the confessions of the accused, insisting that they were under no duress. A clear indication that the regime intended to conduct an open trial of the Mojahedin, mainly for the consumption of Western governments, came with the opening statements of the presiding judge, who warned against supporting a terrorist organization that did not hesitate to murder Christians. Both the open trial and the lenient sentences that the court meted out created more suspicion.

After the trial, the officials in the Foreign Ministry often insisted on presenting the prisoners for interviews with international human rights observers who managed to get to Iran. The Government allowed the Special Rapporteur to speak with the three women in Evin prison in Tehran.[123] The regime had previously denied the requests by Amnesty International and Human Rights Watch for visits to Iran. The regime made an inexplicable exception by allowing one particular human rights monitor, the Iranian-born Elahé Hicks, from Human Rights Watch/Middle East, to visit Iran. Foreign Ministry officials showed a keen interest in taking Hicks to Evin prison to meet the prisoners. In the interview, the three women told Hicks that they were among the Mojahedin prisoners in the 1980s, spending five years in prison. Not surprisingly they also repeated what every repentant prisoner, still in the clutches of the security officials, had said: "that throughout that time they were well treated and never witnessed any ill-treatment or torture in the prisons."[124]

Against the background of the accumulated records of prisons and prisoners in the Islamic Republic, the entire story, as told by the three unfortunate women, simply sounded incredible. This case provided a clear indication of the process by which human rights observers often arrived at their judgments. A violating state was extremely reluctant to provide clear evidence either to validate or invalidate allegations of human rights violations. Paradoxically, however, when it did offer "evidence" to disprove the charges, the result often reinforced suspicions. The ineptitude of the servants of the authoritarian state and clumsiness of the evidence further muddied the field, reinforcing the observers' negative impressions. It was counterintuitive to accept the logic of the official tale.

The Special Rapporteur Amor remained unconvinced by the official explanation. He accepted the more plausible one offered by the international organizations, noting that they "also regarded the trial of the three women accused of murder as a travesty of justice." Some even suggested that the women might be agents of the regime.[125]

The murder of the three Protestant ministers and the official debacle in handling it seemed to have had a cooling effect on the anti-Protestant activities of the intelligence agents. However, they did not end. News of sporadic persecution continued to reach the international human rights community. Then, in November 1995, security agents arrested the Rev. Harmik Torosian, who suffered torture and other ill treatment. A year later, Muhammad Baqer Yusofi (also known as Muhammad Ravanbakhsh), a Protestant Christian pastor, was found dead. He was closely associated with Dibaj in the city of Sari.[126] The Iranian authorities told Special Representative Copithorne that the clergyman had committed suicide.[127]

By 1997, Copithorne was sufficiently alarmed by official intolerance toward religious minorities that he called "upon the Government and the Islamic Human Rights Commission [a state body] to address this situation with an urgency that reflects its seriousness."[128]

In the context of cultural relativistic debates, it is important to note that UN provisions with regard to this right are provided to protect individuals from precisely the kind of abuses against religious minorities discussed above. Left unprotected, the world's Mormons, Rastafarians, Baha'is, Ahmadis, and others who are accused of having false revelations will suffer greatly at the hands of majorities from whom they are seen to have broken away in faith. Individual Muslims are free to feel that Islam is superior to other religions, but a contemporary state institutionalizing that superiority creates human rights violations. Such a state lacks legitimacy among those relegated to inferior positions. International human rights law prohibits states from creating different categories for treating adherents of different faiths. Moreover, it is unacceptable for a state to declare certain groups protected religious minorities. Such a "protection" sets them apart for different treatment that is by definition unequal to the one accorded the majority. International human rights law forbids a state to declare a faith illegitimate, leaving its followers unprotected under the law; the law also rejects a modern state's enforcement of the ancient concept of apostasy. It is high time to take back the ancient "favor" of "protected minority" and let all Iranians be citizens entitled to equal respect and concern.

Bizhan Namvar, an Iranian intellectual living in the United States, described, with a touch of nostalgia, the tapestry of life in his Tehran neighborhood, where many Jews and Baha'is lived alongside their Muslim neighbors during the 1950s and 1960s. Before going to the university, he attended an excellent high school, financed by a Zoroastrian endowment, where most students were Muslims, Jews, and Armenians. Moreover, as a young man, he frequented those fashionable streets in north-central Tehran where shop owners belonging to many faiths courteously offered their goods and services and where a Russian Orthodox woman owned a pastry shop whose heavenly aroma drew in young Tehranis. The notion of *najes*, ritual and physical impurity associated with the infidels, was receding from consciousness, at least in that particular district, where a strolling mullah would most likely be ignored, instead of overtly respected, feared, or despised.

For religious minorities in Tehran's relatively modern middle-class neighborhoods, life was not as idyllic as the sensitive young Bizhan saw it at the time or as the idealistic intellectual Namvar reconstructed it in exile. However, it was much better than in the traditional, lower-class districts, where the mullahs could still arouse the young ruffians to anti-Baha'i mob violence and create anti-Jewish hysteria. Nevertheless, Namvar was accurate in characterizing the departure of thousands of minorities from Iran as a cleric-induced calamity for the country. He observed that Jews, Armenians, Assyro-Chaldeans, Zoroastrians, Baha'is, and others had been citizens of Iran and had contributed to the creation of a modern lifestyle there. The exodus also included Westerners who had married Iranians. Moreover, the relations of those minorities who stayed behind had been largely severed from Muslim Iranians. He considered the presence of minorities a valuable asset for the country and bemoaned the fact that the clerics managed to chase them out of the country with relative ease. "How many centuries will it take for Iran to overcome this vacuum and to repossess minorities who would consider themselves Iranian?"[129]

Chapter 10

Official Responses to the United Nations

Countering the Charges of Violations in the 1980s

In their earlier responses to the UN's inquiries, reports, and resolutions, the Iranian regime's diplomats vacillated between ideological/religious exaltations and outright denials that were sometimes expressed in a calmer, bureaucratic language. Perhaps the most salient feature of the first period (1980s) was the use of inflammatory rhetoric, denouncing the United States and its European allies for sponsoring critical resolutions on human rights violations in Iran. The hysteric Islamist political discourse for domestic consumption largely shaped the diplomatic responses to the international community.

Two examples will suffice to show the tone of the official responses in the early years of the Islamic Republic. One was meant to counter the charge that the Islamic Republic used boys not yet mature enough for military service, in its human wave attacks against the Iraqi aggressors. A diplomat expounded on the virtue of suffering and martyrdom: "It was an honour for their country that those young people had become sufficiently mature to understand the seriousness of their country's situation. Their heroism and enthusiasm were based on the notion of martyrdom, which materialists were unable to understand. Martyrdom formed part of the ideology of the struggle by the Iranian people against imperialism and colonialism, as had always been the case in the Muslim world."[1]

Most likely the language remained incomprehensible to his Western interlocutors and international human rights monitors. A more bureaucratic response that contradicted the first one came from Iran's Permanent Mission to the United Nations, rejecting the allegation that the use of children in the war was "an established practice or one that is encouraged by the Government." The practice was an honor, but the government did not encourage it! The second response was meant to counter the charges of torture: "Detainees, and more particularly persons imprisoned for espionage, violation of the moral order of Iranian society or terrorism, were held in university-like conditions; they had the right to read, they were treated with kindness and respect and they were provided with possibilities for social rehabilitation. The results of that treatment were evident in the voluntary public confession made by many detainees." [2] The authors of the prison memoirs were at that time in the crucible of torture, confession, and repentance, and the UN human rights officials had no detailed knowledge of conditions inside the prisons. However, the diplomats were blissfully ignorant of the fact that such a statement would appear utterly unconvincing to the international human rights community, recalling the memories of the "reform-thought" camps.

The regime's diplomats remained cold, if not hostile, toward the first Special Representative Andrés Aguilar, who had already requested permission to visit Tehran. One diplomat stated that Aguilar's "line of questioning as well as his conclusions clearly point out that he was also affected by the misinformation campaign of the imperialist media." [3] The Permanent Representative of the Islamic Republic to the United Nations in New York rejected the request on December 7, 1984. The diplomat was saying in effect that if the United Nations agreed with the Islamic Republic's description of the human rights "situation" in Iran, then it would permit a visit to the country. [4]

Outright denial continued to be the crudest diplomatic response. A typical denial would read: "Torturing the prisoners in Iran is forbidden in accordance with the Islamic law. . . . No one in the Islamic Republic of Iran is threatened or detained because of his ideological beliefs." [5] Or "The Islamic Republic of Iran categorically denies the question of torture of prisoners and detainees." [6]

After the initial confusions of the early 1980s, the diplomats became resourceful, giving responses that went beyond ideological exhortations or denials. Eventually they came up with a number of countercharges, rationalizing and justifying their refusal to cooperate with Reynaldo Galindo Pohl. I have organized the official countercharges and tactics into four categories: politicization of the process, drawing structural equivalence between their own state and other modern states and pointing to the formality of written law, setting two preconditions for cooperation, and demanding respect for Islamic *différance.*

Politicization of the Process

During the 1980s, Foreign Ministry officials always complained that the decision to create the mandate for the Special Representative on Iran was politically motivated and that using the special procedures mechanism to select Iran for public scrutiny was highly politicized, due to manipulation by the

Western powers.[7] Having made the valid charge of the politicization of the UN process, the diplomats went on, in the course of the next two decades, to outdo the Commission on Human Rights, raising the level of politicizing to a fever pitch, making it even more difficult for UN human rights monitors to form a clear understanding of violations in the country.

On December 4, 1985, Sa'id Raja'i Khorassani, the diplomat in New York, lent academic backing to his political arguments by approvingly quoting Richard Falk of Princeton University: "The promotion of human rights has often served as a propaganda vehicle for a particular foreign policy." Then Raja'i Khorassani expressed his "profound" concern for the future of the human rights community, because it was being threatened by politicization and by political manipulation: "The roots and causes of such political manipulations and misuses of this concept can be found, *inter alia*, in the ambiguity of the concepts enshrined in the international instruments on human rights, which, instead of giving rise to factual and legal discourses and debates about observances of certain norms, provide sufficient means for certain States to manipulate and abuse these concepts for their political objectives. It is imperative for the international community to study and examine both problems in detail, in order to prevent the politicization of human rights concepts and human rights organs from becoming a *fait accompli*." [8]

It did not occur to the diplomat that without the existing violations there could be no manipulation. Nor did it occur to him that his own government was equally guilty of engaging in the same practice. The Islamist officials have readily denounced human rights violations of their international adversaries—Israel, Iraq, and apartheid South Africa. They have praised, with equal persistence, the repressive governments they considered their own international allies—notably Sudan, Syria, North Korea, and the People's Republic of China. They often sought the votes of such friends, themselves egregious violators, to remove Iran from public scrutiny. Needless to say, throughout the past two decades, the regime's officials often approvingly quoted UN condemnations of U.S. human rights violations.[9]

Using the case of the Islamic Republic of Iran, I want to reiterate a point that is accepted by human rights scholars, but often misunderstood by other academics, concerning how the human rights record of a violating state is compiled. The officials in the Foreign Ministry argued that Iran's human rights record was concocted by the mendacious propaganda of their enemies and by "a well-organized campaign," resulting in "the production and dissemination of baseless allegations." [10] The fact is that in today's world, where professional human rights organizations have established credible voices, no state is capable of concocting, with any credibility, a negative human rights record for another state. Any attempt by a powerful state to fabricate false records for a state it does not like will be dismissed as crude propaganda by the international human rights community. Then how is the record of a recalcitrant state made? Simply, a state's record is made through practices that violate human rights, which are then monitored by international human rights NGOs.[11] Human rights scholarship shows that the assistance of the NGOs providing credible and reliable information has been invaluable to the United Nations.[12] Advancing their own short-term political interests, all states can only use, or abuse, records already compiled. Nothing could politicize human rights discourse more than the essentially inaccurate assertion that U.S. government propaganda fabricated a bad human rights record for the Islamic Republic of Iran or any other states. The actual allegations listed in the Special Representatives' reports were often only a portion of what Amnesty International collected and disseminated for Islamist rule during the 1980s. And the concerns expressed by Amnesty and other human rights organizations were far more influential in bringing the abuses to the world's attention, although the United Nations is capable, if politics allow, to exert more pressure on a recalcitrant state. Even Amnesty's reports lacked the prison memoirs' painful detail.

"If law is politics," writes Louis Henkin, "enforcement of law in the inter-State system is also heavily political. In such [UN] bodies, human rights are more susceptible to being subordinated to non-human rights considerations. There, voting, including 'bloc-voting,' has led to 'selective targeting' of some States, sometimes exaggerating their violations, and overlooking those of other States. . . . Smaller political bodies, such as the Human Rights Commission, are also inhibited by government representatives concerned for State values and friendly relations, but increasingly they are able to be somewhat less 'political,' more evenhanded, as well as more activist in the cause of human rights."[13]

This study shows that UN human rights monitors did not exaggerate the violations, at least in Iran's case. Surely, the United States does have sufficient weight in the Commission to selectively influence the process, and it has used double standards to advance its political interests; the fact that the records of some states are more closely scrutinized than others undermines the overall integrity of the Commission's work. The confusion it also creates is detrimental, not to the violating state but to the cause of human rights, as well as frustrating to the monitoring organizations, since the state uses it as an easy excuse to divert attention from its own record of violations.

Moreover, no human rights advocate can be disturbed by a process that, though allowing many states to escape scrutiny, enables the Commission's independent experts to report on the violations committed by other delinquent states. The policy of double standards is obstructionist and unfair not because the records of states like Iran are openly examined by the Commission on Human Rights but because the records of others, like China, are not.[14] It denies the citizens of many countries with records of abuses the chance to use the UN's resources to scrutinize those records. Of course, the regime's diplomats never acknowledged the fact that the Special Representatives, though often embarrassingly cautious and diplomatic, were independent, judicious experts.[15]

Equivalency in Institutional Architecture and Formality of Written Law

Modern states around the world exhibit remarkable similarities in their formal institutional structures, legal codes, and procedural arrangements, apart from differences in culture or actual practices. The Third World architects of authoritarian states of the modern era never invoke cultural relativist arguments in erecting state institutions, superficially modeled on the Western patterns. Authoritarian rulers often present their state institutions and procedures as the structural equivalent of those found in liberal democracies.

For example, in 1992 this tendency revealed itself fully in Iran's much delayed periodic report to the UN Human Rights Committee, supervising the implementation of the Covenant on Civil and Political Rights.[16] Much of the report was a comparison of the Covenant's substantive articles (1 to 27) with their domestic equivalents, showing that many of the Covenant's rights were also enshrined in the Constitution of the Islamic Republic and other domestic legal codes and regulations.

The report gave examples of domestic laws and the procedural arrangements that protect, on paper, individuals against unlawful seizure and arrest; it also stated measures guaranteeing due process and proper treatment of prisoners. In twelve paragraphs, some covering more than a page, the report presented comprehensive domestic legal protections, including freedom of expression and the press and prohibitions against torture. It even listed some laws that existed under the Shah.[17] It is significant to note that the diplomats chose not to reveal the macabre nature of the Islamic Penal Law (*hodud, qesas, ta'zirat, diyat*), which formed a critical part of the domestic legal structure (see Chapter 6).

Most important, the report to the Human Rights Committee presented the Islamic Judiciary as an "independent power"[18] and cited the formality of due process of law as provided by the Constitution.[19] The claim to an independent Islamic Judiciary was a gross distortion, since it lacked the essential checks and balances that exist in well-functioning democracies, where an independent judiciary is a blessing to defenseless individuals facing the might of the modern state.

An Islamist diplomat wrote: "It is important to note here that—contrary to the ignorant assertion of a delegation in the Third Committee—the judiciary of the Islamic Republic of Iran, because of its composition and its relations to the masses, is not constitutionally or practically accountable to the executive branch. The mechanism for oversight and review of the decisions of the courts in the Islamic Republic of Iran exists within the judiciary itself, upon which the other branches of government have no control. It is exactly this ignorance in the West about our system of justice and about our system of government in general that has given rise to such baseless allegations and ridiculous claims." [20]

As discussed in Chapter 6, the very independence of the Islamic Judiciary, tightly controlled by a clique of political clerics, has been a curse for individuals who have been caught in its clutches. "Independence" has meant unaccountable—to anyone, or any law, especially on political offenses. As late as 1998–99, the unaccountability of the Judiciary under Ayatollah Muhammad Yazdi proved to be one of the main obstacles to the reforms promised by President Khatami, whose stated intention to bring about the rule of law in the country was hardly an endorsement of the record of the past two decades.

The diplomats sitting on the UN's influential Third Committee, constrained by bureaucratic habits, often failed to offer a proper response to false claims. Amnesty International and other human rights organizations did not suffer from similar constraints and responded to such distortions. Amnesty International emphasized that the United Nations had already formulated the basic principles by which an independent judiciary should be judged. "The methods of judicial appointment should include safeguards against judicial appointments for improper motives and should ensure the non-discriminatory selection of individuals of integrity with appropriate training and qualifications in law." [21] Basic Principle 2 on the Independence of the Judiciary defines judges with judicial independence as those who are free to "decide matters before them impartially, on the basis of the facts and in accordance with the law, without any restriction, improper influence, inducements, pressure, threats or interferences, direct or indirect, from any quarter or for any reason." [22] Political prisoners judged by clerics in the Islamic Revolutionary Court would have to be rescued, not from any undue influence from the executive branch but from the judicial clerics' own ideological zealotry and vengeful temperament.

As time passed and the Special Representatives' reports piled up, the government's statements made more references to the written constitutional and legal guarantees. High government officials kept asserting that there was no torture in the Islamic Republic because it was forbidden by the Islamic Constitution and that "anyone using torture during interrogation is punished himself." [23] "If a prison staff, or one of the judicial officials molests or applies corporal punishment to the accused to extort a confession, he shall be sentenced to a term of imprisonment ranging from six months to three years." [24]

The prison memoirs expose these official misrepresentations. Amnesty International stated that it "knows of no specific cases in which individuals have been charged or tried for the infliction of torture or ill-treatment of prisoners in the Islamic Republic of Iran."[25] Thus Amnesty focused not on formal constitutional guarantees or written penal codes, but on those practices word of which has escaped the cloistered walls of Iran's prisons.

International human rights jurists are aware of the fact that the mere presence of laws prohibiting mistreatment of prisoners is not proof that such mistreatments do not take place. To the contrary, constant law-enforcing vigilance is required, even in democratic countries that enjoy much stronger traditions of the rule of laws. As Galindo Pohl reminded the regime's officials, the formal presence of laws, regardless of their normative assumptions, loses its significance if the process of "implementation is faulty."[26]

One interesting aspect of the interaction between the UN monitors and the regime was the attempt by lay officials with modern university educations to portray the clerical legalism of the Islamic Republic as somehow normal and comparable to prevailing practices in other states. As if embarrassed, they wished to overcome the impression that the Islamic legal system was esoteric or outmoded. Interestingly, their clerical mentors have often tried to claim legitimacy by accentuating the difference between their Islamic practices and those of secular states. Dr. Hossein Mehrpur presented the government's report to the UN Human Rights Committee. In his oral responses to the Committee, Mehrpur even tried to draw a parallel between the religious *fatvas* and the modern jurisprudential doctrine that provides for judges deciding cases that have no clear precedent in law.[27] He concluded that "in the absence of codified law, the principle of resorting to *fatva* and Islamic sources to issue a judgment is not a strange phenomenon that would be considered unthinkable or outside of recognized legal standards."[28]

In front of the Committee Mehrpur argued that application of *fatva* procedure was relevant only to civil cases and that "in principle" it does not apply to criminal procedure. A criminal act was specified in a codified law and would be considered as such by a judge.[29] He also implied that in practice a judge in a criminal court seldom faced a case where the law was silent on the criminality of the act. The law also provided the punishment.[30] In his writing for domestic readers, however, he presented this as a problematic issue that had to be resolved in the Islamic Republic of Iran. He clearly implied that there were many instances where resorting to *fatva* was practiced in criminal cases.[31] Like many other lay officials, Mehrpur spoke differently to domestic and international audiences (Chapter 17).

Preconditions for Cooperation

In addition to the good old tactic of denials, without which the diplomatic world plunges into periodic disarray, the regime's diplomats formulated two major preconditions which, they insisted, had to be met before they could consider responding to the Special Representatives' inquiries. These two preconditions were presented to both Aguilar and Galindo Pohl. The first was related to the issue of terrorism, as practiced in Iran by the militant organizations that were driven into exile or underground by the clerical rulers after the ouster of President Bani Sadr in June 1981. The second was the government's insistence that the Commission and its Special Representatives must cease referring to Iranian Baha'is as a religious minority.

The Militant Groups

Above all, the officials maintained that the Mojahedin and, to a lesser degree, the Kurdish resistance were responsible for producing "all the baseless allegations of torture and arbitrary and summary executions—forging some evidence that cannot hold up in any respectable institution of domestic or international law." They demanded that the Special Representative disregard the allegations of human rights violations, since they were nothing but forgeries. A diplomat wrote: "There is a wealth of documents, including televised confessions by the members of this organization, concerning their terrorist activities. They have also confessed to have tortured 17- and 18-year-old revolutionary guards in a most brutal and inhumane manner in order to extort information from them. One wonders how a judicial authority of Ambassador Aguilar's caliber could take seriously the claim of the members of this organization and their forged evidence."

Again, the diplomat seemed unaware of the implicit admission in his own statement and the possible negative impact that his reference to the "televised confessions" would create. The Special Representative had gotten his information partly from the testimonies of members and sympathizers of political groups in exile, whom the government considered illegal because they were not "registered as a political party or a minority in the Islamic Republic of Iran." This gave the officials an excuse to justify their lack of responsiveness to the Special Representative's formal inquiry: "To respond to these specific sections of the Report would implicitly imply recognition of the status the Special Representative has granted them. A situation that would run contrary to Iranian law." [32]

By the time Galindo Pohl assumed responsibility for monitoring Iran, the state functionaries had further elaborated the first precondition into a major obstacle, frustrating all his attempts to gain cooperation. In the summer of 1986, the Mojahedin leaders who had escaped to France had to depart from that country. [33] It was unlikely that any other country except Iraq would harbor them; Mas'ud Rajavi set up his camp outside Baghdad, thus committing what amounted to political suicide for himself and the organization he controlled like a religio-political sect. This played into the hands of their nemesis in Tehran.

The Foreign Ministry responded to Galindo Pohl's specific inquiries into violations of the individual's *right to life* in Iran:

On this basis, it is clear that the people's Mojahedin organization cannot, by any means, be considered a political group eligible to enjoy the same rights as other legally recognized political groups and parties. On the other hand, our information related to the names of members, and sympathizers of this group, particularly those with whom the Special Representative has met, reveals that they have acquired citizenship from Iraq and are not recognized as Iranians. At the same time, these members, along with their leadership, are being handsomely paid by Iraq. . . . [T]hey are therefore collaborators with the enemy in wartime and may, at best, be considered as mercenaries whose definition and rights are described in article 47 of Protocol I, supplementary to the Third Geneva Convention of 12 August 1949. Before addressing any individual case, therefore, the legal status of these persons needs to be clarified by the Special Representative.[34]

In another response, Muhammad Hossein Lavasani, Deputy Minister for International Affairs, wrote: "So long as the Commission's information is virtually based on the self-serving, politically motivated allegations of certain armed terrorists to the extent that 7 out of 8 so-called witnesses and claimants of human rights violations in Iran bear their membership in the armed, fifth-column group of hypocrites, i.e., the self-proclaimed Mujahedden [Mojahedin], there remains no room for responding to such baseless allegations. Allegations of human rights violations can be raised only and only after the terrorists have been excluded as a source of information from the fact-finding and information-gathering system of the Commission on Human Rights."[35]

These official responses distorted the history of the Islamic Republic and its suppression of all political and civil groups who opposed clerical rule. The diplomats could not be expected to appreciate the irony inherent in their statement concerning the illegality of the political groups, who were declared "illegal" by the same repressive government. It could not escape Galindo Pohl's attention that the response failed to name any opposition group or party that enjoyed the rights that the government denied to the members of the groups it denounced as illegal.

The Special Representative submitted a number of specific allegations with regard to the right to life. To counter them, the Foreign Ministry's bureaucrats invented the right to "life of the nation," which was supposedly threatened by an armed organization in exile. They came up with the absurd charge that the Mojahedin members who were named by the Special Representative were Iraqi citizens. Of course, the Special Representative had only mentioned those individuals who suffered human rights violations when in custody in Iran.

Surely the Mojahedin were active in their campaigns to discredit the regime by publicizing, and of course exaggerating, the cases of individuals who were executed or who died under torture. By the late 1980s, their efforts had become well organized.[36] However, other groups and individuals also provided testimonies. The Baha'i international community was also effective in disseminating information concerning the assaults on this religious minority in Iran. Another significant source of information were the Islamic Republic's official pronouncements and actions. Above all, the diplomats undermined their own credibility by ignoring the professionalism achieved by the NGOs' human rights monitors and their expert capacity in sifting through diverse evidence. The NGOs have gained a considerable measure of trust from the international community.

As if wanting to teach a human rights lesson to the officials, Galindo Pohl observed: "The political affiliations of those persons are not under discussion. They may or may not be members, sympathizers or simply acquaintances of any of the groups referred to by the Iranian Government. They are human beings entitled to the enjoyment of protection of human rights." [37]

It was not surprising that many individuals who offered their testimony were former members of the radical groups or Baha'is who relied on the support of their international community. As is often the case, a nonactivist citizen would most likely carry the burden of political and social oppression in silent indignation, seldom becoming the target of torture and persecution. It should have been clear to Galindo Pohl that isolated individuals not supported by an organized group were hardly capable of finding their way to Europe to offer testimonies. The fact that individuals mostly connected with the Mojahedin were able to do so was due to the organizational supports they received, after they managed to escape from Iran. They also had a high degree of commitment; most had burned all bridges behind them, not expecting to return to Iran under clerical control.

In this context, Professor Peter H. Kooijmans of the Netherlands, who served as the Commission's chair in 1984 and then as the Special Rapporteur on torture from 1985 to 1993, offered a valuable insight:

Almost invariably torture is practiced in secluded places and it often leaves no directly recognizable physical marks. For this reason, torture lends itself easily to a campaign carried out by political opponents of a government in their effort to discredit those in power. Since false accusations can only be disproved by the governments themselves, it is their responsibility to start an investigation of the allegations or to invite the Special Rapporteur to do so. In actual practice, however, the opposite reasoning is followed: since it is assumed that allegations come from sources which belong to oppositional groups, it is also assumed that such allegations are politically motivated and therefore unreliable. It is true that alleged victims of torture are often opponents of the government in power. It is, therefore, logical that in many cases information is provided by oppositional groups. The fact that allegations of torture come from politically motivated sources does not mean, however, that the allegations themselves are merely politically motivated.[38]

Galindo Pohl added a significant judgment: "In the course of the informal hearings, the Special Representative reached the moral conviction that the persons appearing before him referred to facts that certainly happened to them, and that their declarations were not the product of feverish imagination or of mere fabrication guided by political or religious motivations.

These persons presented the traces of maltreatment, and exposed their account of events in a convincing, articulate and coherent manner." [39]

The Islamist officials proved themselves to be clumsy practitioners of diplomatic diversions and evasions. In 1983 the UN Secretary-General issued a report discussing the rights of minorities, in which he made references to human rights violations of Kurdish citizens of Iran. [40] In 1988, Galindo Pohl reported a new allegation concerning a forceful evacuation and resettlement of twenty-three Kurdish villages. The Democratic Party of Iranian Kurdistan presented the information. The names of the villages were provided and the affected number of people was given as 3,680. [41] Two months later, the Permanent Representative of the Islamic Republic of Iran to the United Nations at Geneva responded. He made a reference to Galindo Pohl's report in which he stated the allegation of the forceful resettling of the civilian Kurdish population in Iran. Instead of responding to the allegations concerning Kurds in Iran, the diplomat diverted the question to the Kurds in Iraq. "Thousands of Kurds have been deported by Iraq forcefully and involuntarily. Most of these deportees are now sheltered in Iran." The letter went on to substantiate the crimes committed by the Iraqi regime against Iraqi Kurds. The allegation stated on behalf of Iran's Kurds is never mentioned again in the letter. The Special Representative was invited to interview not the Iranian Kurds but the Kurdish refugees from Iraq. The Special Representative had to remind the diplomat that he was the Special Representative for human rights situation in Iran and not Iraq, although he volunteered to transmit the contents of the letter "to the competent organs of the United Nations." [42]

The issue of diversion apart, it did not occur to the diplomat that he had repeatedly objected to the Special Representative receiving testimonies from the Mojahedin's supporters, who were portrayed as agents of the Iraqi government at war with Iran. Presumably, it was proper for the Special Representative to accept as facts what refugees from Iraq, who were under Iranian control, could tell him against Iraq. A process is considered politicized and tainted by a double standard only if it works against one's effort to hide human rights violations in one's own state.

Iranian Baha'is

Iran's second precondition for cooperation with the Special Representative was the demand that the UN should stop referring to Baha'is as a religious minority in Iran. This demand makes it even clearer that the preconditions were intended as mere excuses, enabling the diplomats to offer a rationale, however flimsy, for their failure to cooperate with the Commission and its Special Representative. No savvy diplomat could have expected that the Commission on Human Rights would ever deny Baha'is the status of a religious minority. In fact, this issue continued to be the real problem for the diplomats; their clerical mentors had been blinded by their hatred of Baha'is, and the diplomats could hardly hope for a change in the treatment of this minority that might be acceptable to the international human rights community.

As late as March 1988, Syrous Nasseri, the Permanent Representative of the Islamic Republic of Iran to the United Nations Office in Geneva, asked the Commission to "clarify precisely on what basis" it used the term minority for Baha'is. As support, he referred to a resolution passed by the Islamic Assembly of Jurisprudence in Jidda, Saudi Arabia, which "decided that Bahaism does not represent a religion." [43] Apart from the problem that this reference amounted to a late twentieth-century version of accepting the verdict of the Spanish Inquisition on the heretics, the diplomat misrepresented the Jidda pronouncement. Rather than saying "Baha'ism" cannot be considered a religion, the statement says, in effect, that it is a false religion and that its adherents are infidels.[44] The UN human rights instruments are meant to protect those whose religions are rejected by the powerful majorities and their clerical establishments.

In another pronouncement, the Islamist diplomats demonized the faith as:

a foreign-affiliated political movement established through the then tsarist Russia and Great Britain as a means to ensure their colonial interests and long-term objectives in Iran. All activities of this political movement, disguised as a religion, either directly or through other conspiratorial means, have been aimed at the subversion of the Governments in Iran and gradual obliteration of Islam as the established faith and unifying base of the Iranian people. Such subversive activities were only diminished during the latter period of the Pahlavi regime when they infiltrated all segments of the government and held high positions in the Army and the SAVAK, the Shah's notorious secret police. Most of the Shah's policies, in respect to both internal and external affairs, were practically formulated and executed by the Baha'is. This is despite their claim that Baha'is are forbidden to become involved in partisan politics or to hold any political post. The Baha'is also maintain that they are obedient to the Government of the country in which they live, and preach non-violence. Their brief history is, to the contrary, filled with long periods of riots and armed rebellion against the established Governments in Iran and other countries in the Islamic world.[45]

A *brief* history filled with *long periods* of rebellion in Iran and other Islamic countries! The diplomats were just like their turbaned mentors, experts in word manipulation and distortion. There has not been a challenge by religious dissidents in Iran since the middle of the nineteenth century, when the oppressive Qajar Shah, on the urging of the Shiite ulema, crushed the Babi movement. By all historical accounts, the Babi sect exhibited all the characteristics of indigenous and chiliastic movements that took place in some parts of Africa and Asia in the middle of the nineteenth century. Moreover, it was the Babi movement which transformed itself into what is today the Baha'i faith.

The Islamist hatred of the Baha'is has been unbounded. Their responses show a total lack of awareness that their statements, reminiscent of Nazis' description of the Jews, create a revulsion among international observers, setting off alarm bells in the human rights community. A human rights monitor would immediately want to know how a government with the power to take life has arrived at such conclusions about a religious community. What kind of independent scholarly research and judicial investigation established the allegations of wild conspiracies, surreptitious infiltration, and subversive activities attributed to Baha'is? What results would such charges have in a country that has no tradition of respect for due process of law, or in a state whose judiciary is controlled by a clerical caste, whose leaders are themselves the spinners of this conspiracy theory?

Even a cursory reading of the argument advanced by the officials reveals an interesting fact: the regime rejected the Commission on Human Rights because it had "politicized" the human rights procedure with regard to the Islamic Republic of Iran. It is hardly a secret that the Commission on Human Rights reaches its decisions through a politicized process. However, the diplomats' responses and their depiction of the victims of human rights violations in Iran were themselves so blatantly political and extreme that only the most strident Islamists could accept them. Instead of conducting an internal investigation into allegations of the Special Representative, the government issued political denunciations; more ominously, it demonized all members of the militant organizations and the Baha'i faith. From the perspective of a human rights observer, an authoritarian government that showed such a vehement hatred toward its political enemies and a religious minority was conceivably capable of violating their basic human rights.

Thus ironically, the shrillness of the official responses most likely strengthened the view concerning the validity of the allegations of human rights violations in the country. Listening to the official demonization of Mojahedin, other militant activists, and Baha'is, the Special Representative could easily imagine what would happen to them if they fell into the hands of Islamist security agents; that image was reinforced by a political culture that considered torture to be normal, whether under the Shah or the Ayatollah.

Demanding Respect for Islamic *Différance*

In the early stage of interaction with the UN, one diplomat, raising the issue of Islamic laws, contemptuously reminded Andrés Aguilar that he was not "at all familiar with the prevailing school of jurisprudence in the Islamic Republic of Iran," and that it was imperative for him to thoroughly study "the theoretical foundations of that system" before conducting his investigation.[46]

Demands for respect for Islamic *différance* became more persistent as the issue of Islamic norms and laws gradually entered into the diplomatic response, even as the state-controlled press reported regularly on amputations of limbs and stoning of the accused. By 1987–88 the officials openly spoke of the incompatibility of certain universal human rights provisions with Islamic laws and demanded respect for those laws.

The Islamic defense would only be used in instances that involved recognized Islamic punishments or cases related to the freedoms of conscience and religion. There could be no defensible Islamic legitimization for summary executions of political opponents, for inflicting torture on prisoners to extract confession, for arbitrary arrests, and for the grossly unfair trials behind closed doors in prison. To counter these kinds of violations, the regime's diplomats used different tactics, including the denial of charges, rejection of allegations, or recourse to the two preconditions.

The most obvious and contentious issues with respect to the state's public practices that officials could not deny were related to the traditional Islamic punishments of lashing, amputations, and stoning. The Islamists also believed that their religion placed no limits on the number of death penalties. In his report of January 26, 1989, Galindo Pohl commented on certain provisions of the Islamic Penal Code, suggesting changes in the provisions of the laws of *hodud* (crimes against divine will), *qesas* (retribution), and the law of *ta'zirat* (discretionary punishment). He hoped that the government would use the "golden opportunity" that was offered by the expiration of the provisional period "to consider not only the domestic experience, but the views of international organs entrusted with the protection of human rights."[47] As discussed before, Galindo Pohl consistently objected to the excessive use of the death penalty and rejected the official Islamic rationalization for its occurrence.

Muhammad Hossein Lavasani, the Deputy Foreign Minister, delivered the official responses in June 1989:

> The punishment currently practiced in Iran under *Ta'zirat* after a verdict by court of law . . . are entirely based on indisputable laws and regulations stipulated in the Islamic legal system. Having been derived from the Islamic judicial system and having met the consensus of all Islamic sects and persuasions throughout the world, they are being enforced in some other Islamic countries as well. . . .
>
> By its divine outlook, the Islamic judicial system embodies far more superior values than any other judicial system for man and life. . . .
>
> Undoubtedly, no other system, not even present international laws and standards, has ever placed such a higher, exalted value on man's life. Imposition of the death penalty in the Islamic Republic of Iran, therefore, is permitted only and only within this divine framework for maintaining human values and for preserving the integrity of human society as a whole.[48]

All Muslim dictators ruling the contemporary states can hide behind this Islamic edifice of "divine outlook," disguising their repressive practices and rule. In Afghanistan's Islamomania in the 1990s, Mullah Mutaqi, the Minister of Information and Culture in the Taliban government, spoke of the eternal nature of the Islamic principles that have endured without changes "in the last 1,400 years."[49]

From 1987 on, Galindo Pohl began to comment increasingly on the peculiarities of Islamic rule and its disturbing implications for the universality of human rights. His general observations conveyed sympathy for the Islamist arguments: "The peculiarities of the Iranian situation present problems of application that are, to some extent, new, and as such, enrich the practice in this field and involve novel views and arguments regarding the protection of human rights at worldwide level."[50]

The Special Representative upheld the universality of human rights standards and the fact that they have become a part of the international customary law. He stated that a number of provisions in the Islamic Penal Code were not in agreement with some provisions of international human rights laws. Galindo Pohl approached the issue in the same fashion that he would have considered any state's domestic laws. In his view, Islamic laws may provide a foundation for a country's constitutional laws, but the question still remained whether the domestic constitutional law or international law was to be considered as the standard of judgment.[51] It was the responsibility of the government to resolve the discordance. No derogation might be allowed on the basis of domestic constitutional peculiarity or cultural-historical backgrounds.[52]

Having properly asserted the preeminence of international laws, he veered appeasingly away from this firm legal ground toward the political-philosophical deliberations that had preoccupied generations of Muslim reformers.

The study of Islamic history and culture shows that from its beginnings Islam established a tradition of respect for human rights, notwithstanding differences of religion. At the time of its appearance in the seventh century, Islam represented a step forward in the protection of human beings. Its contribution to the development of mankind came at a time when Europe was living in the so-called Dark Ages. . . . Islam has been able to adapt to the changing circumstances of the countries that have adopted it and to new developments in the world through the unanimous findings of jurists. . . . The history of the way Islam has operated throughout the millennium and a half of its existence leads to the expectation that the question of potential conflict could be solved in such a way that the international instruments on human rights would remain untouched as one of the most notable achievements of world-wide international co-operation.[53]

In his report of February 12, 1990, Galindo Pohl again pointed out that there were many Iranian Muslims whose opinions on Islamic punishments, especially execution, stood in opposition to those offered by the government officials.[54] Galindo Pohl stated with approval the familiar arguments and positions advocated by liberal Muslims who believed in the possibility of reconciling the provisions of the Universal Declaration of Human Rights with the "traditional Islamic tenets."[55] This was a well-beaten track, some-

times also traveled by sympathetic western observers who periodically reminded the Islamic traditionalists of the positive contributions of the "good"
Islam in history.

For an international monitor like Galindo Pohl, this might have been in
fact a futile tactic. These kinds of arguments have preoccupied Muslim activists for years, without yielding any meaningful result or clear consensus,
even among practicing Muslims, let alone secular citizens whose conception
of law was grounded on human reason. Galindo Pohl continued to vacillate
between his legal position, which upheld human rights as customary international law, and his desire to facilitate a cross-cultural dialogue by engaging
in political-philosophical arguments.

In his report of January 26, 1989, Galindo Pohl seemed to have conceded that the problems in Iran emanated, at least in part, from the government's adherence to "the traditions of a genuinely Islamic people." [56] He
even suggested that it was necessary to hold discussion, presumably with
Iran's Islamist officials, concerning "the question of compatibility of international law with Islamic law." [57] According to an Iranian official who met with
Galindo Pohl during his first visit to Tehran, the Special Representative recommended to the officials that an "international seminar" should be held on
Islamic views on human rights.[58] Galindo Pohl suggested that the Commission on Human Rights and similar international bodies should "take into account the peculiarities of the Iranian situation" and facilitate "the full compliance of Iran with the provisions of the international instruments." [59] He
suggested that the international community should make "efforts in order to
meet some of the misgivings and concerns of the Iranian Government." This
reader began looking forward to specific suggestions the Special Representative might propose to satisfy the Government's "misgivings and concerns."
None seemed possible, and none was suggested. Galindo Pohl offered no
elaboration as to how an international recognition of the Iranian "peculiarities" could lead, practically or theoretically, to the possibility of the Islamic
Republic's full compliance with the provisions of the UN human rights law.
All these efforts were made against the background of the Islamic Republic's
total lack of interest in anything that remotely resembled an acknowledgment of rights violations in Iran.

Yet the ultimate goal of Galindo Pohl's attempts to establish a dialogue
was to prepare Islamist rulers to accept the universality of human rights
by ignoring Islamic precepts and rules. As he observed: "The statement on
compatibility of certain international provisions with Islamic law may be
understood as an effort of accommodation to the international obligations
and as the beginning of a sustained trend that may eventually reach the
point of acceptance of the positions adopted by the General Assembly of the
United Nations and the Commission on Human Rights in their successive
resolutions." [60] Galindo Pohl's incursion into Islamic peculiarities brought
him to the same discursive cul-de-sac faced by other advocates who searched

for that elusive cross-cultural dialogue in the charged political atmosphere of the 1980s. The international monitors, charged with monitoring human rights as stated in UDHR, should have stayed clear of the debate over Islam and left it to the Muslims to reinterpret Islam and make it accord with universal standards.

In practice, Galindo Pohl's commentaries on the issue of Islam encouraged the regime's spokesmen to pursue fully what they may have thought a God-given avenue of diversion from a concrete examination of existing violations of human rights, sending the international monitors chasing after fruitless theoretical arguments. In comments to the session of the Commission on Human Rights on March 9 and 10, 1988, Syrous Nasseri, a diplomat in the UN Geneva office, raised the issue again by welcoming "the initiation of the discussion on the very important issue of compatibility between Islamic law and international law." In what seemed to be the only time that the diplomats had something positive to say about the Special Representative, Nasseri praised Galindo Pohl's decision to engage in this theoretical dialogue as "positive and fruitful." This tactic was fully developed later by the diplomats who sponsored international conferences, held in Germany and Iran, for theoretical debate on the issue of Islamic *différance*. The regime's diplomats admonished the Commission for maintaining that "adherence to international law is a must for all States." It was not only the Islamic Republic that was affected but "all Islamic countries and Muslims the world over." He charged again that "Islamic doctrine had very limited presentation and reception at the time the Declaration and the two Covenants were formulated." [61]

In the meantime a large number of concerned individuals and international monitors were to be kept engaged ad infinitum in a mostly futile debate over "human rights in Islam." No specific proposal came from the Foreign Ministry as to how its officials intended to consider the "matters raised by the Special Representative in practical terms" or to "reflect" on the "true situation" of human rights violations any differently than they had done theretofore.

Chapter 11

Change of Tactics After
Ayatollah Khomeini's Death

Ayatollah Khomeini died midway through two decades of clerical dominance. The acute period of human rights crisis lasted from 1980 until 1988.
Then began the chronic period, during which the regime denied the rights
of the mostly intimidated citizens without many cases of active violations
being reported. Violations produced relatively fewer visible victims. The
relative quiescence in the arena of political executions signified not an improved situation but a dormant state for human rights of many Iranians.
During the first phase of acute human rights crises, numerous violations
were reported because many Iranians, especially the politically mobilized
young people, exercised their rights openly or claimed them assertively.
After the suppression, resistance became passive, the language returned to
its familiar allegorical and symbolic constructs, and secular women could
only discreetly defy and ridicule the imposed dress code. From 1989 to the
late 1990s, rights were disregarded, mainly because human rights could not
be openly asserted.

As indicated before, a sharp increase in the number of executions for
common crimes, especially narcotics trafficking, matched a drastic reduction in the number of executions for political offenses. Meanwhile, the relative abatement of the most egregious human rights violations opened the
possibility in mid-1990s for monitoring and reporting of other significant
rights violations, such as freedom of conscience and expression and rights
of women. These were rights that hitherto did not receive proper attention,
perhaps because of the extreme urgency of political executions and torture
and/or because of the international community's deference to the "cultural
sensitivities" of the Islamist rulers.

At the same time, the Special Representative and the international human rights organizations no longer faced an undifferentiated aggregate of
names of executed prisoners, for whom little or no biographical information
was available. The mass executions of the regime's opponents had ended;

its new victims were no longer mere statistical figures and unknown individuals. Those who were threatened, arrested, and prosecuted in the new period were often recognizable individuals, sometimes well-known personalities from Iranian politics, religion, journalism, and literature. The cleanup of prisons and torture chambers may have ironically made the task of the regime's diplomats harder and more complicated. The international monitors now asked them to provide specific information about the relatively smaller number of individuals about whom they knew enough to recognize clearly the discrepancies in the responses. A simple denial no longer did the trick. The international human rights organizations registered the details of the cases of Reverend Mahdi Dibaj, Ali Akbar Sa'idi Sirjani, Faraj Sarkuhi, and Daryush Foruhar, to mention only a few.

New Diplomatic Initiatives

The abatement in massive political executions offered the diplomats an opportunity to change the Republic's unfavorable image in the world—or at least they hoped so. The officials in the Foreign Ministry were long aware that their previous positions were untenable. The fact that the Islamic Republic continued to be under the UN Commission's special procedure cast a shadow over the self-projected image of the Islamic Republic as a paragon of Islamic morality and ethics. Perhaps the diplomats also considered it a professional defeat for themselves. An official book describing the Islamic Republic's interactions with the Commission repeatedly referred to the UN condemnatory resolutions, indicating where the diplomats' sensitivities lay.[1]

The Foreign Ministry officials needed the cooperation of Ayatollah Yazdi, the Head of the Judiciary and a ruthless defender of the clerical system. Returning to Tehran in the fall of 1989, the Ambassador to the United Nations explained to Yazdi the need for a new policy of cooperation with the United Nations, especially in the area of human rights.[2] Yazdi appointed his lay deputy, Dr. Hossein Mehrpur, to attend the UN sessions and become familiar with Iran's case in the Commission and the covenant-based Committee (Chapter 17).[3]

One diplomat told Galindo Pohl that the end of war with Iraq placed the government "in a better position to turn its attention to the question of human rights."[4] One can also see a connection between the new diplomatic initiatives and the cleansing of the prisons in the massacre of 1988 and the subsequent amnesties. Whatever the link, in 1989 the diplomats trumpeted the news of the amnesties for 2,500 political prisoners. They claimed that only 900 political prisoners remained in custody by late 1989.[5] As we have seen, the authors of the prison memoirs who were in prison at the time duly noted the amnesty. In the light of what we know about the new diplomatic initiative of 1989, Raha's puzzlement about the prison authorities hastily sending prisoners home may no longer appear puzzling.

If the diplomats could show that in the 1990s the human rights "situation" in Iran was no worse than in other countries in the neighborhood, then all the denials they had asserted for the 1980s would appear credible.[6] They could conveniently attribute the previous allegations to the fabrications of the terrorist groups and the manipulations of "certain malignant Western sponsors" of resolutions against the Islamic Republic of Iran.[7] Hopefully, they would not have to appear periodically in front of the Commission on Human Rights.

Mehrpur and the Foreign Ministry officials also prepared and submitted the long-delayed report to the Human Rights Committee, the implementing organ of the Covenant on Civil and Political Rights. The imperial government of Iran ratified the Covenant in the spring of 1975, and it did so without offering any reservations. The Islamic government did not revoke the international treaty. It was therefore legally obligated to comply by submitting the required periodic reports to the Committee. It seemed that the officials had come to a tentative understanding that the Covenant did not, in its most important provisions, contradict Islamic principles—all on paper. They could point out that the Constitution of the Islamic Republic enumerated many of the rights in the Covenant. Of course, they conveniently forgot that the clerics restricted the application of these rights by placing Islamic qualifications on them. "Based on this position, it was decided to prepare the second periodical report and defend it accordingly."[8] They submitted 262 paragraphs to the UN office in Geneva on May 22, 1992. The Committee considered this report in three sessions, and its recommendations to the government were similar to what the Special Representative had already recommended.

The new policy of active engagement somewhat changed the previous hostile rejection and refusal to cooperate with the Human Rights Committee and the Commission on Human Rights. It also further politicized the process and added new confusion, making Galindo Pohl's task even more difficult. The previous policy of rejection and denial was less complicated and easier to dismiss as deceitful. An important part of the new initiative was to grant Galindo Pohl's long-standing request for a visit to Tehran. The first two visits took place in 1990, January 21–28 and October 9–15. His third and final visit came in 1992.

The new diplomatic initiatives showed some novel features. The first thing the officials intended to do was to present their own account of the Islamic revolution and the Republic. This clerical historiography would not only exonerate the clerics of all charges of human rights violations but also present them as the true victims of so many evil forces in the contemporary world. During his first two visits, Galindo Pohl often listened to the officials, who faithfully followed the official narrative, which offered him a distorted picture of the political events that had mired their Republic in blood since 1979. They desired to elicit sympathy by reciting the problems faced by the revolution and the difficulties the Islamic Republic experienced in the international community. Of course, they did not say that many of these problems were of their own making, nor did Galindo Pohl remind them.

Deputy Foreign Minister Manuchehr Mottaki lectured "that terrorism had begun one month after the Revolutionary Government had come to power." He recited the official titles of all clerics and their lay protégés who fell victim to terrorism.[9] Later, he observed that many governments violated human rights around the world. Those violations often followed certain policies adopted by the top leaders. However, he hastened to add that the Islamic Republic did not belong in such company; rather, it belonged to "those countries which occasionally commit a few violations."[10] The clerical Intelligence Minister, Ali Fallahian, said that the function of his ministry was "to prevent and bring to light cases of espionage and to preserve the culture and integrity of the Iranian nation."[11] Galindo Pohl did not write what he thought of the Intelligence Minister preserving the culture and integrity of the nation. Fallahian, who was directing the state terrorism's killings in and outside of Iran, even attempted to redefine the Special Representative's mandate. "The Special Representative should focus the attention of world public opinion on the acts of aggression committed against the Iranian nation and adopt a clear stance denouncing and condemning acts perpetrated by terrorist organizations."[12]

Mehrpur, the Judiciary's liaison with UN human rights organizations, spoke of "the publicity campaign being waged abroad against the government of the Islamic Republic of Iran."[13] Ayatollah Ahmad Jannati, later the hidebound defender of the *hezbollahi* vigilantes, conferred his self-serving insight: "The Revolution that occurred in Iran has been under constant threat from those who wish to destroy it. It is difficult for those who live in a peaceful environment to understand this situation. As long as these points are not understood, it will be impossible to solve the problem."[14] Judicial authority Ayatollah Morteza Moqtada'i reiterated the same complaint.[15]

Perhaps diplomatic discretion prevented Galindo Pohl from pointing out the fallacies of the official narrative. The counternarratives of all oppositional groups and Iranian intellectuals, as well as western academics, often begin with Khomeini's deliberate plans to establish his Shiite theocracy, despite serious opposition and regardless of the predictably high cost. There was an element of incongruity between the clerics' posture of being aggrieved (*mazlumiyyat*) and the political reality of the 1980s, when they were the most aggressive actors in the political drama. The clerics continued brewing conspiratorial theories, forgetful of the fact that the Ayatollahs were no longer a politically irrelevant religious caste, surviving in a state that was no longer attuned to their dogmas and was often dismissive of their social significance. The clerics had unleashed an act of such political aggression as to be unrivaled in the modern history of Iran. Yet they continued to project fragility, as if they were truly menaced by a multitude of internal and external enemies—and not themselves menacing. The mullahs continued using the aggrieved language that was their vocational trademark.

During Galindo Pohl's first visit to Tehran, Interior Minister Hojjat al-Islam Abdollah Nuri lamented the fact that the record of the Islamic Republic was being scrutinized, while other countries escaped unscathed. Were there any problems in the early years of the revolution with reference to human rights violations in Iran? Nuri characterized them as "many problems of public order." He asserted, however, that "the security and confidence of citizens has now been restored. Islamic law and the government of the Islamic Republic of Iran respect human dignity and have organized the institutions of the Islamic Republic of Iran on the basis of that essential principle."[16] Nuri could not imagine that one day he would become a dissident and be convicted by one of those institutions (Chapter 14). In an understatement of the year, the President of the Supreme Court informed the Special Representative that in the early years of the revolution "some abuses were committed." He gave no further explanation, nor was one demanded, concerning the nature of those abuses. Who had been responsible for them? Did the government hold anyone accountable? The Special Representative did not ask. The Ayatollah added, however, that established institutions such as the Judiciary are "functioning normally." The regime was attempting "to remedy shortcomings and errors in the enforcement of the law."[17]

The Minister of Justice repeated the official line that the government did not prosecute anyone for holding a religious or political view; it brought to trial only those individuals who had broken the law. He further claimed that the record of execution under the Islamic Republic was much better than that under the Shah's regime; he complained about the "grossly exaggerated" figures for political prisoners and executions that Galindo Pohl presented in his reports. He wanted to inform the Special Representative that the enemies of the Revolution supplied the UN with erroneous information. "These figures are wrong and they are a manipulation for propaganda purposes."[18] The Minister could not appreciate the irony of his comparison between the figures of human beings executed under the two successive regimes. Most likely he had believed the inflated numbers that the Shah's opponents threw around to be a true measure of political executions in the 1960s and 1970s.

Presenting the Outlawed Political Groups as the Only Human Rights Violators

Apart from these self-justifying complaints and mostly empty promises, the government made a shift in its tactics. It discreetly dropped the two previous preconditions for cooperating with the Commission. More accurately, it no longer insisted on the first precondition on Baha'is and added a new dimension to the Mojahedin precondition. The diplomats had realized that the regime would have to change its openly repressive policy toward the Baha'i community if the rulers ever wished to achieve a measure of normalcy in their international relations, especially with the Commission and its European members. The government began to be much more careful in its handling of that persecuted religious community. The new policy removed the most odious pressure and tried harder to conceal the less egregious acts of persecution.

As for the second precondition, the diplomats still insisted that the Mojahedin should be "excluded as a source of information from the fact-finding and information-gathering system of the Commission on Human Rights."[19] But that demand was no longer a precondition for cooperation. The new policy was to reverse the human rights situation in Iran by making the militant opposition organizations—especially the Mojahedin and the Kurdish groups, both of which were by then marginal and mostly based abroad—as the principal *violators* of human rights in Iran.

The Mojahedin's incursion from Iraq into western Iran in the summer of 1988 gave the officials an excuse to further discredit the testimonies of its members who had suffered human rights abuses in Iran. Thereafter, the Mojahedin members were not only "terrorists" but also "war-time traitors," conducting military operations from enemy territory (Iraq) and "treacherously" engaging in espionage activities for the enemy. The officials now presented them as murderers of "thousands of defendants of their own country and fellow countrymen.[20] The diplomat Muhammad Ja'far Mahallati denounced "this petty group's activities," which "are neither political nor confined to a party or legal framework," as if the regime allowed any independent political activity to take place legally. He added that the Mojahedin had launched "joint military operations along with our enemy" and committed treason by espionage "against our national security." He asserted that the organization "has assassinated the President of the Republic . . . as well as tens of thousands of ordinary people."[21] A "petty group" capable of assassinating tens of thousands of people! The opposition groups were not alone in adding zeros to the numbers of their imprisoned or executed members.

Facing a mountain of allegations and considerable evidence that the international monitors had accumulated since 1981, the regime's spokesmen now presented themselves as human rights champions. Once more they announced their intention to strengthen the UN human rights regime: "The representative of the Islamic Republic of Iran said that it was absolutely necessary to establish the responsibility of groups and organizations which . . . carried out activities and committed offences that comprised violations of human rights and to hold them accountable for their acts. In his view, that very important matter had not received appropriate consideration from the United Nations."[22]

Creating "Nongovernmental" Delegations and Groups

Presenting the opposition, particularly the Mojahedin, as the sole violators of human rights in Iran, the regime's diplomats turned the table on the Special Representative by bringing "delegations" of Iranians to Geneva to give testimonies to that claim. Abusing the language of human rights, the agents of a theocratic regime named their first dispatched group the "Special Human Rights Delegation." These delegations periodically showed up at the UN Human Rights Centre in Geneva, expecting the Special Representative to interview them. The government also sent a number of written reports on the Mojahedin's violations of "the rights of the people of Iran."

In the first meeting with a five-person delegation on July 17, 1989, three individuals claimed that the Mojahedin had killed their family members. The government could present any Revolutionary Guard who had lost his life in confrontation with the radical groups, especially the Mojahedin and the Kurdish guerrillas, in the early 1980s as a victim of antigovernment terrorism. One woman said that the Mojahedin assassinated her son and then killed her husband two years later. She gave no date for these assassinations. Other members told equally painful stories. The other two men introduced themselves as former Mojahedin members who saw the true light of Islam and the terrorist nature of the Mojahedin Organization.[23]

Apart from plausibility, the reported killings seemed to have taken place during the bloody period of 1980–81, when the new rulers were tightening their grip on Iran and mercilessly decimating the Mojahedin and all other organized groups. Some stories strained credibility with respect to possible motives for the enumerated murders committed by an organization whose survival was gravely threatened. An older man told the story of his dentist son, whom the Mojahedin assassinated. The father was not clear about the reason, but he thought it had something to do with his son's offering dental treatment to individuals "the Mojahedin considered as their enemies."[24] Again, he offered no date. The diplomats expected the Special Representative to believe that the Mojahedin ordered its otherwise constantly hounded members to go out and kill a dentist because he treated their enemies.

Galindo Pohl listened to many ex-Mojahedin readily denounce the organization as terrorist. One man said that he realized his error in time. As he was going to a political demonstration, the Mojahedin leaders told him to arm himself and use the gun at his discretion. He went on to say that at the time of his active involvement with the organization, "he participated in the kidnapping and torture of three persons." Wanting to help the Special Representative to gain a true measure of the Mojahedin activities, he offered his estimate that some 57,000 persons lost their lives during the Mojahedin incursions into Iran.[25] He did not explain how he was in a position to know such exact information, nor did Galindo Pohl ask.

The last person in the delegated group offered the most incredible story.

If Galindo Pohl wanted to know what happened to political prisoners in Iran, he better examine what happened to him. As an active member of the Mojahedin, this "witness" said, he participated in armed struggle before and after the revolution. At the time of his arrest, he occupied a high position, responsible for two hundred members. Arrested in the house that he used as a base for armed operations, after a few months in prison, he received a trial. Of course, "he could have had legal counsel, but he chose not to, as he recognized he was guilty of the criminal charges against him." Upon his release, the only condition that the authorities demanded was that he report to the prison once a month. His family suffered no repercussions, and the authorities left his home untouched.[26] It seemed that the diplomats assumed that the government's stories about political prisoners would sound more credible if the ex-prisoners repeated them. It is against this background of official misinformation that the value of prison memoirs becomes apparent.

It is not that the Mojahedin were incapable of murdering the Revolutionary Guards during their suicidal confrontation with the regime in 1981–82. The irony was that the government accused the Special Representative of wrongdoing by collecting allegations from members of the Mojahedin who could not be trusted. Now the government displayed ex-members who had changed their views in captivity and remained under the regime's control to validate the government's credibility and to counter the charges of human rights violations. The diplomats expected Galindo Pohl to believe those ex-members who repented in captivity, but not those members who were free, living in Europe.

This was the first time that the Special Representative was looking at the repentant ex-prisoners, without, of course, being fully aware of the painful process through which the prison officials had turned the young revolutionists into docile *tawaban*. It was as if the ex-prisoners were delivering to Galindo Pohl a second reading of their gory confessions-recantations in prisons.[27] The testimonies were coming from a government that paraded its political opponents in televised broadcasts.[28] Again, the prison memoirs offer glimpses of relevant information. Ghaffari reported that during his last months in prison in 1990 the interrogators pressured him to write a letter to Galindo Pohl. They believed that his Ph.D. degree from an American university and his ability to write well in English would add a measure of credibility to such a letter. They asked him to explain how well the authorities treated him in prison and to condemn the political groups "that have destroyed" his life.[29] Had he agreed to write such a letter, the diplomats would have presented it as the genuine testimony of an ex-prisoner.

Shortly after the first dispatch of government witnesses, Muhammad Hossein Lavasani, Deputy Foreign Minister, forwarded a letter to Galindo Pohl, stressing the "significance" of his meeting with the "special human rights delegation." He referred to the individuals he had dispatched to Geneva as "messengers," bearing the testimonies of "numerous bereaved fathers, mothers and wives in Iran." "With the sincerest sentiments and while still suffering from pain and distress caused by the violation of the most fundamental rights of their dear ones, that is, the right to life, each one of them revealed undeniable cases that demonstrated the savage nature and cruelties of terrorists."[30] His concern for the right to life would have been touching, had he not been trying to conceal the human rights violations of the clerical state he served.

After the debut of "the human rights delegations," the regime began creating "nongovernmental organizations." Their success, as far as the Islamists were concerned, was in the confusion that they were capable of adding to the monitoring process. The discordant chorus of claims and counterclaims created a bewildering mixture of truths, half-truths, and lies. Under such conditions and in the absence of domestic governmental accountability, the Special Representative could not arrive at a clear conclusion, especially with the meager research assistance and other resources the UN made available to him.

During Galindo Pohl's first visit to Tehran in January 1990, the Islamist officials continued their efforts to turn the Mojahedin into the main object of the Special Representative's inquiry. In doing so, the clerics showed their penchant for public spectacles. Politicizing the process further helped to increase the already apparent sense of confusion, if not desperation, among the international observers. This time the government presented its witnesses in mob actions. Galindo Pohl had already announced his desire to receive oral testimonies from aggrieved Iranian citizens. On January 22, the bewildered Special Representative saw a "tumultuous" crowd blocking the entrance to the UNDP office, which housed his mission. He noted that the government-sponsored witnesses "impeded the access of witnesses who had previously asked for appointments." The crowd followed him to the hotel, "so that it became impossible to hear all those who had wanted to see him." The disorderly crowds wanted the Special Representative to hear their testimony about Mojahedin crimes, and Galindo Pohl felt obliged to hear them.[31]

The government-sponsored crowd and the activities of security agents overwhelmed those Iranians who were the victims of the state's violations of human rights. One such person was the bereaved wife of an ex-prisoner who had been executed in the summer of 1988. She was among a group of mothers and wives who came to present their complaints to the Special Representative. The women were harassed and detained as they gathered near the UNDP Office. The security agents did not arrest them but told them to report to the prosecutor's office later. She believed that the authorities waited until the Special Representative left the country to summon them for further intimidation.[32]

The government witnesses repeated stories similar to those others had offered earlier in Geneva.[33] In one interesting encounter with four repentant

Mojahedin members, one of them passed a note to the Special Representative, informing him of the government's deception and that he had been forced to testify the way he did. The note added that "many ex-prisoners had been induced by the authorities to make similar statements under threat of execution."[34]

After Galindo Pohl's first visit to Iran, the government continued sending witnesses to Geneva to testify about their "personal experiences." On February 23 and July 12, 1990, the witnesses were mostly members of the Organization for Defending Victims of Violence, the first government-sponsored "nongovernmental organization." On July 12, the regime even managed to produce an ex-Baha'i, who asserted that Baha'is were totally free and experienced no discrimination in education at any level, including universities. "Indeed, he said, it was better to say you were a Baha'i to get work or get a passport more promptly."[35] These assertions were untrue.

When Galindo Pohl again visited Tehran in October 1990, at the request of the Foreign Minister he met with a number of "nongovernmental organizations," including the Organization of Iranian Women, whose representatives assured him that "women enjoyed freedom in absolute terms without any limitations." Not only had women "freely chosen the law of Islam" but they seemed not to get enough of it, since they complained that "not all Islamic rules were as yet fully implemented." They dutifully repeated the clerical position that it was "a cruelty to pretend that men and women are equal, since the two sexes had very distinct characteristics." Other governmental "nongovernmental organizations" presented themselves as representing Iranian "Workers," "Victims of Violence," "Families of Martyrs," "Teachers," "Writers," and even "High School Students." Like the Iranian hawkers of secondhand goods, they all recited the positions already repeated by the clerical power holders. The Association of Families of Martyrs advised the Special Representative to "reaffirm the specific rights of the martyrs of terrorism." It also offered information on Iranian Baha'is, accusing them "of financially supporting the State of Israel."[36]

Despite the inherent problem of credibility associated with the stories offered by the ex-prisoners who had repented in captivity, Galindo Pohl felt compelled to give them some sort of recognition. This was in part indicative of the considerable degree of confusion that the government created in the monitoring process. Before receiving an invitation to go to Iran, the Special Representative was perhaps anxious not to undermine the prospect for what he hoped would be an imminent visit. Not wanting to anger the regime's officials, he took a middle position, as if the state and an armed opposition in exile were equal players in this deadly game of human rights violations. Galindo Pohl observed: "Just as the deposition of witnesses is not to be discounted because of the political position of the organization promoting their appearance, nor can the testimony of those who have appeared through the offices of the Government of the Islamic Republic of Iran be rejected, because it is not a question of statements by one or other of the interested parties but of individuals relating their personal experience." [37]

This was a diplomatic contrivance, since a critical aspect of the personal experience of the government's witnesses was their captivity and almost certain forced repentance. Moreover, some of the testimonies from government witnesses emanated not from their own personal experiences but from official scripts.

Nowhere did Galindo Pohl comment on the obvious fact that the "nongovernmental organizations" that paraded their witnesses in front of him were entirely government creations. He took cognizance of reports from witnesses, nongovernmental organizations, and "other independent sources confirming torture." He added: "On the other hand, some of the witnesses heard, when relating their experience in Iranian prisons, had stated they had not been subjected to ill-treatment or torture. In conformity with that testimony, some prisoners are apparently not so badly off in some prisons, but, of course, this testimony does not invalidate that of less fortunate persons, perhaps much more numerous, who were very badly treated in those prisons." [38]

The phenomenon of the *tawaban*, as amply described by the prison memoirs, explains convincingly why those "witnesses" offered Galindo Pohl a favorable picture of their incarceration. In this light, his picture of bad and not-so-bad prisons appears simplistic.

At the end of this particular discussion, Galindo Pohl gave a lesson to the diplomats on the fundamentals of human rights, perhaps trying to remind them that they represented a state that had ratified the Covenant: "Human rights . . . remain integral in extreme emergencies, even in those that endanger the existence of the nation itself, and admit only of the restrictions expressly laid down in the International Covenant on Civil and Political Rights. . . . Moreover, it is precisely in emergency situations, even acute emergencies, that adherence to human rights and their careful and constant application is most necessary." [39]

Nevertheless, the government's strategy to divert Galindo Pohl's attention from the state's human rights violations appeared partly successful, at least in the eyes of the diplomats, as shown through their writings in Persian for the domestic audience. As Galindo Pohl observed, during his visit to Tehran, terrorism "featured a great deal in the statements by Iranian officials and many witnesses." [40]

A careful reading of the UN reports will show that the officials' creativity in diversion somehow compounded Galindo Pohl's task. This official muddling made it harder for the international observers to establish a clear responsibility for the state's violations of human rights. On the one hand, Galindo Pohl faced a state that was a signatory of the Covenant on Civil and Political Rights. On the other hand, state officials inundated him with reports of real and fabricated atrocities by an armed political insurgency that the regime had largely driven out of the country and thus was no longer a weighty factor in domestic politics. The accusations and counteraccusations by state officials and Mojahedin supporters might have made it appear that there were two insurgent rivals engaged in internecine warfare. Galindo Pohl must have felt that these two sides offered mirror images, the allegations of each validating those made by the other. If he was supposed to believe that the Mojahedin were capable of committing horrendous crimes, he could hardly be expected to believe that similar acts were beneath the dignity of the Islamists in power. But the clerics wielding the state's repressive apparatus were obviously far more powerful and dangerous in seeking the annihilation of their nemeses.

In an atmosphere already saturated with allegations, the rulers introduced a heavy dose of accusations, which "private citizens" presented to the Special Representative. Maurice Copithorne of Canada, who succeeded Galindo Pohl in 1995, expressed his view that "the politicized tone of much of the dialogue is so pervasive that human rights are in danger of becoming a vehicle rather than an end in themselves." [41] The government not only contributed a lion's share to this murky state of affairs but was also its main beneficiary. Overall, it was a testimony to Galindo Pohl's competence that they did not succeed in totally distracting him by their smoke screen. Although the official guilefulness managed to distract him temporarily, Galindo Pohl's subsequent reports established a new and extended list of human rights violations in the Islamic Republic of Iran.

We should avoid juxtaposing an armed opposition group and a state in evaluating a state's record of human rights violations, especially a state that is a signatory to the International Covenant on Political and Civil Rights. The Covenant defined the limited circumstances under which a signatory state may derogate from its treaty obligations. The government must, moreover, declare the existence of such a state of "public emergency," allowing the international human rights community to evaluate the credibility of that claim.

Eventually the flurry of activities aimed at turning the outlawed political groups into the primary violators of human rights subsided. The maturing bureaucratization process reduced the tendency to create ad hoc "nongovernmental organizations" or send "human rights delegations" to Geneva to counter the charges of violations. As will be shown in Chapter 17, the different branches of government created three bureaucratic human rights organizations in the second half of the 1990s. Their task was less to place blame on the Mojahedin than to project the sincerity of the regime as an upholder of the Islamic version of human rights for the country and the world.

Chapter 12

The Special Representative's Meetings with the Judiciary and Security Officials

Reynaldo Galindo Pohl visited Tehran three times between 1990 and 1992 and met with clerical jurists and the security officials in charge of the Intelligence Ministry and Evin prison. They failed to convince him to recommend to the UN Commission on Human Rights the removal of Iran from its special procedures of public scrutiny.

UN Visits to Evin Prison

With an uninterrupted history from the Shah's regime to that of the Ayatollah, Evin prison has carved a place for itself in the world's prison literature. Galindo Pohl's visit to Iran would have been incomplete without a tour of the prison, where he met the infamous Assadollah Lajvardi, by then promoted to director general of all prisons in Iran. At the gate, Galindo Pohl received a taste of Lajvardi's theatrics, one of the most grotesque moments in his visit to the land of the Ayatollahs. A docile choir of repentant prisoners, accompanied by a small band playing an odd assortment of musical instruments, sang an Islamic revolutionary song welcoming the UN delegate. It was probably the band of *tawaban* singers Azadi contemptuously referred to in his memoirs. Perhaps the seasoned Galindo Pohl saw it as pleasant chicanery. In front of a prison well known for its bloody past, it must have been a disquieting spectacle for the well-informed international observers, some of whom may have recalled the agonies of all the tortured men and women who had passed through that gate since the Shah's time.

It looked as if the entire young radical population of Evin had vanished. Lajvardi did not allow Galindo Pohl to see the young prisoners remaining from the first period. The repression of the first period had made the leftist opponents of the regime invisible in the larger society. Raha wrote in her memoirs that in the winter of 1990 she and other prisoners became aware that Galindo Pohl had visited their prison. Prison authorities moved them to a different ward, which they then concealed from the main corridors by building a wall, which explained the sounds of construction they heard. Raha's testimony points out an interesting dynamic: a state that commits human rights violations, though capable of stonewalling, is hardly able to conceal forever all information and evidence of those actions. Galindo Pohl could not meet Raha in Evin, although she had resolved that if he did she would inform him about prison conditions, regardless of the probable punishment. A few years later, when she was living in Europe, Raha met Galindo Pohl. He told her that at the time of his visit to Evin he had been aware that authorities had hidden some prisoners from his view.[1] In the prison, cleaned as much as possible of the most obviously incriminating prisoners and all traces of their previous existence, Galindo Pohl managed to collect evidence of torture (Chapter 4).

During his second visit to Iran, Galindo Pohl went to Evin prison again, without the welcoming fanfare of the singing inmates at the gates. Better prepared, he had collected information on twenty-six prisoners whose names he submitted to authorities a few days before the scheduled visit. "The Special Representative was told upon arrival at Evin prison on 13 October 1990 that, for various reasons, it was impossible to see all twenty-six persons. The Special Representative, therefore, handed to the authorities an additional list of six persons."[2] Prison authorities told him that two of the prisoners had been released, four were on "leave," two were kept in other prisons, and six could not be seen, "since their cases were still under investigation."[3] The last reason in particular appeared incredible to Galindo Pohl, and he expressed his view to the officials. He was allowed to see only two of the six prisoners whose names he had submitted in the second list.

Galindo Pohl was particularly interested in two groups of prisoners: the signatories to the critical letter drafted by the ex-premier Mahdi Bazargan and the individuals arrested in connection with Jamshid Amiri Bigvand. The prison officials presented only six of the first group. In his report, Galindo Pohl expressed his deep regrets for being unable to see everyone he wanted to interview.[4]

During his first visit, Galindo Pohl asked to see Roger Cooper, the Englishman incarcerated since 1985. The authorities refused. The prison warden would not present Cooper because he "was a self-confessed spy who was in solitary confinement." In addition, his "sentence had been handed down a month earlier and was currently being translated from Farsi into English." Galindo Pohl asked about the penalty specified in the verdict. One prison official told him that Cooper had been sentenced to ten years in prison; the warden's answer, however, was that "he was not sure exactly how many years he had received." The entire story was an instant fabrication by the prison officials, as Roger Cooper's account of his experience in the Ayatollah's prison later showed. The reference to translation was also ironic, as Cooper did read Persian and was asked, while in prison, to translate into English a book written by his main prosecutor, who requested his services.[5]

The case of Roger Cooper came up again during Galindo Pohl's second visit, and the Islamist jailers seemed unable to offer anything but misinformation. The warden of Evin said that Cooper's trial "was still pending." The Special Representative recalled that, on his first visit, prison authorities had told him that Cooper had been sentenced to ten years in prison and that his sentence was being translated into English. But the warden said that the trial was not over because the sentence had been appealed. The Special Representative said he did not consider this a valid reason for refusing to let him see Cooper, for the interviews were neutral and had nothing to do with the status of trials. The warden replied that a new accusation had been made against Cooper and another trial had begun, related this time to moral issues. He then confirmed that Cooper had been sentenced to ten years' imprisonment.[6]

During his final journey to Tehran, prison officials refused his request for a meeting with a number of prisoners on his list because those particular prisoners were still under investigation. He objected, since the reason offered by Evin's director appeared unconvincing. Judging from his report, the exchanges between him and the officials at Evin seem to have been tense.[7] Of those who were allowed to meet with Galindo Pohl privately, several prisoners said that they felt unsafe to speak with him or answer his questions. "Other prisoners whom the Special Representative had interviewed on previous occasions declared that their complaints had resulted in reprisals against them and in one case in a particularly heavy sentence compared to other cases in which the accusation had been identical."[8]

Discussions Meetings with the Judiciary Officials

Assuming that a major improvement in the workings of the justice system would have a positive impact on the human rights situation, Galindo Pohl paid considerable attention to the Islamic Judiciary. In his visits to Tehran, he met with a number of Ayatollahs in charge of its different branches. The regime's new policy toward the UN Commission coincided with a major reorganization of the Judiciary in 1989. The political fortune of Ayatollah Abdolkarim Musavi Ardabili declined, and he was removed from the Supreme Judicial Council. The Council itself was abolished. At the same time, the political fortune of Ayatollah Muhammad Yazdi, for whom the office of the Head of the Judiciary was created, was on the rise.

During the second visit, Galindo Pohl interviewed Ayatollah Yazdi, whose conservative and conspiratorial mind-set could conceive "justice" in a contorted way and only through highly politicized lenses. He showed no understanding of the link between justice and due process of law. He also exhibited ignorance of the modern notion of human rights.

Galindo Pohl presented Ayatollah Yazdi with a number of specific problems relating to due process of law. Many trials had been inappropriately conducted in prisons; many people had been condemned to death without the benefit of defense lawyers; and one who had been accused of espionage went through a trial, yet two years later he had not been informed of the sentence.[9] Avoiding the specifics, the Ayatollah's response was both instantaneous and predictable, often ruminating on empty generalities. He pontificated that "the interests of society must prevail over the interests of the individual." Galindo Pohl summarized the Ayatollah's next words: "The international community paid little attention to that principle because the issue of human rights had been politicized. Such politicization undermined the enjoyment of those rights. In eight years of war, the international community had never concerned itself with the crimes perpetrated against the Iranian people. He then referred to recent events in Palestine and to the [Persian] Gulf crisis."[10] The Special Representative must have felt bewildered by this kind of political exhortation in place of proper responses to his specific questions, even though the Ayatollah's points could have been raised in a different context.

In a meeting with Ali Fallahian, the Intelligence Minister, Galindo Pohl again focused on specific problems related to the Ministry's tasks. He inquired about "the role played by information or intelligence officers and agents in the trial of prisoners, chiefly in cases submitted to the revolutionary courts; the specific role of intelligence agents who worked with the prosecution and, particularly, their participation in interrogations; the hierarchical relationship between intelligence officers, Komitehs [Revolutionary Committees] and Pasdaran [Revolutionary Guards]; and the degree to which intelligence agents could act on their own initiative without express orders from their immediate superiors."[11]

Direct and honest answers to these questions would have revealed the true nature of much of the human rights violations in Iran. The answers, however, were all according to the official scripts, short on specifics and long on generalities. The clerical Minister depicted Iran as a country that enjoyed the kind of due process of law that could be the envy of the most democratic European countries. Judges who in many cases rejected officers' testimony and denied them "permission to arrest suspicious persons," he asserted, controlled the entire process. Moreover, it was not true that they used any means, including violence and torture, to obtain confessions. In emergency cases, such as when someone planted a bomb, they might take the initiative, but they must inform "the judge within 24 hours, and he must decide whether or not there are legal grounds for the arrest." He added that many of the intelligence agents had been dismissed or sentenced to prison terms.[12] None of these assertions was true, as demonstrated by the prison memoirs and by the reformist press in 1997–2000 (Chapter 13).

During the first visit, Galindo Pohl was particularly concerned about the slapdash procedure through which a person accused of a capital crime was rushed through the revolutionary courts. He raised the issue with the President of the Supreme Court of Justice, Ayatollah Morteza Moqtada'i, and with the Special Prosecutor for Drug Trafficking. The responses were mostly confusing. Different officials said different things. Galindo Pohl brought up the discrepancy by pointing out the fact that another high government official "had mentioned those time limits in a radio broadcast." The Special Prosecutor retorted "that not all high Government officials were well informed."[13]

In the meeting with the Special Prosecutor for Drug Trafficking, Galindo Pohl again discussed the need of the accused to have ready access to a defense lawyer. The Prosecutor informed him that in some cases, the defendant refused to have an attorney, and in other cases, lawyers refused defendants they considered indefensible. "Moreover, there was no sense of appointing a lawyer in cases of *flagrante delicto* in which the accused had confessed to the crime."[14]

Galindo Pohl belabored the points as if the problem were technical and not structurally inherent in a political system that was built to preserve clerical dominance. He lectured the Prosecutor, who probably listened with an outward expression of sincerity, as if the discussion were relevant to his political task.

> It was necessary to establish a procedure effectively to ensure without any room for doubt that no accused person, unless he himself was a lawyer, was without a defence counsel; that, on the basis of that principle, it should be considered that the right to a defence council could not be waived; and that, if a lawyer refused to take on a case, others should be chosen until one finally accepted. Although it might sometimes be difficult to find legal arguments for the defence, there were always humanitarian reasons for asking if not for acquittal, at least for a lesser sentence. The law should also take account of the position of lawyers who refused without good reason to be court-appointed defence council, for that was part of their professional function, just as doctors must not refuse to treat patients.[15]

This was again one of those surrealistic moments in the long discussion over the formality of law when the seemingly logical appearance of things stood in an incongruous relation with the hidden realities. The disjuncture was amusing. A proper legal term, *flagrante delicto*, stood in the place of a tortured confession. To continue the dialogue, the Prosecutor's claims had to be accepted at face value, as shown by the Special Representative's recommendations: the defendant refusing an attorney, the confessed criminals deserving to have a lawyer to plead leniency, lawyers violating the professional code. Torture and confession had no place in the abstract, legalistic dialogue, which had only a formal bearing on the well-known realities of the interrogation that had made an indelible mark on the prisoners.

However, that moment in the dialogue was as transient as it was devoid of reality. It should have been obvious to Galindo Pohl that the clerics' political imperatives had often taken precedence over law. This fact has influenced the conduct, attitudes, and expectations of all those who worked for the system, from its highest judicial authority to prison wardens. During the same visit to Tehran, Galindo Pohl interviewed a secular lawyer who reminded him how difficult it was "for attorneys to function effectively within a framework of illegality." He added that in the Islamic Revolutionary Court "no legal representation was possible and no appeals were admitted."[16] Another attorney and a former judge told the Special Representative that lawyers were not allowed to appear before the Islamic Revolutionary Courts. "But even in ordinary penal cases lawyers had to be very careful." The secular attorney "referred to the example of one of his colleagues who after having asked for an additional hearing in a suit was indicted and condemned for undue interference in the procedure."[17] Galindo Pohl was well aware of the background of the issue under discussion.

Notwithstanding the secular attorney's information, the Special Representative continued to present the problem in his report as if it were technical, assuming that by adding another rule in the books, the problem would be corrected.[18] Galindo Pohl could not have been unaware of the fact that in all likelihood the new rule could easily be ignored in critical political cases, just like all other constitutional guarantees.[19]

It is interesting to note again that during Galindo Pohl's visits the lay protégés of the ruling clerics presented a more moderate view on certain aspects of Islamic law that have proven problematic for human rights. For example, the archconservative Ayatollah Jannati was adamant in his defense of Islamic rules, often repeating the traditionalist position that international norms and laws cannot be accepted if they are contrary to Islamic principles.[20] In contrast, Hossein Mehrpour, the lay deputy to Ayatollah Yazdi, refrained from mixing legal infractions with sins and suggested the possibility of some reforms in Islamic judicial practices. He tried to placate the Special Representative by saying that Iranian "experts in charge of legislative reform have taken account of the legal opinions which the Special Representative has stated in his reports." He added that they were studying Galindo Pohl's recommendations "to determine whether it is possible to incorporate them in Iranian legislation."[21] He was just being polite, considering the abuses the Members of Parliament regularly flung at Galindo Pohl. What is even more revealing was that he was not totally truthful and was substituting his own desire for reality.[22]

As far as Galindo Pohl's clerical hosts were concerned, these legalistic discussions hardly constituted the pivotal axis around which they wanted to manage his visit. They did not allow the Special Representative to come to Iran to lecture them on due process of law; they mainly indulged him during those long, legalistic discussions. Their main goal was to turn Galindo Pohl's visit into a fact-finding mission on "the human rights violations committed by the terrorists." The clerics responsible for the judiciary devoted more attention to vilifying the "terrorist" organizations than to figuring out, with the assistance of the Special Representative, how to make the Judiciary function more effectively in protecting the rights of the accused.

The Special Representative Remained Unconvinced

Perhaps Galindo Pohl felt that his first visit to Iran was successful. He managed to conduct interviews with a number of politically moderate individuals whose testimonies he could reasonably trust. These testimonies reiterated the allegations he had collected outside Iran; they pointed to executions without due process of law, torture, trials in the absence of defense attorneys, and continued imprisonment even after a prisoner served the specified time.[23] "Reports of torture and ill-treatment during imprisonment continued to be received since the first visit of the Special Representative. . . . It was also alleged that mutilations and corporal punishment are being applied." [24] "Testimony collected privately and statements taken at Evin prison in the presence of prison officials again spoke of ill-treatment and torture." [25] These reliable testimonies also indicated that the government most likely did not execute political prisoners under false charges of drug trafficking.[26]

On the issues of executions and the absence of due process of law, especially for those who stood accused of drug trafficking, the officials left Galindo Pohl with the impression that his pleading with the clerical officials might produce some results. He informed the judicial officials that a policy of rehabilitation for the accused might prove more effective in the long run. He seemed to have believed the official assertion that no execution had taken place "in public for five months." But he added "that many persons, probably hundreds, are still awaiting execution," and he hoped that the hitherto "harsh policy could become a good deal less severe." [27] Soon after, however, he learned that the information given to him in Tehran, that the regime had not executed anyone in public, was inaccurate; a number of public executions had occurred.[28]

The regime's diplomats expected Galindo Pohl to return to Geneva convinced that some Islamic practices must be tolerated by the international community, since they were based on indigenous Islamic traditions, and that reforms in several areas of concern were under consideration. During his first visit, officials wanted him to believe that whatever violations might have taken place in Iran were unintended consequences of the two interrelated tasks they faced: overcoming constant foreign threats and subduing domestic terrorism.

Galindo Pohl's meeting with the Foreign Minister during his second visit was revealing. The Minister began by second-guessing the Special Representative, as if trying to "spin" his next report to the UN Commission: "The minister said he hoped that at its next session, the Commission on Human Rights would change its attitude to the Islamic Republic of Iran. Otherwise, a sector of national public opinion might interpret the official attitude of co-operation with the Special Representative and the Commission on Human Rights as a mistake. . . . If the Commission on Human Rights did not change its attitude to the country, some hard-liners within the country would argue that the conclusions of the Special Representative's reports and his visits to the country, as well as the voting within the Commission, were politically motivated." [29]

The Deputy Foreign Minister hammered on the same themes.[30] The Foreign Ministry officials were unambiguously telling Galindo Pohl that in return for the favor of allowing him to come to Iran for the second time and to visit Evin prison, they expected him to recommend that Iran be removed from UN special scrutiny. That would have been the end of his mandate as the Special Representative on Iran.

How could the Foreign Minister hope for such a thing? Like all bureaucrats serving authoritarian regimes, he wanted to focus Galindo Pohl's attention on the appearance of things rather than on their substance: the court trials and convictions, rather than the process by which the verdicts were reached; the confessions that justified convictions, rather than the concealed torture that elicited them; the visit to the prison, rather than what transpired during the visit, or what failed to transpire due to official subterfuge; and the promises of reforms on paper, rather than their implementation.

It appeared that the Islamists were culturally grandstanding, evidentially stonewalling, and cosmetically primping their laws and practices, painting a more humane face for their Republic, which they hoped Galindo Pohl would present to the Commission on Human Rights. But the report he submitted after his second visit to Tehran provided a more direct and less equivocal evaluation of the government's records: "The enormous quantity and variety of allegations and complaints received from very diverse sources, even allowing for the fact that they may contain errors or exaggerations, provide a credible factual basis for the belief that human rights violations occur frequently in the country and that government action to prevent and remedy such violations has not been sufficient to put an end to them." [31]

The diplomats were incensed by the report. Their official reaction was swift, and the attack on Galindo Pohl was *ad hominem*. On February 5, 1991, the diplomats sent him a letter that posed a number of polemical questions, the central point of which was to show that he had no "objective criteria" for recommending that the monitoring mandate be continued. In a meeting in Geneva, Syrous Nasseri, a Foreign Ministry official, described Galindo Pohl's latest report as "negative," with "various specific features which he considered to be lacking in balance." [32] The diplomats seemed to be arguing that the Special Representative could not make such a recommendation on the basis of his own reports, since the information gathered in those reports could not yield such a conclusion.

They also implied that the Special Representative could not properly be allowed to use his "personal judgment," and they wanted to know what criterion he used to make his recommendation. They suggested that since UN Special Representatives did not monitor most countries of the world, Galindo Pohl logically should have recommended the removal of that status for the Islamic Republic of Iran. The officials were in effect arguing that Iran's record had become "normal," no worse than those of other countries in the region. This was considered a logical conclusion based on the officials' assumption that they had accepted Galindo Pohl's recommendations and that "practical steps have been taken for their implementation." They continued to pretend that they had supplied enough replies "to the so-called allegations."[33]

In Galindo Pohl's view the government had failed to provide the detailed responses he had demanded for years. He continued sending letters of inquiries to the diplomats and reminded them that during his second visit in October 1990, the Deputy Foreign Minister, M. Mottaki, promised him "that investigations on the allegations transmitted so far were already under way." Galindo Pohl insisted that he wanted replies not only to the allegations he had submitted in 1990 but also to all allegations from previous years.

The Islamist diplomats wished to run away from the state's accumulated records. They demanded that the Special Representative base his recommendation only on the post-1989 human rights situation. The clerics had established their institutions and created a political system in which very few individuals dared to claim their rights. Galindo Pohl would not dismiss the history of egregious violations of human rights. Given his legal background and his commitment to human rights, Galindo Pohl could not simply recommend the removal of a state that was currently under scrutiny by the Commission on Human Rights.

If it was "unfair," as suggested by the diplomats, to have Iran under scrutiny and not other states with similar repressive policies, it was so only to the citizens/victims of those states. Galindo Pohl wrote: "The fact that a number of countries that ought to be under supervision are not is an interesting topic for debate, but the decision in that regard lies with the Commission on Human Rights and does not affect the human rights situation in the Islamic Republic of Iran, since it makes it neither better nor worse."[34] It would have been a forfeiture of moral and ethical responsibility to recommend the removal of such a state from UN scrutiny. The international comparative argument, placing the record of one violating state against another's, is a statist argument that makes a mockery of the Universal Declaration of Human Rights as the standard of judgment. Considering the Iranian victims of human rights violations, it becomes even less relevant. It was only fair not to let it off the hook until a meaningful reversal of policies occurred.

After four and a half years of monitoring violations and two visits to Iran, Galindo Pohl was in a position to write recommendations that were more comprehensive and thoughtful than anything he had hitherto written. He recommended that the government should take specific measures in fifteen areas that needed attention and reforms.[35] It appeared that he intended to remain focused on them in the months ahead by submitting any new allegations he received in the light of his recommendations.[36] The list was far more complete than the list of the 1980s, which covered only five categories of rights. Reflecting a better knowledge of the country's human rights situation, his new list covered almost all areas of human rights violations, including recommendations concerning the death penalty, torture, reforms in the administration of justice, equal treatment and equal rights for all citizens, due process of law, the right of association, and freedom of publication and other artistic works. It also recommended ways to improve respect for human rights, including legal procedure against agents and officials guilty of human rights violations.

Galindo Pohl's third journey to Iran in 1992 seemed to have added to his aggravation. He commented "that in most of the areas of concern to the Special Representative there had been no substantial progress since the last visit."[37] He went on to offer a negative evaluation of the lack of progress with regard to his list of fifteen recommendations. In certain key passages his language became less diplomatic. In his postvisit report, he reiterated the criteria for his evaluation. He would "go through each of the aforementioned recommendations that the Commission decided to use as a benchmark against which to judge the progress in Iran in applying international human rights standards. The considerations and observations deriving from the reports gathered over the year . . . are inserted after each recommendation."[38]

On January 20, 1993, Galindo Pohl met with Syrous Nasseri, Permanent Representative of the Islamic Republic of Iran to the United Nations office at Geneva. The diplomat complained, rightfully observing that Galindo Pohl had changed his "tone and position" in the 1992 report.[39] Therefore, the government gradually decreased its "cooperation" with Galindo Pohl, and when he requested a fourth visit that July,[40] the government of the Islamic Republic of Iran declared he was no longer acceptable. For a few more years, Galindo Pohl continued from Geneva and New York to monitor and report new violations. After nine years of admirable service to international human rights law, in March 1995 Reynaldo Galindo Pohl resigned as the Special Representative and retired to El Salvador.

Chapter 13

The Right to Freedom of Opinion, Expression, and the Press

During the 1980s, the UN Special Representatives did not create a separate category for this critical human right to freedom of opinion, expression, and the press, and they revealed almost nothing on its violations. An inert period of human rights violations is one during which no overt claim to rights is made and hence no open violation is reported. After the bloody suppression of the early 1980s, all appeared quiet on the secular front of the Islamic Republic, and the regime's secular outsiders did not appear in international reports in this category of violations, since the regime had eliminated all meaningful possibilities for their open participation in the national debates. In effect, the clerics had muffled the secular voices in the fields of politics and literature; those who tried to hide their voices in symbolism and allegory presented no serious political threat and were mostly ignored by the intelligence officials. The secular intellectuals and writers dared not apply for the needed permission to engage in open journalistic activities. An authoritarian regime overtly violates human rights if individuals claim them openly. Thus, in the period of inert human rights violations in the early 1990s, the cases that Galindo Pohl reported in this category could not be considered as a true measure of the human rights situation in the country.

In general, during the late 1980s and early 1990s, two small groups of writers and journalists still dared to claim cautiously their rights to freedom of expression and political participation, thus forcing visible violations. The first group were liberal Muslims—mainly the associates of Mahdi Bazargan, the former premier of the Islamic Republic—who originally supported the Islamic revolution. Ayatollah Khomeini grudgingly tolerated their marginal presence during the 1980s. The second raised within the system's own ranks but gradually became discontented because they lost their previous official positions or influence.

Thus, many of the restrictions noted by international monitors in the early 1990s related to those that limited the freedom of expression of these two groups. Almost no one uttered a word that the clerics could declare as "serving the enemies of Islam."[1] Galindo Pohl observed "that while the Iranian media do not lack variety, they are by no means free and that radio and television broadcasts are subject to extensive self-censorship and censorship."[2] The dissident voices of the second group accounted for that little variety in the early 1990s. Galindo Pohl quoted an interesting comment made by an insider, the editor of the semiofficial newspaper *Tehran Times*, on July 27, 1992: "Most newspapers were afflicted with self-censorship or with a kind of party and group vengeance because, after the victory of the revolution, officials in charge of the country's important newspapers were mainly comprised of two parts: Those who desired to use the newspapers as a ladder of success to reach higher state posts or those who left posts as ministers and top officials and fell in status and turned to the press to be present in the country's political-economic scene."[3]

Political Context of the Violations

Violations of the right to freedom of expression, as well as the closely related right to freedom of conscience, dominated the country's human rights discourse in the second half of the 1990s. To return briefly to the issues of authenticity and cultural relativism, this chapter will show that the state's claims to Islamic legitimacy were severely undermined by the mid-1990s, since the regime's façade of unity began to show serious signs of strains. The Islamic Republic of Iran, constituted as a religious/ideological state, now experienced serious religious/ideological confusion on critical issues.

The crisis in the religious state was indicative of a failure, and anxieties over this failure created the tense political climate for violations of the right to freedom of opinion and expression. More than fifteen years of clerical rule had passed, and the youth of Iran continued to drift away from politicized Islam. Evidence was everywhere; the secularists saw a poetic justice in the poignancy of the sense of failure expressed by the disappointed Islamists.

One Muslim journalist bemoaned the fact that the authorities had superficially divided the young generation into two groups of "*hezbollahi* and non-*hezbollahi*" (Islamists and non-Islamists), who confronted each other across the ideological divide. "What should be done?"[4] He directed the question to Ayatollah Abdolkarim Musavi Ardabili, who played a significant role in the first decade of the Islamic Republic but fell by the wayside in the 1990s. Carefully choosing his words, the elderly Ayatollah conceded that the number of "non-*hezbollahi*" was increasing. He then questioned the appropriateness of the division between *hezbollahi* and non-*hezbollahi* that he himself had helped to create. "The non-*hezbollahi* has not come from abroad; he belongs to this society." He placed blame on the tactics used. "I too did not like those arrests and those prosecutions. I always warned [them] not to rely on the sword, imprisonment, and exile."[5] Of course, Musavi Ardabili had never publicly expressed such sentiments when he was the Prosecutor-General in the Judiciary that brutalized the secular youth for much of the 1980s. He was not the only Ayatollah who felt he had failed to communicate with the youth.[6]

The youth were subverting the Islamic Republic. The Muslim intellectual Ali Hozuri, whose critical comments caused the banning of a magazine in 1998, observed sarcastically that the Islamic Republic created a new, non-religious generation. "We raised a generation who does not believe in us, and that was not a small task. We know that to raise devout human beings is hard, but to raise a generation who is uniformly devoid of faith is not easy either." [7] Without stating how he had arrived at the statistic, a clerical official reported to Tehran's City Council in July 2000 that 75 percent of the country's inhabitants and 86 percent of students did not perform their obligatory daily prayers.[8] The news would ring sadly ironic for the prison survivors of the 1980s.

However, the hard-line Islamists refused to look in a mirror and locate the cause of their failure among themselves. The enemy was always external. Thus in the 1990s, the central theme in the official propaganda of the hard-line clerics became that of Western cultural invasion (*tahajom-e farhangi*). Following the lead of the Supreme Leader, different authorities made numerous references to the culture war that the Western powers, especially the United States, had supposedly waged on the Islamic Republic. "The enemies of Islam want to make our youth indifferent, negative and pessimistic toward Islam, the Qur'an, and the rule of the Imams, and the efforts of the people and authorities must defeat this conspiracy." [9]

Like the battle against the insufficiently veiled women, the culture war appeared to be a losing arena for the clerics. As early as 1988, officials in the Islamic Cultural Propagation Organization were tacitly admitting failure for what they had hoped to be a new genre of arts and literature submissively following the dictates of politicized Islam. They, however, attributed the failure to attract the youth not to the message but to organizational ineptitude and lack of coordination between different state organs in charge of Islamic propagation.[10]

The officials pursuing Islamic propagation failed to appreciate that cultural habits denounced as un-Islamic dazzled and seduced; the mullahs, now endowed with guns and prisons, were unable to offer an attractive alternative. Some Ayatollahs attributed the problem to the lack of communication; other Ayatollahs saw it as the result of not using enough force. By the end of the 1990s, the latter were using force against the former and resorting to prosecution and imprisonment. The Islamic Republic, which began with a war against secularists, was entering the new century at war with itself. Its fate seemed to have been aligned with other ideological states of the twentieth century.

Against this foreboding background, many propaganda campaigns were launched to win a battle in a war that was already lost. To mention one, in 1994 the issue of an unhampered access to international satellite television became a major conflict among the factions within the regime, adding to existing social tensions.[11] The hard-liners managed to outlaw dish antennas in 1994.[12] The new law gave another task to the morality police: confiscating the dishes in the market. It also offered the unscrupulous agents of official Islam another opportunity for extortion. Galindo Pohl noted that the penalty for a repeat offender was three to six years in prison.[13] Few went to prison, many paid bribes, and most dishes remained operational in creative camouflage.

Targeting the *Digar Andishan*

By the mid-1990s, the new political development increasingly pushed the violations of the rights to freedom of opinion and expression from the inert state of the 1980s to the contested arenas of printed pages and Islamic prosecution. The number of individuals who felt ready to make discrete claims for their rights increased, creating a new environment for overt human rights violations.

The upholders of the Islamist paradigm disliked the prospect of hearing again publicly the detested voices of Iranian secularism, rising from beneath the lava of the Islamist volcanic eruption that seemed to have buried them in 1980–81. They viewed with extreme suspicion the secular intellectuals' loyalties to non-Qur'anic discourses. They considered the secularists as traitors and apostates, outside the faith community. The clerics had expected that the secularists would remove themselves intellectually from the path of the clerically envisioned Islamic redemption for the country. Ayatollah Khomeini had constantly denounced the "wielders of pen" who could not be allowed to publish unless they learned the values of true Islam. They did not. Their nonconformist behaviors in the mid-1990s constantly suggested that the Islamic communal solidarity Ayatollah Khomeini painfully advocated had failed to embrace the country's well-known literati. The younger ones were even more hostile.

The hard-liners who controlled the state's disciplinary institutions, cultural agencies, and the media coined the epithet *digar andishan* (literally, those who think differently) in the mid-1990s. This new pejorative word covered visual artists, novelists, poets, playwrights, filmmakers, and scholars—anyone whose artistic and literary works did not fit the mold of the Islamist ideology. The renewed attacks on the secular intellectuals was a testimony to their tenacious and annoying (to the mullahs) presence in the Iranian society. The epithet was damning; nevertheless, it showed a diminution of evilness in the real and potential enemies. In the revolution that had spent itself, the secular intellectuals were characterized as *digar andishan* and not as *mofsedin fel arz* (those who sow corruption on earth).

As the sense of failure became more acute and political conflicts intensified, this damnation was generalized to include people other than intellectuals. In the late 1990s, the hard-liners often spoke of "insiders" (*khudi*) and "outsiders" (*ghir-e khudi*) with an unmistakable assumption that the former are privileged over the latter in rights and freedoms.

The hard-liners had expected intellectuals and artists to devote their works to the furtherance of values supportive of the clerical rule. According to a cleric's characterization of the conflict, "Whatever God and his prophet have enjoined is value and whatever God and his prophet have prohibited is anti-value."[14] They saw the true Islamic arts and literature as a refined extension of the Shiite discourses, venerating the Imams and lamenting their tragic lives, all adorned with the necessary religious trappings. Always the nemesis of Persian poets, the mullahs, armed with Qur'anic certitude, posed as final arbiters of the works of imagination. They put restrictions on the creative genius of literary figures and artists and subjugated them to an outmoded, regressive standard of clerical judgment. The late secular novelist Hushang Golshiri recalled that a censor once told him: "We have inherited a house from the Shah. This house has a lavatory, and that is literature."[15]

On every occasion, the semiofficial press denounced the secular intellectuals not only for their secular worldviews but also for their "corrupt" lifestyle. For example, when one hundred of them wrote a letter to the Head of the Judiciary, expressing their concerns over the humiliating arrest of the popular writer Sa'idi Sirjani, the hard-liners referred to them as if they were a pack of narcotic-crazed debauchers, who moreover had the temerity to complain about Islamic justice.[16] The implied threats escaped no one.

Even more sinister only because of its outreach, the state-controlled television produced and broadcast in 1996 the infamous serial called *Hoviyyat* (Identity), in which the Islamic reformists were ridiculed and secular intellectuals were demonized. The secular Iranians saw it as a rather insipid ploy of intimidation, as it depicted the "intellectuals as social misfits or foreign spies."[17] As revealed later, Sa'id Imami, then Deputy Intelligence Minister and the mastermind of extrajudicial killings, was behind the despised television show.[18] As in other authoritarian states, the Intelligence Ministry was the country's cultural watchdog.

Resurfacing of Islamic Reformism

As explained in Chapter 2, the reemergence of the bureaucratic state and President Rafsanjani's desire for reconstruction and normalcy changed the political atmosphere. Rafsanjani's men found the dominant Islamist paradigm too restrictive, preventing them from reaching out to the youth and gaining their support for the state policies. While leaving the issue of political security in the hands of the Islamist commissars, the technobureaucrats wished to create a new climate more conducive to the state-directed developmental projects. The publication of a few journals, magazines, and newspapers, especially the daily *Hamshahri* (Citizens) by the reformist Mayor of Tehran in 1992, signified the opening of a crack in the regime's façade.

They initiated changes but failed to control the process for their own purposes. Others who did not share Rafsanjani's visions of the authoritarian state directing developmental projects renewed their activities with vigor. The majority of liberal Muslim intellectuals and politicians had failed to fade away. Moreover, they were joined by a new generation whose understanding of Islam clashed with the underlying premises of *velayat-e faqih* and the Leader's views.

At the same time, a significant return to the older trend of Islamic reformism enlarged the ranks of reformist Muslim intellectuals. As noted in Chapter 2, Khomeini had derailed the Islamic reformist movement. His revival of the obscure concept of *velayat-e faqih* went against the grain of Islamic reformism, which had tried to revalidate Islam by adopting modern political norms and institutions borrowed from the West. During the populist revolution of 1979, some reformist Muslims were both mesmerized and rendered politically impotent by Khomeini's enormous capacity for mass mobilization. However, his populism was authoritarian. Among the educated youth, almost all of the real and potential Islamic reformists rallied around Khomeini's antiliberal paradigm. Once he gained power, many of them suppressed their reformist thoughts, hoping to retain a presence within the regime. The philosophy professor Abdolkarim Sorush, who participated in the forced Islamization of universities under Khomeini, typified the young generation of Islamic reformists, who had temporarily submitted to *velayat-e faqih*. Less philosophical and more political, other men who formed the pro-Khatami movement in 1997–2000 were the former intellectual and journalistic storm troopers of *velayat-e faqih*. They continued to support, with varying degrees of intensity, Khomeini's regime until his death in 1989. In exercising expedient dissimulation when necessary, some had remained truthful to the Shiite tradition. Others had genuinely learned from the failure and changed their views.

The return to Islamic reformism was facilitated by the political development in the early 1990s. The radical Islamists (the Old Left) who had previously harbored state socialistic views shifted their positions, once the conservatives and Rafsanjani's pragmatists removed them from power after 1992. Awakened to the reality of the failure and unpopularity of *velayat-e faqih*, they returned to the basic premises of Islamic reformism. The collapse of the world's socialist movement helped in this transition, since the old Islamist Left was competing during the 1970s and early 1980s with the anti-free-market sloganeering of the secularist Left on behalf of the poor, popular among the revolutionary youth. The forced disappearance of the Iranian Marxist Left allowed them a breathing space in which they rediscovered the mundane ideas of tolerance, real political participation, and the rule of law.

In the mid-1990s, moreover, they had to adapt their "Islam" to their own latest discoveries from the West, concepts such as pluralism and feminism. They were up-to-date.

In the return to Islamic reformism, the writings of the scholarly cleric Muhammad Mojtahed-e Shabestari, who valiantly grappled with the notions of faith and liberty, gained popularity among a growing number of Muslim reformists.[19] Anyone who accepted his interpretations could no longer accept the Islamic validity of *velayat-e faqih*, since he rejected the notion that the Islamic jurists were entitled to make laws for the contemporary state. At the same time, Sorush was advocating a democratic Islam and urging the clergy to reduce their control over the political life of the country. The Western postmodern trend assuming different readings of the text reached the intellectual world of Islamic reformists. Sorush's works gave credence to the notion that historical Islam was the product of a particular reading, no more authentic than the one he was capable of offering. He had already asserted that only the individual could attain faith; therefore, there could be no collective faith. The assertion of private faith and different readings of Islam subverts the notion of the Islamic State formulating and implementing public policies according to Islamic principles. By the late 1990s, Sorush concluded that the clerics in power had turned the religious establishment into a despotic establishment—or created political despotism in the name of religion.[20] At the same time, daring Muslim journalists such as Akbar Ganji kept contrasting their modernist reading with the "fascistic reading of Islam." [21]

Of course, even without the fascism analogy, the notion of different readings of Islam infuriated the hard-line clerics, who had the necessary qualification to pass judgment on Islamic matters. Without mentioning Sorush, the Supreme Leader chided those lay intellectuals who were unjustly criticizing the clergy and "earning a living on Islam." [22] The Head of the Judiciary, Ayatollah Yazdi, expressed anger at those who had not been trained as ulema but presented themselves as authorities in Islam (*Islam-shenas*).[23] Of course, the Islamic reformists reminded the ruling clerics that the politicized Islam offered by Khomeini was itself a novel reading of the religion.[24]

In the forefront of the struggle against undue limitations on the press in 1997–2000 stood the new generation of Islamic reformists who had supported the Islamic Republic in the 1980s with the characteristic fervor of young radicals. By the mid-1990s, they had joined an amorphous band of graybeards, weary both of their own past radical shibboleths and of the Ayatollahs' empty promises. They had realized that their anti-imperialist posturing and flag burning activities in front of the U.S. embassy had done nothing to improve the country's rule of law or the worsening economic conditions.

The self-reflection of the former radicals turned Islamic reformists sounded touching. The daily *Salam*'s editor, Abbas Abdi, the former hostage taker, seemed to think about his own past when he observed: "Many individuals within the regime realized that they would get nowhere by physically eliminating others, by driving people to extreme opposition to the system, or by monopolizing power." He saw a change in the 1990s "from the discourse of black or white, zero or hundred, revolution and anti-revolution, to the discourse of gray areas, compromise and dialogue, tolerance and reform from within." [25]

Of all former radical Islamists, Akbar Ganji was perhaps the most thorough in "reconciling religion with modernity," for which he would pay a heavy price in prison. He had drastically scaled down his former ambitions "to create new kinds of human beings." [26] This reversed the main goal of the Islamists who criticized the Western-inspired "normal human" (*ensan-e normal*) and wished to create a new perfect human (*ensan-e kamel*) before considering his rights. By the end of the 1990s, Ganji associated such utopian views with the traditional religious paradigm "that revolves around duties." Discarding it, he was now willing to advocate "the modern paradigm that revolves around rights." [27] The "perfect man is non-existent among us, the fallible," declared Ganji. "Average human beings populate the entirety of human societies; all rulers from the highest to the lowest are average humans, and all governments are the governments by the average for the average." Earthly humans should not be sacrificed at the altar of the utopian ideologies. "The value of a human being is more than the value of an ideology." [28] In this perfect reversal, it appeared as though he were answering his own ideological teachers of the 1980s (see Chapter 1). Ganji called for democratic reform and transparency in government, which banned his paper and landed him in prison more than once.

The daily *Salam* was a representative of this radical Islamism gradually returning to Islamic reformism. It was published by the cleric Muhammad Musavi Kho'iniha, a radical Islamist in the 1980s. The former radicals who now advocated reforms had been ousted from positions of power and influence by President Rafsanjani in alliance with the conservatives in control of the Majlis and other institutions. However, in the second half of the 1990s, the outside reformers were in a tacit alliance with Rafsanjani's technobureaucrats. The latter were still authoritarian, only wanting to encourage active but controlled participation of educated Iranians in the reconstruction efforts.

Within a short period, several hundred publications appeared, covering a wide range of interests from sports to sciences and technologies. Although pursuing different, and often contradictory, political agendas, these publications advocated an expansion of the country's narrow and monotonous press.[29]

Thus, the mellowed Islamists began printing their updated versions of Islamic reformism in the pages of *Negah-e Now* (Mohsen Sazgara's platform), *Iran-e Farda* (1992, Ezzatollah Sahabi's paper), *Kiyan* (1991, Sorush's mouthpiece), *Zanan* (1992, a women's monthly, edited by Shahla Sherkat), and *Bahman* (1996, Mohajerani's paper). The bimonthly *Iran-e Farda* (Future's Iran) boldly presented the moderate views of men associated with *Nehzat-e Azadi Iran* (Freedom Movement of Iran), the late Mahdi Bazargan's organization, and emphasized the right to freedom of association, without which they were unable to reactivate their political group. *Kiyan* (Universe) became the main journal of Islamic hermeneutics, advocating the acceptability of different readings of Islam. Under Sorush's influence, its editors and contributors eventually argued for Islamic acceptance of the separation of religion and politics.

Against this background of misgivings and second thoughts, a major, though temporary, political realignment began to take shape in the second half of the 1990s. It placed the radical-turned-reformists, Rafsanjani's Islamic technobureaucrats, and the Muslim liberals (associated with the late Bazargan's Liberation Movement) in a tactical alliance against the hard-line Islamists. In turn, the hard-liners, supported by the Supreme Leader, responded aggressively to meet the challenges presented by this "unholy alliance." The hard-line writers associated with the Supreme Leader never ceased scolding their misguided brethren for betraying Khomeini's legacy.[30] The conservative *Resalat*, for example, accused the former firebrand Muhammad Musavi Kho'iniha, *Salam*'s publisher, of sacrificing *velayat-e faqih* on the altar of the Western philosophy of liberal democracy. He was doing so by arguing, in the pages of *Salam*, that the *faqih*'s right to power was bestowed on him by the people and that the limits on his authority should also be decided by the expressed wish of the people.[31] It was an accurate charge. Following its banning in July 1999, *Salam* included among its achievements the attempt to make *velayat-e faqih* function within the limits of law.[32]

With the approaching election of a new president in the spring of 1997, the hard-liners bitterly pointed out the convergent political views of the former radical Islamists (the Old Left) and the liberal Muslims. The daily *Kayhan*'s editor announced ominously that the political "line of the enemy is establishing a connection with some political trends within the regime." He criticized the positions taken by Behzad Nabavi, a former radical, as indicative of the joining of enemies and former friends.[33] *Resalat* lamented the fact "that a group of the insiders (*khudi*) expressed concerns about dictatorship, political monopoly, repression and stifled freedoms that were similar to those expressed by the enemies."[34] In 1998, the hard-liners might have been incensed by the former Islamists' attempt to reach out even to the secularists. The Islamic reformist editor of *Rah-e Now* (New Way) said that he and his colleagues did not determine their allies on the basis of their commitment to Islam. The new criterion was democracy: democratic "us" versus the antidemocratic "them."[35]

The newly invigorated conflicts within the ruling circles produced a political side effect. The secular *digar andishan*, watching the process with distrust, took their first steps toward claiming their right to freedom of expression. Amid the regime's discord, an opportunity presented itself to the secular outsiders: to extend the existing threshold for tolerating dissent, for discreetly expressing views that fell outside the bounds sanctioned by the clerics. A number of closet secularists (writers and journalists), professing a mild allegiance to Islam and/or the Islamic Republic, published their magazines. As the intellectuals began claiming their rights, new cases of human rights violations arose and were reported.

"We Are Writers"

On October 25, 1994, 134 intellectuals, mainly writers and translators, tested the limits of tolerance possible under President Rafsanjani's claim to normalization. They drafted an open letter, "We Are Writers," addressed to no particular authority, asserting the necessity for reactivating the Writers' Association and requesting an end to censorship. The right to freedom of expression had become the main demand in the Islamic Republic.[36] The letter became a watershed in the history of intellectuals' resistance to the theocracy. Other intellectuals and academics followed the tactic of writing open letters.[37]

The international human rights community noted with pleased surprise the appearance of "We Are Writers" and understood its importance. However, its significance for the history of human rights violations in the mid-1990s lay in the underlying fears of its drafters, in the circumstances under which it was drafted, and in the disturbing things that happened to its signatories afterward. The censor did not allow it to be printed in the dailies, although two magazines published it. Its publication by *Takapu* was one of the causes of its being banned, and *Gardun* managed to print it in the middle of an article written by one of its writers.[38]

The writers were anxious to protect themselves against the likely misreading of their intentions in issuing such a letter, since Islamists' intentional misreading was often followed by prosecution or the *hezbollahi* attacks. They were careful what to write; they were even more careful how to write it. In a text that contained only nine short, substantive paragraphs, they gave at least three paragraphs to reassuring everyone that their intentions were purely cultural and professional.

An unspoken fear became the subtext of "We Are Writers," as it made its way through preliminary drafts, collections of signatures, and the after-the-fact acrimony among its illustrious signatories. The fear of official prosecutions and the *hezbollahi* retaliations snapped the already frayed nerves. "Within a month, 10 of the 134 writers had officially withdrawn their signatures from the letter."[39] Also within a month, the official press agency printed a small news item, reporting the death in custody of the popular writer Sa'idi Sirjani. However, the first truly frightening news for the signatories came on October 24, 1995, when one of them, Ahmad Mir'ala'i, was discovered dead in an alley in Tehran. The suspicious circumstances under which he died were never clarified, and within a few years three more of the signatories were murdered. One of them, Muhammad Mokhtari, had already defined their lives as being lived in a "situation of anxiety."[40]

Despite the fear, the secular intellectuals and writers kept jabbing, prodding, and poking fun at the dominant paradigm. The more Rafsanjani's technobureaucrats advocated normalization and reconstruction, the more proponents of alternative paradigms agitated for their rights to freedom of expression. They could not allow Rafsanjani's normalization to gain credibility unless it also normalized the intellectual life to such a degree that the secularists could also breathe. It appeared as if the technobureaucrats knew that they could not claim full normalization without the secular intellectuals' tacit acquiescence. Paradoxically, any cultural, literary, or artistic endeavor had to receive the endorsement or participation of secular intellectuals, if it did not want to appear propagandistic. The hard-liners' incessant attack on Iran's secular cultural producers was ironically indicative of the fact that the secular intellectuals had remained, in many ways, the validators of literary and artistic works. They were still the real arbiters of society's creative cultural works.

What followed was a precarious political situation where a new crop of mainly secular publications was added to the already existing and expanding Islamic reformist ones. Journals like *Adineh, Jame'eh-ye Salem, Doniya-ye Sokhan, Gardun, Takapu,* and *Goft-o-Gu* published articles reflecting secular sensitivities and concerns. Their political articles used the allegorical and symbolic language that would be easily deciphered by middle-class readers, as well as by the intelligence officials who themselves were political pros. Significantly, *Goft-o-Gu* (Dialogue) was devoted to, among other reformist goals, a dialogue between the secular and Muslim intellectuals—a frightening aberration for the supporters of *velayat-e faqih.*

The Supreme Leader, Ayatollah Ali Khamenei, reminded everyone of the "Islamic Redline," setting the limits for the freedom of expression. In May 1996, he rejected the term that his associates had coined for the liberal Muslims and secularists. He asked his supporters not to call them *digar andishan,* since the term might imply that the regime was opposed to those who think differently. As far as he was concerned, freedom of thought existed in Iran. This was based on his Islamic assumption that a citizen was free to hold any views and opinions, so long as he did not express them in public. The reformers challenged this traditionalist Islamic view: "Freedom of thoughts without freedom of expression (writing and speech) has no tangible meaning. What is it good for if a human being is free in his privacy and in isolation from the rest of society to think in a particular way but is not free to share his thought with others?"[41] For the Leader, however, the issue was not about freedom of thought. "It was about contumacy (*anad*) and opposition." The dissidents were "tendentious," opposing the system and intending to harm it "to the degree that their courage would allow them." However, they were not "very courageous." He denounced them further by associating them with the previous regime. "Everyone must pay attention to the Redline," and beyond its limits no one could express opinions. Where was it drawn? He did not say. However, he indicated that it would not allow anyone to question the righteousness of the Islamic revolution, its principles, and the system of the Islamic Republic.[42] Of course, he would also be the final arbiter of who crossed the Islamic Redline.

The Chasm Separating Conservative Clerics and Secular Intellectuals

During the early days of the Islamic rule, Ahmad Shamlu, the most celebrated poet of modern Iran, expressed what he felt about new rulers aggressively imposing the ancient moral code, in particular, "smelling the mouth" of suspected alcohol drinkers. It reads in part:

> They smell your mouth
> To find out if you have told someone:
> I love you!
> They smell your heart!
> Such a strange time it is, my dear;
> And they punish Love
> At thoroughfares
> By flogging.
>   We must hide our Love in dark closets!
> In this crooked dead end of a bitter cold
> They keep their fire alive
> By burning our songs and poems;
> Do not place your life in peril by your thoughts!
> Such a strange time it is, my dear!
> He who knocks on your door in the middle of the night,
> His mission is to break your Lamp!
>   We must hide our Lights in dark closets![43]

During the second half of the 1990s, the chasm that existed between the clerics and the intellectuals revealed itself openly, as secular intellectuals cautiously began expressing their views in reformist publications. Everything that the intellectuals did displeased the clerics in charge of the Judiciary, the Majlis, and the Intelligence Ministry, causing many of the violations of the right to free speech.

For example, the Iranian cinema produced a number of internationally recognized films in the 1990s. The winner of the Palme d'Or at the Cannes International Film Festival in 1997, Abbas Kiarostami, was perhaps the most exciting of many culture producers pursuing a secular future for Iranian culture. His cinema, in the words of one eminent scholar, "puts forward a radically subversive reading of a cultural inhibition brutally institutionalized by a theocratic revolution."[44] The conservative clerics could hardly contain their disdain for the success of the filmmakers, perhaps the most seductive exponents of the secular paradigm. Ali Akbar Nateq Nuri, the Speaker of the Majlis, attributed their success at film festivals to the evil intentions of Western jurors who, in his opinion, granted prizes to the Iranian filmmakers because they presented values other than those espoused by the Islamic regime. Declaring the films worthless, even if they received prizes, he called upon the filmmakers to give priority to stories that would propagate the spiritual values of Islam.[45]

In the trial of the magazine editor Abbas Ma'rufi, the clerical judge of the Press Court wanted to know what his goal was in his writings, where he included "subjects related to sexual issues." He further demanded to know Ma'rufi's real aim in using "unethical words." The clerics' puritanical impulses often carried sexual undercurrents. Slightly baffled, the secular writer responded that if that perception were allowed to control the country's publications, no novel would ever be published in the country. Without the slightest sarcasm, he remarked that novels do contain words like "kissing" and that, without "a few words like that," there could be no stories.[46] Similarly, when the novelist Parsipur found herself again in prison in August 1990, she was charged, among other things, with the crime of writing a dialogue about virginity in her novel *Women Without Men.* After months in prison following her second arrest, an Islamic court considered her crime for writing about virginity and thus offending Islamic sensitivities of the *hezbollahi*; the judge also objected to the use of the word "whore" (*jendeh*) in a passage of another novel (*Dog and the Long Winter*), prompting the novelist to observe politely that a good novel must come close to the colloquialism used by common people.[47]

On the topic of authoritarian rulers selecting cultural themes for intellectuals and aesthetic inspirations for artists, it is appropriate to quote two of the intellectuals who were killed by intelligence agents in 1999. In an interview published posthumously, M. J. Puyandeh spoke at length about the world's intellectuals and the problems created by authoritarian regimes demanding that arts and literature follow their political dicta. "The dominant thought says that in this country a great revolution and a costly war had taken place. Then, it asks the artists to depict the war and the revolution, expecting them to transfer, immediately and without intermediaries, the present social phenomena into the works of art." This view "subjects the arts to the imperatives of power." He observed that "the greatest and the most extensive manifestation" of this official expectation came to "an absolute defeat in the Eastern Bloc."[48]

On the same subject, Muhammad Mokhtari, another talented intellectual whose life was cut short by the extrajudicial killings in 1999, observed that under the Islamic Republic, culture and propaganda had become one and the same thing. "In this way, priority is given to politics and not to culture." This meant "the *khudi* [insider] cultural producers who had accepted that priority would subordinate culture to politics and propaganda." The outsider cultural producers were "rejected and placed under restrictions." The cultural life of the country had been placed in the hands of the third-rate cultural officials who were opportunistically attuned to the political leaders' wishes.[49]

Puyandeh's and Mokhtari's words indicated the absence of a common discourse between the clerics who ruled the country and the intellectuals who, for almost two decades, had barely kept their heads above the muddy waters of politicized Islam. The clerics could not allow the freedom of opinion and expression that they demanded without undermining the foundation of the theocracy. That demand, costing their lives, partly defined the context of the violations of this right in the second half of the 1990s. Secular intellectuals were not alone in lamenting the subordination of culture. The more far-reaching among Islamic reformists also bitterly complained that culture had been reduced to propaganda.[50]

In the more open climate of Khatami's presidency, the dissident writer Mohsen Khalili criticized the Press Law in a way that was most revealing of the intellectual chasm that separated him from the clerics in power. It also revealed the type of issues that modern Iranian intellectuals had to grapple with under the religious state. The Law defined missions for the press, but to him the missions were confusing and contradictory. He explained that the Law made the press responsible for the "edification of public thought and opinion." He then asked: "What is the meaning of edification of public thought and opinion? How can we achieve it? Were the ongoing denunciations in the [semiofficial] press examples of that edification effort?" The law demanded that the press negate "the false and divisive political lines of demarcation among the people" and avoid "pitting the existing social strata against one another." Khalili asked: "What is the divisive line? What is a line of demarcation? How is its falsehood determined and by whom?" The law demanded that the press struggle against the colonialist culture and its manifestations such as prodigality, dissipation, and indulgence in luxuries. He asked: "What is the colonialist culture? Are there any concrete and agreeable meanings for prodigality, dissipation, and indulgence in luxuries?" The law demanded the propagation of the true culture of Islam. He asked: "Is there any consensus on the meaning of the true culture of Islam?" What does it include? Is the debate over the true culture of Islam reserved only for the qualified clerics? Can lay scholars and philosophers participate?

His answers were all inherent in the questions he posed. Nevertheless, Khalili concluded by saying that there was too much disagreement among Iranians, making the task of identifying the true culture of Islam impossible.[51] In the end, Khalili emphasized the fact that the institution of *velayat-e faqih* had introduced into the contemporary state the numerous disagreements that had existed in Islam, especially in the Shiite jurisprudence (*feqh*). Thus, in state affairs "we Iranians have become involved in theoretical disturbances and in endless, irresolvable disputations." [52] The last comments clearly violated the Redline.

In 1998, a young intellectual resorted to the allegorical and sarcastic prose that was a distinctive mark of Iran's political literature facing censorship. Appearing to address the Supreme Leader, he linked the necessity of freedom of expression to the cherished propensity of the modern mind to doubt. "Not knowing—and the curiosity to know—drives human beings to freedom," he observed.

That is why I ask and ask. However, you by yourself seem to know everything.
Incidentally, what is the shape of the question mark in your mind?
You still believe in that kind of certainty that died a long time ago, at least since Einstein.
In your mind, all roads end with you; looking at everything, you only see yourself. . . .
I ask, "What is freedom?"
You say "Shut up!"
I ponder where in history the thought process has been shut up, so that your attempt may succeed here.[53]

The secular commentaries in the examples described above enraged the hard-liners, who saw them as a frontal assault on the institution of *velayat-e faqih* and as insults to the divine convictions of the people. The hard-liners reinvigorated their attacks on secular intellectuals, and to a lesser degree on liberal Muslims. Vulgar, impudent, and almost thuggish, their words reeked with contempt and rude sarcasm. Scores of articles that depicted the intellectuals as pestilence polluted the pages of the semiofficial press.[54] The editor of *Resalat* thought that the dissident intellectuals did not belong to Iran. Their real "homeland" was the secular Western lands, to which they all will eventually escape.[55] They imputed sinister intentions to the intellectuals' words or mistakes. A lecture given by philosophy professor Sorush to a German foreign policy association was depicted as an act of betrayal, a sellout to the enemies. A meeting of a few intellectuals in the home of the German cultural attaché in Tehran was considered proof of their treacherous tendencies, if not of espionage. The dissident newspapers and journals were often referred to as foreign-dependent publications and their writers as obstinate enemies (*mo'aned*), foreign-worshipers (*ajnabi parast*), and corruption-mongers (*ebtezal gara*).

Normalization could not be truly attained for the *digar andishan* without unnerving the hard-line custodians of *velayat-e faqih* and alarming the security apparatus that was not under the technobureaucrats' control. President Rafsanjani and his pragmatist associates, both clerics and laymen, faced a problem they could not resolve or even contain. The bureaucratic side of the state was being unhinged from the security side. Confusion reigned, since there were no clear rules about the new political interactions, nor was there a clearly defined limit to freedom of expression. Violations of the right ensued.

Emerging Pattern of Violations During Rafsanjani's Presidency

With intensification of factional conflicts, the Islamic prosecutors used the Press Law to keep the *digar andishan* in line, hoping to prevent them from expanding the boundaries of permissibility. The law stipulated a Press Court to investigate the transgressions of journalists. In practice, the only mitigating factor that could allow certain individuals to escape punishment was the increasing level of disagreement among the competing ruling factions. To drive home the stiff warnings to the nonreligious dissidents, the Majlis passed a law in 1995 that made "insulting" the rulers a crime punishable by imprisonment for six months and up to seventy-four religiously mandated lashes. The law made the entire power elite of the Republic sacrosanct.[56] Another law made insulting the memory of the late Ayatollah Khomeini punishable by death.[57] All dictators of the twentieth century were capable of passing such laws; in this case, however, Islamic sanctification added the curse of the religious state.

Galindo Pohl observed that the intellectuals desired a less restricted space for expression and that the existing regulations were stifling.[58] Abid Hussain, the UN Special Rapporteur on Freedom of Opinion and Expression, clearly saw that the existing constitutional limitations violated the right to freedom of expression. He also saw the probabilities for abuses inherent in the constitutional stipulations that made freedom of expression, assembly, and association contingent on the unspecified criteria of the "principles of Islam." He was aware of the fact that those who decided what was in accord with the "principles of Islam" were the same people who also wielded the instruments of political power.[59]

There were indeed plenty of abuses. The next chapter presents a few cases that exemplified the harassment and prosecutions of dissident intellectuals and clerics who claimed their right to freedom of expression and the press. Here, I outline a pattern that emerged in the early 1990s and continued into Khatami's presidency after 1997. The three most familiar features of the pattern of violations were the use of judicial prosecution, violent and abusive actions by the *hezbollahi* vigilantes, and the privatization of legal claims. Already in 1990–91, writers and intellectuals were the targets of renewed verbal attacks in the hard-line press. These appeared far more sinister than the ordinary criticism leveled against works the critics did not like. These attacks were understood to be part of what Iranians called "preparing the atmosphere" for further actions, including physical assaults and imprisonment. After her first release from prison, the novelist Parsipur was terrified by these verbal attacks.[60]

A clear outline of the pattern emerged in 1993. No sooner had the security-judicial authorities fixed their forbidding glares on a publication than the *hezbollahi* vigilantes attacked its offices and security agents arrested its editor or the editorial staff. As discussed in Chapter 2, the *hezbollahis* had become an integral part of the security apparatus. Galindo Pohl mentioned the attacks by the cleric-sponsored *hezbollahi* gangs on newspapers and magazines that were legal but deemed insufficiently Islamic—or that were critical of the rival groups in power. He also noted that the *hezbollahi* vigilantes issued death threats, "with the tolerance of the authorities and without fear of prosecution."[61] *Kiyan* and *Doniya-ye Sokhan* were among the earliest targets. *Kiyan*'s publication of an interview with the ex-premier Bazargan had provoked the anger of Ayatollah Yazdi's Judiciary and of the *hezbollahis*.[62]

The powerful backers of the *hezbollahi* vigilantes were always ready to rush to their defense. Most outspoken was Ayatollah Ahmad Jannati, a member of the Guardian Council and president of the Islamic Cultural Propagation Organization, the regime's largest propaganda machine. In his views, the *hezbollahi* vigilantes "had done what the authorities should have done in accordance with Ayatollah Khomeini's political testament." The reference to the testament reminded the technobureaucrats of Khomeini's warning that the regime should never allow the press to be influenced by the Western-style liberties. Jannati asserted that Khomeini's "Will" stood above the law.[63] Other high officials, including the powerful commander of the Revolutionary Guards, impressed upon the *hezbollahis* and *basijis* (the irregular force) that it was their singular duty to protect the Islamic system from the liberals. To make his point very clear, the commander identified the "war between the *hezbollahi* and the liberals as the fundamental issue of the time."[64]

The most novel feature of the new pattern was the privatization of legal claims. The hard-line clerics asserted that the printed or spoken words of the dissidents had caused "emotional distress" for the favorite children of the Islamic revolution, especially those who had sacrificed so much in the war against Iraq. In the second half of the 1990s, they used the pretext to bring libel suits in the Judiciary controlled by their political allies. Thus, insulting Islam and its self-appointed custodians was a crime; so was injuring the political-religious sensitivities of the *hezbollahi* groups.[65] To silence dissent, this was eventually developed to a tactic that charged reformers with libels that offended the prestige (*haythiyyat*) of bona fide Islamist revolutionaries— a tactic that the Islamic editor of *Zanan* (Women) called "libel-suits terror-ism."[66] The Judiciary was becoming creative in the mid-1990s. The clerics eventually introduced into their court procedures a privatized legal claim to "emotional injury."

Abbas Ma'rufi was the editor of the monthly magazine *Gardun* in June 1996, when the prosecutors ordered his arrest and sentenced him to six months' imprisonment and twenty lashes, which were never administered.[67]

He was eventually driven into self-imposed exile. This became the first well publicized case in which the *hezbollahi* groups within the regime brought charges against the intellectuals. They claimed that Ma'rufi's journalistic activities were hurtful to their political-religious sensitivities. They hoped to preserve the "legality" of the procedure, while preventing the expansion of the boundaries of permissibility of freedom of expression. In August 1996 in exile in Germany, Ma'rufi "noted that no private claimant had accused him of a private crime but he found himself facing private complaints of his having committed public crimes." [68]

Musavi Kho'iniha recalled that during the ten years that he published the daily *Salam* he was summoned to courts more than thirty times to respond to an endless string of complaints. He believed it was the goal of the Intelligence Ministry's "war of attrition" to exhaust reformist editors by getting hard-line individuals and groups to file complaints against them. [69]

The pattern continued, and scores of newspapers and editors were subjected to official harassment through the courts. Attacks by the *hezbollahi* vigilantes also continued. [70] Intellectuals were also attacked and suffered injuries. [71] These unlawful activities clearly undermined the technobureaucrats' agenda of creating normalcy in the country. They grumbled, and their supporters in the press objected to the disturbing pattern and criticized the *hezbollahi* activities. However, President Rafsanjani was committed to keeping the working arrangement between the bureaucratic side and the security side of the state intact.

In his report for 1996, Copithorne wrote that "the social climate in the Islamic Republic is becoming less tolerant." [72] Human Rights Watch observed: "Nothing has had a more corrosive influence on the climate of respect for basic freedoms than the government's toleration of, and in some cases even open encouragement for, the violent activities of groups of religious zealots." [73]

Pressure on Mostafa Mir-Salim, the hard-line Minister of Culture and Islamic Guidance, was intense. He had reluctantly given in to Rafsanjani's policy of normalization; however, by the end of 1995, he concluded that the policy of trusting writers and publishers had been a mistake. In February 1996, he admonished the press by saying that the editors did not understand the limits for freedom of expression and lacked wisdom and common sense. Some 190 journalists answered back, protesting and criticizing the arbitrary restrictions imposed on the press. Soon afterward, the Minister imposed further restrictions on the publication of books. [74] The imposition of prepublication censorship added pressure on the Deputy Minister, Ahmad Masjed-Jam'i, who had been responsible for relaxing many of the "rules" that allowed new newspapers and magazines to appear. He resigned. The Rafsanjani administration was proving incapable of maintaining only a limited range of freedom of expression, just enough to allow it to claim a state of bureaucratic normalcy. The technobureaucrats had opened a floodgate, but they did not expect the deluge of 1998–99 that threatened to sweep away the Redline.

Khatami's Presidency and the New Political Context

The Islamic reformists' invigorating voices that called for the rule of law and more tolerance of dissent found a receptive national audience in young Iranians, who also followed the secularists' courageous attempts to create a space for articulating nonreligious views. Together, they played a significant role in creating the intellectual and political ferment that shaped the 1997 presidential race. The ferment indicated that the country's experiment with Islamization had reached an impasse that could no longer be negotiated within the narrow political framework created by Ayatollah Khomeini.

Muhammad Khatami's surprising victory brought together the otherwise heterogeneous political groupings that desperately sought reforms, and they named it the Do-e Khordadi Movement—*Do-e Khordad* being the second day of the Persian calendar month in which Khatami won the presidency. As such, it was not a political movement. Rather it signified an outpouring of written words against the authoritarianism of *velayat-e faqih* and reflected the desire of many Iranians to change the sociopolitical direction of the country by advocating bold reforms heretofore deemed impossible. The master craftsmen of these words were the cleric Abdollah Nuri and the lay Islamic reformer Akbar Ganji, whose collections of articles and trial defense became national best-sellers.

In Khatami's election and the unmistakable votes of discontent, a Supreme Leader more secure than Ayatollah Khamenei, who never appeared self-assuredly ensconced in *velayat-e faqih,* would have recognized the widespread hopes that diverse classes of people had expressed for the regime's transformation. Not until the end of the 1990s did he realize the danger that the regime faced, and even then, he remained unsure about how to stem the tide of the reformist discourse or come to terms with it. He kept vacillating between verbally appeasing the reformists and acquiescing with their prosecutions and imprisonment.

As mentioned before, Khatami's election disturbed the delicate balance that existed within the regime, between its bureaucratic and its security sides. Within the constraints of *velayat-e faqih,* President Khatami tried to build on the momentum of his election campaign. As the head of the visible state, the President could no longer remain silent concerning the illegal actions of the invisible state of the security agents. The judicial authorities had sanctioned the vigilante actions and protected the security agents. They were able to carry on their illegal security work with impunity, mainly because the bureaucratic side of the regime, especially the former President, Rafsanjani, remained publicly reticent about them. Khatami's political agenda of the rule of law, giving him legitimacy with the youth and women, clashed with the previous tacit arrangement between the bureaucratic and security sides of the regime. The turban-wall of silence cracked.

One way for President Khatami to claim a new legitimacy was to blur the sharp line of demarcation the clerics under Khomeini had drawn between themselves and culturally literate Iranians. It was not that Khatami and his associates entertained any hope of gaining the allegiance of the secular intellectuals. They did, however, try to be more accommodating to them, despite the fact that Khatami, as a Shiite cleric, viewed secular intellectuals in Islamic terms as outsiders.

Attaollah Mohajerani, a target of the hard-liners' criticism, became the Minister of Culture and Islamic Guidance. The appointment heartened the Islamic reformers.[75] In his view, "Islam is not a narrow and dark alley into whose constraining wall human beings constantly clash," making it impossible for them to conduct their lives effectively and reasonably. Mohajerani also argued that attacks on public meetings, publishing houses, and newspapers had proven counterproductive. If the Minister of Culture gave permission for a publication, "the revolutionary brothers" had no business disturbing and attacking the premises of that publication. "Do we live in a system based on laws or not?"[76] Especially encouraging was Mohajerani's deputy in charge of publications, Ahmad Burqani, a sincere Islamic reformer who issued new licenses and allowed the reappearance of a number of banned publications. He had spent more than a decade in the United States as a student. According to one official estimate in mid-1998, there were some 850 publications throughout Iran with more than two million copies in circulation. Some 220 of them were born in the first year of Khatami's presidency. There were some 800 more applications pending for governmental licenses.[77]

In January 1997 in an open letter, more than 350 journalists had demanded that their profession be officially recognized. They pointed out the difficult circumstances under which journalists worked in Iran, dealing with psychological stress and physical pressures. Shortly after Khatami's assumption of the presidency, the Islamic reformers in the press managed to establish the Union of Journalists.

The unrelenting attacks on reformists failed to intimidate them into submission during the critical years of 1997–2000, although their future is fraught with danger. They boosted their resolve to such a degree that by 1998 they began to describe themselves as the "New Islamic Left" struggling for the rule of law. In a highly charged political environment that encouraged the breaking of the taboos heretofore untouched, scores of new publications appeared.[78]

Mashallah Shams ol-Va'ezin and his friends felt confident enough to launch the first daily that claimed total independence from the established order. The appearance of *Jame'eh* (Society) in 1998 signified a new phase in the struggle for the right to freedom of opinion, expression, and the press.

Jame'eh began with a circulation that exceeded by far those of the semiofficial dailies, sometimes reaching up to 300,000 copies.

The daring language of the paper explained its popularity. "*Jame'eh*'s independent and inquiring spirit constituted a watershed event in the history of the Islamic Republic's press. More surprising than its attacks on political foes (the conservative and ultra-conservatives), were its cutting remarks and criticisms aimed at reformists."[79] Other new, popular publications included *Sobh-e Emruz* (Sa'id Hajjarian's daily), *Rah-e Now* (Akbar Ganji's bi-monthly), and *Khordad* (Abdollah Nuri's daily). Scores of young Islamic reformists contributed articles, and some like Alireza Alavitabar and Emad ed-Din Baqi moved from one publication to another with ease.

The Islamic reformers were increasingly questioning the taboos of the security state. It was one thing to engage in theoretical debates about the "true" meaning of Islam and another to reveal information about the illegal actions of security agents. For example, *Jame'eh* ran a long interview with Abbas Amir-Entezam, the Republic's longest held prisoner, who gave an account of his experiences in prison in the 1980s. At the time when *Jame'eh* had come under serious attack, Shams ol-Va'ezin told Elaine Sciolino of the *New York Times* that the paper was "a test case of how much openness the Government can tolerate."[80]

Rational Political Discourse De-legitimating *Velayat-e Faqih* and Revealing Past Violations

The central institution of the Islamic Republic began to face its most serious challenges, as reformers of the old and the new generations began whispering doubts about the suitability of *velayat-e faqih* in today's world.

In the late 1990s, well-reasoned arguments in the pages of the reformist press presented a major problem for *velayat-e faqih*. When Ayatollah Khomeini was alive, his followers were in awe of him. Under his stern gaze, critical issues could not be openly debated, and the opinions expressed by a few of his trusted clerical associates usually went unchallenged. Alternative political discourses were incapable of advancing rational counterarguments. Divine imperatives silenced everyone. Khomeini's successor, Ayatollah Khamenei, lacked the power of a charismatic leader, and his supporters failed to elevate him to the august position that Khomeini had enjoyed.[81] Hardly anyone was in awe of him.

In the second half of the 1990s, Islamic writers and journalists began to analyze the controversial issues and to show the irrationality in the regime's institutional setups and the illegality of many of its repressive measures. Their approach was logical and sociological, patterned on Western academic styles. The Leader's words could no longer put an end to the controversial issues. To illustrate, *Neshat* was shut down in September 1999 because it had published, among other things, two articles that questioned the appropriateness of the death penalty, thus questioning the Islamic *qesas* laws (retribution). Its editor, Shams ol-Va'ezin, was sentenced to three years' imprisonment. The articles attracted the hostile attention of the conservative clerics, and the Supreme Leader sought to put an end to the debate by pronouncing that opposition to the *qesas* was an act of apostasy. Ignoring his words, the reformist commentators pressed on, debating the issue.[82] To give one more example on another major conflict, the Guardian Council claimed that it possessed approbatory supervision allowing itself the power to reject applications of candidates it deemed undesirable (see Chapter 15). The Supreme Leader approved of such an extensive interpretation of the constitutional role by the Council. Ignoring him, scores of articles and books continued to appear, logically showing that such interpretation of Article 99 was in violation of other constitutional provisions. One well-argued legal book stated calmly and factually: "Any interpretation of constitutional principles that negates other principles of the same Constitution means abrogation or cancellation of a part of the Constitution."[83]

Velayat-e faqih could function as an authoritarian system only if the writs of the Supreme Leader (*faqih*) were obeyed and not subjected to logical examinations more in a social scientific style than a religious manner. In the second half of the 1990s, no argument could be discredited by merely branding it as contradicting Khomeini's words, serving the interests of the Western enemies, or belittling the cherished memories of the heroes of the revolution and the war. Akbar Ganji called these tactics of silencing logical arguments a premodern relic and a revolutionist habit (*enqelabi-gari*), a term with a clear negative connotation.[84] The far more cautious Musavi Kho'iniha observed that the regime's propaganda machinery had always tried to place certain state personalities above and beyond logical questioning, *fara-manteqi*; these were individuals whose words could not be evaluated for their logical soundness. "When they speak, we must accept." He added that his banned daily *Salam* tried to subject the words of even the highest authorities to "the crucible of logic, causing much anxiety and anger."[85]

The Supreme Leader understood that a relatively free press presenting logically constructed arguments would seriously undermine the apparent sanctity of *velayat-e faqih* (the vice-regency of the Islamic Jurist). In the late 1990s, Islamic reformers openly questioned what they could only whisper earlier: the religious imperative of *velayat-e faqih*. Theoretically, every Shiite Muslim would have to follow a Grand Ayatollah as his/her *marja taqlid* (source of emulation). The reformers asserted that if a particular *marja taqlid* expressed disbelief in *velayat-e faqih* as a proper Islamic institution, his followers would have to follow.[86] The reformers hastened to remind everyone that a number of Grand Ayatollahs did not believe in *velayat-e faqih*, the foundation of the Islamic Republic's legitimacy. In the meantime, the only thing their followers had to do was to obey the constitutional laws, a proper civil duty until laws are changed. The argument, patently modern and secular, in effect deflated the sanctity of the institution on which the Shiite theocracy rested.

The problem emanated not only from rationally constructed sociopolitical articles that indirectly reinforced secular views. Iranian journalism has often shown, during relative freedom, an abiding penchant for a biting sarcasm. Ridiculing state policies and poking fun at stiff, pompous, and bumbling officials always increased circulation. In the late 1990s, journalistic sarcasm contributed to the debunking of the clerics' claim to a divinely inspired state. The reader-response column in the daily *Salam* carried on that tradition with considerable success. Even more popular was the column written by the witty Sayyid Ibrahim Nabavi, which appeared in *Jame'eh, Tous, Neshat, Asr-e Azadegan,* and *Arya.* Political satire was subversive of the religious rule that blurred all distinctions between politics and God, approaching both with the same humorless certitude. The Redline lost its significance as a bulwark defending *velayat-e faqih.*

Many observers, inside and outside of Iran, paid close attention to the new political dynamics that began with Khatami's presidency. Some of them, including Copithorne, hoped that they could lead to fewer human rights violations in the future. For this history of human rights violations, the significance of Khatami's presidency lay in what it had revealed about the past. The relative freedom of expression in 1998–2000 allowed the reformist press to initiate a rational, journalistic discourse, implicitly validating many of the charges of violations that almost everyone within the regime denied previously, including those who became Khatami's supporters in 1997–2000.

The reformers often discussed all the reforms they intended to implement. Foremost among them was the rule of law, which in the minds of many reformers still included constitutional provisions that circumscribed rights according to the "Islamic criteria." Their prognoses had often revealed more about the past than about the promised future and possibilities of improvement. Many writers enumerated the desirable changes that had to occur before a possible realization of the civil society. They based their entire arguments on the implicit assumption that respect for human rights did not exist, thus necessitating the recommended changes.[87]

One author stated that the Islamic revolution of 1979 had promised "liberating concepts." He pointed out that a long time had passed since 1979, but "it is never too late for liberty." He asserted that "the process must continue until the rule of law is fully established and violence is forever rejected."[88] Another article posed a question that spoke volumes about the past. First, it stated that the President had emphasized that the rights of all citizens, including the law-abiding opponents of the regime, must be respected. Then, it questioned those in power who granted no political freedom to "even the devoted friends of the Islamic Revolution" and who expected others to accept their restrictive interpretation of freedom. Addressing those who set the limits on liberties and freedoms, the writers of the article asked: "Why can't these gentlemen tolerate criticism? And why do they impetuously describe every criticism as a threat to national security?"[89] Sa'id Hajjarian, another former radical Islamist, identified the significance of Khatami's election in the fact that the "excluded society" announced its desire to enter into political space and claimed political participation as a right and not as a religious obligation.[90] Hundreds of such poignant questionings of past practices appeared in the reformist press between 1998 and early 2000.

Unmanageable factionalism undermined Rafsanjani's old arrangement for upholding the autonomy of the invisible side of the state in charge of security agents and the *hezbollahi* vigilantes. The reformist press began to discuss torture and extrajudicial killings. The cabinet ministers and their deputies on the bureaucratic side could no longer maintain the wall of silence. Now some of them too had fallen victim and were being tortured by the security agents. They told their stories and produced medical evidence.[91] Their main newspaper, *Iran*, revealed that nine high-ranking city officials in Tehran had been "blindfolded, battered, tortured, and humiliated."[92] *Iran Times* in Washington observed: "While thousands of opponents of the regime have alleged torture, those allegations could be dismissed as propaganda because they came from opponents. But the latest charges come from people with revolutionary credentials."[93]

The reformist *Hamshahri*, published by the accused Mayor of Tehran, quoted a Khatami supporter as saying that "the discussion about the torture of the children of revolution in prison has saddened and worried many people." The conservative *Resalat* retorted: "And it made the UN Commission on Human Rights happy!"[94] The hard-line Islamists considered the exposure of human rights violations as an act of betrayal. They thought that internal criticism of state practices would provide evidence to international human rights organizations. To prove the point, one angry Majlis deputy impeaching the reformist Interior Minister Nuri quoted from a letter sent by Hanny Megally, the Executive Director of Human Rights Watch/ Middle East, that resembled what Nuri had said about the illegality of Mayor Karbaschi's trial.[95]

Renewed Violations

In early August 1998, Ayatollah Yazdi delivered a forceful attack on the new policy of the Ministry of Culture and Islamic Guidance for allowing newspapers and magazines to "grow like mushrooms."[96] The Supreme Leader, Ali Khamenei, renewed his attacks on secular writers and journalists. In a speech to the top brass of the Islamic Revolutionary Guards in September, he came to the Redline again and delivered an ultimatum to the responsible authorities. They "must act in this regard and find out which newspaper steps outside the limit of freedom of expression."[97] Again, in Khomeini's time, such a chastisement by the Supreme Leader would have smothered the rumblings of discontent; in Khamenei's time, it fueled the debates.

The day after the Leader's threatening remarks, Revolutionary Guards raided the office of the newspaper *Tous* and arrested its editor, the publishing managers, and a staff writer, who spent up to five weeks in solitary confinement before being released.[98] The hard-line daily *Kayhan* praised the closure of *Tous* and the arrest of its staff as a step toward reversing the "cultural coup."[99] Orders went out for the closure of four other publications, including *Rah-e Now* (Akbar Ganji, editor) and the monthly *Jame'eh-ye Salem.*

The arrests and intimidation of reformers also took place. To give only one example here, Akbar Ganji, who coined "the fascist reading of Islam," was arrested on November 30, 1997. During that particular incarceration, which lasted fifty days, one week of it in solitary confinement, he was housed among common criminals. The security agents blindfolded him, placed him on a chair facing the wall, and interrogated him for hours. He sarcastically called the interrogation a "dialogue, intimidating and humiliating, that was supposed to bring [me] to the righteous path."[100]

The attack on *Tous*, which had replaced the banned *Jame'eh*, revealed the old dynamics at work with reference to freedom of expression and the press. The attacks were initiated politically and outside of the judicial process by the powerful hard-liners in the security network. *Hezbollahi* gangs then ransacked the *Tous* offices, and the Judiciary ordered the offices closed down, all of which clearly lay outside the legal procedure for revoking a press license.

A new trend, however, showed that the working arrangement created under Rafsanjani between two sides of the state was unraveling as the bureaucrats in charge of the ministries, all Khatami's supporters, were now in open conflict with the security apparatus, working at cross purposes. The police raids on the offices of three reformist dailies in April 1998 revealed the intensity of the disagreements between the two sides. The hardline Head of the Judiciary, Ayatollah Yazdi, was directing the new phase of attacks on the reformers. Police searches were conducted without prior knowledge of the Ministry of Culture and Islamic Guidance, which was supposed to be in charge of the press. Minister of Culture Mohajerani demanded an explanation for the judicial authorities' actions, and his less opportunistic deputy, Ahmad Burqani, pointed out the illegality of the actions.[101] Frustrated by attacks on the press, Burqani resigned in protest in February 1999.

The Ministry of Culture and Islamic Guidance under the reformist Mohajerani issued press licenses to individuals without the kind of ideological scrutiny that the security officials demanded. The hard-line clerics in charge of the security apparatus used other instruments, including the Judiciary and the Special Court of the Clergy, to harass and close publications licensed by the Ministry. Upon closure, the Ministry would not prevent the publication from reappearing under a new name. The fastest way to resurrect a banned publication was to find a fellow reformer who held a publishing license that was not in use. The best example was the successive resurrection of *Jame'eh* under four names, published by more or less the same group of journalists, including Sham ol-Va'ezin and Hamid Reza Jala'ipur.[102] The journalists called the sequence "a cat-and-mouse game." When an Islamic prosecutor asked Sham ol-Va'ezin how long this game must continue, he replied, "Until the cat realizes that the mouse has a right to live."[103] The "cat" was not about to arrive at such a realization any time soon, as the banning of all reformist, pro-Khatami newspapers showed in April and May 2000.

The closing of *Jame'eh* in the summer of 1998 started intense debates in the press and allowed Islamic reformists and secularists to expose the political nature of the legal actions against reformist publications. *Hoquq va Ejtema* (Law and society) devoted an entire issue to the closing of *Jame'eh* and its replacement by *Tous*. In a series of well-written and legalistic articles, *Hoquq va Ejtema* argued that the specific charges (spreading lies, creating a disturbance in public opinion, and publishing slanderous materials) that the Judiciary used to close down *Jame'eh* were subterfuges. They were hiding the real reason, which was the judicial authorities' dislike of the political views advocated by the Islamic reformers. Such political manipulations, the articles argued, were unlawful.[104]

It is important to note that during the period of inert human rights violations in the late 1980s and the early 1990s, the Islamic Republic's 1984 Press Law had never been seriously tested. Political repression in the early 1980s had created a press, uniformly monotonous, that gave the officials' versions of the news, praised Ayatollah Khomeini and the revolution, and denounced their real or imagined enemies. The Islamists had tailored the Press Law to the political conditions of the 1980s, when the regime's insiders toed the official lines and the secular outsiders were effectively silenced. For a decade, the Minister of Culture and Islamic Guidance found no vagueness in its restrictive clause that prohibited writings that were "harmful to the principles of Islam" or to the "public interests." During the second half of the 1990s, as the united façade of the Islamist camp cracked, the limitations of the Press Law began to reveal themselves. By the late 1990s, the Islamist camp had lost its consensus as to what constituted harm to Islamic principles; the reformist Minister Mohajerani found the law lacking in clarity.

The hard-liners, however, saw the problem as one not of ambiguity but of enforcement, especially under the supervision of such a minister who lacked religious zealotry. In October 1998, the conservative Majlis began drafting a new press law that would impose a tighter rein over the reformist journalists and commentators and create an enforcement mechanism outside the Ministry of Culture. The draft stated, among other things, that the Revolutionary Courts should also investigate press offenses, a clear violation of Article 168 of the Constitution, which allowed only the Press Courts to adjudicate press cases. The bill made it more difficult for the reformist editors to start a new newspaper or magazine when their previous ones were banned.[105]

The Extrajudicial Killings of the *Digar Andishan*

Legal prosecutions and illegal vigilante actions alone could not silence the vociferous opposition of Islamic reformists and the reinvigorated secularists. The zealots in the state security apparatus knew that the ongoing rational political discourses undermined the authority of *velayat-e faqiq*. The intragovernmental conflicts over the boundaries of freedom of expression intensified and led to extrajudicial killings of secular dissidents. It was as if the hard-liners in the Intelligence Ministry wanted to send a message to the dissidents that President Khatami might continue giving verbal assurances to the Muslim intellectuals, but until the Supreme Leader was in power, there could be no safe place for the outspoken secularists in Iran. The intragovernmental fissures widened precipitously; predictably, the secular dissidents paid the price. The security agents still did not dare to target the Islamic reformers who were more openly vocal in their criticism of the regime. Ironically, the vigorous debates concerning freedom of expression, hailed by Special Representative Copithorne, led to the worst open violations of the right to live since the murders of the Protestant pastors and the Sunni religious leaders in the early 1990s.

The first news that jolted the reformers and intellectuals was the killing by multiple stab wounds of Daryush Foruhar and his wife in their home on November 22, 1998. Foruhar had been a political activist since the late 1940s. In the months leading to his murder, he had spoken frequently with the international media, criticizing the Islamic Republic and denouncing the *hezbollahi* vigilantes.[106]

Then the body of Majid Sharif, a dissident writer, was found on November 25. As the secular dissident community was mourning the deaths, passionately appealing to President Khatami and denouncing those who had stepped outside the rule of law, the news came that two other writers had been murdered in December. Muhammad Mokhtari and Muhammad Ja'far Puyandeh were active participants in the effort to reorganize the Writers' Association in Iran; they had also signed the famous letter "We Are Writers" in October 1994. The murderers had strangled them and left their bodies in the streets of Tehran. "The December killings sent a shudder through Iran's intellectual community."[107] Many intellectuals in Iran, as well as the international human rights monitors, could not believe that these killings were unrelated, especially in light of their similarity to another string of deaths in 1996–97. Many remembered Ibrahim Zalzadeh, the writer and editor of the magazine *Me'yar*, and the gruesome multiple stab wounds that killed him in March 1997.[108] The reformist journalists began to discuss these killings and other mysterious deaths: Sa'idi Sirjani (1994); Hossein Barazandeh (1995); Ahmad Mir'ala'i (1995); Ghafar Hosseini (1996); Professor Ahamd Tafaz-zoli (1997); and Ma'sumeh Mossadeq (1997), a granddaughter of the 1950s nationalist hero.[109]

Two UN Special Rapporteurs (on Extrajudicial, Summary, or Arbitrary Execution and on Freedom of Opinion and Expression) joined with Copithorne and forwarded a letter to the Foreign Minister, asking the government to investigate the murders and announce its findings.[110]

The families of the murdered individuals had no doubt that responsibility lay with the intelligence agents. President Khatami's insistence on investigation proved what the families believed. Some thirty security agents led by Sa'id Imami, a former Deputy Intelligence Minister, were identified as the "rogue elements" responsible for the killings. Mostafa Kazemi, Executive Director of the Ministry, was arrested in January 1999, and Imami was taken to Evin prison in February 1999. Five extrajudicial killings in late 1998 and early 1999 seemed to have unraveled the arrangement between the two sides of the state. Now the intrastate conflicts had reached into the Intelligence Ministry as well, creating a split between those who wished to support Khatami and the hard-liners who wished to remain hidden behind the wall of denials. On similar occasions in the past involving intelligence agents, the regime would have spoken in one voice—with only minor differences in emphasis—as the example of the Mykonos murders in Berlin had shown. A group of defectors from the Intelligence Ministry provided Khatami with evidence of the security agents' involvement in the Foruhar murders.

Obviously, no outsider could know what happened behind the closed doors of factional politics. It appeared that President Khatami and his men saw the killings as a direct assault on their credibility with the middle classes. Nowhere did the significance of Khatami's election for human rights present itself more clearly than in the cases of the extrajudicial killings of late 1998 and early 1999. However, the tug of war between different factions within the regime continued, without decisive victory for Khatami's men. The debacle allowed the reformers to suggest the regime's responsibility in the extrajudicial killings.

The most daring reformers focused their attention on the Intelligence Ministry's past activities. Even the more cautious Musavi Kho'iniha denounced the leadership of the Ministry as a "political club," bent on "ousting their political adversaries from the scene." He charged that these men disguised and justified their destructive activities as the needed measures supportive of the Supreme Leader.[111] In a well-argued theory that reflected popular opinions concerning extrajudicial killings, Akbar Ganji popularized the Persian equivalent of "the dungeon of ghosts." This referred to a secret committee in which "the éminence grise" discussed the regime's enemies and issued fatvas for their demise. Ganji then linked that deplorable state of affairs with the much needed and often discussed transparency in state affairs; it would shine light into "the dungeon of ghosts." His collection of articles went into numerous reprints.[112] For the purpose of this study, the significance of Ganji's discussions was not that he named names, which he could not do, or offered conclusive evidence, which he did not possess. The popularity of his book reflected the widespread distrust of the state's hidden side. As people read Ganji's theory, they had no doubt in their own minds as to who were "the *éminence grise*" and the figures pulling the strings behind the scene of the "death squad committee."

In the second collection of articles, Gangi's arguments linked the *hezbollahi* storm troopers, through their leaders Hajji Bakhshi and Hossein Allah-Karam, to a number of middle-rank clerics who occupied important positions in the Islamic Judiciary and the security apparatus.[113] They included Ali Fallahian, Ruhollah Hosseinian, Ali Razini, Mohseni Azhei, and Dorri Najafabadi. He also showed that since the late 1980s the Intelligence Ministry was controlled by the same cabal, many of whom had been closely linked since their student days at the Haqani religious school in the city of Qom. They had also established their influence in the office of the Supreme Leader. They all subscribed to "a fascist reading of Islam" whose master proponents were such Ayatollahs as Khaz'ali, Mesbah-e Yazdi, and Mahdavi Kani. A number of publications, including the resourceful *Kayhan*, presented their hard-line arguments to the public, and the commanders of the Revolutionary Guards often repeated their threats against the reformers. Ganji's arguments pierced the regime's shield and rejected the argument that the extrajudicial killings were done by the "rogue elements" in the Intelligence Ministry. The security apparatus that recruited and trained men like Sa'id Imami grew out of the imperatives of preserving an authoritarian rule that sanctioned violence by resorting to religious edicts (*fatvas*), perhaps the deadliest curse of the religious state.

As for the Khatami administration, Ganji revealed that Dorri Najafabadi was not Khatami's free choice as the Intelligence Minister; rather, he had been imposed on Khatami by hard-liners in charge of the security apparatus. Ganji recommended policies that the new Intelligence Minister had to follow in order to bring the Ministry in line with the President's reformist agenda: Unlike his predecessors, he should not define national security so broadly as to include every criticism of the regime; he should refrain from entering into political and factional conflicts and orienting the ministry's duties and goals to one political faction's advantage; and he should not interfere in the country's cultural and educational affairs. He observed that dissident thoughts could not be stifled by threats and imprisonment.[114]

The reformers kept up the pressure in the press and pointed out the Intelligence Ministry's involvement in earlier extrajudicial killings. Many of the past murders, including those of the Christian pastors in 1994, appeared to have been the work of Sa'id Imami and his associates.[115]

The dailies *Salam* and *Khordad* even asked the former Intelligence Minister, Fallahian, to clarify the extent of his Deputy's involvement in the extrajudicial killings, including those in the Mykonos restaurant in Berlin.[116] *Salam* editorialized: "All evidences point out that the political, economic and ethical deviations in the Intelligence Ministry had began when Mr. Fallahian was the minister, and the bitter crops that we reap today are the result of the seeds that were sown at that time."[117] Akbar Ganji wrote that Sa'id Imami's overseas extrajudicial killings "were surely against national interests, and in some instances against national security and the system of the Islamic Republic."[118]

In a second extensive investigative report, the monthly journal *Payam-e Emruz* concluded that Ali Fallahian was involved in the more than eighty assassinations during his tenure as Minister, not counting those that occurred outside Iran. Furthermore, it suggested a reason for the sudden halt in the official investigation in 1999. Fallahian had dropped hints that he would name names, including that of the former President, Rafsanjani, if the official investigation implicated him.[119]

For the first time, Iranians read about circumstantial evidences and tacit acknowledgments of extrajudicial killings in and outside Iran that the international human rights organizations had alleged occurred in the 1990s. The reformists also discovered evidence that implicated Imami in the persecution and torture of editor Faraj Sarkuhi (see Chapter 14).[120]

Ganji continued to hammer on the issue of Rafsanjani's responsibility in the serial killings. Rafsanjani's supporters hinted, in their typically obscure style, that the Rafsanjani was restricted in his selection of the Intelligence Minister, who sat in his cabinet. This argument followed the logic of what I have described as the Islamic state's division into a visible, bureaucratic side and an invisible security side, for which the President claimed no responsibility. Ganji retorted by saying that the real issue was that Rafsanjani continued to deny the truth by insisting that no extrajudicial "killings took place during his presidency."[121]

Rafsanjani responded to the Sarkuhi case by saying that he did not know what was happening because the Intelligence Ministry had lied to him about Sarkuhi's whereabouts.[122] As the electoral campaign for the sixth Majlis got under way in January 2000, Rafsanjani, who returned to active politics by standing as a candidate, fired back against the former radical Islamists who now wished to make him accountable for the past human rights violations. "Some of these gentlemen now disguised as reformers and liberals used to make problems for us by their extremism." He stated that he had suffered greatly in trying to curb their "excesses—hanging, trials, and confiscation of private property in the early years of the revolution." He added that he had not divulged their "secrets" and that he had "protected everybody" within the regime. "But if they go too far, I will answer."[123] One can only wish he would. These men were partners in the bloody repression of the 1980s. A decade later, their revelations about each other's unsavory past were testimonies to human rights violations that took place during the first fifteen years of their unified rule.

The Wholesale Banning of Reformist Newspapers and Magazines

The political ramifications of the extrajudicial killings further complicated journalist activities in the country, with the reformist editors taking advantage of the debacle to expand the permitted range of free expression and the judicial authorities increasing their prosecutions of the most daring editors, especially of the dailies.

Salam, the popular alternative to the semiofficial newspapers, published an Intelligence Ministry memo reportedly written by Sa'id Imami, the mastermind of the killings. In this memo, Imami warned that the reformist journalists presented a security risk to the regime, and he proposed that the new press law, under consideration by the Majlis, should make writers responsible for what they write and punish them for infractions.[124] The former law made only the editors of publications accountable to the Press Court. His goal was to eliminate "hostile elements" from the press by proposing strict rules of "professional conduct" and issuing a "cultural code" to each journalist, the same way a code is issued to a physician. Thus, journalists could be sued for malpractice. He concluded: "In this way, the insiders (*khudi*) will be strengthened and the contumacious elements (*mo'aned*) will be ousted from the scene."[125] The timing of the publication of the memo was significant, since the hard-line deputies in the Majlis were drafting a bill that included some of the measures recommended by the disgraced Imami. A storm engulfed *Salam*, as the hard-liners denounced the publication of the memo and the editor responded, calmly and sarcastically, by insisting that the newspaper had done no wrong. If anything, it had done a public service.

Accused of publishing a classified document, *Salam* was banned on July 7, 1999. Many of the reformists believed that the judicial process, either in the Press Court or in the Special Court for the Clergy, that closed the reformist press only finalized the decisions that had been made elsewhere, most likely in consultation with the Supreme Leader, who had always watched the press carefully. The beleaguered publisher of *Salam* seemed to concur.[126]

When *Salam* was banned, university students demonstrated in Tehran. Security police and *hezbollahi* vigilantes retaliated with a predawn raid on a Tehran University dormitory.[127] These events set off six days of violent protests, the worst since the 1979 revolution. Scores of people were killed and injured, and hundreds of students who were arrested faced an uncertain future at the hands of the Islamic Judiciary, which treated them as political enemies of Islam.

Despite new leadership in the Intelligence Ministry, its security officials continued issuing alarmist announcements, complete with videotaped confessions of those who were arrested. The tapes repeated the experiences of the state television shows in the 1980s: despondent-looking men and women confessing to their "crimes" and attributing them to foreign plotters. Among the foreign enemies, the Ministry named the Persian Services of the Radio Free Europe/ Radio Liberty and the Voice of America, which "fed information" to and "received information" from the accused students in Tehran. One communiqué said that this particular group had asked Radio Free Europe/ Radio Liberty for funds.[128] It seems that after twenty years of struggling against external enemies, the Ministry faced a paucity of real, frightening enemies to be denounced by its captives in tortured confessions.

Gholam Hossein Rahbarpur, the zealot head of the Tehran Revolutionary Court, resurfaced with the announcement that forty-nine people who were arrested during the July student riots had been secretly tried and convicted; four were sentenced to death. Such an announcement would have met with absolute silence in the 1980s; in the late 1990s, the reformist press reacted loudly and angrily. The same would have been the case with the Intelligence Ministry's communiqué. But the reformist press was able to publish the views of those who questioned the circumstances under which confessions were wrung from student protesters.[129] Two student testimonies were mentioned in Chapter 4 dealing with torture.

The wholesale banning of the reformist press began after the reformers captured a solid majority in the Majlis elections in 2000 (Chapter 15). Hardliners were alarmed by the possibility of a reformist Majlis pursuing liberal legislation and a reformist press giving vociferous support to such measures. Perhaps they thought that, without the benefit of widespread publicity through such a popular press, the reformist Majlis could be contained by the Guardian Council and the Expediency Council, both under antireformist factions. Following another of the Leader's denunciations of the reformist press, the Judiciary issued several rulings. By July 2000, they closed down twenty pro-reform publications, including the popular *Asr-e Azadegan*, edited by Shams ol-Va'ezin, and *Fath*, edited by Akbar Ganji. Both editors were sent to Evin prison in April 2000. The daily *Bayan* was also banned.

The new century began with the Islamic Republic at war with itself and with conflicts revolving around the freedom of public discourses, reflecting a country exhausted by Islamization. Khomeini's legacy for Shiite Islam was laden with crisis. A decade after his death, no one had any clear idea how to put the *jinni* of the politicized Islam back into the bottle and return the power-intoxicated clerics to their mosques and seminaries.

The Most Revealing Cases of Violations of the Right to Freedom of Expression and the Press

The cases that I have selected from among many ordeals experienced by intellectuals and dissident Shiite clerics best captured the intimidating climate in which they tried to assert their freedom of expression in the 1990s. Of the two secular intellectuals, one died in custody, and the other ended up in exile in Germany. The cases of Ali Akbar Saʻidi Sirjani and Faraj Sarkuhi generated considerable publicity in the Western press, in the international human rights community, and among Iranian émigrés in the United States and Europe. Each in its own way revealed the dynamics of the human rights discourse in the Islamic Republic during most of the 1990s, underlining not only the shared characteristics with other authoritarian rules but also the added curses of the religious state. The latter was further underlined by the ordeals of the dissident Shiite clerics who suffered more prosecutions and harassment in the Islamic Republic than under the secular Shah's state. I see no irony here, since the suffering was inherent in the mixing the contemporary state and religion, negatively affecting both.

The Death of Saʻidi Sirjani

Saʻidi Sirjani was a popular writer, scholar, and cultural commentator. I could have included his case in the categories of the rights to life, to security of the person, and to a fair trial. It is best considered here because his claim to freedom of expression led to the violations of his other human rights.

The clerics' anger toward this remarkably independent writer and brilliant satirist was brewing for a long time; perhaps he was the only writer who hardly hesitated to express his criticism of the Ayatollah's rule, even after the general suppression of the early 1980s had silenced almost everyone. The case of Saʻidi Sirjani showed the Intelligence Ministry's style of attacking intellectuals who refused to bend to the theocracy. It also revealed the dynamics of the interaction between the UN Special Representative and his diplomatic interlocutors. The authorities ordered the arrest of Sa'idi Sirjani and his literary colleague, Muhammad Niyaz Kermani, on March 14, 1994, holding them incommunicado. Indicative of the destructive style of the Intelligence Ministry, the semiofficial press reported the news on March 16 as the arrests of two drug traffickers. The intelligence agents had apparently arranged for the antitrafficking units to arrest them. It came, the officials said, as the result of a police follow-up, after busting a number of addicts and distributors of drugs and alcoholic drinks, leading to their doorsteps. The semiofficial press named the two men without mentioning their profession, or that one was a well-known writer. The news stated that "their houses were searched, and opium, alcoholic drinks and pornographic videotapes were discovered. They had confessed to their crimes."[1] This was typical of the controlled press, where the security officials decided when and how sensitive news should be presented to the public.

It took three months for Sa'idi Sirjani's tortured repentance to hit the press, confessing to an assortment of vaguely defined crimes, denouncing past activities, and asking for leniency. Perhaps Sa'idi Sirjani had a premonition about the outcome of his insistence on freedom of expression. A decade earlier, he told an interviewer that in case that he was arrested one day and spoke strange words expressing regret about his past activities, those words should be considered "untrue." Elsewhere in his typical satirical style, he wrote that one day he would be accused of all unimaginable crimes and added a surrealistic script for his future confession to impossible political activities.[2] In the alleyways of his youth, Sa'idi Sirjani had grown up with the provincial clerics, many of whom now controlled the Islamic Judiciary and Intelligence Ministry. He knew too well his tormentors' political culture.

Galindo Pohl reported Sa'idi Sirjani's arrest in his interim report to the General Assembly in 1994.[3] Parroting the official press reports, the diplomats responded to Galindo Pohl's inquiry: "The person in question is arrested and now in detention on charges of espionage, acts against the moral health of society, including drug possession and use. This individual is at present in good physical and psychological condition."[4] Soon after, the diplomats had to tell the world that the individual "in good health" had died of a heart attack in prison. The official press agency reported the death on November 27, 1994. This was one of the many cases on which the Iranian diplomats had no accurate information; they generally knew little about the events that transpired in the darker side of the state, within the cloisters of the security apparatus. The Special Representative had difficulty believing the story of the heart attack. "It was reported that his body was buried in Tehran and the necessary autopsy had not been carried out."[5]

The charges against Sa'idi Sirjani were typical of the Judiciary controlled by Ayatollah Yazdi. They were, especially in political cases, an amalgam of odious condemnations for several of which official Islam prescribed the death penalty: membership in a band of drug traffickers, production and consumption of alcoholic drinks, and receipt of money from antirevolutionary forces abroad. The admixture was seasoned as usual by a sexual crime, this time homosexuality. The reference to accepting money abroad was to the prize from the Lillian Hellman and Dashiell Hammett Foundation of New York. Sa'idi Sirjani and Parsipur, the novelist and author of the prison memoirs, were the corecipients of the prize in 1993. Galindo Pohl noted that the Foundation informed the public that Sa'idi Sirjani had refused the money that came with the prize.[6] Interestingly, Human Rights Watch had nominated him for the prize that appeared among his crimes.

Again, the tragic fate of Sa'idi Sirjani testified to the irrelevance of cultural relativism in human rights discourse, especially in a complex state society like Iran. If one were to look for a genuinely "authentic" Muslim-Iranian intellectual, Sa'idi Sirjani would have been an ideal candidate. In a 1990 letter to Khomeini's successor, Ayatollah Ali Khamenei, Sa'idi Sirjani wrote: "Contrary to your unequivocal verdict, Your Excellency, I am a Muslim in pure faith, and proud of my religion, and of my belief in it. No anti-Islamic idiot would spend fifteen years of his life editing the most extensive commentary of the Holy Koran. . . . No one less than totally committed to Islam would dare break the silence of the present moment to protest the injustices that are imposed on the people, and that are shaking the foundation of their faith."[7]

Moreover, his unique literary genre delved deeply into the subterranean cultural storehouse of the country, mockingly drawing parallels between current events and individuals and well-known legends in Iranian folklore. His skillful, satirical use of traditional cultural motifs accounted for his popularity with readers; it also pricked the sensitivities of the clerical rulers who perceived a threat in his mastery of cultural references, directed against the banalities and absurdities inherent in the mullahs' rule of a modern state.[8] The arrest and charges against Sa'idi Sirjani, if not his death, showed that the case was devoid of any cultural signifier. This Muslim intellectual died in custody only because he expressed his views in his own sarcastic way, which had infuriated the Supreme Leader.

The Case of Faraj Sarkuhi

Challenging the limits of permissibility, Sarkuhi's journalistic ventures exposed again the conditions of hidden human rights violations that existed in the late 1980s, when very few individuals dared to claim their right to freedom of expression and the press. Like Sa'idi Sirjani, once he claimed his rights, he became the visible victim of human rights violations. Unlike Sa'idi Sirjani, he survived the ordeal, and the Press International Association in Zurich honored him with the prestigious Golden Pen of Freedom in 1999.

At the height of the Intelligence Ministry's campaign of harassment and intimidation against the *digar andishan*, Sarkuhi became involved in the web of a security operation that was truly Kafkaesque, elaborate and inept, typical of security operations of many authoritarian states.

Sarkuhi took advantage of the fissures in the façade of Islamist unity and began publishing the monthly journal *Adineh* (Friday). He was a signatory to "We are Writers," the path-breaking statement of 134 critics of the regime. Moreover, in 1995–96, he and a handful of other writers pursued the formidable task of revitalizing the Writers Association, which truly alarmed the security directors. Becoming the uninvited guests at the home of the German cultural attaché Jens Gust on July 25, 1996, security agents took Sarkuhi and five other writers from the dining room of their German hosts to the interrogation room of their tormentors. At the dinner table, they found the forbidden items of eternal damnation, bosoms and booze, and promptly videotaped the unveiled women and the bottles, the two most prized pieces of evidence of anti-Islamic illicit activities. The news of the detention was withheld from the press for a while, but once the semiofficial newspapers were informed, they referred to the meeting as the "secret banquet in the German embassy."[9]

On November 3, 1996, Sarkuhi was arrested again in Tehran, as he was about to board a flight to Germany, where his wife and children live. Thus began an incredible ordeal that lasted for forty-seven days. In his youth he had experienced the Shah's prison for eight years, which "could not be compared in pain and distress with a mere five minutes during these forty-seven days."[10] He was released on December 20, only to be arrested again on January 27, 1997. This was the fourth time that intelligence agents had arrested him, causing an alarm in the international human rights community. By that time, Sarkuhi had every reason to be apprehensive for his life. Shortly before his arrest on January 27, he penned a moving open letter, handwritten, some 14 pages in length, that has since found its rightful place in the annals of prison literature.[11]

The intelligence agents revealed their conspiratorial mind-set by seizing on Sarkuhi's "German connection," his family living in Germany and his arrest in the German diplomat's home in Tehran. The security officials planned to use Sarkuhi in an anti-German scheme that could only be conceived by intelligence men, deficient in foresight and efficient in hatching incredible plots. The plot was aimed at the German government, in response to the trial of an Iranian agent and his four Lebanese accomplices in the murders of opposition Kurdish leaders in Berlin's Mykonos restaurant. The reader recalls that the German prosecutor linked the murder to the top officials in Tehran and issued an indictment against Ali Fallahian, the Intelligence Minister. Sarkuhi was to be charged with unlawful contacts with the German government in a propaganda blast that was intended to counter the negative publicity of the German trial. Sarkuhi himself understood that his arrest was part of a plot "to counter the Mykonos case." He also understood that the plot was aimed at "frightening the intellectuals into silence."[12]

His ordeal began with his "secret" detention at Tehran's international airport on November 3, 1996. His panic-stricken wife, anxious for information about his whereabouts, announced his disappearance to the German press. The security agents told Sarkuhi that he had "disappeared," that he had left Iran and his arrival in Germany had been documented. Later they produced a German entry stamp on his passport, but the German officials believed that officials in Tehran faked the passport.[13] Sarkuhi wrote: "Based on the documents they showed me during the interrogations and things they were saying among themselves, I found out than on that day, they had changed the photograph on my passport, and put someone else's photo in place of mine. That person . . . went to Hamburg with my passport and my name, since my passport now has the Hamburg airport stamp."[14]

They told him that he would stay in solitary confinement for some time. "After the interrogations, interviews, and other inquiries, we will kill you and bury you secretly—or we'll dump your body in Germany." The interrogation, as usual, was preceded by physical and psychological pressure that "crushed" him. The story is reminiscent of the prison memoirs of the 1980s. The interrogators wanted the interrogation forms to reflect the date of his previous detention. "They forced me to write the September date," apparently to show that he had confessed to espionage before his "trip" to Germany. "They forced me to memorize and 'recite' the texts they had prepared in a staged TV interview, which they were taping with a video camera. They taped these forced, false, and fabricated interviews in that same prison. The 'interviews' included a discussion about other writers; they provided the text, and most of it was lies."[15]

They forced him to confess to being a paid spy for both the French and German cultural attachés. Moreover, he "confessed" that the German provided him and his journal *Adineh* with "ideological instructions." It did not occur to his tormentors that international monitors might wonder what constituted "ideological instructions" and how the German could give them to a seasoned journalist in Iran. To make the confession credible, the interrogators wrote down some details about the lives of the German and Frenchman and asked him to repeat the information. Sarkuhi confessed to everything. "They beat me into performing this interview credibly. They repeated the interviews several times, and each time they would tell me to plead for forgiveness and clemency."[16]

Having extracted their confession, the security directors had perhaps no clear idea what to do next. International human rights organizations reacted with flurries of activity. The German government made official inquiries and filed protests. Particularly effective were the heart-wrenching appeals of his courageous wife, Farideh Zebarjad, who embarked upon a publicity tour in

Europe and the United States.[17] It is important to note that the interrogators forced him to confess to espionage, but the Judiciary did not charge him with that crime. The entire event was an intelligence charade. It is likely that President Rafsanjani intervened and the security directors agreed to release him for a while to let the storm of international outrage subside. They also probably felt that they had frightened their unassuming victim into permanent submission.

Security agents told Sarkuhi that they would release him if he followed their scripts. He agreed but there was a logistical problem, since he was supposed to be in Germany, from which he had to be returned. In one of the most bizarre episodes in the history of the Iranian secret police, Sarkuhi reappeared on December 20 in the same airport from which he had disappeared seven weeks earlier. At a prearranged "press conference" in the airport, he repeated what security agents had dictated: he had been in Germany, but did not visit his wife and children, since he was estranged from his wife; on his way back to Tehran, he stopped in Turkmenistan to get assurance from Iranian authorities that no charges would be leveled against him once he reached Tehran.[18] Moreover, he told the reporters "that he hoped that his return to Iran could contradict the widespread and negative propaganda by the Western media, whose only goal is to oppose the Islamic Republic's independence and progress."[19] This line often appeared in scripts penned by intelligence officials.

Badly shaken, Sarkuhi went home and in those moments of the after-arrest, with its mixture of despondency and suppressed anger, aggravated by the absence of his loved ones, wrote the open letter, from which I quoted above. It begins: "Today is January 3. I, Faraj Sarkuhi, am writing this note in great haste in the hope that one day someone or some people will read it so that Iranian and international public opinion and especially my loved ones—Farideh, Arash, and Bahar—will learn of the terrifying experiences I have had."[20]

The letter found its way to Europe, where a German newspaper first published it. Three weeks after he wrote the letter, the security agents took him back to prison. This time the government announced that Sarkuhi and his brother were arrested as they intended to cross the border on the Persian Gulf coast.[21] They released his brother. In an authoritarian regime, no one dares to ask the authorities why they arrested a man, released him, and re-arrested him. None of the semiofficial press editors, who always responded to human rights charges with angry assertions about freedom of the press, dared to question the implausibility of the tale the security officials had forced Sarkuhi to tell. Sarkuhi was in prison in late June 1997, when the Head of the Judiciary announced that he had scheduled a trial for him. The immediate speculation was that Ayatollah Yazdi wanted to dispose of Sarkuhi's case before his political adversary, Muhammad Khatami, took office as the new President in August. The Ayatollah charged Sarkuhi with spying for a foreign country and attempting to leave the country illegally.

This time the international community responded with a sense of outrage, since the charge carried the death penalty.[22] His wife pointed out that during his "disappearance" for forty-seven days, his "reappearance" for thirty-seven days, and his latest detention for five months, no official charge of espionage was leveled against her husband. She questioned why, on June 24, 1997, the Head of the Judiciary unexpectedly indicted him with such a serious charge. Up to that point, the only official charge against Sarkuhi was the attempt to leave the country illegally. She expressed her anger by adding that the Ayatollah did not even trouble himself "to disclose the name of the country Faraj allegedly spied for."[23] Germany remained focused on the case. Prior to the trial, the German Foreign Minister had publicly said that "Iran's handling of the Sarkuhi case was key to the question of improved relations."[24]

The court convicted Sarkuhi of a relatively minor offense in late September. No outsider could know what took place behind closed doors. The political leaders of the Islamic Republic perhaps reached a compromise between the hard-line factions around Ayatollah Yazdi, who wanted his head, and the moderate technobureaucrats around Khatami, who wanted his release. The new president wanted to begin his term on an amicable note with the European states. It was a measure of the politicized Islamic Judiciary that the charge of espionage did not appear in the announcement of the verdict. The Head of Judiciary had leveled such a charge against him only a few weeks earlier. It was also a crime to which Sarkuhi had "confessed" in the taped interviews. The court convicted him of "activities against the country's security through negative propaganda against the Islamic regime."[25] He spent one year in prison before being allowed in May 1998 to join his family in Germany.

The story of Faraj Sarkuhi clearly indicates how violation of the right to freedom of expression leads to other human rights violations, notably the rights to security of person and fair trial and the right not to be subjected to torture.

Sarkuhi's ordeals also revealed the precarious positions in which the regime's diplomats often found themselves, scrambling between the international human rights monitors and the clerical-controlled Intelligence Ministry and Judiciary, over whose actions they had no control. In fact, they often lacked accurate information about what went on behind the closed doors of the security apparatus. On March 7, 1997, the Permanent Representative to the United Nations Office at Geneva wrote a response to Copithorne's inquiry. He stated that Sarkuhi had been arrested in February 1997 "while attempting to leave the country illegally." Then the diplomat tried to mischaracterize Sarkuhi's famous letter, which had become a new reason for his arrest. He wrote that foreign agents had encouraged Sarkuhi to write the letter and send it abroad and that the "letter's contents are groundless." He further informed Copithorne: "Soon, a court will examine publicly his charges."[26] As shown below, the diplomat's explanation of the letter was un-coordinated with the story the security agents were brewing for the same letter. On July 16, 1997, the same diplomat informed Copithorne of the charge of espionage and repeated the security officials' claims: "As he had stated in an interview, Mr. Faraj Sarkuhi left Tehran for Germany in November 1996. Therefore, any allegations about his detention in this period is baseless."[27]

The story had an equally absurd postscript. Sarkuhi and his brother were arrested on January 27, 1997. They released the frightened brother after a few days. Then, on February 6, 1997, the Islamic Republic News Agency ran a story entitled "Sarkuhi's Brother Rejects Foreign Media Hype about His Brother." In the story, the brother was quoted to the effect that Sarkuhi had not been arrested "since his return from Germany and Turkmenistan." The brother also characterized the content of Sarkuhi's anguished letter as fictional: because Sarkuhi knew that he was under suspicion for his connections with foreign embassies, he had "sent the letter in a bid to attract support in Germany." He also called his brother "a suspicious man suffering from illusion." The brother claimed that he had personally faxed the letter to Sarkuhi's wife in Germany without reading it, indeed assuming that it was a private letter dealing with Sarkuhi's "extra-marital relations with a female journalist in Iran for five years." He also said that his brother was in contact with "one of the ringleaders of counterrevolutionary grouplets, during his trips to Europe."[28] It certainly defied logic. Why did a man divulge such information about his own brother in a state that punishes adultery by lashing and counterrevolutionary activities by execution? Not long after that strange interview, Sarkuhi's wife received a telephone call from the distraught brother-in-law, during which he told her how sorry he was and asked for forgiveness. She responded by saying that there was nothing to forgive, since she understood his situation and what the pressure and torture could do to a person.[29] The machinations could have come from any intelligence ministry in the region.

The Cases of Dissident Ayatollahs and Their Associates

Perhaps it will come as a surprise to Western cultural relativists, who demand consideration for Islamic *différance*, that many of the Shiite ulema, including Grand Ayatollahs, were among the victims of human rights violations since the establishment of the Islamic Republic. Again, we can understand the character of a regime by looking at its victims. Not even during the secular, politically repressive monarchy could Amnesty International prepare a twenty-three-page report documenting violations of the rights of Iranian Shiite clerics. History is full of surprises. The Shah's imprisonment of several of the clerics in 1975, following a short period of political agitation linked to Khomeini, appeared outrageous. They were the victims of an authoritarian regime. Describing the plight of clerics under the Shah, Ervand Abrahamian, an authority on the history of modern Iran, observed, "Never before had so many prominent clerics found themselves imprisoned at the same time."[30] What happened to dissident clerics under the Islamic Republic somehow absolved the Shah, making the bleak days of 1975 appear not that dark after all. For the 1990s, one can make a bleaker observation. In almost two centuries under two monarchies, it was inconceivable that the Shahs would have a score of Grand Ayatollahs, Ayatollahs, and Hojjat al-Islams serve in prison or under house arrest for such a long duration.

The nonpolitical clerics and those who entertained views other than Khomeini's were the targets of verbal and physical attacks from the early days of the Islamic Republic. After Khomeini's death, the dissident clerics spoke their minds more openly and suffered prosecutions and harassment. As discussed earlier, the central institution of the Islamic Republic could claim legitimacy among its supporters when a Grand Ayatollah, who had already been recognized as a *marja-e taqlid* (the source of emulation), was willing to assume the position of the *faqih* (the Islamic Jurist) in *velayat-e faqih*. Already during Khomeini's rule a number of prominent clerics had expressed theoretical and practical reservations about the clerics exercising executive power. Early in the Islamic republic at least four Grand Ayatollahs experienced hardship as the result of their opposition to *velayat-e faqih*. The most senior among them was the Grand Ayatollah Shari'atmadari. In a move that could have shocked the previous generations of the Shiite ulema, Khomeini stripped him of his position as a *marja-e taqlid* in 1982. Shiite tradition had never granted such a power to anyone.

After Khomeini's death, it had become apparent that some Ayatollahs were unwilling to accept the middle-ranked Ali Khamenei (the successor to Ayatollah Khomeini) as a senior religious figure to be qualified as a *marja-e taqlid*. For him to claim being the *faqih* appeared simply incredible. An increasing number of Shiite ulema, particularly the most senior ones (*maraj'e-ye taqlid*), discreetly began to challenge the religious legitimacy of the concept of *velayat-e faqih*. Politicized Shiism created havoc in the Shiite establishment, and the religious state threw the religion into confusion.

Several senior religious figures were held under house arrest in the 1990s, and hundreds of their close associates have been detained and reportedly tortured. Some were unfairly tried in the Special Court for the Clergy, while others were held in total disregard of due process of law.[31] In his February 1997 report, Copithorne observed that a significant number of dissident clerics were among prisoners of conscience.[32]

By Khomeini's order in 1987, the regime set up, in an unprecedented move in the history of Shiism in Iran, the Special Court for the Clergy (*dadgah-e vizhe-ye ruhaniyyat*) to keep recalcitrant clerics in line. Only a religious state needs to set up a separate court for its clergy. Hojjat al-Islam Ali Fallahian, later the crafty Intelligence Minister, served as its first prosecutor. According to its regulations, completed in late 1990, the court had jurisdictions over such crimes as corruption, fornication, and other unlawful acts and behaviors not compatible with the clergy's status. Its primary function, however, had been political. It aimed at silencing the opposition voiced by the clerics, some of whom had never reconciled themselves with *velayat-e faqih*, while others had broken away from the ruling clerical factions. The court apprehended, prosecuted, and imposed sentences without the convicts having any right to appeal.[33]

Against the backdrop of increased tensions between the official ulema and their disgruntled brethren in 1995, the debates revolved around the question of the appropriateness of the ulema's direct involvement in government. Grand Ayatollah Sayyid Hasan Qomi remained critical of the central institution of the Islamic Republic, *velayat-e faqih*, and spent more than fifteen years under house arrest. Rather than reciting all such ordeals, I will limit the discussion to three cases that best indicate a pattern that emerged in the 1990s.

Grand Ayatollah Muhammad Sadeq Ruhani showed exceptional courage opposing the rule of Ayatollah Khomeini. After Khomeini's death, he advocated limiting the power of his successor, making him more accountable to the people. Ruhani issued two public pronouncements, in the form of letters to President Rafsanjani. The first was written in January and the second in June 1995; both criticized, among other things, arbitrary detention, torture, and extrajudicial killings. In his first letter, he wrote that life in Iran had become "unbearable for those who abide by the true principles of our Islamic faith."[34] He also indicated that "armed criminals" associated with the regime had posed a threat to his life. He wrote that he was unable to "remain a spectator while Islam is violated daily and while true religious leaders are forced to remain silent in a country claiming to be an Islamic republic."[35] The security agents arrested the Grand Ayatollah's sons and his immediate associates, almost all clerics of low to middle ranks.[36]

Perhaps the least political among the Grand Ayatollahs was Sayyid Muhammad Shirazi, who enjoyed a considerable Shiite following. He stayed clear of political involvement during the Khomeini era. However, he became indignant over Khamenei's attempt to gain recognition not only as the Supreme Leader but also as an eminent *marja taqlid* (source of emulation), a position only reserved for the Grand Ayatollahs. Shirazi seemed to have favored a committee of Grand Ayatollahs to provide leadership for the country.

The security authorities targeted the Grand Ayatollah's son, Morteza Shirazi. They accused him of forming an illegal organization and arrested him and his associates on November 21, 1995. They released him conditionally in January 1997, but a few of his associates were still in prison in 1999. Amnesty International reported that the arrests took place at night, during which most of them were beaten. The security agents even harmed some of their relatives in the process. The wife of one cleric suffered a broken hand, and the young son of another received an eye injury. The following morning, the security agents conducted a raid on a religious school in Qom and carried away some 120 seminary students. "Most were released several hours later, but seven remained detained. Despite repeated requests to the Iranian Government for clarification, their fate is unknown to Amnesty International."[37] The authorities continued arresting people in Qom in the next two months.[38] They arrested Mahdi Shirazi, the fourth son of the Grand Ayatollah, on June 19, 1996. The arrests of staff members and their relatives followed.[39] Copithorne noted the arrest, on October 15, 1997, of two more clerics who supported Grand Ayatollah Shirazi.[40] Copithorne observed that the authorities apparently demanded from them a public confession to the effect that they and the Grand Ayatollah Shirazi were "cooperating with foreign powers." He also noted the "allegations of physical and mental torture."[41] The strategy behind these operations was one of intimidation to induce silence.

Grand Ayatollah Hossein Ali Montazri continued to be a thorn in the side of the Supreme Leader. In the late 1980s, the regime arrested hundreds of his supporters and executed a dozen of his close associates. Following his removal as Khomeini's designated successor, he was denounced repeatedly throughout the 1990s. In this case, too, his close family members and associates became targets of prosecutions and harassment. One can only surmise the depth of his contempt for the middle-rank Khamenei assuming the office of *velayat-e faqih*.

In January 1997, Montazeri issued an open letter to Khamenei. He asked him to allow unrestricted participation in the regularly held elections and warned that unless the government respected the right to freedom of elections, he and his followers would initiate a hunger strike. On November 14, 1997, he publicly criticized the authoritarian function of *velayat-e faqih*. He even considered it improper for the Supreme Leader to issue religious *fatvas*. He urged the regime to strengthen "people's rule," which meant reducing the power of the Leader. Since 1998 Montazeri seemed to be honing his arguments for placing drastic restrictions on *velayat-e faqih* and whispering them to a close network of admirers. Montazeri asked: "How can the President implement the Constitution when the military and security forces are not under his command?" He added: "Whereas all social expectations are directed at the President and he has to respond to almost everyone, all institutions of power are under the command of the Supreme Leader."[42] Surely, this influential voice behind the scene encouraged the mid-ranked clerics such as Kadivar and Nuri to openly debate the tabooed subjects. In fall of 1997, Ayatollah Ahmad Azari Qomi gave support to Montazeri's positions and was promptly placed under house arrest by security forces.[43]

The *hezbollahi* gangs attacked Montazeri's office and residence in the city of Qom on November 19, 1997, five days after his denunciatory sermon, and the security agents placed more restrictions on his public activities. In the province of Isfahan and even more so in the city of Najafabad, his birthplace, people protested publicly and vociferously the harassment of their *marja-e taqlid* (source of emulation). The official propaganda tried to abuse the name of Mahdi Hashemi, the executed brother of Montazeri's son-in-law, by depicting the social unrest as a political manipulation by the remnants of the "Hashemi gang." In February 1998, the Special Court for the Clergy froze all the funds that Montazeri's followers had sent him as religious tithes. No longer able to pay the stipends to his seminary students, his educational activities ended. In response, 385 of Qom's seminary students and teachers issued an open letter strongly denouncing the actions against Montazeri. In the Islamic Republic an increasing number of the Shiite clerics were expressing concerns about the independence of the religious institutions.[44] True to its authoritarian nature, the religious state had become a major curse to its foundation of legitimacy.

The authorities imprisoned his relatives, including his son and son-in-law, and their close associates. One report indicated that the security agents arrested some 240 of his supporters.[45] In March 1999, the court ordered the press not to publish Montazeri's statements, which the reformist daily *Khordad* had periodically published.[46] The court charged Abdollah Nuri, *Khordad*'s publisher, and brought him to a trial for offenses against the state.

In the summer of 1998, the Special Court for Clergy arrested Hadi Hashemi, Ayatollah Montazeri's son-in-law. Three months later, Ashraf Montazeri, the Ayatollah's daughter, issued an open letter addressed to the ulema, in which she described her husband's mistreatment in Evin prison. An interesting part of the letter was the comparison Ashraf Montazeri drew between what she had witnessed during the Shah's imprisonment of her father and what she experienced now, visiting her husband in the Islamic Republic's prison. She provided a few examples of how the Shah's prison authorities treated the family during their visits with her father. Although he was not even an Ayatollah at the time, they were treated as would be proper for the family of a religious figure. In contrast, for sixty-five days the Islamist authorities prevented Ashraf Montazeri from visiting her husband. When they did allow a visit, she was humiliated and harassed. She found this comparison "unpleasant, disturbing, and disheartening." She noted that the judicial authorities leveled no formal charges against her husband, who had been arrested and mistreated in order to put pressure on her "esteemed father."[47]

Reports indicated that on December 26, 1998, Hadi Hashemi was released from prison after seven months.[48] The authorities accused him of igniting a series of protests in Isfahan and Najafabad, the main areas of Montazeri's popular support; there was no news whether he was ever charged or tried. Almost at the time of his release, the authorities arrested another group of dissident clerics. In April 1998, Gholamhossein Nadi, a two-time Majlis deputy from Montazeri's hometown, was sentenced to thirty months' imprisonment for supporting his longtime mentor.[49] In July 1998, more than four hundred clerics wrote an open letter to President Khatami protesting the arrest and prosecution of two other cleric associates of Montazeri. The signatories complained about the lack of due process of law, as no one knew for what crimes the Special Court convicted them in a secret trial.[50]

The cases discussed above reveal a pattern that was indicative of the dynamics of the Shiite state. The intelligence authorities dared not punish the eminent Grand Ayatollahs by subjecting them to prolonged imprisonment and torture. They placed them under house arrest. To induce silence or political acquiescence, they harassed and prosecuted their associates and relatives, especially their sons, subjecting them to periodic incarcerations, mistreatment, and torture.[51] They arrested when they wished, charged with crimes as they wished, and released from prison when they wished, many times without even the formality of a trial. The curse of the religious state was that it privileged a group of clerics with power and money but brought the recalcitrant clerics distinct disadvantages and agonies. The religious state needed the Special Court for Clergy, which served its purpose well.

Like other authoritarian rulers who are sticklers for formal institutional setups, the powerful clerics added, in November 1998, a fourteen-member press jury to the Special Court for Clergy. Its goal was to control the journalist activities of dissident clerics. Copithorne saw "the appointment of a press jury in the Clerics' Court as an ominous expansion of its jurisdiction, and a prescription for further confusion in the press regulation regime established by the Press Law."[52] Ominous it indeed became for the two most outspoken clerics whose provocative interviews and articles had adorned the pages of the dissident press since 1997.

The Cases of Mohsen Kadivar and Abdollah Nuri

The middle-ranked cleric Mohsen Kadivar was perhaps the best example of the younger generation of clerics freeing themselves from the suffocating constraints of Khomeinism and returning to the earlier Islamic reformism. He saw himself as the representative of "a current of Islamic thought that considers religion as the fountainhead of tolerance and compassion, and that condemns violence and exclusionary politics."[53] His views in 1998–99 spoke volumes about the clerical impasse in politics, since he was among those young men of 1979 who were attracted to Khomeini's rule. Having received a degree in electrical engineering, he went to the city of Qom for advanced religious studies and donned the clerical robs and turban. As an educated cleric, he held posts in a governmental research institute and taught Islamic studies since 1991. Reflecting the renewed tensions within the clerical caste after 1995, his scholarly articles showed that there was no consensus among the Shiite ulema on the theological basis for *velayat-e faqih* (see Chapter 2). He also spoke critically about the country's sociopolitical situations and suggested, among other innovative things, the possibility of selecting the Supreme Leader through direct, popular elections.

There could be little doubt about his devotion to a system that upheld religious values; however, his thoughtful political judgments on the regime's shortcomings infuriated the men in power. On February 27, 1999, after being held in custody for forty-seven days, Kadivar was taken to Tehran's Special Court for the Clergy. Rejecting the Special Court's jurisdiction over his case, which he considered to be related to freedom of expression, he offered a well-reasoned argument on the illegality of the Special Court. Conveniently ignoring the fact that Khomeini had created the court, he declared it unconstitutional because it operated outside the Judiciary, the only adjudicating body recognized by the Constitution.[54]

Even more interesting was Kadivar's sense of disappointment. He rejected the prosecutor's indictment because it sounded "like a political statement or a propagandistic oration." Revealing of the defendant's modern sensitivity was his attention to the indictment's language, characterizing it as unworthy of a court of law. He lectured the clerical prosecutor: "The judicial language possesses its own quality, which is different from that of the political language. . . . The judicial language is formal, weighty, precise, and free from emotion and propaganda. It is also scientific, logical, judicious and polite."[55]

Like Ayatollah Montazeri's daughter, he remonstrated: "In my entire life, no one had insulted me in this way. Not even in my student days in 1979, when the SAVAK arrested me on charges of activities against national security did the Shah's prosecutor use these insulting and demeaning expressions. . . . Who could believe that in the Islamic Republic such an indictment could be issued?"[56]

Kadivar took the indictment as an example of practices for which he had expressed his concerns in his writings and public lectures, expressions that had brought him to the trial. He had expressed his worries in a lengthy interview with the reformist *Khordad*, published by Abdollah Nuri, who would soon join him in Evin prison. In the interview, he passed an entirely secular judgment on the Islamic revolution and saw only two major achievements: overthrow of the 2,500-year-old monarchic system and Iran's independence from foreign influence. He then somewhat emptied these two victories from their potential value. "Eliminating the monarchic system is one thing and eliminating its old institutions and social habits is another thing. We have succeeded in discarding the system. However, similar to the aftermath of other revolutions that we have witnessed, the old relations have reproduced themselves under new guises. A revolution must succeed to bring about profound changes not only in forms but also in substance and content."[57]

Illustrating his point in an example, Kadivar added that in the old system one person made decisions for the nation who had no role in electing him,[58] implying that the Supreme Leader was a replica of the Shah. As for the second ostensible achievement, he said that the real value of independence would reveal itself when national leaders make independent "decisions that are wise, in accord with the real needs of the society and based on today's possibilities,"[59] implying that decisions made by the Leader lacked these qualities. Kadivar was clearly implying that the regime had failed to alter the psychological basis of the country and in effect perpetuated the authoritarian attitudes already ingrained in Iran's political culture.

As discussed in Chapter 13, the Supreme Leader considered the expression of such rational arguments dangerous to the regime, since they created doubts in people's minds about the viability of *velayat-e faqih* as the central institution of the Republic. In Islamist legal terms, it was a crime of "disturbing public opinion," for which Kadivar was charged. His other offenses were propaganda against the Islamic Republic and dissemination of fabrications. In April 1999, the court sentenced him to a year and a half in prison.[60]

In 1999, when the Special Court indicted Hojjat al-Islam Abdollah Nuri, he was the publisher of the reformist *Khordad*, a paper whose name was associated with the month in which Khatami's electoral victory occurred. A former Interior Minister until his interpellation in June 1998 and an outspoken critic of the conservative establishment in 1998–99, Nuri had become a charismatic politician who had received more than 40 percent of the votes in the Tehran City Council elections in March 1999, collecting some 200,000 votes more than the second person elected to the council. The third reformist winner was Jamileh Kadivar, sister of the imprisoned Mohsen Kadivar. Nuri's triumph at the polls gave the impression that he would be a top vote getter in the next parliamentary election, with a good chance of becoming the Speaker of the Majlis in 2000, a real nightmare to the hard-line clerics (Chapter 15).

On November 27, 1999, the Special Court for the Clergy imposed a five-year prison sentence on him, and armed guards whisked him away to Evin prison. Throughout the trial, he "maintained a scornful attitude toward the court and a seeming indifference to his own fate, which characterized his defiant speeches at his trial."[61] These were familiar postures of Iranians who would become national heroes.

The Court made a mistake in opening the two-week trial and allowing reporters to report extensively on Nuri's defiant speeches, which in effect put the hard-line clerics on trial for their unconstitutional and antidemocratic policies.[62] The younger clerical judge, a crony of the Supreme Leader, was no match for Nuri's quick mind and tongue, even less so for his comprehensive knowledge of the Islamic issues under discussion. "Tell me, who is challenging our Islamic system here? Is it I, or is it those who ignore our Constitution?" Speaking more to the nation than to the Court that he considered illegal, Nuri declared that his advocacy of improved relations with Washington was no crime, nor was his high regard for Grand Ayatollah Montazeri.[63] He suggested that the regime was responsible for the human rights violations of Iranian citizens and made a direct reference to the extrajudicial killings of the 1990s by naming dozens, including Sa'idi Sirjani and the Protestant pastors. He wanted to know "why the names of the murderers were not announced so that the citizens become aware of the depths of the crimes that have been committed in this country."[64]

Before the trial, Nuri had spoken openly of creating a measure of control over the enormous power of the Supreme Leader. He pointed out the improper constitutional arrangement whereby the Assembly of Experts, empowered to certify the qualification of the Leader, was the one whose judging members the same Leader appointed.[65] Nuri repeatedly asserted that the Supreme Leader, like any other citizen, must remain within the law. The larger implication of this assertion could not escape the attention of both conservatives and reformists. It was a challenge to the Supreme Leader's prerogatives that—the reformists now believed—had proven to be the main obstacle to the development of true republican institutions accountable to the people. And Isfahan's senior cleric, Ayatollah Jalaledin Taheri, a mentor to both Nuri and Kadivar, said: "Nuri revived the dead questions of the revolution. What Nuri said in court was what everyone knew but would not dare to express."[66]

The seemingly unconnected strings of past judicial and security abuses had become tangled in a tug of war. On its opposite ends the rival clerics tugged on the political rope, each trying to outmaneuver the other. The Grand Ayatollah Montazeri, the Dissident in Chief in the religious camps, declared Nuri "the pride of every freedom-loving cleric," adding that the "conviction by an illegal court only booted his credibility and honor." He further observed that his imprisonment was part of "the struggle for religion and free thought."[67] The Grand Ayatollah who had helped to create the Islamic State was now in struggle against what it had become. Reacting to Nuri's conviction, Ayatollah Yusof Sane'i, now a senior teacher in Qom's theological seminary, said to a group of students: "Islam is a religion with thought and understanding at its service, rather than whips and batons. Islam is a religion of mosques, not of prisons and torture."[68] He too had conveniently forgotten his own cracking of whips and blistering denunciations of the "enemies of Islam" in the 1980s.

The Rights to Participate in the Political Life of the Country and to Peaceful Assembly and Association

As discussed in Chapter 2, although the Islamic Constitution allowed for a republic, *velayat-e faqih* (the vice-regency of the Islamic Jurist) circumscribed the right to participate directly in elections for the Majlis (parliament), the presidency, and other elected positions. This contradictory constitutional arrangement bedeviled the political clerics in the 1990s.

The Guardian Council acted as the political watchdog of *velayat-e faqih*. It was composed of six clerical jurists who were appointed by the *faqih* (Supreme Leader) and six lay jurists who were nominated by the Head of the Judiciary, himself an appointee of the *faqih*. The Constitution bestowed upon the Guardian Council the power of rejecting parliamentary bills that it deemed contradictory to the *shari'ah*. The Council's main task, therefore, was to deal with the conflicts inherent in the juxtaposition of the sovereignty of the *faqih* and the sovereignty of the people. Up until the Majlis elections in early 2000, it accomplished the task in favor of the *faqih*.

The Extraconstitutional and Constitutional Exclusions

A successful implementation of *velayat-e faqih* depended on forceful exclusion of all secular nationalist and leftist forces from Iran's political scene, since such a rule by definition left no room for legislative interactions and compromises with political parties that did not believe in the Shiite theocracy. The earliest regulations for parliamentary elections passed by the clerically dominated Revolutionary Council in 1980 made sure only those who had expressed strong allegiance to the Islamic Republic could stand for election. The reality was that all prospective candidates who remained truly independent of clerical factions were forcibly prevented from seeking elected offices. It was an unofficial and extralegal exclusion. The institutionalization of *velayat-e faqih* in the 1980s was contingent upon prior suppression. The powerful clerics eliminated, forced into political dormancy, or drove into exile all groups and individuals who could have actively participated. It was as if the secular groups, nonreligious intellectuals, and the entire leftist movement had vanished. This unofficial and extralegal exclusion mediated between the sovereignty of the people and the sovereignty of the *faqih*. The political clerics created a system that operated on the foundation of widespread exclusion, even before commencing the formal electoral process. They achieved it by the use of bloody suppression and continuous intimidation.

What could justify the claim made by the political clerics and their lay protégé that they alone determined the political life of the country? Their rhetoric employed two tactics to justify their exclusive legitimacy. Using the language of politicized Islam, they argued that it was the religious duty of the Shiite clerics to create an Islamic government. In addition, they exploited the revolutionary sentiments of the year 1979, specifically the "sacrifices made by the Muslim nation of Iran" in creating the Islamic Republic. Those sacrifices remained the clerics' exclusive political asset, a kind of collateral that they could draw on in perpetuity to legitimize their hold on power. Of course, they ignored the fact that much of the original popular support had dissipated through official corruption and intolerable zealotry. This official version left little room for acknowledging that violations of human rights had been committed against secular political activists and intellectuals who opposed the clerical dominance. Such an acknowledgment would be tantamount to recognizing that their opponents had the right to be politically active or to enter electoral politics. The audacious and the foolhardy who opposed *velayat-e faqih* were Islam's enemy, forfeiting their rights, if not their humanity.

The hidden suppression that prevailed after 1982, when very few individuals dared to claim any right, simply prevented them from raising their heads and signaling their intention to run in elections. The process left few visible victims of violation of this right. Perhaps this was the reason that the UN reports paid no attention in the 1980s to the violation of the right to participate in the political life of the country, in the same way that they ignored the right to freedom of opinion and expression.

The secularists dared not even submit the required application. However, this extraconstitutional exclusion of considerable sectors of politically active citizens was not sufficient to guarantee the smooth functioning of *velayat-e faqih*. Thus, the clerics created a system by which they approved the suitability of all individuals who dared to announce their candidacies for the Majlis, the presidency, and other elected offices. They had to submit applications for prior examination of their candidacies. However, as political tensions between the factions within the regime increased, the patently manipulative process, controlled by the hard-line clerics, rejected candidates mainly based on political disagreements and factional affiliations.

With reference to the parliamentary elections, a scholar sympathetic to the Islamist rulers described the manipulation of elections in the early 1990s "as a method of controlling, discrediting, and eliminating rival factions." The struggle was over which of the official factions would control the Majlis. "The victorious faction shrewdly capitalizes on this perception to consolidate its control and power in other important institutions of governing."[1] This explained the dynamics of factionalism among the officially tolerated groups, without considering the larger polity where prior exclusions had already taken place through violence in the early 1980s.

During his visits to Tehran in 1990, Reynaldo Galindo Pohl inquired about the right to freedom of association that is needed for political participation, but he could only do so by interviewing liberal Muslims like Mahdi Bazargan.[2] The regime granted the right to peaceful (and not so peaceful because of the *hezbollahi* vigilantes) assembly and association only to its supporters. In fact, the clerics in power organized and financed such assemblies and associations. There were few possibilities in the mid-1990s for liberal Muslims or secular Iranians to form organizations. It was indicative of the narrow limits of official tolerance that Bazargan's Freedom Movement of Iran was the only group that continued its precarious existence. It occupied a borderline political position between those groups that the clerics had forcefully banned and those that enjoyed clerical sponsorship. It played a painful game of hide-and-seek with its former allies in the Islamic Revolution of 1979.

During Galindo Pohl's visits to Tehran, Bazargan presented a cautiously worded indictment of the government's anti-human rights practices. He explained that his organization had barely survived, since its offices were taken over in June 1988 and four of its leaders were arrested. "Its newspaper had been confiscated illegally and attempts to obtain a judicial decision on this matter had failed." The ex-premier further informed the Special Representative that the authorities never clarified the legal status of his political organization. He explained that the Act of Parliament that was supposed to regulate the formation of political parties dated back to 1981. Article 10 of the Act provided for a Commission to implement the law. The Commission met in late 1988 and paid no attention to the application submitted by Bazargan's group. The so-called Article 10 Commission only approved those associations belonging to the ruling circles within the regime.[3]

Ignoring the prior suppression that had circumscribed the right to political participation, the officials resorted to bureaucratic formality in explaining away the absence of independent political groups. Ali Muhammad Besharati, the Interior Minister, asserted "that in the past 12 years no organization had asked to be registered as a political party." This was a testimony to the prior suppression discussed above. In fact, the only group that dared to ask was Bazargan's political associates, one of whom pointed out the fallacy of the Interior Minister's assertion. He said "that his organization had requested formal registration in 1983 and had still not received any reply to its application."[4]

Other individuals close to Bazargan spoke of similar woes. They tried to establish the Association for the Protection of Freedoms and Human Rights. They wrote a charter and submitted it to the Interior Ministry. Three years passed without an official response. "Last year [1989] they received forms from the authorities which were duly completed, but no reply was given to their request for official recognition. The authorities had occupied the Association's offices one and a half years ago and its chairman was arrested on that occasion."[5]

During the second visit, Galindo Pohl interviewed the Majlis deputy who chaired the Article 10 Commission (the Commission on Political Parties). The Commission's real function was to keep the outsiders out. The chairman offered the same explanation that human rights monitors have often heard in other countries. He said, "Certain groups claim to be defending human rights in order to mask political activities—at times, political activities designed to destabilize the Government."[6] Presumably, he had no problem with the government-sponsored groups that embellished themselves by tacking "human rights" to their titles.

The Guardian Council's Abuse of Its Power

The Constitution envisioned for the Guardian Council a supervisory role in elections for the presidency, the Majlis, and other representative bodies. Again, this took place after violent exclusion of secularists, which prepared the conditions for this "legal" vetting of prospective candidates. As the Third Majlis was approaching its end in 1992, a major political realignment pitted the radical Islamists (in the 1990s they were called the Old Left) who enjoyed a majority in the Majlis against the tactical alliance of the pragmatist supporters of President Rafsanjani and the more conservative Islamists. The latter preferred the bazaar economy to the state-controlled economic policies of the radical Islamists. Both sides began their political maneuverings to ensure a majority in the Fourth Majlis (1992–96).

The radical Islamists lost at the end, and the Guardian Council played a major role in the process. Offering a new interpretation of Article 99 of the Constitution in 1992, the Guardian Council gave itself approbatory supervision (*nezarat-e esteswabi*), rejecting applications of candidates it deemed undesirable. The daily *Salam*, which was launched to counter Rafsanjani's policies, lamented the loss of the right to stand for election. It questioned the process that had transformed "the citizen's fundamental rights to privileges" by restricting the eligibility to such a degree that a large part of society could not "find the persons it wished amongst the candidates."[7] Of course, the radicals-turned-reformists did not care to express such a concern at a time when secular Iranians were unable to exercise their right.

No objective criteria existed for excluding those who had registered their candidacies. The Council could use elusive notions such as a candidate's Islamic piety to decide his qualification for election. It was also arbitrary in its decision. For example, it twice approved Behzad Nabavi's applications to stand for the Majlis elections and rejected him once. The rejection came in the 1997 by-elections, when he had closely allied himself with Khatami's presidential campaign. A lay supporter of Khomeini, Nabavi had been a fixture in the Islamic system since its inception, and he would become one of the organizers of the pro-Khatami reformist victory in the 2000 elections for the Majlis.

The elections for the Majlis in April 1992 attracted Galindo Pohl's attention. He noted that of some 3,000 applications that were sent to the Guardian Council for approval, one-third were rejected. Rejected applicants included dozens of the former Majlis deputies and cabinet ministers, six of whom wore clerical turbans.[8] One was Sadeq Khalkhali, who as the clerical judge in the revolution of 1979–80 had Khomeini's blessing in sentencing hundreds of the Shah's high officials to death. He wanted to know why he was excluded from the list of candidates, but he received no reply. If insiders like him "are treated in such a manner," he wondered, "think what will happen to others."[9] He was not the only former revolutionary cleric who highlighted his own plight as an insider by wondering about others.[10] Even the official, conservative Association for Women of the Islamic Republic objected to the disqualification of several of its candidates.[11]

The vetting policies of the Guardian Council reflected the ruling circle's political divisions, which manifested themselves in two major clerical associations and a number of smaller groups. By the mid-1990s, many of the leading conservative Islamists were members of the Association of Combatant Clerics (Jame'eh-ye Ruhaniyyat-e Mobarez), who also controlled the Guardian Council. All six appointed clerics on the Council were leading members of the Association. They disliked the latest modernist interpretations of Islam, demanded strict adherence to the Islamic dress code for women, supported a free market economy, and expressed xenophobia in cultural policy and anti-Americanism in foreign policy. They strongly supported an absolutist interpretation of *velayat-e faqih*, which they considered the source of all legitimacy. They advocated total state control and censorship over all cultural products. They were the main forces behind the violations of the right to freedom of expression and the press. They strongly supported the candidacy of Ali Akbar Nateq Nuri in the presidential election of 1997 and experienced a crisis of self-confidence after Khatami's surprising victory. The daily *Resalat* reflected their views in the second half of the 1990s.

Defending the absolute power of *velayat-e faqih*, the Association of Combatant Clerics received critical support from an influential network of "official clerics," who were appointed by the Supreme Leader as the Friday prayer leaders in the provinces. Standing ready to give critical and, if necessary, violent assistance were other hard-liners who had coalesced in smaller groups, mixtures of laymen and middle-rank clerics. The most militant was an old group of traditionalist activists referred to as the Mota'llefeh (amalgamation), led by men such as Habibollah Askaroladi and Assadollah Badamchian, who were both closely allied with conservative bazaar merchants. They were prone to using violence to advance their fundamentalist politics. Muhammad Reza Taraqi actively represented the group's views in the Majlis. Mota'llefeh published a monthly magazine (*Shoma*) that regularly demonized the secular intellectuals and lampooned liberal Muslims. Of course, the conservative supporters of the Supreme Leader controlled scores of other semiofficial publications such as *Kayhan, Jomhuri-ye Islami,* and *Abrar.*

These organizations offered practical support to the Supreme Leader, especially in mobilizing crowd actions in critical political junctures. However, behind them lay a web of personal relationships entangling many of the regime's leading personalities. Many of them belonged to an informal, cabalistic affiliation (the "graduates" of Refah or Haqani religious schools) and cultivated a mysterious aura for most of their activities. The reformist clerics disliked the Haqani graduates as a group who held narrow political views and exercised control over the Judiciary.[12] They also belonged to patronage networks that benefited from financial resources of the semiofficial organizations such as the Mostazafan Foundation and the Fifteenth of Khordad Foundation. The latter placed a bounty on Salman Rushdie's head. They engaged in mutually profitable partnerships where nepotism ran rampant. Thus, their considerable assets and personal fortunes—in the hands of those who controlled them and those who were the beneficiaries of their patronage machines—depended on the security of *velayat-e faqih.* The best known men in this web of patronage and power were Ayatollah Ali Meshgini, Ayatollah Makarem Shirazi, Hojjat al-Islam Muhammadi Reyshahri, Ayatollah Mahdavi Kani, Ayatollah Nateq Nuri, Ayatollah Jannati, Ayatollah Yazdi, Habibollah Askaroladi, Assadollah Badamchian, and Mohsen Rafiqdust. Several of them enjoyed a close relationship with the security network controlled by Ali Fallahian. President Rafsanjani ostensibly kept his political distance, but his family members were involved with and benefited financially from the web of patronage.

This powerful Association of Combatant Clerics and its allies faced the oppositional clerics who had developed political and personal dislike of the dominant groups. They had their own organization, the Society of Combatant Clerics (Majma-e Ruhaniyyun-e Mobarez). After several years of political quiescence following their parliamentary defeat in 1992, they reentered politics in the late 1990s. Hojjat al-Islam Mahdi Karrubi spoke for them in public. They were less hostile to the outside world and less enamored of the open market economy or traditional bazaar. Some of them were former radical Islamists who used to advocate a social welfare state assisting the poor; some had turned to Islamic reformism in the early 1990s. The daily *Salam* represented their views, at least in the earlier years of its publication. Their rivalry with the Association of Combatant Clerics, who gave unconditional support to the absolute power of the Supreme Leader, had led the Karrubi group to advocate some limits on the power of *velayat-e faqih*. Of course, they presented such a moderate position only after Ayatollah Ali Khamenei assumed that office. Thus, they supported halfheartedly political reforms that would strengthen the existing republican institutions.

Several smaller groups, the best known of which was the Organization of the Mojahedin of the Islamic Revolution (Mojahedin-e Enqelab-e Islami), supported this clerical oppositional group. Muhammad Salamati headed this organization in the late 1990s, and Behzad Nabavi was behind the biweekly *Asr-e Ma* (Our Era), advocating reforms and supporting Khatami's presidency.

Open Protests Against Exclusionary Practices

The Guardian Council's blatant abuse of its power for political purposes incensed many within the regime. The tempo of public criticism of the Council increased among the supporters of the Islamic Republic. Liberal Muslims outside the regime also kept up the pressure. The critics only saw a supervisory function for the Council and not an exclusionary power serving the political preferences of its members who belonged to the dominant faction.

The conservative powerholders reacted by adding amendments to the elections law. Passed on July 26, 1995, the amendments sought to provide a legally sound ground for the exclusionary power of the Guardian Council. However, they failed to create logical, coherent criteria for the Council's acceptance or disqualification of prospective candidates. The conflict over the arbitrariness of the Council decisions continued into the 2000 elections for the sixth Majlis.

The Guardian Council's exclusionary practices marred the elections for the Fifth Majlis held in early 1996. It rejected the candidacies of 40 percent of 5,121 prospective candidates for the 270-seat Majlis. It also nullified the results of a score of the elected individuals.[13] Human Rights Watch published an excellent report on the exclusionary electoral procedure: "In practice, the council has excluded candidates who, in its view, 'lacked a practical commitment to Islam,' or 'failed to uphold the principles of *velayat-e faqih*. . . .' The council is not required to give reasons for its exclusions. Its decisions are final and not subject to appeal."[14]

UN Special Representative Maurice Copithorne also noted that the elections were marked by irregularities in eight electoral divisions, "which led to the nullification of the results."[15] This was the same report at the beginning of which Copithorne restated his desire to discuss progress that had already been achieved or still had to be accomplished. Obviously, Copithorne had also adopted a limited perspective for his reporting on the right to political participation, ignoring the prior extralegal exclusion of secular individuals and liberal Muslims who did not dare to submit applications. Copithorne only mentioned the official disqualification of some of those who submitted applications for their candidacy. This offered an opportunity for the regime's diplomats to respond: "Since 1979, the Islamic Republic of Iran has held five rounds of parliamentary elections and six rounds of presidential elections and so many other elections. The mere suggestion that some irregularities were alleged during the recent election would indeed not constitute strong argument to question the entire democratic system, as democracy in the Islamic Republic of Iran is institutionalized."[16]

The diplomats went on bragging about the people's active participation in the process of elections and the "lively competition and free debate between the candidates in a free political environment."[17] Within Copithorne's narrow perspective, this official fustian in expression may not appear strained after all. Human Rights Watch offered a wider perspective and a clearer focus that provided little opportunity for false diplomatic claims of institutionalized democracy.[18]

The details of the Guardian Council's exclusionary power revealed how a cultural relativist claim led to an argumentative closed circle. Limits on rights were originally defended on religious grounds; however, when devout coreligionists with different political views objected, they were declared to be misguided citizens or misfits. Moreover, the details of many elections indicated another curse of the religious state in that the Shiite religious tradition was abusive of modern electoral processes, essential for the right to political participation in a state society like Iran. By the mid-1990s, many people had become disillusioned with the political process, especially with the limited choice of candidates, and refused to participate in elections. Some disgruntled Muslim activists even demanded free election, without which they would not cast their votes.[19] The main demand was for the removal of qualification procedures by the Guardian Council.

This protest prompted a response from the Supreme Leader. He showed sensitivity toward any suggestion that the decreasing number of people casting their votes signaled diminished popularity of the regime. In the election of 1996, he became creative again by extending a traditional Islamic edict to modern electoral practices, hoping to intimidate those who spoke of the lack of popular participation in elections. In a speech to provincial governors and officials in charge of the elections, he attacked those who said that people either did not participate in elections or should not do so. "If you carefully examine these people, you will see that they are dependent on the [foreign] enemy. If they are not in practice the hired agents, they serve, in the way they think, the enemies of this nation." Then he came to his innovative Islamic ruling: If a person expressed his intention outside his private house, saying that he would not participate in an election, he must be punished because he had committed a crime. He said that Islamic punishment was applied for a sin that was demonstrated in public. He made his new ruling clear by drawing an analogy with a more familiar Islamic ruling: A person not fasting inside his own house during the month of Ramadan had committed a sin but would not be punished; if he ate in public, he would be subject to the punishment of Islamic *ta'zir*.[20]

The opposition to the Guardian Council's rejection of prospective candidates gathered steam following President Khatami's election on May 23, 1997. As discussed in Chapter 2, the clerical establishment rejected 234 presidential candidates who dared to apply, allowing only four to compete in an open election. Copithorne expressed a positive judgment on the election of the new president.[21]

On March 2, 1998, the association of students at Tehran University held a public rally in front of the university. The association had long supported the Islamic regime. Khatami's administration had permitted the rally, which was intended to give support to the President and voice objections to the Guardian Council's rejection of a number of candidates for the midterm elections for the Majlis. The *hezbollahi* groups attacked the rally. There was widespread discussion about the event in the reformist press.

The next nationwide election was for the Assembly of Leadership Experts (Majlis-e Khobregan-e Rahbari), empowered to appoint and dismiss the Supreme Leader, the occupant of the office of *velayat-e faqih*. Since only a *faqih* (Islamic Jurist) could assume that office, it was expected that the Guardian Council would only accept the candidacy of the qualified clerics for the Assembly. Only clerics, it was assumed, could properly determine the qualifications of a *faqih*. This generated an intense debate. The Constitution envisaged the Supreme Leader as an Islamic Jurist, who was moreover familiar with the affairs of the state and knowledgeable about "the circumstances of his age" (Article 5).

The maverick Abdollah Nuri, among others who were perhaps influenced by the writings of Mojtahid Shabestari, argued thoughtfully that the clerical members of the Assembly were qualified to pass judgment only on the religious qualifications of the prospective Leader. However, Nuri pointed out that the "circumstances of the age" were very complex. To judge these complexities properly, other (lay) Iranians must be elected to the Assembly, those who were conversant with the worldly affairs of government, society, sciences, and technology. The Assembly should be "an admixture of diverse groups, each of whom specialized in specific areas and capable of forming sound opinions on such subject matters." [22] This essentially Islamic reformist argument, which was also endorsed by his mentor, Grand Ayatollah Montazeri, could undermine the Khomeinist construct of *velayat-e faqih*. More forcefully criticizing the procedure that allowed only the clerics to sit in the Assembly and select the Supreme Leader, Akbar Ganji wrote: "If the senior clerics consider the selection of the Leader to be their exclusive right, why don't they set up their own Vatican and like the Catholic cardinals limit the governance to themselves and not to citizens?"[23]

In the elections for the eighty-three-member Assembly of Leadership Experts held in October 1998, the Guardian Council misused its "approbatory supervision" and rejected the candidacies of a large group of individuals, many of whom were Khatami's supporters. Of some 400 applicants, only 160 men (and no women) were declared eligible. Of those approved, not more than 40 men could be considered as the President's supporters. UN Special Representative Copithorne noted widespread complaints about the undemocratic process.[24] The people's turnout was limited, reflecting the fact that prior exclusion by the Guardian Council had a negative impact on the people's desire to participate. President Khatami's objection to the manipulation was as usual mild: "The honorable Guardian Council has endorsed these candidates as suitable. Of course, there are many more suitable and qualified people than those in this list. At any rate, . . . there is still the opportunity to vote for a variety of candidates—that is, the list is still relatively diverse."[25] The result should have been obvious to him. Very few of his reforming supporters were allowed to run, so that even if all of them had won, they would still be a minority in the Assembly of Experts.

Objecting to this obvious political meddling in the election, Hojjat al-Islam Mahdi Karrubi, the leader of the competing Society of Combatant Clerics, wrote an open letter to the Secretary of the Guardian Council, Ayatollah Ahmad Jannati, who responded. That exchange of accusations between these two clerics of rival camps revealed the policies of mutual elimination practiced within the ruling circles of the Islamic Republic. Karrubi listed the names of the well-known individuals, many of them clerics, who had previously served in different official capacities and whose candidacies the Council rejected. After enumerating the services that those individuals had rendered to the regime, he asked what could possibly justify their disqualification. He reminded Jannati how they, as Shiite clerics, had closely cooperated with each other for many years since the revolution. Karrubi in effect accused Jannati and his associates of religious arrogance, because Jannati's group considered their own preferences and their own understanding of the issues to be identical with the precepts of the religion. Conversely, they considered every other person who thinks differently to be antireligious. Jannati's response in essence reiterated that the Council had no obligation to reveal its reasons for disqualifying prospective candidates, adding that it was only answerable to the Supreme Leader. As for the propriety of rejecting so many good and qualified believers, Jannati retorted polemically by pointing out that Khatami had himself dismissed many good and qualified Muslims from their official positions—a clear reference to the replacement of hard-line officials in Khatami's administration with his reformist followers. Were those many dismissals "based on right and justice and without consideration of the political currents?"²⁶ The hard-liners were truly angered by Interior Minister Abdollah Nuri's dismissals of many hard-line officials in all provinces (1,689 of them, according to a hostile Majlis deputy).²⁷ This became a main cause of Nuri's impeachment by the conservative-controlled Majlis in June 1998.

Among the Shiite clerics, the most influential dissident voice belonged to the Grand Ayatollah Montazeri. Referring to the fact that he had been a main figure among those who drafted the Constitution, he issued a religious *fatva* in which he pointed out that the Constitution did not allow the Council the power to veto candidates. He pointed out that the vetting power had in effect made the process a two-stage election, which was against the intentions of the drafters of the Constitution. He pointed out, inaccurately, that the drafters wanted direct election by popular votes and that the Council's supervisory role was intended only to prevent the executive branch in charge of elections to engage in vote frauds.²⁸

Formation of New Political Groups and the Reformists' Electoral Victories

As intrastate conflicts intensified during the second half of the 1990s, political factions within the system formed new political groups to advance their agenda. The so-called Commission 10, responsible for giving licenses to political parties, could only delay its approval. It could not postpone its decision indefinitely, nor could it reject their applications outright, as it had done to Bazargan's political associates.

Under the leadership of Tehran's Mayor, Gholam-Hossein Karbaschi, the technobureaucrats around President Rafsanjani formed the Executives of Construction (Kargozaran-e Sazandegi) in 1995, before the elections for the Fifth Majlis. Its members had to be Muslims and loyal to the Constitution of the Islamic Republic. Its leaders wished to grant membership to the protected religious minorities, but the Commission 10 rejected such an un-Islamic inclusiveness.²⁹ The Executives became one the three main reformist groups competing in the critical Majlis elections in February 2000.

After the 1997 presidential election, Islamic reformers close to President Khatami also realized the need for a political party to further the reformist agenda of what they referred to as the Do-e Khordadi movement. The men and women in this movement possessed a political temperament different than the one exhibited by the Rafsanjani group. The latter maintained a correct, but mostly contrived, fidelity to *velayat-e faqih* and the Supreme Leader. Less authoritarian, Khatami's supporters formed the Islamic Iran Partnership Front (Jebheh-ye Mosharekat-e Iran-e Islami), which was eventually led by Muhammad Reza Khatami, the president's younger brother. Its election platform advocated less state control over the press and fewer state intrusions into private lives. It also wanted a redefinition of *velayat-e faqih*, making it more compatible with the representative institutions of the Republic. The country entered the February 2000 elections for the Majlis with this group as the most popular reformist contender, competing against the conservative power holders and hard-line supporters of *velayat-e faqih*. They cooperated with the Rafsanjani group, but their relationships were fraught with distrust and competition.

The pro-Khatami Islamic Iran Partnership Front and the pro-Rafsanjani Executives of Construction were supported by dozens of smaller political groups, such as the Office for Strengthening Solidarity (Daftar-e Tahkim-e Vahdad), a university group that often sponsored pro-reform student rallies, and the Islamic Party of Labor (Hezb-e Islami-ye Kar). Scores of "professional associations" also joined in the campaigns for change. Together they provided a semblance of reformist political organizations for national elections.

The third main reformist group was the much older Society of Combatant Clerics, led by Karrubi. This group plus the pro-Rafsanjani Executives of Construction and the pro-Khatami Islamic Iran Partnership Front became the three groupings that showed their popularity in the elections for local councils in March 1999. In the race for Tehran's City Council, the pro-Khatami candidates did remarkably well, and the cleric Abdollah Nuri drew far more votes than the second-place candidate. Observers began to refer to him as the next Speaker of the Majlis, since they expected him to run in the 2000 race.[30] In early September 1999, Nuri announced his intention to resign from City Council, which he served as chairman, and to prepare for the Majlis race. He resigned but ended up in Evin prison, as described in Chapter 14.

In the 2000 race for the Majlis, the pro-Khatami reformers presented themselves as candidates who would strengthen the rule of law, curb the illegal activities of the intelligence agents, and expand the boundaries of freedom of expression in the press. In particular, the Islamic Iran Partnership Party advocated significant changes in the Judiciary, including the elimination of the Special Court for the Clergy and the reversal of Ayatollah Yazdi's court reform that combined the roles of prosecutor and judge.[31] A few months before the elections it launched the daily *Mosharekat* that filled the void created by the banning of Abdollah Nuri's popular *Khordad*.

Rafsanjani, who had been the patron of Karbaschi's group, announced his intention to run for the Majlis, and he was placed at the top of the Executives of Construction's list of candidates. Karbaschi, the nominal leader of the Executives of Construction, was released from prison in January 2000 to help Rafsanjani's election campaign, and his release underlined the fact that political expediency could easily supercede proper judicial procedures. One kind of politics placed him in prison, and another kind of politics set him free.

These three main groups of reformers, squabbling among themselves, offered three separate lists, which convinced some observers that the division would increase the chances of the conservative clerics to keep their seats in the Sixth Majlis. A dozen smaller groups supported these reformist lists.

The proponents of the status quo and the absolute power of *velayat-e faqih* also managed to create an umbrella coalition of 15 groups, referred to as the Coalition of Followers of the Line of the Imam and the Leader. Central to this coalition was the Society of Combatant Clerics (Jame'eh-ye Ruhaniyyat-e Mobarez), conservative clerics who controlled such main institutions as the Guardian Council. It offered its own list of 30 candidates for Tehran and 210 for other towns and cities around the country.

Months before the 2000 elections, the conservatives in the Majlis, assisted by the Guardian Council, and the reformists in Khatami's administration maneuvered to increase their chances in the pivotal elections. Each move and countermove created spirited debates in the press. The Guardian Council's prerogative to screen all candidates generated more open opposition than ever before. In May 1999, the Supreme Leader again denounced those who intended to weaken the Council and "pave the way for election to the Majlis of people opposed to Islam." [32]

The 2000 campaigns began with the rejected candidates denouncing, bemoaning, and sometimes ridiculing the process that had officially eliminated them. Outside the regime's competing camps were the liberal Muslims, who had participated in the 1979 revolution and who were ousted afterward but never violently suppressed. They hoped for a better treatment in 2000, when the President was advocating tolerance. They formed the Nationalist-Religious Coalition and pleaded to be recognized. They sponsored thirty candidates for the Majlis, but their applications were promptly rejected, including that of Ibrahim Yazdi, the leader of the Freedom Movement of Iran. President Khatami was unwilling or unable to take any steps toward legalization of the Muslim organization. Some high officials around the President still expressed typical conspiratorial views, shared by the conservative clerics, to the effect that those who have "any connection to foreigners" (meaning Yazdi and his associates) should not be granted official recognition as a party. [33] The Yazdi group wrote a letter of protest to President Khatami and held new conferences. [34] Nevertheless, having declared themselves the Nationalist-Religious Coalition, they supported five independent candidates who were included in other lists approved by the Guardian Council. [35]

The Guardian Council's approach to Khatami's supporters was more complex and manipulative. It barred the leading Islamic reformists, particularly the activist journalists whose spirited articles in the press had made them household names among the educated public: Abdollah Nuri (applying from prison!), Abbas Abdi, Hashem Agha-Jeri, Hamid Reza Jala'eipur, and Azam Talaqani. All of them remained defiant and expressed outrage at the Council's decision. Azam Taleqani told a reporter that the conservatives in power must realize how they had misdirected the Islamic Republic over the past twenty years. "The exclusionary exercise of power," she asserted, "was indicative of their weakness." [36]

The Council, however, allowed other individuals associated with the three main reformist groups to run. It became apparent that the debate over the Council's "approbatory supervision" had made an impact not only on public opinion but also on the conservative allies of the Supreme Leader. Since the elections for the Assembly of Leadership Experts in October 1998, the Council had come under enormous pressure from all sides, with unmistakable expression of public dislike for its veto power. It ultimately decided to exercise restraint and allowed many reformers who had agreed to work within the regime to stand for election. It behaved more moderately also because the Intelligence Ministry and the Judiciary, which in previous elections had recommended rejections, exercised much more restraint in 2000.[37] Both institutions had less confrontational leadership following the extrajudicial killings of 1988 and Ayatollah Yazdi's "retirement" from the Judiciary. The Intelligence Ministry was also forced to give up the money-generating enterprises that it ran as a corporate conglomerate.

John F. Burns, writing for the *New York Times*, was accurate in his observations: "While key reform leaders have been jailed in recent years, and some killed, and reformist newspapers have endured a relentless campaign of harassment and closure, the conservatives have given the reformers enough leeway to prevent popular restlessness from boiling over. The prime tactician in this appears to have been Ayatollah Khamenei, who has at times made concessions to the reformers, and at other times hit back hard." [38]

Many observers perceived the 2000 elections as a referendum on the state's religious nature and its many restricted practices, imposed in the name of Islam. The diehard conservatives, on the other hand, felt that the reformist desires would undermine the religious nature of the state founded by Ayatollah Khomeini. The elections for the enlarged 290-seat Sixth Majlis, involving 5,800 candidates including 424 women, engaged the imaginations of the youth. Tehran, where 861 candidates competed for 30 seats, was buzzing with campaign excitement.

The result was an amazing validation of the young people's desires for change. People elected a much younger and less clerical Majlis, more then 75 percent of whom were new faces. In the first round, 225 of the 290 seats went to those candidates whose names had appeared in the endorsement lists of the three main reformist groups. Even after the second round, the conservatives managed to hold onto only 20 percent of the seats. Of Tehran's thirty representatives, no one associated with the conservative factions that controlled the Fifth Majlis was elected. The first twenty-seven went to those whose names had appeared in the reformist list headed by Muhammad Reza Khatami, the President's brother. From Tehran, only four clerics were elected, three of whom counted among the well-known opponents of the Supreme Leader, including his younger brother, Hadi Khamenei. He had stood up to his older brother and opposed the conservative power holders at a time when few insiders dared to be outspoken, and he was handsomely rewarded by the voters. No less significant was the victory of the cleric Muhammad Musavi Kho'iniha, the publisher of the banned daily *Salam*. The most significant political message that Tehran's voters sent to the Supreme Leader was that the candidates with the second and third highest votes each had a brother who had been convicted by the Special Court for Clergy and was in prison at the time of the elections. The first was President Khatami's brother.

In contrast, the majority of voters in Tehran humiliated the former president, Rafsanjani, who more than any other person symbolized the Islamic state in the first half of the 1990s. Rafsanjani portrayed himself as an elder statesman of Islamic moderation, capable of bringing together different factions in the new Majlis, the same way he claimed he had done as the Speaker from 1981 to 1989. He received the least number of votes among the thirty persons who were elected in the first round in Tehran. The man who finished thirty-first charged irregularities in counting votes. The humiliation was compounded by a popular rumor that he was squeezed in by officials who resorted to cheating by adding to his tally thousands of votes cast in the name of his daughter, Fa'ezeh Hashemi Rafsanjani. Despite the humorous nature of the rumor, it further undermined the Rafsanjani clan. The daughter, the Islamic feminist who had become the darling of some Western scholars, was also rejected by Tehran's young voters, mainly because her father was seen as representing the status quo. The Pro-Rafsanjani party as a whole did poorly compared with the pro-Khatami party.

The surprising results of popular elections since 1997 have severely undermined the legitimacy of the Islamic rule as constituted in the absolute power of *velayat-e faqih*. They also created a crisis of confidence in the conservative clerical establishment headed by the Supreme Leader, Ayatollah Khamenei. The fact that a substantial majority of Iranians wanted systemic reforms could no longer be credibly dismissed by twisted polemics against real and imagined foreign enemies. In a significant speech to his diehard supporters in mid-1998, Khamenei seemed to be downplaying the significance of the majority votes and what they entailed for his office. He resorted to a modified version of the insiders and outsiders (*khudi* and *ghir-e khudi*), but it appeared that the ranks of the insiders had greatly diminished. He seemed to be saying that it did not matter much what millions of people were thinking, since "the real protectors of the Islamic revolution and the legacy of Imam Khomeini were the devoutly Muslim youths and the *hezbollahi* and *basiji* [irregular militia] forces." These were the real people "who had proven themselves in the eight-year war [against Iraq]." The real strength of the nation "resides in their power." Disregarding the fact that millions of voters cast their votes in support of candidates who no longer employed such a binary vision, the beleaguered Supreme Leader added that his devotees were in total control and would frustrate those who "dreamed about restoring the past system and establishing relations with the United States."[39] He was right in the last point; whereas his critics had votes, his supporters had raw power and institutional muscles, capable of frustrating the reformist desires of the new Majlis.

In the mid-1990s, every time the Supreme Leader faced an issue that cast a dark shadow over the legitimacy of the system, his followers gathered together thousands of people in street demonstrations in Tehran. However, at the end of the 1990s the crowds, although still large in absolute numbers, no longer signified the presence of real popular support. In three elections since 1997, a much larger percentage of people, those whom the Islamic regime had marginalized, cast their votes trouncing the well-known conservative defenders of the Leader. The system seemed to have reached its limit. The Leader could not rant and rail against "those people" and then expect them to vote for his supporters. The potent political slogan that the most progressive reformers devised for the elections was "Iran for all Iranians," a clear counter-expression against the clerics' binary vision of insiders-outsiders. In a typical scapegoating tactic, the conservative Ayatollah Mesbah Yazdi denounced the slogan by saying that it was most appealing to Baha'is. The republic side of the Islamic Republic was undermining its Islamic side, as reflected in *velayat-e faqih*. That august Shiite office had become gradually dysfunctional since the death of Ayatollah Khomeini, for whom it was tailored. The revolution had spent itself, and so had *velayat-e faqih*. Inspirational references to either could hardly create Islamic authenticity for the clerics in power.

After the news of the crushing defeat of the hard-line supporters of the Leader in the 2000 elections, the familiar political arsenal of *velayat-e faqih* was rolled into place. In a clear indication that the Leader was not about to hand over control of his regime to the reformist-dominated Majlis, the Expediency Council under the embittered Rafsanjani's control issued a ruling in April 2000 to the effect that the Majlis had no power to investigate any institution under the Leader's control. This ruling would exclude the military, the police, the state broadcasting, the Judiciary, and the wealthy state foundations from the Majlis's jurisdiction. The reformers objected to the unconstitutional decision.[40] As noted in Chapter 13, the new reformist press was banished by the Judiciary after the overwhelming victory of the reformers in the 2000 Majlis elections. The Fifth Majlis had passed a more repressive Press Law; one of its provisions was meant to restrict the ability of reformist editors to reopen their banned publications under new names. The new Majlis, which was dominated by the pro-Khatami reformers, introduced a bill that would in effect repeal the former law; moreover, it would prevent prosecutions of editors by courts other than the Press Court. The combination of a reformist Majlis and a relatively free press was deemed dangerous by the Supreme Leader. On August 6, 2000, he intervened again by issuing a "state order," forbidding the Majlis to pass a new press law. Negating the main constitutional prerogative of the people' representatives, *velayat-e faqih* showed that it could at any moment trump the Majlis, whose reformist members tasted a dose of its oppressive reality after the recent exhilaration of an electoral victory.

Having suffered a humiliating defeat in his drive to become once again the Speaker of the Majlis, the mercurial Rafsanjani "drew explicit parallels between the current political tension and the civil strife between secular nationalists and Islamic militants following the Iranian revolution in 1979." Reminiscent of his alarmist talks in 1980–81, he thundered against "agents" of foreign powers: "What is being attacked is the Islamic content of the revolution. . . . Now they're putting freedom before Islam, freedom before faith." [41] Rafsanjani was as accurate in his evaluation of the political conditions in the early 1980s as he was for those in the new century: The struggle was over *velayat-e faqih*. The future of the Majlis, as the main institution of the republic, as well as that of the free press depended on the outcome of the ongoing political struggle over the future of *velayat-e faqih*.

Chapter 16

The Rights of Women

> In December of 1979, Ms. Farrokhrou Parsa, the first woman to serve in the Iranian cabinet [Minister of Education, appointed 1968], was executed. . . . A few hours after the sentence was pronounced she was wrapped in a dark sack and machine-gunned. . . . At the time of her death she had been retired for four years. . . . She was not a heroic figure but a hard-working, disciplined woman who struggled to achieve her position in government. She was a practical, level-headed feminist. The significance of her position for the Iranian women's movement rested not so much in her considerable personal achievement but in that she was one of hundreds of thousands. Those who executed her also understood this and staged the event as a symbolic attempt to reduce her— and through her the type of women she represented—to an insignificant, lifeless shape in a dark sack.
> —Mahnaz Afkhami, Secretary-General of the Women's Organization of Iran under the Shah

During the early 1990s, UN Special Representative Galindo Pohl took a wider look at Iranian society and saw, apparently for the first time, the secular women who since 1979 had endured insults, intimidation, and discrimination.[1] He improved his coverage of the violations of women's rights and increasingly expanded his reports to include almost all discriminatory laws and humiliating practices directed at them. As mentioned before, international human rights reports during the 1980s devoted no section to the rights of women. Perhaps out of deference to Islamic sensitivities of the rulers, the forced *hijab* (Islamic dress code) was not generally perceived— even in the 1990s when the violations of women's rights were noted—as a violation of the right to freedom of conscience; it was certainly not exposed as rigorously as the violation of the same right was exposed in the case of religious minorities.

Many Iranian women, and not only modern secularists, suffered greatly under the new Islamic restrictions imposed in the early 1980s, when angry young men turned the streets of Tehran into a veritable "cultural" war zone, harassing and attacking women in contemporary international dress. Re-inforcing *hijab* became a vocation for Islamist men who were sent out to the streets in sorties and an avocation for the mischievous among them who seem to enjoy the new opportunity for abusing women in "improper *hijab*" and gain satisfaction for their frustrated sexual fantasies. Thus, women have been placed at the center of the debacle created by the Islamists over culture and authenticity. They are also central to the issue of control and exercise of power in the country. As discussed in the section on Islamization of prison in Chapter 7, in particular the clerics trampled violently on secular women's rights to freedom of conscience and expression. This chapter focuses on this aspect of women's experience.

Dr. Homa Darabi can best be presented as a symbol of the hardships emancipated women were subjected to under the Islamic Republic. A gradu-ate of the University of Tehran's medical school, she pursued residencies in a number of the finest U.S. teaching hospitals before returning to Iran to become an accomplished professor of psychiatry in her alma mater. On Feb-ruary 21, 1994, Dr. Darabi walked into a crowded square in northern Tehran, removed the headscarf required of women by the *hijab*, and doused herself with gasoline. As she shouted, "Death to tyranny! Long live freedom! Long live Iran!" she set herself on fire. It was as though her anger and defeat could be expressed only through the fire that killed her, sending a message to the world that only she possessed her body. Dr. Darabi's final act was a rebuke to the standards of morality of the Shiite clerics' wives and daughters who were unwilling to emancipate their minds by first emancipating their bodies.

In a moving book, her sister described the multiple causes that drove Dr. Darabi to commit suicide. She had endured the humiliations of living in a misogynist culture, the official harassment that aimed at imposing a particular Islamic conscience she despised, and a grossly insensitive hus-band who dismissed all the symptoms of a deepening depression. Himself a physician, the husband seems to have enjoyed the brotherhood of men in a reinvigorated patriarchal web of social and familial relationships that had suffocated her spirit. By late 1980, Dr. Darabi continued to express despair at the conditions of her life in the grip of strict religious rules, while her husband worked within the system and enjoyed privileges due to him be-cause of his gender and profession. She felt "like a caged bird" and stated, "If it wasn't for work, I don't think I could survive."[2] In December 1990, she lost her faculty position because she refused to comply with the Islamic dress code.[3] As a psychiatrist she could still practice. However, the head of the hospital told her that she must adhere to the correct dress code. "She told him she would rather die than wear a chador."[4] She told her sister in 1992: "I love my husband and I love my country and neither one of them is treating me properly."[5]

After more than a decade in which the Islamic regime failed to bring about any fundamental change in Iran's economic position in the increasingly globalized economy—or to identify itself with any economic model (be it a capitalist market economy, state capitalism, or socialism) over which it could assert any exclusive, divinely sanctioned claim—the regime was increasingly compelled to wage its power struggle in cultural terms. Thus, women became the signifier of the anti-Western credentials of the Islamists, the veiled ones as a positive testimonial and the "badly veiled" ones as the evidence for continued Islamist vigilance against the collaborators with the West.

Being placed on the edge of what seems to be the sole slippery terrain for deviation from the true path of Islam, women became the raison d'être of *velayat-e faqih*, the unwilling bestowers of its legitimacy. The sight of bare-headed women was a challenge to the legitimacy of the religious state. Other vices like Western and Iranian popular music, videos, films, and alcohol were produced locally, smuggled, distributed, and consumed at homes whose morality the Islamic Republic failed to "Islamize." Unlike the secular women's dress, these were hidden vices in which men of all ideological stripes partook without feeling threatened in their public domination.

Discriminatory Laws and Practices Limiting
Human Rights of All Women

After the victory of the revolution, Ayatollah Khomeini wasted no time in reversing the reformist legal trend that Iranian secular women had helped to establish under the Shah. The clerics discarded the 1967 Family Protection Law (amended 1975) that the Shah's government had enacted. The Shah's law offered some meaningful protection to women by making divorce and polygamy more difficult for men. It also took away men's automatic custody over children and placed the issue at the discretion of the court.

The new Islamic regulations placed men in control of divorce and the custody of children. The Islamic rules neatly measured the worth of a woman as half that of a man. The clerics reimposed the medieval practice of Islamic laws of retribution and punishment. In the Islamic Penal Code's section on the *diyat* (compensation or blood money for murder or injury), the price for a woman killed by a man was set at half the price for a murdered man. Inheritance law codified the worth of a woman as half that of a man. The law also defined the unacceptability of women's testimony in judicial determination of certain crimes.[6] And in cases where women's testimony was accepted, its value was equal to half that of a man's testimony. The traditional culture had taken for granted that a female's sexuality was a concern to all her male relatives. Thus, the new law also empowered male relatives to "protect" women's chastity. It sanctioned the outraged husband who killed his wife if she offended his honor by engaging in a relationship with another man.[7]

Dr. Hossein Mehrpur, the regime's liaison with the UN Commission on Human Rights, acknowledged in his Persian writings that all these limitations stood in violation of the UN Covenant on Civil and Political Rights. However, Mehrpur reiterated the official position that the state's policies were not to "belittle women and violate their rights."[8]

The UN Special Representative, Galindo Pohl, provided information on the increased incidence of polygamy. Men could legally marry up to four wives; they could also have "temporary" wives. He noted an increase in the practice of short-term marriages. The newly enacted Islamic Family Law gave men the exclusive right to divorce. The law also severely circumscribed a mother's right to custody of her children; she could automatically lose custody of a son after the age of two and of a daughter after the age of seven.[9] Galindo Pohl mentioned that the law sanctioned the marriage of nine-year-old girls.[10] Women also had to secure written permission from their husband to travel abroad.[11]

New Islamic regulations denied women professional opportunities in some areas of public life. Limitations were also imposed on many fields of higher education and professional training for women, who were denied the opportunity to advance to managerial positions.[12] In November 1992, Galindo Pohl offered the figure of 40,000 female teachers who were dismissed by the state between 1980 and 1985. Like Dr. Darabi, they did not fit into the Islamic model of proper women. Amidst an uproar of protests by legal professionals, the regime also dismissed female judges, since Islam reserves the occupation only for Shiite clerics, who were by definition men.[13] The Islamic Republic appeared as a bonanza for traditional Muslim men. However, appearances were deceiving, as the strength of secular habits became apparent.

Women Fighting Back to Recover Lost Rights

Discriminatory laws and practices created a negative reaction that was eventually reflected within the regime. Islamization of women's spheres of life proved more difficult than what Ayatollah Khomeini had assumed. Despite the inadequacies of the Shah's Family Protection Law, the urban women's knowledge of its progressive direction—as well as their knowledge of educational opportunities that the Shah's regime had opened to women—worked against the Islamist projects. Having come of age in the late 1970s and early 1980s, women whose voices and actions frustrated the total Islamization project were the graduates of the previous regime's high schools, if not the universities. Even the practicing Muslims among them might struggle to make sure their daughters' legal protections in family and their right to higher education would not be curtailed. Mothers who had not gotten the chance to go to universities would do their utmost to have their daughters graduated from the universities, whose values and upward mobility functions remained intact, despite the Islamist propaganda emphasizing motherhood.

An impressive surge in private educational activities hoping to give proper training to children of both sexes—even in Western languages, arts, and music—and prepare them for a university education occurred despite the Islamic Republic. "Government officials have stated," Copithorne observed in 1999, "that female students enrolling in university in 1998 outnumbered male students."[14] This was hardly remarkable, since it indicated at best a continuing trend from the Shah's time. A year before the fall of the Shah, "33 percent of all university students were women and they began to choose fields other than traditionally female occupations."[15] Leaving aside the poor quality of tertiary education and low standards of education in the new Islamic universities,[16] the credit for this and other educational achievements must properly go to women themselves, as well as to the tradition of secular higher education that had developed strong roots in the 1960s and 1970s.

It did not take long even for Islamist women to learn the real implications of the Ayatollah's rules. These women began to find an "Islamic" way to fight back, hoping to remove or modify some of the newly imposed limitations. Since they could not question Islam, they returned to the earlier Islamic reformist practice, blaming traditional interpretations of Islam that sanctioned discrimination. This struggle in turn spawned an Iranian version of Islamic "feminism," whose proponents raised their voices within the regime's fluctuating limits on freedom of expression. Like the Islamic reformers of previous generations, they claimed that the discriminatory practices, especially in family laws, were inconsistent with the moral precepts of "True Islam." Through their reinterpretation, Islamic "feminists" hoped to offer a better, improved Islam. Therefore, Islamist women seeking changes in law and practice were the first group of Iranians to make a tacit return to the basic tenants of Islamic reformism that were derailed by Khomeinism.

A list of the heads of Islamic women's organizations was almost identical with a list of politically or socially active wives and daughters of clerics or their laymen associates.[17] As Haleh Esfandiari observed, these women "had to adopt a posture that at once met new standards of propriety for women in a regime determined to 'Islamize' society and that also responded to the concrete needs of women."[18] A secular woman in Tehran observed in 1996 that Islamic women's organizations and publications were linked with the competing factions within the regime. At any moment, some of these factions were in power and some were struggling to gain more power. At best, these women did "support some pro-women reforms within the framework of Islam."[19]

Challenging the conservative clerics who had long assumed that the privilege of Islamic interpretation was theirs alone, Islamic "feminists" wished to remove *fiqh*, Islamic jurisprudence, from the male monopoly. They argued that, throughout history, men had inappropriately defined the perimeters of *shari'ah* laws and kept women secluded in subordination. They asserted that "True Islam" had always encouraged learning for women as well as for men. Therefore, a learned woman was as qualified as a learned man to offer interpretations, with the goal of removing layers of misguided limitations that male interpreters had placed on women's lives. Like philosophy professor Sorush, they offered their own reading of Islam, and like him they became targets of clerical attacks.

Despite threats and harassment, Islamic women continued to put pressure on the regime. The moderates among them participated in the larger Islamic reformist debate for a more open society and a less restrictive press law. For example, Shahla Sherkat, the editor of the magazine *Zanan* (Women), indignantly rejected the simplistic notion of Western "cultural invasion" introducing elements of corruption into Iranian society. The real problem that could open the doors to such an "invasion," she asserted, emanated from the conservative restrictions that had created a culturally barren land.[20]

Islamic reformists argued that certain norms governing women's position in an Islamic society were derived not from immutable laws of the Qur'an but from cultural practices that had accumulated over years. The argument blamed an amorphous patriarchy, which had apparently grown in an ideological vacuum and inexplicably drawn no inspirations from Islamic teachings. UN Special Representative Copithorne noted the argument and repeated the reformist view that these patriarchal practices "can and are being changed."[21] This is similar to the neo-feminist positions among some Western academics with Islamic backgrounds, who reject the misogynist Islamic tradition as a foreign contribution to Islam.[22] Copithorne also stated the position of the struggling Islamic women who believed in gender complementarity. Thus, men and women could not be granted equality, since they function in different but complementary spheres of life. What these women demanded therefore was equity, as determined by benevolent Islamic values toward both sexes.[23]

Islamic "feminists" in Tehran focused their attention on those aspects that could improve women's social and economic well-being, such as reducing the required age for women's retirement or providing national insurance for women and children. They faced a very difficult situation. As one moderate female Majlis representative said in 1998, women increasingly wanted change; however, it meant that they would have to go against the law, since "patriarchal beliefs have somehow assumed legal forms."[24] They succeeded in changing the law that allowed honor killings. The amended law made men who killed their wives subject to the existing legal procedure for murder. They also succeeded in removing many of the restrictions that the Islamic

Republic had imposed on higher education for women. As a sympathetic scholar observed, it was a notable achievement "since at the time there were discriminatory measures against women in 119 academic subject areas."[25]

For more than fifteen years, almost all Islamist women were activists who expressed no major objection to *velayat-e faqih* and its authoritarian political structure, as long as it kept secular outsiders from freely participating in public policy debates. However, they wanted more than a handful of Islamist women in high governmental positions. They also demanded from their Islamist brethren more female representation in the Majlis. Standing outside the regime, a few secular feminists began in the mid-1990s to encourage their Islamic counterparts to demand further changes. One of them, Mehrangiz Kar, observed that in the first five parliaments, the regime allowed only loyal Islamist women to enter the Majlis. These few women generally "believed in the foundations of the system and were all in agreement with official principles." Kar compared them to the Shah's female representatives in the Majlis, who also were all cut according to the same pattern.[26] "The presence of women in legislation in itself is not a solution to gender inequalities." She pointed out that the homogeneous female representatives seemed to prefer glorification of motherhood to the hard task of legislation to improve women's standing in law.[27] Kar called for a real reform through which women from all walks of life and diverse ideological views would be empowered to enter the Majlis.[28] It was unlikely that many of the Islamic "feminists" could agree with such a proposal, which would have undermined the claim to Islamic legitimacy and to an exclusive right to parliamentary seats.

During Khatami's reformist presidency, Islamic women increased their pressure for a more equitable share in governmental posts. A female adviser to a ministry observed that although 30 percent of state employees were women, only 2.8 percent of them occupied managerial positions. A female deputy in the Majlis observed that the presence of two women in subministerial positions in Khatami's cabinet has helped to dispel doubts about women's capabilities. She demanded that serious attention be given to their employment in higher offices, especially in the Ministry of Education, where half of the employees were women. Zahra Shuja'i, adviser to President Khatami on women affairs, complained that cabinet ministers could have done better than appointing only one woman to the position of vice minister.[29]

Islamic "feminists" have also argued that the rules regarding marriage, divorce, and child custody had been made by men and were contrary to the true intents of Islamic law. They argued for revision of the prevalent interpretations concerning the value of a woman's testimony, the amount of *diyat*, and the extent of women's employment in the Islamic Judiciary, including judgeships.

The story of the revision and re-revision of the family laws was very revealing of the dilemma the clerics faced in ruling a complex state society.

There were strong indications that after the establishment of clerical rule, the imposition of strict Islamic rules governing marriage and divorce came face-to-face with realities of women's expectations, which had been largely shaped by secular practices of the past half-century. In the cleric-run family courts, thousands of women struggled over the consequences for them and their children of newly reinstated polygamy, easy divorce by men, and child custody laws that favored fathers. Making the job of judges very difficult and distinctly unpleasant, women seeking justice in courts had been instrumental in creating a countermovement to revise the Islamic family law. The Muslim women demanding better treatment in divorce and custody cases showed few inhibitions in letting the clerical judges hear their true feelings. This practical struggle was also reflected in public discussions in newspapers and magazines that demanded modification of the newly enacted Islamic regulations.[30] They highlighted the plight of lower-class women by reporting on their painful stories. Islamic "feminists" challenged the patriarchal trend in codification of Islamic laws.[31]

In the early 1990s, the rulers reversed themselves partially by passing new regulations that placed divorce cases under the jurisdiction of the courts.[32] And in November 1997, another new law allowed judges to grant, in some specific cases, child custody to a divorcing mother, a measure in violation of the *shari'ah* law, which automatically gave custody to the father.[33] The passage of the new laws meant, in Schirazi's words, "if not explicitly, nonetheless in terms of actual meaning, that the law of 1967 . . . was partially rehabilitated."[34] Or, as the feminist scholar Parvin Paidar observed, in 1979 the Islamic Republic nullified the Shah's Family Protection Law in two weeks. Then it took "ten years to rebuild it again bit by bit."[35] The struggles of women in Islamic family courts for over ten years forced some changes in divorce laws. However, women were far from being satisfied, since most judges usually followed the traditional spirit of Islamic law. Passing legislation was one thing; properly implementing it was another.[36] In Tehran the secular human rights lawyer Shirin Ebadi tirelessly argued for the applicability of the UN human rights covenants and defended women's and children's rights, especially in cases where family courts failed to give custody of children to mothers, even in cases where fathers were patently unfit or even criminal.[37]

The clerics in power had circumvented the *shari'ah* rules where practical necessities and state expediencies demanded the continuation of established practices inherited from the Shah's secular regime. The ideologues hastened to offer a new Islamic interpretation and justification for changes whose motivations, born in the actual experiences of running a government, appeared nonideological and could be traced back to Western-influenced practices that have become normal, losing their ideological colorings. The mullah power holders and their female supporters in the Majlis engaged in ideological backpedaling in order to justify, in Islamic terms, the secular practices that had struck roots and proved impossible to uproot. It remained unconvincing; the makeup behind the veil had become too glaring. In 1999, when the hard-liners charged the maverick cleric Abdollah Nuri with the crime of advocating practices that violated Islamic laws, he retorted that the prosecutors should take a look at current laws covering women "that are contradictory to Islamic ordinances as defined by *fiqh* (jurisprudence)."[38]

Thus, during much of the 1990s, the discourse on women was, with the exception of *hijab*, no longer constructed mainly in terms of culture and authenticity, since some women in governmental circles began to speak in terms of unequal power and gender inequality. The unintended consequences of the actions and words of the rulers redirected attention to the issues of male domination and the violation of women's basic rights.[39]

In his first substantive report, UN Special Representative Copithorne did not mention any specific violations of women's rights. Instead, he devoted the section on women to various discussions about the possibilities of improving women's status. However, he concluded that the women's status was "indeed not equal to that of men in very many ways."[40] In his following report, Copithorne was more forthcoming in identifying certain violations, while listing a number of improvements. In 1997 he concluded, "Iran has considerable distance to go to bring itself into compliance with international standards, but there are clear signs that this may be a time for progress to be made. The change must be real and the momentum must be sustained."[41]

The debates continued, as did the violations. The hard-line clerics disliked Muslim women's intruding freely into an important subject in Islamic law, wielding feminist interests and offering new interpretations that had little resemblance to the ulema's understanding of Islam. Ayatollah Yazdi, the Head of the Judiciary, dismissed them as dangerous elements tinkering with Islamic law. For him Islam's "primary ordinances" concerning "inheritance, judicial testimony, and *hijab*" were beyond question.[42] In 1998, conservative deputies passed a law that they hoped would put an end to Islamic women's vogue of reinterpretation. The law forbade all interpretations about women's position that took place "outside the legal and *shari'ah* framework." They conveniently ignored the fact that they themselves were guilty of the same infraction. They implicitly accused the reformist women of creating discord between Muslim men and women through new interpretations.[43]

The backlash against Islamic "feminists" who advocated a more tolerant regime for women reached other areas of public life. In 1998, the conservatives proposed two more restrictive laws. The first called for segregated hospitals based on gender, allowing the patients to be treated only by doctors of the same sex. The second bill that the Majlis passed on August 12 tried to impose a stricter censorship on newspapers and magazines that published photographs of foreign women whose hair was not properly covered. The deputy from Isfahan argued not only against un-Islamic photos but also against "poems and novels that describe direct relations between woman and man." He added: "Some novels and photos stimulate the youth and awaken their instincts."[44]

In 1979, the Islamists understood accurately that under the Shah's secular regime, Western-style modernity was undermining old Islamic habits, especially in Tehran. They had only underestimated the depth of the subversion. In early 2000, it appeared that the Islamic "feminists" were also becoming the agents of that creeping modernity; they were even pushing its dispositions into the clerics' own households. The younger "feminists" were mischievously subversive in their conversations with some clerics who held elective offices and worried about votes. They sometimes tried to get clerical validation for modern habits by placing a cleric in an unenviable position where he either had to express conformity with contemporary norms or appear to be a diehard, out of touch with modern gender relationships. Questioning the hard-line candidate for president in 1997, a reporter asked about the cleric's relationship with his wife. In another such conversation, an interviewer began with political questions and then unexpectedly shifted to the personal realm:

Q.   Hajji Agha, do you go to movies?
A.   I don't have time, but when the state art institutes or the Ministry of [Islamic] Guidance invite, I go.
Q.   Do you go with your family [the code word for wife]?
A.   Yes.
Q.   If your son says that he has fallen in love with a young lady and wants to go to cinema with her, what do you say to him?
A.   I would say . . . if she also wants him, he should go and marry her, that is if it is advisable.
Q.   What if after some time, he did not like her?
A.   It is not advisable [to get to know each other] without marriage.
Q.   Well, he just wants to get to know her—no?
A.   To get to know is different than to become friends. A relationship that they would enjoy is different from a mere meeting in which he would ask if she would be willing to marry him and reach an agreement. If they go to cinema holding hands and having their bodies touched, etc.—all problematic in Islamic law.

The conversation continued with the reporter wondering if the Majlis clerical deputy believed there could be any healthy (code word for nonsensual) relationship between a man and woman and the cleric insisting that any such relationship of two physically healthy persons would lead to sen-

sual activities, forbidden outside marriage.[45] The cleric was Ali Movahedi
Savuji, a five-term Majlis deputy, who lost his seat in the landslide victory of
the reformists in the 2000 elections.

The Absence of Secular Voices

In the climate of reform in 1998, a female secular filmmaker said in Tehran: "I think there are as many different types of women in Iran as there
are women who live in Iran. Because these many different types, thoughts
and opinions do exist, it is impossible to collect them all in one category
and issue abstract prescriptions for them."[46] Some Islamic "feminists" must
have realized the truth in this statement, since they published it in their
newspaper.

For a long time, however, the Islamic "feminists" fell far short of adequately addressing the grievances of the emancipated, secular women. The
voices of secular women who had refused to hide their real views had been
absent from the national debates. While engaging in their own hermeneutic
debates over Islam, the Islamist men as well as women suppressed the human rights of secular women. The emergence of Islamic "feminist" voices
must be understood in the context of the suppression of the voices of secular women. A few courageous secular women tried to beat the Shiites at their
own game by exercising *taqiyyah*, expedient dissimulation of one's true beliefs, and presenting their demands for change in Islamic terms. Scholars
in the West, understanding Iran's political realities through published texts,
paid close attention to the voices of Islamic "feminists." Since the political
views of the secularists who did not exercise *taqiyyah* could not be expressed
in the press, they were largely absent from the text-based studies of Western
academe.

The intra-Islamist debates no more adequately reflected the entire reality
of violations of the rights of women than the debate over the formal exclusion of candidates for elected seats reflected the entire scope of the violations of the right to political participation, since it ignored the informal,
prior exclusion of the secularists (Chapter 15). In the second half of the
1990s, Iran under the Ayatollahs appeared to me as an extended family
whose patriarch had gagged several of the nonconformist members of the
family and locked them in the cellar. Their "free" cousins upstairs fervently
discussed their possible courses of action for the future of the family, while
being acutely aware of the existence of the constrained members. What appeared possible to those who were upstairs was contingent on the continued
gagging of those downstairs. There was an air of unreality in the house, and
the nature of debates would change if the gagged kin were to free themselves
and openly participate in debates.

The price that secular women paid had been high. However, during the
relative opening of 1998–2000, Iranian women's secular voices began to re-

emerge, exhibiting a much wiser disposition than their predecessors showed before the revolution. Disjointed efforts were being made. Khatami's government was unable or unwilling to grant licenses to secular women for publishing newspapers or journals. However, a number of young, courageous women began to publish their secular views. For example, Nushin Ahmadi Khorassani published collections of articles in book format, which in effect functioned like a journal. In one collection, there was a biographical essay about Nur al-Hoda Manganeh, president of a women's organization in the early 1900s. In addition to her photos, the collection featured a photo of the executive committee of the organization: twelve women, all young, unveiled, posing for the camera in dignified modern dresses.[47] Modern Iranian women are beginning to reclaim their secular history.

Cultural Authenticity Reveiling Secular, Emancipated Women

The Islamist women in revolution appeared menacing to secular women. The historian Homa Nateq, who was active among intellectuals during the revolution, expressed her fears: "Women's role in this revolution was extremely reactionary as it has been in all democratic movements of this century. The first demonstrations in the early stages of the revolution simply horrified me: all women in black chadors. When I heard what they were chanting, my hair stood on end: 'O beloved Khomeini, order me to shed blood.'"[48]

In the first decade of the clerical rule, thousands of women lost their jobs for their improper *hijab*.[49] During the 1980s, many scholars in the West described, with considerable sympathy, the Iranian women's outrage toward the new Islamic restrictions and the fact that "the veil was once again becoming compulsory."[50] In the 1990s, some of the same scholars became enthusiastic about the efforts of Islamic "feminists" trying to remove, partially at best, the burdens that they themselves had helped to impose in the early 1980s. The perception that these women belonged to "popular classes" added legitimacy to their voices, at the expense of the dismissed voices of secular women who belonged to the "bourgeoisie." This perception ignored the fact that the aggrieved popular classes could be equally indifferent to human rights. One feminist scholar expressed appreciation for "the indefatigable struggles of Islamist elite 'feminists,' such as Azam Taleqani, Maryam Behruzi, Shahla Sherkat and Zahra Rahnavard."[51] No longer was historical stress placed on the painful period between March 1979 and July 1980, when thousands of modern women demonstrated and staged sit-ins.

Of course, the female Islamists derived maximum advantage from the opportunity the regime accorded them. As Maryam Poya observed, it "gave them access to material and ideological resources and provided them with a space to exercise power." Financial rewards were not insignificant. These women consented with "their subordinate position and some participated in the reproduction of their own subordination by policing the patriarchal state . . . . In this sense the ideology had a material basis, which women used to improve their status."[52]

The Islamist women denounced emancipated women who had refused to accept *hijab* willingly. Zahra Rahnavard, who wore revealing modern dresses in the sixties, reveiled herself during the revolution and asserted that keeping the Islamic veil was more important than keeping the Persian Gulf for Iran. A hard-line ideologue on *hijab*, she claimed: "The veil frees women from the shackles of fashion, and enables them to become human beings in their own right."[53] And Maryam Behruzi "compared the women who did not observe *hijab* to people who trampled on the Qur'an. . . . For her such women, with their made-up faces, belonged to the swamps of Europe." Another female deputy asserted that *hijab* was "God's command and an unconquerable fortress in which the personality of women is preserved."[54]

In traditional Islamic understanding, *hijab* was associated with man's unalterable weakness in resisting sexual temptations when facing any woman (other than grandmothers, mother, aunts, and sisters) not made invisible by a total physical separation. It was a divinely ordered requirement, so self-evidently accepted as an inherently Islamic ordinance that it needed no further explanation or rationalization.

The traditional Islamic rulings for *hijab* had become embarrassing for the contemporary defenders of the indigenous culture. Thus, Islamic "feminists" in the 1980s and 1990s argued that reveiling in Iran, as in other Islamic countries, presented an authentic manifestation of cultural conformity. They often repeated a claim that Muslim women, by adopting the Islamic *hijab*—a manifestation of chastity, dignity, and modesty—regained their female autonomy. *Hijab* was said to be the affirmation of the female in Islamic terms, "enabling women to negotiate in the new world while affirming the traditional values of their upbringing."[55] Emptied of its traditional Islamic rationale, *hijab* became an enabling social outfit, a liberating banner of the new ideology. Distorting traditional meaning, this view could be understood as yet another attempt to counter the influence of secular women who had emancipated themselves from the traditionalist imperative of *hijab*. The religious ideologues seldom presented their current interpretation of the social-enabling function of the veil as something new, as a novel understanding of Islamic norms, arrived at under the influence of Western feminism. They often presented it as something that has always existed "in Islam." In Tehran, an Islamist argued that *hijab* has always guaranteed women's presence in the public: "Contrary to malicious propaganda, the law of *hijab*, far from imprisoning the woman, has liberated her to enter the social domain; *hijab* grants woman human identity, allowing her to engage in social activities free from sexual attractions."[56]

What if a secular woman refused to accept such an affirmation of the "traditional value" of her upbringing? The writings of female prisoners in the

Islamic Republic offered an answer. Other Islamic "feminists" told the world that Islamic women were contributing to the national struggle by reasserting the authenticity of Muslim men who were under attack by Western cultural imperialism. Does it matter that a female prisoner like the novelist Parsipur was "extremely hateful" of the imposed *hijab*? Many secular women from middle and upper classes reacted viscerally to *hijab*. As one such woman reacted in 1980: "But no chador. Never a chador, I swore, no matter what they did to me."[57]

Dare to make a simple demand that you did not want to wear that despised headscarf! The discursive universe of some frustrated intellectuals from Islamic backgrounds crashed on your head. It spewed forth incessant concepts that explained, beyond your patience or comprehension, everything that they had learned from books published in the West: the Orientalist reading of Islam; the colonialist design to depict Muslims as backward by focusing on the veil; the imperialist fetishisation of the veil as the signifier of Oriental women; the West's "perpetual attempt to undress Muslims and make them available to its gaze"; the cultural betrayal of the first generation of Westernizers who advocated the removal of the veil, and on and on.

The issue was further trivialized by the argument that the women who resented *hijab* might "only be interested in conforming to trends in international fashion."[58] Such commentators ignored the real lives of women in a country like Iran, where conforming to international fashion saw little abatement even under the chadors. Journalist Geraldine Brooks observed: "At first, I'd naively assumed that hijab would at least free women from the tyranny of the beauty industry. But at the Iranian Women's Conference, locked up day and night with a hotelful of Muslim radicals, I soon learned I'd been mistaken."[59]

Western travelers to Tehran often noted the regime's obsession with *hijab*.

On the inside of the taxi's passenger door, . . . was a decal that I soon realized was ubiquitous throughout Iran. Showing the silhouette of a women's covered head, it stated, "For the respect of Islam, *Hijab* is mandatory." The same four-inch-wide decal was on display in stores, restaurants, and every public building I visited. A storekeeper would later tell me, "It means we are forbidden to serve you unless you wear a proper *hijab*." As we traveled through the city, other *hijab* signs were common. "Bad *hijab* is prostitution," . . . Another that was intended to be more threatening than insulting stated, "Lack of *hijab* means lack of man's manhood."[60]

Ignoring the Islamic "feminist" reinterpretations, the *hijab* signs were more truthful to *hijab*'s Islamic cultural underpinnings. Yet, if *hijab* was so atoned to the people's culture, why did it need so much coaxing and coercing?

"Getting to the truth about hijab was a bit like wearing it, a matter of layers to be stripped away, a piece at a time," observed Geraldine Brooks. "And under all the talk about *hijab* freeing women from commercial or sexual exploitation, all the discussion of *hijab*'s potency as a political and revolutionary symbol of selfhood, was the body: the dangerous female body that somehow, in Muslim society, had been made to carry the heavy burden of male honor."[61]

The Islamic *hijab* also created confusion among human rights scholars, mainly because Iran specialists had failed to explain fully, for the benefit of nonspecialists, the plight of secular women. The trauma that secular Iranian women experienced made even a weak relativist position that allowed respect for cultural *différance* in dress code indefensible. While defending the universality of human rights, Jack Donnelly advocated a weak cultural relativist position; it sounded credible in theory, but the specific example he provided rendered it indefensible. His position allowed the imposition of "dress codes to protect public morals and decency, such as the Muslim requirement that women wear veils in public."[62] Here Donnelly engaged in a theoretical discussion without any detailed account of actual practices or any consideration of the fact that secular women considered the veil an assault on their human dignity. Using Donnelly's own criteria of an internal judgment and an external (Western) judgment,[63] I would argue that the Islamic dress code lacked the required consensus in Iran (internal judgment) for Donnelly to consider it as a "requirement." The authoritarian rulers and their female subordinates considered the imposition of the veil to be a legitimate state policy in the interest of public morality.

The same kind of sentiment may have caused the international human rights organizations to pay insufficient attention to the imposed *hijab* as a violation of freedom of conscience and thought. As late as 1998, even the Human Rights Watch deemed it sufficient to include only one short paragraph about the Islamic dress code and the related harassment of emancipated women in the twenty-one paragraphs of its yearly report on Iran. Amnesty International annual reports failed even to mention women. Human rights discourse generally failed to consider the violations of the rights of emancipated, secular women. The discourse had at best reduced the issue to women's inability to choose the dress they liked or the inconvenience that the all-enveloping chador created in the everyday life of professional women. On the larger scale of things, how important that could be?

Driven by regressive societal norms, the mullahs had authored the ascriptive categorization imposed on modern, secular women, in particular the degrading and humiliating position ascribed by the veil—denying them, as it did, autonomy in public space. The female identity bestowed by the veil and the particular sort of social respect it entailed were in conflict with the inner sense of self-respect of such women, who saw the imposed veil as a violation of their freedoms of conscience and expression. The Islamic *hijab* signified the wearer's self-definition and announced the presence of a particular conscience and a uniform worldview. The public display of that identity was unmistakable. Donning an aesthetically loathsome symbolic reference to a religious value they did not share, secular, emancipated women were forced to pretend to be what they were not—a violation of their freedom of conscience and expression.

Many traditional women might have voluntarily adopted *hijab* as a practical necessity if they were to function in a public space whose rules the patriarchy set. For them—not secular women—it was a "necessity" that the Islamic ideologues turned into a universal virtue. As an "affirmation of female autonomy and subjectivity," it was perhaps illusory, more a symptom of a deeply rooted sociocultural malady than a sign of female autonomy. It was illusory because the precondition that necessitated adoption of *hijab* was set by the patriarchal reinvigoration of control and dominance. It was illusory because the wearer's notions of propriety and modesty had internalized the androcentric norms of the culture.[64] It legitimized women's presence outside the home, but it did so in male terms—and to the detriment of modern, secular women who were forced to don the veil. The imposition of the headscarves inflicted psychological scars on young, secular women.

Haleh Afshar characterized the views of Islamic "feminist" writers as believing that, if "adjusted to local needs and circumstances," the "new interpretation of Islam [is] as liberating, if not more so, than feminism has been for women in the West."[65] A liberating paradigm cannot be a source of human rights violations of others.

Freeing themselves from Khomeinism and reverting to older Islamic reformism, Islamic "feminists" in Iran focused their struggle on discriminatory laws and other practices that denied women equal opportunity in employment and advancement. However, almost all of them have continued to support, in principle, the Islamic Republic and remained largely impervious to the imposed *hijab* as a violation of the rights to freedom of conscience and expression. A daughter of the former president, Fa'ezeh Hashimi (Rafsanjani), the Islamic "feminist" celebrated in Western academic discourses, considered *hijab* as "an indisputable trademark for Muslim women." Oblivious to the fact that the Islamic Republic imposed *hijab* by violence, she regretted that in Turkey "Western dress norms" have been imposed on women.[66]

In fact, daughters, sisters, and wives of the Shiite clerics were yet to free their thoughts from the discursive fixation that Ayatollah Morteza Motahhari had developed in the 1970s about unveiled women. He and other ideologues like Ali Shari'ati created that enduring image by viewing—and largely stereotyping—secular women's experiences under the Pahlavi Shahs from the 1930s to the 1970s. They saw a vast conspiracy in the irksome historical process of modernity. They had set about to "liberate" secular women from their infatuation with the West, or from what they called westoxification. As Fa'ezeh Hashimi editorialized in 1998, on one side of the divide stood the virtuous Islamic woman who covered everything "except the face and the palms of two hands"—a *hijab* that did not "hinder any educational, social and economic activities" in public. On the opposite side stood "the exhibitionist women in tight cloths and colorful modes—a lecherous, pleasure-seeking appearance that caused paralyses in society and sullied the work environment." Muslim women adopting the contemporary international dress were the agents of the conspiracy: "Behind such an appearance lay a perspective that sought not only to change faces and figures but also to destroy the essence of the national-religious identity. . . . If a woman does not have a mental illness and does not want to appear in public naked [*lokht*, a code word for appearing in fashionable international dress], the wearing of a simple dress that covers all her body and head, with the exception of face and hands, does not hinder any activities in public." [67]

This seemingly defensive language, which might be misconstrued as cultural relativist, assassinated characters and sought to silence secular women. It went beyond the more familiar, traditionalist language that chastised the emancipated women by depicting them as loose, shrill, and strident. Casting all secular women who detested *hijab* into one mold, such depictions aimed at preempting secular women from presenting themselves as real individuals possessing free wills, discarding traditional values and acquiring new tastes.

Thus, the Islamist historical judgments on secularism, and on what it entailed for women under the Shahs, became irrevocable. Reza Shah's "original sin" removing *hijab* by edicts in 1936 was permanently hung like an albatross around secular women's necks. They were, in Shari'ati's words, "the unquestioning" slaves of promiscuity and immorality. Lacking "consciousness or control," they allowed the West to prescribe for them norms and attitudes.[68] The Islamists could never see these women as individuals struggling to escape cultural-religious prescriptions. No sympathy was shown for those who were caught in the heedless and often confusing experiences in the 1960s and 1970. As far as Islamists were concerned, these women and their daughters were unable to think, reflect upon their lives, step out of their environs, and learn from their experiences and possible mistakes. They were beyond self-reflection and reevaluation. This was indeed ironic coming from the Islamic "feminists" who gave themselves such a generous hermeneutic leeway, casting aside fourteen centuries of actual Islamic experiences and rediscovering "True Islam."

To the new generation of secular women who grew up under the religious state that was truly independent of the West, such reductionist views appeared anachronistic. The young secular women developed a different perspective and were no longer preoccupied with Western imperialism, as their leftist predecessors had been under the Shah. For them, the wounds had been self-inflicted. Their views of the West have also changed. Nushin Ahmadi Khorassani said in Tehran in early 2000: "In Iran, every time Western culture entered, it meant freedom for women. If you look at appearances—what you can wear, for example—for millions of young girls, the West holds a great attraction. Precisely with all the anti-American rhetoric that has been espoused by the regime over the past twenty years, any wariness that once existed has lost all meaning." Addressing the suffocating weight of the Islamic tradition on women, she added: "Western culture was just different enough to sweep in like a breath of fresh air that could shatter what was seemingly impenetrable. It was very appealing to Iranian women. Something different, finally. It offered itself as an alternative." [69] Interestingly, a general impression had been created in the second half of the 1990s to the effect that some older secular women who had reached majority before the 1979 revolution were less resentful of the imposed *hijab*. They were more concerned with other human rights. Their daughters, young women who were raised under Islamic indoctrination, showed no such reservation and wanted "to be themselves." This yearning for individual autonomy seemed at times stronger than the desire for political activism for reforms.

The voices of Islamic "feminists" belonged to those who had voluntarily accepted the veil. Their difficult struggles to modernize Islamic laws and practices should receive proper recognition, regardless of their historical distortion and selective amnesia about the immutable *shari'ah* laws and fixed doctrinal points. Their valiant struggle to make the traditionally bounded women "believe" in themselves—as the first editorial of *Ruznameh-Zan* put it—might be their lasting contribution.[70] Rather than intending to minimize the significance of their struggle or the positive results that it may bring to traditional women in a transitional period, I wish to highlight the violations of the right of secular women to freedom of conscience. For the sake of historical justice, it needs to be emphasized that Islamist women were themselves partly responsible for those violations. I wish to reiterate that the human rights violations of women who despised *hijab* have been one of the central issues of human rights discourse and practice in Iran.

As far as freedom of conscience was concerned, Islamist women and men belonged to the same tabernacle, and their true vocation was to give legitimacy to the politics endorsed by the sacred text. Both sexes sanctified their politics by recourse to Qur'anic discourse. The women did not offer radical, alternative sociopolitical postulates to religiously sanctioned views of the political mullahs concerning the role that Islam ought to play in a modern state. Their revisionism only aimed to make that role less harsh and more enlightened in *some* aspects of social life, but made no allowance for removing Islamic precepts from the realm of public policies concerning women. All Islamists asserted that laws and policies must follow the clearly stated Qur'anic rules and general Islamic principles. From the beginning, Islamist women insisted on the imposition of religious laws in public domains. Having done so, some of them began to offer a reappraisal of Islamic rules only on *certain* aspects of the compendium of Islamic rules that they helped to impose. Aspects of Islamic public policies that remained beyond revision have been violating the rights of thousands of secular women. For more than fifteen years, Islamist women helped to impose Khomeini's Islam on women. Having discovered that many of its laws and practices were alien to "True

Islam," they began offering women another version of Islam, never realizing that secular women might be tired of being the guinea pigs of the state-driven religious experiments.

The most moderate Islamic "feminists" had only advocated a less severe imposition of the Islamic dress code. And by demanding that Islamic "modesty" in dress should apply to men as well, they wished to extend the Islamic fashion fascism: "Furthermore all these musts and must nots which continuously demand of women not to speak, not to walk, not to choose the colour of their clothes fail to address the disturbed males and demand of them . . . not to appear in an arousing fashion."[71] Some Islamic women tried to make the wearing of scarves and loose overall dress—instead of the all-enveloping chador—acceptable. They wished to impress on their more strict Islamist sisters that wearing color in clothing had no Islamic prohibition. Such slackening of restrictions, even if successful, did not sufficiently address the question of free choice for secular women.

Violations of the Rights of Secular Women

The Islamists in Iran were losing the "battle of the veil" to progressive and educated women who were holding up their "badly veiled" heads. After many years of Islamic propaganda and coercion, they refused to change their "satanic manners," efface their conscience, or remake themselves permanently in the image of the Ayatollahs' wives and daughters. However, the political clerics were equally relentless. They made sure that President Rafsanjani's normalcy did not extend to women's appearance in public; their continued use of coercion belied any faith in cultural relativist arguments.

Bad-hijab was the term used for a woman who deliberately broke the rules by, among other things, showing a strand of hair under her headscarf and using makeup. The hard-line power holders often renewed their efforts by launching campaigns to bring the secular women of Iran into full compliance with the Islamic dress code: The Plan to Combat Immorality and Improper *Hijab* (*bad-hijab*), 1990,[72] or, the Plan for the Superior *Hijab* (*tarh-e hijab-e bartar*), 1994. The latter intended to persuade modern women to replace their all-covering coats (*manteau*) and scarves with the superior all-black chador. An influential cleric told his followers that "from the view of Islamic custom, the covering of chador has always been in use among Muslims and from the beginning of Islam has occupied a special place." He added that "the chador has always covered women's chastity" and that "for the people the chador has been the only acceptable criterion for the Islamic *hijab*."[73] And a group of conservative clerics in the Assembly of Experts issued a statement defending the Plan for the Superior *Hijab*, referring to the chador as a strong fortress, "protecting the spiritual atmosphere of the society."[74] The political prisoners of the 1980s often heard similar exhortations. In the 1990s, *hezbollahi* marchers were organized in major cities as part of the renewed campaign on behalf of *hijab*.[75]

At last, ten years after severe restrictions were imposed on the appearance of women in public, Galindo Pohl discussed the issue of *hijab* in 1992. Women accused of "*bad-hijabi*" might receive a maximum of 74 lashes. Other punishments included prison terms or fines. The confrontations continued in the streets, where official and semiofficial morality patrols sought out young women who flouted the Islamic dress code and displayed an odd strand of hair in public. They especially targeted middle-class neighborhoods, where defiant young women could be easily spotted. In a campaign of harassment on April 22 and 23, 1991, some 800 women were detained. The morality police renewed pressure on shopkeepers and retailers not to sell goods to women who appeared without proper Islamic covering. The proprietors of public places like hospitals and cinemas were ordered to police their establishments to prevent women with *bad-hijab* from entering.[76] The only relief came because of the prevailing official corruption, as the morality police were often eager, like the rest of the state officials, to supplement their insufficient salaries by openly demanding bribes to overlook a violation of the Islamic law or an offense against Islamic sensitivities.

Galindo Pohl noted this campaign of harassment in 1992.[77] For example, he listed a number of street clashes involving such women.[78] In a response dated October 27, 1993, the regime's diplomats repeated one of their typical understatements: "Modest attire and appearance in public is an Islamic requirement for both men and women. Those violating this norm may be stopped and discreetly counselled."[79] In his February 1994 report, Galindo Pohl wrote: "It was reported that, on 20 and 21 June 1993, security agents set up several checkpoints and covert and undercover patrols in different cities, particularly in Tehran, arresting and imprisoning hundreds of women on the charge of improper veiling and non-Islamic attire, during a campaign for the promotion of virtue and prohibition of vice."[80]

In response, the diplomats simply wrote, "This allegation is denied."[81] In another example, Galindo Pohl referred to a news report in the daily *Salam* of March 4, 1993, that a morality patrol visited a girls' school and "divested the girls of their jewels and adornments." He also quoted another Tehran newspaper that reported on June 24, 1993, that a number of women had been charged with violating the Islamic dress code and were sentenced to flogging.[82] For both cases, the diplomats responded by denying "the accuracy of this allegation."[83] Galindo Pohl quoted Tehran's police chief informing the public that his men had arrested some 800 young people and taken them to the Office for Combating Corruption. Some were arrested for wearing dark sunglasses.[84] In response, the diplomats said that the story was distorted, adding that "those arrested simply received counselling at the Office for Combating Corruption, and then were freed."[85] Galindo Pohl noted that

Interior Minister Ali Muhammad Besharati had announced in September 1994 another of the regular campaigns against women who refused to abide properly by the dress code.[86]

At the time when the diplomats were making their habitual denials, a modern Iranian woman in Tehran revealed to an American journalist the pain and humiliation she, along with a group of women, endured following their arrest for flouting the Islamic dress code. Jan Goodwin's passage is worth quoting:

> Faridah was herded into the basement of the building with the other women. . . .
> "Two *Pasdaran* [revolutionary guards] took me into a cell. One was holding a whip in his hand. They handcuffed me facedown on a wooden bed. All I could think was, This is not really happening . . . then they started whipping me."
> Faridah pauses and exhales as if she has been holding her breath while talking for the last couple of minutes. "What they did to me hurt me more mentally I think than physically. Somehow I was numb to the pain, I was so shocked that this was happening. But it was the total helplessness and subjugation. The lack of power, being robbed of all dignity. It was a disgusting experience, so degrading, and as violating in its way as rape. And it has changed me in so many ways."[87]

Copithorne noted in 1997 the statement by a morality watchdog group, reiterating the legal threat of imprisonment "up to 12 months, fines and flogging up to 74 lashes for some offences relating to the dress code." Moreover, in August 1997, the conservatives came up with yet another campaign called "Extension of the Culture of Chastity," demanding stricter enforcement of Islamic dress.[88]

As indicated earlier, the UN Special Rapporteur on Freedom of Opinion and Expression had visited the country. In his report dated March 11, 1996, Abid Hussain paid attention to the violations of the rights of women and accurately characterized the restrictions imposed on them as violations of their right to freedom of opinion and expression. Abid Hussain saw, better than any other UN representative, the imposed *hijab* as a human rights violation.[89] In his report of February 1997, Copithorne cautiously broached the issue of veiling and saw no improvement in the treatment of women who appeared in public in "improper veiling." Instead of drawing on UN universal standards, he reverted to the discussion among different Islamic groups. "There appear to be differences of view, drawing on religion and on culture, as to the appropriateness of norms concerning *hijab*, and particularly the tolerance with which such norms are applied." He added "that in his view some more tolerant regime needs to be introduced, one that would respect non-conforming behaviour."[90]

After Khatami's election, the most daring of the dissidents voiced their concerns about the use of force in enforcing the Islamic dress code. One such woman, Shahla Sherkat, who herself always appeared in a correct *hijab*, stated in 1999 that no one should step outside "the Redline" of prohibition. "For example, you never see us writing that women are free not to wear the scarves. However, in our magazine we may pose the question as what constitutes the best form of *hijab*, and our readers then can express their views. Only in this way, we can deal with this subject. . . . Herein lies the secret of our resistance."[91] It was, however, the maverick Abdollah Nuri, who in his political trial in November 1999 spoke most openly what many women had expressed for two decades: "You cannot enforce *hijab* with clubs and batons. You cannot claim religion is limited to your own particular interpretation of it."[92] In addition, among the non-clerical, Islamic reformists, a new discussion has begun, at least in private, about the principle that *hijab* is a private matter and "coercion . . . should never be permitted,"[93] a recognition that had come a lifetime too late for emancipated women such as Dr. Homa Darabi. Perhaps the foundation under this final fortress of Islamic legitimacy had also begun to erode from within.

Chapter 17

UN Monitoring, 1984–2000

Mixed Results

Let me return to the UN monitoring process and reporting procedures and examine not only their limitations but also their possible influence on Iranian officials who were assigned to deal with the charges of human rights violations. The results were mixed, mostly ineffective in forcing the recalcitrant state to change its practices but somewhat adequate in helping the society to arrive at a better understanding of human rights. However, the visible changes in Iran in the late 1990s and the reformers' discussions about past violations had no real impact on Iranian diplomats who continued upholding the façade of rejections and denials in the United Nations.

The Limitations of the UN Procedure

To counter the charges of human rights violations in the first phase of their encounter with the Commission on Human Rights, the regime's diplomats made use of every arrow in the state quiver of obfuscation, distortion, and denial. By the end of the 1980s, it had become apparent that the tactics used by the diplomats proved ineffective in removing the state from the UN special procedures or changing the highly negative judgments of international human rights organizations. Nevertheless, they had considerable success in adding confusion to the monitoring process. The more politically confused the process of monitoring human rights becomes, the more difficult it is to establish a clear responsibility for the state that violates the rights of its citizens.

Like other authoritarian states, the regime played other parts of the UN human rights machinery against Special Representative Galindo Pohl, who refused to recommend removing Iran from the special procedures. While denying him access to the country, the Iranian Foreign Ministry invited the newly appointed High Commissioner, José Ayala Lasso, to visit in 1995; he wisely deferred. Following the same track, the Ministry invited the Special

Rapporteur on Religious Intolerance (Abdelfattah Amor) and the Special Rapporteur on Freedom of Opinion and Expression (Abid Hussain), hoping that these two UN experts with Islamic backgrounds would produce reports that were more sympathetic. They were disappointed; as discussed earlier, the Rapporteurs' familiarity with Islamic culture enabled them to look behind the veil and see through the state's religious pretenses.

Galindo Pohl used all available sources to collect his information and submitted "detailed allegations" to the government with the view that they would help the responsible officials "to verify their accuracy." The UN's official expectation was that the government would conduct its own investigation.[1] For example, the Special Representative wished to know whether Mrs. Robabeh Boudaghi's husband was kept in a prison in Gilan, as she claimed. He wanted to know whether or not a Baha'i Council with six members existed in the city of Urumiyeh and what had happened to them. He wanted to know whether Mrs. Zhaleh Fallah's husband was executed in September 1986.[2] Only the government was in a position to verify the relevant facts. Take the case of Mrs. Fallah's husband: Was there a file on him in Evin prison, what did it contain; what was he charged with; did the prosecutors observe due process of law; who was the judge; who was the attorney for the accused; how well informed was his family about his case and conviction; how did an independent press cover the case; and did he exhaust all appeals available to him by law? Did the officials who wrote the response to Galindo Pohl's allegations order an independent inquiry into the circumstances of his presence in custody? Could the Special Representative have a copy of the inquiry and response of the prison warden? The UN monitor never received responses that would satisfy such specific, relevant questions.

In its well-publicized expectation, the Commission had set for itself the improbable task of gaining the cooperation of a recalcitrant state to validate the embarrassing record that the international human rights organizations have compiled for it. Moreover, the UN's official expectation of a governmental investigation of the allegations presented to it by the Special Representatives was paradoxical in the sense that the diplomats who wrote the responses had no meaningful access to the state security apparatuses and had no real power to conduct any investigation or ask questions concerning the individuals whose lives were destroyed in prison. That forbidden territory of the state was the domain of the powerful clerics in charge of security apparatuses and the Islamic Judiciary, none readily answerable to the Foreign Ministry in the bureaucratic side of the state.

Thus in the 1980s, the Foreign Ministry officials conducted a diplomacy of evasion, diversion, and rejection. With such interlocutors, the expectations of the UN Commission on Human Rights revealed its limitations. There was plenty of diplomatic pretension on all sides, making the UN correspondence and reports sometimes surrealistic. As Galindo Pohl wrote:

The communication of allegation of violations of human rights has a positive aspect, as it gives information to the Government concerned on facts that may have escaped its knowledge and may orient the investigation and contribute to the possible redress of any weakness in the national system of protection of human rights. The communication of such allegation thus contributes to the fair functioning of national institutions. The furnishing of circumstantiated replies to such allegations also has a positive aspect for any Government.

. . . The objective of the exercise is to ensure compliance with international obligations on the basis of co-operation of each State. . . . It is not a judicial procedure. It appeals to good will, to moral and political standards and to legal norms whose enforcement is, for the time being, imperfect. Its goal is not to condemn a Government but to redress a given situation.[3]

The UN's official expectation would have been realistic if a state under consideration were democratically established and willing to advance human rights in order to enhance its legitimacy in the eyes of its citizens. However, the most egregious human rights violations take place in authoritarian states, and the equally authoritarian officials who prepare the state responses live in a diplomatic world that considers deception and denial to be the arts of the state. The procedure becomes problematic where the government is undemocratic and unresponsive to the views and sensitivities of its own citizens, where there exists no viable political opposition that is allowed to turn the shortcomings of those in power into political assets in free elections, and where the public remains uninformed about the details of the allegations leveled against its government. Thus, the state under consideration turns the procedure into one of hiding and denying, while maintaining a façade of cooperation with the Commission, hoping to make the otherwise sufficiently reliable information suspect and unworthy of consideration by the United Nations.

To their short-term advantage, the regime's diplomats muddied the field in such a way that nothing appeared to have been proven and everything remained as allegation. Yet in the long run, the UN monitoring of the regime's human rights violations was not devoid of positive results, especially in changing attitude over a long time.

The Embarrassed Cultural Relativists

It appeared that the Iranian lay officials—not diplomats—who had to defend Islamic punishments in front of international human rights monitors often reflected on those charges and experienced difficulties justifying certain human rights violations. The Special Representative Copithorne spoke with Ali Akbar Ash'ari, the Deputy Minister of Culture and Islamic Guidance in Rafsanjani's cabinet. In front of international human rights monitors, the Rafsanjani "pragmatists" whitewashed the unsavory actions of the security apparatus. Ash'ari claimed that "there is a great freedom of the press in the Islamic Republic of Iran, but if a person feels insulted he can bring the publisher/editor before a jury in the Press Tribunal. The jury is the personification of the culture of the society."[4] Accepting this cultural logic, the international monitor should not have been surprised when an editor was sentenced to flogging in accordance with the same cultural norms. Like Dr. Mehrpur, the Deputy Minister spoke differently to his domestic audience. His sentiment on personification of culture was contradicted by his own comment to the Iranian press that the punishment of lashing for a journalist was "not very appropriate."[5]

Dr. Hossein Mehrpur's Persian writings reflected his experiences with the UN reporting procedures. He was the Judiciary-appointed human rights liaison in the early 1990s.[6] Despite his misrepresentations of the UN reports, his Persian writings might reflect the positive influence of the sustained pressure of the international monitoring process, leading to his tentative reconsideration of some laws and practices. The fact that lay officials grappled with certain Islamic punishment was nowhere better shown than in his Persian writings. Apparently he felt a sense of failure in the effort to rationalize the violations in the United Nations, where he had to defend amputation and stoning as Islamic practices that his clerical mentors believed were beyond criticism and reconsideration.

In his writings for domestic readers, Mehrpur struggled to find a way to communicate to clerics in power that an effective defense of the Islamic penal laws and practices had proven difficult in international human rights forums. He informed the clerics that the international community considered corporal punishments like flogging, amputation, and stoning to be cruel and inhuman, even if they were administered in accordance with laws. He pointed out that the UN human rights experts and representatives considered them torture.[7]

Mehrpur cautiously suggested to his clerical superiors that they should take more seriously the task of codifying laws that would be appropriate for and responsive to the needs of the "contemporary world," while retaining basic Islamic principles. In essence he was calling for a more aggressively innovative approach to Islamic legal interpretation, *ejtehad*.[8] He appealed to those clerics "who are profoundly knowledgeable about Islamic principles, are capable of rendering *ejtehad*, . . . are free from unscientific and irrational pre-judgments, and are familiar with . . . human rights discourse." Without indicating how to find such clerics, he invited them to debate the Islamic rules and human rights and determine those Islamic principles and rules that are immutable and valid in every time and place. "Then, their goodness and usefulness should be explained to the society in a scientific and rational language, using statistics and results derived from experience."[9]

Mehrpur informed his readers that amputating the hand of a thief and lashing adulterous men and women are specified punishment in the Qur'an. He observed that stoning for adultery is not specified in it; however, the ulema of all schools of jurisprudence consider it an appropriate Islamic pun-

ishment.[10] He was embarrassed by these punishments. Even Hashimi Rafsanjani, then Speaker of the Majlis, was reported on August 10, 1987, to have
stated that stoning was imposed by "tasteless judges," indicating his belief
that this form of Islamic punishment should not be used.[11]

As though agonizing in an internal debate, Mehrpur continued his discussion with an acrimonious defense of corporal punishments. "That every
corporal punishment is fundamentally contradictory to the inherent human
dignity, and that it should not be imposed on anyone for any reason, is a
question that can be debated. It can be argued that human beings possess
inherent dignity that must be protected." He then asked the reader to imagine a human being who "puts aside the essential human characteristics and
violates, like a wild beast, the life, property and the *namus* [wives and daugh-
ters] of the people." How could "striking a few lashes to the body of such a
person for punishment and admonition be considered as belittling or degrading [of him] and in violation of inherent human rights?" He added that
"the Qur'an grants inherent dignity to humanity but reduces bad and low
humans to the level of animals and sometimes compares such a person to a
dog."[12]

However, Mehrpur seemed to be uncomfortable with his own defense of
Islamic punishments. In an earlier article he recommended that unchanging Islamic rules be clearly designated and explained in a rational way. He
also indicated, in what seemed to be his main argument, that some corporal punishments could be replaced by imprisonment and fines. Leaving it
to the ulema, he took no position as to which punishments might be interchangeable. His advocacy of innovative *ejtehad* seemed to be directed toward
a modernist reconsideration of Islamic ordinances.[13] Later, he seemed to
have become bolder, offering a mild criticism of the current laws that specified lashing for minor crimes and infractions.[14]

Mehrpur was caught on the horns of a dilemma. As a Deputy to the Head
of the Judiciary, he had to walk through the labyrinth of clerical politics and
gingerly tread a path littered with political mines. At every step, he had to
submit to the ever-present imperative to adhere to the formality of Islamic
ordinances, as enjoined by his clerical mentors. On the other hand, as a
layman and product of the prerevolutionary educational system and as the
Judiciary's liaison with the UN human rights organs, he understood the im-
probability of ever succeeding in the international arena in presenting a convincing defense of the human rights record of his clerical mentors. He could
not have succeeded, even had he limited discussion to formal law, with little
consideration of practice. Facing international forums, he defended the Republic's laws and practices; in Persian for his domestic readers, he argued
discreetly for paring the parameters of Islamic laws to what was absolutely
necessary. He objected to what he considered to be excesses, especially in
cases where lashing was prescribed for "many simple misdemeanors in our
penal laws." This, he believed, was difficult to understand and justify even by

"those who are familiar with the Islamic principle—leaving aside criticism by international observers and human rights organizations."[15]

In traditional Shiite jurisprudence, penalties for crimes that qualify for discretionary punishments (*ta'zirat* category) were left to religious judges. Mehrpur grappled with the problem faced by the Islamic Republic in adapting the *ta'zirat* to the judicial system of a modern state that required codified laws and fixed penalties. In 1996, the Majlis and the Guardian Council passed the new Islamic Penal Code of *ta'zirat*, in which the punishment was left to the discretion of judges. However, the Penal Code specified lashing as a form of punishment for all offenses that fell into this category. In other words, as Mehrpur observed, according to the Guardian Council, imprisonment and fines are against the principle of the *ta'zirat*. Frustrated by the absurdity of a law that specified lashing for many minor offenses, Mehrpur explained that according to Article 156 of the *ta'zirat* law, the punishment for driving without a license is seventy-four lashes, while Article 102 specifies up to seventy-four lashes for women who appear in public without the prescribed *hijab* (Islamic dress code).[16]

Becoming even more daring, he explained to his domestic readers that international human rights organizations and supporters of women's rights often "scream in commotion," objecting to the existence of such punishments. Faced with those objections, some Iranian officials "tried to pretend that such a law does not exist." Or, they say "that even though such a punishment is specified in law, no one is enforcing it." Mehrpur asserted that if this is in accordance with the Islamic ordinances, they "should not be ashamed of it and hide it." Finally, he asked, "Why make an irrational justification and not repeal the law?" He concluded that the punishment of lashing for *ta'zirat* offenses was not an unalterable Islamic ordinance and should be replaced by another form of punishment.[17]

Thus, the diplomats seemed to be embarrassed to acknowledge the occurrence of certain Islamic punishments. Whenever denial might sound credible, they denied that the alleged cases occurred.[18] The emergence of embarrassed cultural relativists, disguising some aspects of the cultural norms they defend—incongruous as it seems—was truly emblematic of our universal culture in the late twentieth century. Mehrpur offered us an example of the embarrassed cultural relativists.

It was a logical progression that in the presidential elections of 1997 Mehrpur found himself in the reformist camp supporting Khatami. By that time, he had fallen by the wayside in the Judiciary controlled by Ayatollah Yazdi. In December 1997, the new President appointed him to head a new commission to oversee compliance with the much-neglected constitutional provisions. In his own cautious manner, he was critical of the past. In the course of an interview in 1999, he referred to torture as an example of the past violations of a constitutional provision. "Torture-induced confession should not be considered in judicial procedure. In this regard there are also common laws that some [officials] still disregard." He added, "The laws were very clear concerning the arrest of the accused, explanation of the charge, detention not more than 24 hours before formally charged by a proper judicial authority. Yet there are sometimes complaints and reports about violations of these rights."[19] Did he know that much when he testified in the United Nations defending the record of the regime?

Governmental Human Rights Organizations

Interactions with the international community, often shrill with denunciations and denials, gradually gave way to less strident responses and reactions. One notable development in the 1990s was the appearance of three official human rights organizations, attached to different state institutions and controlled by different factions within the regime. Ayatollah Yazdi, the Head of the Judiciary, a key figure in the security network, set up the Islamic Human Rights Commission in March 1995. Its mandate obviously did not include implementing the UN recommendations. Yazdi and his associates envisioned their Commission as an Islamic instrument, parallel to that of the UN Human Rights Commission. It was to articulate "human rights from the Islamic point of view," review the regime's positions concerning "international covenants and conventions in the field of human rights," and identify the "points of convergence and difference between Islamic human rights and international human rights instruments." Official announcements did not mention the task of monitoring human rights violations in Iran, but spoke of monitoring "the enjoyment of Islamic human rights in the Islamic Republic of Iran and other countries." It would also investigate and respond to international human rights organizations on "matters relating to the Islamic Republic of Iran."[20]

The Foreign Ministry established a Human Rights Department that offered responses, often in the form of denials, to international monitors. In 1994, the Majlis set up its own Human Rights Committee of thirteen deputies. One deputy, Sa'id Raja'i Khorassani, the former Permanent Representative to the UN, was mainly responsible for its creation. He now presented himself to international visitors as a human rights advocate, struggling against his more intransigent colleagues who viewed human rights as a political tool used by the West. He told one visitor "that in the early days after the revolution the government purposefully characterized human rights criticism as part of the international conspiracy against it," adding that "it has become extremely difficult to make people understand that human rights is not just propaganda."[21] He failed to remind the visitor that in 1984–85, as the regime's diplomat, he had denounced the UN reports on human rights violations in Iran and asserted that the process had become totally politicized, serving only as a propaganda vehicle for the United States and its European allies.[22] Could it be that he had been partially enlightened as a result of his interactions with the international organizations? Or, did he speak differently now in accordance with his current political affiliation and official position? I certainly hope it was the former, which points out the possibility that UN human rights activities may gradually exert a positive effect on some officials within the ruling circles.

In 1996, the UN Special Representative, Copithorne, entertained some hopes for the official human rights agencies' ability to make a difference. He received a list of the Islamic Human Rights Commission's activities.[23] He took note of a comment made by the clerical head of the Commission. The cleric told Iranian reporters that "the Commission had proposed that all instances declared by international organizations as human rights violations should be collected, examined and reviewed, and a comprehensive report prepared for the authorities concerned with necessary decisions." The bombastic exaggeration is self-evident. However, Copithorne saw the cleric's proposal as a positive development. Copithorne added earnestly that he looked forward to a discussion with the head of the Commission "on an occasion of a visit to Iran."[24] In Geneva in April 1997 Copithorne met with a group of senior Iranian officials, several of whom were Commission members. Subsequently he received copies of some of its publications.[25] By then, perhaps he had developed a degree of skepticism about the official pronouncements issued by the Commission's secretary.[26]

When they were set up, the governmental human rights organizations were mostly smoke-and-mirrors. They often justified mistreatments of citizens or provided misinformation. For example, in February 1996, the director of the Human Rights Department of the Foreign Ministry sent a response to Copithorne's inquiry concerning Sayyid Morteza Shirazi, the son of Grand Ayatollah Shirazi (see Chapter 14). The letter stated that he was the head of an illegal organization that engaged "in unlawful objectives and acts."[27] It named ten other members of his organization who were all charged with similar offenses. The director of the Human Rights Department was perhaps unaware that such a response, which included a list of vague offenses, many political in nature, would increase the Special Representative's suspicion. The response itself was indicative of the fact that the case was a political crackdown on the regime's opponents. The letter repeated many of the charges for his arrested associates, with variations on words that had no significant legal distinctions. Far from being judicious, the charges appeared to have been borrowed from an Islamist political tract. According to the letter, the Special Court charged Sayyid Morteza Shirazi with the crimes of "disseminating lies and rumours, and endangering the right of freedom of expression in some of the theological centers." It also charged him with an "unauthorized collection and dispatch of information and reports to foreign countries." For each of his associates, only the wording of the charges changed.[28]

I wonder how the director of the Human Rights Department distinguished, in a legal sense, between those lies and rumors that tried to provoke people abroad against the Islamic Republic of Iran and those that tried to make psychological war and damage the reputation of the government. How did the prosecutor decide which charge should be leveled against one person and which charge against the next? Did the difference lie in the nature of "the lies and rumors" or did the two men commit different legal offenses with different penalties? The regime's responses did not come close to satisfying the official expectation of the UN Commission on Human Rights, which expected factual accounts that would clarify the allegations. The fact that in the second half of the 1990s the responses came from the government human rights organs did not make them more credible.

The Judiciary's Islamic Human Rights Commission also covered up the regime's human rights abuses. In 1996, the Commission informed the Special Representative that rumors concerning the destruction of the Baha'i cemeteries were false and politically motivated.[29] On November 30, 1997, Zia'i-Far, the Commission's secretary, dismissed Copithorne's latest report as lacking "legal credibility owing to his documentation of false allegations." He added, "Absence of accurate understanding of the Islamic norms, partial interpretation of international human rights and disregard of the social and cultural criteria of the nation are the weak points of Copithorne's report." Zia'i-Far accused Copithorne of ignoring "the positive developments in Iran such as restoring the rights of women, freedom of expression and the democratic presidential election held last May." [30]

Zia'i-Far toed the official line by claiming exceptionality for "a religious society" in which a minority that violates Islamic law is "not allowed to undermine the values maintained by the majority." [31] He did not understand that one of the goals of the UN Commission is to protect minorities from the "offended" senses of the majority.

Nevertheless, as Raja'i Khorassani's change of heart showed, the UN monitoring may have influenced those officials who were assigned to counter charges of human rights violations. Here I assume that the establishment of these human rights organizations by different state institutions can be attributed to the fact that Iran has remained under the UN's monitoring regime. The UN Commission has continued to renew the mandate of its Special Representative on Iran. The political pressure exerted by such organizations as Amnesty International could not have initiated the process leading to the formation of these state human rights agencies. Despite the original intentions, one or two of them may have the potential to acquire a life more honest or adventurous than that intended by their manipulating founders, coming to some disagreement with its mother bureaucracy. The Commission regularly denounced the Western abuse of UN human rights procedures. Nevertheless, denunciation could not remain the only task for a commission with human rights in its title. The Commission's name itself and the discussion about its purported superior goals and activities generated questions and raised expectations. The officials felt it necessary to disavow any connection between the Commission and the Judiciary, adding that it "investigates all the complaints submitted to it."[32]

In September 1998, the Commission held a four-day conference, inviting a number of agreeable international participants for a theoretical discussion of the universality of rights and a consideration of "human rights in Islam." The more these Islamic officials talked about human rights, the more they increased the possibility that one day they might have to protest against certain practices. The existence of a Commission officially recognized as a center to which citizens could make appeals added a new dimension to Iran's human rights discourse.

The secular outsiders had little hope that their appeals might be heard, but the Islamic reformers whose rights were being violated in the late 1990s made formal complaints to the Commission and reminded it of its pretenses. From his prison cell in Evin, the courageous journalist Akbar Gangi forwarded a letter to the Commission on January 24, 1998. After pointing out the existing violations, he asked, "Why is it that the Islamic Human Rights Commission defends human rights of citizens of France, Germany, United States, Algeria, Turkey . . . instead of defending human rights in the Islamic Republic? Should not charity begin at home? Why does the Commission remain silent about the prisoners of conscience?"[33]

Officials carrying human rights in their title could not have remained unaffected, especially when they felt sympathetic to the Islamic reformers and their causes. On some specific cases where the well-known reformers were mistreated, the Commission was willing to express its concerns. After the security officials' mistreatment of Tehran's district mayors and the exposure of torture in the reformist press in 1998, Zia'i-Far had no option but to complain about "illegal detention centers." He implied that the security officials operated those centers.[34] Under the law, all detention centers were supposed to be under the State Prisons Organization, itself under the Judiciary's control. The Head of the Judiciary, casting doubt on the validity of the reports, appointed a committee to investigate the charges.[35] It is highly unlikely that the Head of the Judiciary did not know about the existence of detention centers run by the security agents. Nothing came out of the investigation.

The intensification of intra-regime conflicts may have encouraged Zia'i-Far to become more daring in registering his objections. When the cleric Mohsen Kadivar, an outspoken critic of the regime discussed in Chapter 14, was arrested by order of the Special Court for the Clergy in early 1999, he sent copies of his correspondence with the court to the Commission. Zia'i-Far responded positively by publicly stating that the court had failed to explain the reasons for Kadivar's arrest and to allow the Commission to visit him in Evin prison.[36] The Judiciary had set up the Commission, but the courts ignored its pleas. By the end of the 1990s, Zia'i-Far was clearly defending the rights of Islamic reformers. Reacting to the closure of eighteen publications in April 2000, he issued a statement, calling the Judiciary's action a "press massacre." He added that the act might further "distort" the image of the Islamic Republic in the world's public opinion.[37] Speaking the language of human rights is hazardous in an antidemocratic state; authoritarian power holders who openly parrot the seductive language of human rights may face undesirable consequences. The secretary of the Commission was no longer stonewalling, at least when Islamic insiders were the victims. However, the diplomats' habits of denial seemed impossible to change.

Enduring Diplomatic Habits of Denials and Misrepresentations

Removal of Iran from the UN special procedures remained the regime's constant goal, regardless who was the President of the Islamic Republic or who occupied the position of the UN Special Representative. When, following Copithorne's 1996 visit and his subsequent report, the UN Human Rights Commission failed to act according to the Islamist diplomats' desires, they responded with predictable anger toward the Western sponsors of the Commission's condemnatory resolution. They accused the sponsors of the resolution of only seeing the negatives in Copithorne's reports.[38] The Foreign Ministry's spokesman asserted that the UN had ignored the positive aspects that Copithorne had noted for Iran's human rights situation.[39] The message was that no more visits by the Special Representative would be allowed.

In the second half of the 1990s, Iran was changing and the vociferous voices objecting to human rights violations were heard around the world, yet the regime's diplomatic approach remained largely unchanged. Diplomats continued issuing rejections and denials; there was no diplomatic recognition of serious human rights violations in Iran.

As described earlier, many of the human rights violations in the second half of the 1990s involved intellectuals and journalists. The activities of the *hezbollahi* vigilantes constantly exasperated them and irritated the international human rights community. The misuse of the Press Court and the Special Court for the Clergy harassing and prosecuting dissident journalists had become a major concern of the domestic reformers and international observers.

In their responses, the diplomats continued resorting to the institutional similarities that exist in modern states, regardless of their democratic or authoritarian content (Chapter 10). They stated that "the resolution of all media litigation takes place within the framework of law and lies within the jurisdiction of the judicial branch."[40] Using the similarity with universally accepted institutional norms and practices, they mentioned the cases of litigation of the Press Law in the presence of a jury.[41] Again, this was the most convenient way to explain away the violation of freedom of the press, without having to address specific violations.

With reference to the attack on the reformist theoretical journal *Kiyan*, the diplomats' response combined disingenuous protestations and bureaucratic sophistry: "Following this magazine's interview with Mr. Bazargan and the discussion of issues related to the sacred eight-year defence and relations with the United States, a number of families of martyrs and fighters rallied near the offices of the publication to protest the printing of words that caused them emotional distress. That this magazine has so far been published with no interference invalidates the allegation. It proves that those overseeing the country's media conduct themselves in accordance with the law and do not represent sectarian interests."[42]

In response to a different case, the diplomats stated, "It is a matter of pride for Iran that even the highest judicial authority must file a complaint against a publication like all other citizens."[43] These diplomatic excuses were issued at the time when the reformist press in Tehran was objecting to the emerging pattern of the abuse.[44]

The officials still responded to charges with countercharges, righteous indignation, categorical denials, denunciations, and contrived surprises. As discussed before, the regime's diplomats remained mostly ignorant of the security activities. They presented to the outside world what security officials concocted as explanations. The Sarkuhi episode was such a story. Another one tried to prove that the Mojahedin had murdered the Christian pastors. The official press faithfully reported these stories, and the diplomats parroted them in New York and Geneva. A meaningful acknowledgment that state security agents did violate human rights was still beyond the diplomats. Even when the reformers were able to corner one of the main security directors and implicate him in extrajudicial murders, the hard-line power holders portrayed him and his accomplices as wayward agents who had gone astray. Above all, the officials evaded the issue of accountability for those in the highest offices of the security apparatus.

Even Khatami's reformist presidency did not change the way his Foreign Minister and diplomats responded to charges of human rights violations. As mentioned in Chapter 8, Khatami blamed the outside world's propaganda for creating reports on human rights violations of the Baha'is. Moreover, the Foreign Minister consistently faced the issues in a denial/rejection mode. In a meeting in Tehran with UN Human Rights Commissioner Mary Robinson, Foreign Minister Kamal Kharrazi repeated the official mantra that "the Western powers use human rights in a selective manner and with a political goal."[45] As usual, this was in response to questions about human rights *in* Iran, not the Western powers' abuses of Iran's record.

Shortly after being appointed, Kharrazi reacted to Sarkuhi's case and strongly objected to the German Foreign Minister, who had indicated that a secret trial of the incarcerated editor was an obstacle to an improved relationship between the two countries. Kharrazi expressed surprise that such a statement could come from "a Foreign Minister who ought to be famil-

iar with the international norms and laws." Kharrazi spoke as if he did not
know the bizarre nature of Sarkuhi's disappearance and reappearance and
the government's claim that Sarkuhi had gone to Germany, when actually
he had been detained in Evin prison and tortured (see Chapter 14).

Kharrazi said that the trial of a citizen was an issue that fell within the
competence of the Judiciary of that citizen's state alone. Kharrazi could not
have been ignorant of the involvement of the German government and its
embassy in Tehran with this case, including the forging of Sarkuhi's passport to "prove" that he had gone to Germany. He even added: "This trial
is being processed in the Judiciary and the judicial system is very carefully
observing the process of this just trial." [46] This totally ignored the contradictory aspects of the trial, the trumped-up charges leveled against the victim,
and his repeated arrests and incarcerations without regard to due process
of law. A simple acknowledgment of the fact that Sarkuhi's case presented
a human rights problem for his government was beyond the regime's chief
diplomat.

That the diplomats would say anything to avoid acknowledging human
rights problems was displayed again by Kharrazi's false assertions to reporters in New York on October 2, 1999. The issue was the fate of thirteen Iranian
Jews who had been falsely accused of spying for Israel and kept in prison
for months without being formally charged or tried. International reporters knew that the charge carried the death penalty. The Foreign Minister
assured them that "Iran does not execute spies in peacetime." [47] This was
simply not true. In the 1990s, when there was no war, the Judiciary executed
a number of individuals after accusing them of spying for the United States.
Amnesty International reported the execution of a seventy-seven-year-old
Jewish man in 1994 for espionage. After Khatami became president, two
men were hanged for spying for Israel and the United States in 1997; one of
whom was retired colonel Siyavush Bayani. [48]

In New York, the regime's diplomats issued a long statement on the imprisonment of thirteen Jews in Shiraz. It asserted that the arrests had nothing to do with their religion and that they had "been charged with espionage
and acting against the national security of Iran." They furthermore wished
to assure the international human rights community that once the investigations were completed, "all arrested suspects will receive a fair trial in accordance with due process of law," an assurance that the diplomats were not
in a position to give. [49] The diplomatic statement was issued in June 1999,
three months after the arrests. This was exactly at the time when President
Khatami, concerned with ramifications of the case for his administration,
twice announced that he was responsible for the security of all religious minorities, and everyone understood that he was referring to the arrests of the
thirteen Jews. [50] The diplomats ignored the fact that the case of thirteen had
all the features of political maneuverings conducted through the Judiciary
(see Chapter 9).

Responding to a question, the moderate Mohajerani, the Minister of Culture and Islamic Guidance, tried to justify the parading of the accused on state television to repeat their confession. He said that it took place in response to the Western "big propaganda" for the case of the thirteen Jews. "So our judiciary had to use its instruments to show that the Jews might be guilty, so it used the state television."[51] After two decades of experience, even a moderate high official was unable to grasp the negative impression that a secretive proceeding and confession broadcast could create in the international human rights community.

As discussed above, the rationale for appointing a Special Representative was based on the expectation that the state under consideration would cooperate with the UN monitoring process. The Islamic Republic never complied. No governmental investigation of the allegations presented to it by the UN Special Representatives was forthcoming.

Thus, despite the passage of many years of intense interaction with the UN human rights organs and with the Special Representatives, and the issuance of hundreds of UN reports, resolutions, and pleas, the diplomats still refused to treat the issues related to the charges of human rights violations with a modicum of straightforwardness and honesty.

This attitude toward human rights violations that had occurred in practice seriously undermines the credibility of any cultural relativist claims. The Foreign Minister Kharrazi lectured the UN General Assembly on September 22, 1997, asserting that human rights must be redefined by taking into account his country's spirituality and religious roots. Implying that the UDHR was a reflection of "extremist individualism" of the Western culture, Kharrazi called for the "liberation" of the concept of human rights "from the restrictive bonds and monopolistic claims of a particular culture and ideology." This redefinition must be done "through genuine respect for the plurality of beliefs, religions, traditions, value systems and modes of thinking" of different peoples of the world.[52] Placed against the Foreign Minister's false assertions, denials, and prevarication concerning real violations, his theoretical, cultural relativist pronouncements lack credibility. A state with a proven record of violations is not in a position to lecture the international human rights community on the necessity of redefining universal rights.

In Iran, however, the struggle against the Islamist rule helped to integrate human rights into the political discourse of the opposition to the clerical authoritarianism, notably among Islamic reformers who wish to reform and preserve the system of the Islamic Republic. It is not possible to measure the positive impact of the UN monitoring process on the domestic opposition in Iran. The fact that Iran was under the UN's special procedures and that the Western news media, especially the BBC and Voice of America broadcast news about the UN reports on Iran helped to keep the dissident community focused on human rights.

In the early 1990s, even the emerging moderate reformers had difficulty accepting an international observer. A reader asked the newspaper *Salam* if it were permissible for an Iranian to give a person like Galindo Pohl "information or documents" that were contrary to what judicial authorities claimed. The editors responded that such an act was not only a sin but also an offense against national interest. "We must never complain about ourselves to a foreigner."[53] By the end of the 1990s, when the forces of suppression of freedom of expression had become intolerable even to the Islamic reformers, the editors of the banned *Salam* no longer showed such reservations in listing the support of the international human rights organizations and making references to international human rights laws. *Salam* was ostensibly banned for publishing an internal memo belonging to the Intelligence Ministry. To show the illegality of such a ruling, Mehrdad Mola'i, a *Salam* associate, even made direct references to rulings by the European Court on Human Rights, which rejected government actions that had prevented the European press from publishing what state officials considered confidential documents related to national security.[54]

The daring Islamic reformer even made sarcastic references to the way the old Islamists looked at international human rights:

> Of course we have read the often-repeated words that human rights is an essentially Western phenomenon and that we as Muslims need neither human rights nor such disreputable monitors, watchers, committees, and commissions. Another group thinks that the concept of "Islamic human rights" is the only form that is acceptable to us. However, the problem is that no one elucidates the meaning and scope of this [Islamic] phenomenon. Thus, these general notions are turned into a rampart, from behind which they judge everything and everyone and silence every voice of discontent. The advantage of the existing international human rights laws is that their scope is clearly delineated and a specific implementing mechanism is provided.[55]

Other reformists insisted that officials take the Constitution's right protections seriously, and they referred often to the Universal Declaration of Human Rights.[56] Iran's case confirms Lauren's general observation: "Ironically, visions of human rights have always gained the greatest support during times of greatest human abuses."[57] Never before in modern Iranian history had the language of rights been as loud and persistent as during the second half of the 1990s. It permeated the political discourse to such a degree that speakers were no longer aware of its "Western origin." While under house arrest, the beleaguered Grand Ayatollah Montazeri told the English journalist Robert Fisk of an "expression in Persian": "Rights are something you must seize—they're not given to you."[58] The Grand Ayatollah, a true parochial mullah, was probably not aware that he was giving back in Persian a famous motto that has motivated many Western human rights movements.

In fact, the discourse of political opposition to the Shah's authoritarianism was predominately nationalistic and anti-imperialistic, neither of which was particularly helpful to the development of a human rights culture. The anti-imperialist discourse had all but disappeared. Expressing a national sentiment, Abdollah Nuri asked from prison: "How have we benefited as a nation from slogans like 'Death to America'? Have these slogans developed our economy or promoted our national policy and culture?"[59] Nationalism increasingly expressed itself in a language that constructed national well-being in human rights terms. The future leadership of a reformed Islamic Republic—or another regime—will have to operate in a radically different political landscape than the one left behind by Muhammad Reza Shah and Ayatollah Khomeini.

Conclusion

Darkness will roll back. The light will spread like silver. We await a golden dawn.

—Iranian poet Simin Behbahani

Respect for Human Rights, a Precondition for Cultural Discussions

The Universal Declaration of Human Rights has been a proper response to the menacing presence of modern states. Notwithstanding the intense cultural debates, a universal human rights core exists as an accepted practice, from which no derogation is permissible on grounds of national security or culture. States that stood accused of violating this core have often and predictably resorted to denial and concealment, not to justification based on cultural norms and religious imperatives. A cursory inventory of human rights violations by states that include the Islamic Republic reveals that certain violations, largely of civil and political rights, regularly occur, irrespective of different cultural traditions. They include:

1. the right to life;
2. the right to freedom from torture or cruel and degrading punishment;
3. the right to liberty and security of person and freedom from arbitrary arrest and detention;
4. the right to a fair trial;
5. the right to freedom of conscience, thought, and religion;
6. the right to freedom of opinion, expression, and the press;
7. the right to participate in the state's political affairs; and
8. the rights of women to equal opportunities in public life.

Cultural and religious arguments cannot be credibly offered to justify derogation from these categories of civil and political rights, since all of them are directly related to the state and state-centered politics; moreover, they are considered the core of international human rights law, beyond derogations. The Islamic Republic of Iran has proved capable of violating them despite some relevant provisions that the culturally authentic clerics wrote in the Islamic constitution.

Many sincere Muslims may think that some social practices impacting human rights might be open to plausible cultural considerations based on Islamic imperatives or Muslim citizens' religious sensitivities, as distinct from the political culture of the neopatriarchy in control of the state. The considerations that might have a bearing on implementation of international human rights law may include Muslims' inability to change religion (the apostasy crime), Islamic customs and the *shari'ah* law regulating marriage, unilateral divorce by husband, child custody, inheritance, polygamy, temporary marriage, women's inability to marry non-Muslims, and so on.

On these issues, as well as the eight categories of rights listed above and discussed throughout the book, Muslim liberals and secular citizens have demanded cultural changes and modifications in laws and state practices. The Islamists-turned-reformists have acknowledged, more or less tacitly, the need for modifying cultural attitudes and changing legal practices sanctioned by Islamic traditions. This was also shown by lay officials' apparent embarrassment in the face of certain practices, such as stoning, that their conservative clerical mentors attributed to Islam.

Moreover, given the contentiousness of various Islamic interpretations, adopting any version of Islam as the guiding light for public policy to decide the culturally sensitive issues mentioned above is a political decision subject to the requirements of the authoritarian state, as defined by men in power. The state's requirements and the desire of such men to hold onto political power largely subsume cultural issues, subject them to the state *modus operandi*, and subvert their authenticity. Therefore, a reasonable resolution of any of the culturally sensitive issues is largely contingent upon the satisfaction of fundamental rights that are directly under state control, such as the right to freedom of association and the press, the right to political participation, and the right to security of person. To begin negotiating the sensitive cultural boundaries, people need protection of their civil and political rights. The state must protect the eight categories of rights mentioned above for a meaningful discussion to begin, free from intimidation and prosecutions, on the culturally and religiously sensitive issues.

Many Iranians rely on the Universal Declaration of Human Rights for moral and legal support, since they understand that universal human rights offer a "standard of achievement for all peoples and all nations." International human rights law serves as a prestigious platform for dissident views that demand changes in all cultural practices that sustain and legitimize human rights violations. If human rights, as envisioned by the Declaration, were in agreement with the world's cultural traditions, there would have been no need for them. They would be a meaningless redundancy or a kind of psychological cushion to make all peoples feel good in the comfort of their own cultural home. But almost no premodern culture recognizes the inherent dignity of all human beings, nor do they heed the fact that dignity requires recognition of equal respect and concern at all times. The absence within a traditional culture of the principle of equal concern and respect is often dangerously reflected in an authoritarian state's practices, particularly when they assume divine sanctity.

Human rights are less about what a culture is than about what it should become by incorporating safeguards that the individual requires to live a life of dignity within a modern state and capitalist economy. This is the same treatment historically accorded to cultural norms of the peoples in the West. The agonizing cultural pain endured by the introduction of changes into one's culture, granting everyone equal concern and respect, is an equal opportunity pain, shared by all peoples of the world. Many human rights scholars maintain that international laws do not have a provision for making exceptions for an Islamic derogation of human rights. It would be the beginning of the end of the internationalization of human rights if exceptions were to be made. The world is full of religions with particularistic demands to reduce the scope of international human rights law. As shown in Chapter 9, the criminal conduct toward Iranian Baha'is does not emanate from the victims, nor can the blame be placed on the international human rights advocates who point out the egregious violations of that religious minority's rights. The responsibility in Iran rests with the Shiite tradition, which clerics developed mostly in the nineteenth century, a negligible interval in the life of an ancient people who had shed numerous cultural skins throughout the ages.

A modern state's considerable ability to influence people's cultural attitudes must be recognized. For example, the state would be in a stronger position to effect changes toward less regressive mores if it adopted and sincerely carried out a policy of political and economic equality with respect to the population as a whole. The prejudicial views that Iranian society harbors against Baha'is — and to a lesser degree against other "recognized" religious minorities — can be overcome by the state's protective legal measures, as well as by its ability to frame cultural discussions to effect progressive changes. The Islamic Republic has done the opposite, as it has tapped into a long-standing prejudice that society has harbored against the minorities who are considered *najes*, emitting ritual and physical impurity. The regime has codified the primordial societal prejudices into the state's legal system. It has given political currency to the medieval elements in Iranian culture. As shown on many occasions, the Islamic Republic and ancient intolerance have fed on each other.

If we do not wish to empty the concept of its intrinsic meaning, civil society is the society of citizens who are freed from ascriptive categorizations. Islamic reformers have given unconditional support to the notion of civil society that President Khatami helped to popularize in the press. The point to remember is that a modern state which allows considerable autonomy to a society that still upholds these categorizations of the Self/Other does not bring us closer to civil society. Voluntary associations, formed in accordance with the traditional norms, do not foster a civil society, nor do they encourage experiences that would free the society from its ascriptive categorizations. Shiite Muslims have a long way to go in accepting the right of Baha'is to assert their claim to a universal religion that, in their beliefs, transcends Islam.

In Iran's case, these cultural changes must occur, not because the Western states advocate them, but because a substantial segment of Iranian society demands them.

The Islamic Republic Violates Rights Like Other States

The Islamic Republic has failed to measure up to international expectations. In fact, it has largely reinforced the existing cultural prejudices against minorities and women and granted them legal sanctions. Above all, the details I presented in this study, though by no means comprehensive, show the political contingency of the human rights violations. Perhaps because of a lack of understanding of human rights, as Special Representative Copithorne observed, the clerical rulers have often disregarded their own Islamic constitutional provisions. They have failed to appreciate the significance of constitutional law for a modern nation-state. Putting aside the insufficiency of the Islamic constitutional provisions, they could not transform abstract (Islamic) ideals into a workable legal framework capable of offering protection even to former Islamists within the regime. They failed to protect the secular outsiders. Whatever framework the clerics created kept changing in the shifting sands of Islamist factional politics and the imperatives of holding onto power.

It is possible to assume that the Islamist ideologues of the 1970s were sincere in claiming high moral ground and denouncing secularism's ungodly practices such as "sexual promiscuity and rampant consumerism," to mention only the two that horrified traditionalists the most. Ideological assertions made outside the perimeters of the Shah's authoritarian state became subverted once they assumed a new role within the new state, granting legitimacy to the Islamist rulers who were even more self-indulgent than the ones they removed by the help of such assertions.

Thus, after 1979, I have always approached the Islamist rulers' words of commitment to the superior Islamic paradigm with profound skepticism, since their practices were guided by mundane opportunism. Too much evidence indicates that the system housed ruthless gangs of politicians, antiquarians, clerical buccaneers who saw booty in wealthy foundations (*bonyads*), profiteers, political sharks in turbans, opportunistic technobureaucrats who flocked around centers of power, and the hooligans who had always been endemic to Iran's traditionally cabalistic politics and had now escaped the streets of discontents and moved inside the corridors of power and money.

The fact I want to emphasize here is that even if we grant their sincerity in creating a state-society based on genuinely authentic Islamic norms and then examine their conspiratorial mind-set and practices, we would have to conclude that they, like all other ideological dictators, thought they were justified in using repression, torture, and execution to protect and advance the system they had built in the image of their ideology. Like all other ideological dictators, the Islamists predicated the success of their propaganda machine of distortion and misinformation on the kind of political repression that had silenced everyone. The historian Edwin E. Moise observed: "Dominating the media of public propaganda, they presented their one-sided argument with all the carelessness of people who know that if they confound logic, falsify the facts, or misrepresent the views of their opponents, nobody will dare to point out the errors."[1] Moise's description is not about the Islamists in Iran in the 1980s; it is about Maoists in China during the Cultural Revolution. What is remarkable is how similar they were in their tactics, as well as in the view that the end justified the means, making them all guilty of human rights violations.

What is remarkable about the pattern of violations of the right to life by a regime that claims fidelity to Islamic norms is that there is hardly anything unique about it, as compared with similar patterns observable in almost all rights-abusive states. All of them crack down mercilessly and in total disregard of due process of law on their young leftist activists and national minority groups, especially those who take up arms for resistance; all of them suppress street demonstrations with sufficient ferocity to prevent its spread across the city; all of them level the charge of espionage against anyone deemed to be the enemy of the regime, deserving death; all of them seek added legitimacy by turning antidrug-trafficking measures into a political campaign; and all of them kill intransigent writers who refuse to forfeit their conscience. The tactics the Islamist security agents employed against Saʻidi Sirjani or Pastor Dibaj, to recall only two of their victims, could have been concocted in the office of any Intelligence Minister in any authoritarian state. Even the assassinations of political opponents outside state borders are carried out by the bloodthirstiest among them, hardly a distinguishing mark of a particular culture. The culture that prevailed in the Intelligence Ministry had less to do with Islam as a religion than with the authoritarian state's modus operandi, which is universal, thus requiring universal human rights to curb its abuses.

"Yet again the devouring regime was presenting itself as a victim. A noble victim," to borrow Marguerite Feitlowitz's apt characterization of Argentina between 1976 and 1983.[2] Moreover, when they are pressed hard by their dissidents demanding civil and political rights, the conservative power holders become the champions of economic rights. Having supervised the whole-sale banning of the reformist press in 2000, the Supreme Leader, revisiting an earlier theme of the Islamic revolution, dismissed the desire for civil liberties and identified the most critical task as eradication of massive poverty.[3] What has also become universal is the misrepresentation of all diplomats who, despite the diversities in their cultural backgrounds, mimic each other to please their political masters back home.

Particular Curses of the Religious State

Nevertheless, a religious state inflicts its own political curses. In Iran, curses revealed themselves in many of the cases presented in this study, showing more convincingly than any abstract discussion the necessity of a separation between religion and the state. The fact that this particular religious state has been a Shiite state is significant, since in every state we must focus on the existing patterns of human rights violations and call attention to their victims. Here I will only recap some of its most troubling curses.

This Islamic state demanded from middle-class men and women, inheritors of a century-long tradition of modernization and secularization, allegiance to Ayatollah Khomeini's politicized Islam. Prison memoirs demonstrate that his men turned prisons into a closed social laboratory in which they imposed, under a controlled environment impossible to create in the larger society, a strict regime that demanded religious conformity. This was as close as one could be to the Ayatollah's vision of Shiite Islam and what it envisaged for society. When they failed, they massacred hundreds of the prisoners who refused to acquiesce to the Inquisition's demands.

Seen through the prism of prison memoirs, this painful history of human rights violations sheds considerable light on Islamic cultural relativism in human rights discourse. Article 18 of the International Covenant on Civil and Political Rights protects the right to freedom of thought, conscience, and religion. Is there any provision in the International Covenant that may allow derogation, based on cultural specificity, from the state's obligation under Article 18? Can international human rights law make exceptions for what took place in the Islamic Republic's prisons in the 1980s? The answer is obviously no. What took place in prisons made a mockery of Article 18. At the time when conversion to a *hezbollahi* notion of Islam was forcefully demanded inside prison walls, the regime's diplomats had the audacity to present it as a reeducation process for the good of prisoners. In terms of credibility, no amount of cultural relativist arguments could withstand the memoirs' debunking.

The Islamist official quoted in Chapter 1 declared blasphemy and polytheism strictly forbidden. "Even if it is packaged as freedom of opinion, the thing that human beings have the right to choose is religion. The right to choose is not between religion and irreligion. If they choose wrongly, they will be punished." In light of this assertion, what prison officials tried to do was in character with the expected behavior of a religious state. Given a closed environment, they tried to implement the vision articulated by the ideologues. The fact that they did not succeed in the larger society was not due to lack of resolve or insufficient actions. Urban complexities in Iranian society, which had experienced a century of secularization, defeated the Ayatollah's Islamization project, leaving behind dead bodies and shattered lives.

Even in prisons, the coercive reintegration of the individual into a politically reconstructed Islamic community was successful only in its deception. It largely destroyed or badly injured, physically and psychologically, those young men and women it sought to reconvert and integrate. Secular individuals whose conscience was important for their identity and who survived the Islamization of prisons felt bitter and contemptuous.

Prison memoirs show what I asserted at the beginning of this study: Cultural relativist debate in human rights discourse is not a debate over philosophical anthropology. Any debate that loses sight of the victims of human rights violations is a debate about something else and not about human rights. We must evaluate cultural relativist ideas within their specific historical context, by asking what sociopolitical praxis would result from allowing derogation of human rights law based on claimed indigenous cultural principles. What liberal Muslims profess in their new interpretations of "True Islam" is of little consequence. Iran's historic experience in the past two decades relates to the Islamic Republic as constructed by the politicized Shiite clerics. The details show that secular Iranians have been among the victims of cultural relativist ideas espoused by the regime. They are more than a negligible group of misguided "Westernized" intellectuals who are constantly berated by the Islamists of both genders and more kindly dismissed by Western cultural relativists.

This particular religious state became a curse on Iran's intellectuals. After an intense and largely unsuccessful drive to effect a new conversion to the Ayatollah's politicized Islam, the clerical rulers applied their binary vision in a less frantic manner in public pronouncements, separating secular intellectuals from the community of believers. In the 1990s, many of the problems that secular writers and journalists faced emanated from being branded as the *digar andishan*. The symbol of Islamist gender segregation has, of course, been the Islamic *hijab*, an aesthetically troubling symbol of the existing patterns of human rights violations of secular women.

Implementation of Islamic rules has become another curse on citizens of the authoritarian state. What Dr. Ousiya (Paya) observed in the first months of the revolution continued throughout the 1980s: uncertainty as to what would happen next. Authorities constantly reminded political prisoners that they faced Islamic justice. If the prisoners knew nothing about Islamic jurisprudence, they could have easily imagined that uncertainty and pre-varication were its main features. In the 1990s, the religious state finalized the Islamization of the court system, where the same mullah was prosecutor and presiding judge who issued the verdict and fixed the penalty.

In cases where the accused was charged with political offenses, there has hardly been any improvement in granting him/her due process of law, irre-spective of the passage of new laws or claims made to Special Representative Copithorne about "maturation" of the process. Hardly any trial held could prove that reforms had made any difference. The only new element has been widening of the intra-elite conflict, providing a small window through which international monitors could see miscarriages of justice. The cases of the secular authors discussed in Chapter 14 shows how the clerics made a trav-esty of due process of law. In Sa'idi Sirjani's and Sarkuhi's ordeals, as in the cases of many other intellectuals, no ordinary criminal proceeding was fol-lowed. Arrest without warrant took place. No charges were preferred during the permitted period of detention. The detention was not an initial step in a criminal proceeding leading to judicial investigation of the charges and a fair trial. Between Sa'idi Sirjani's arrest and his death lay a bewildering gap, filled with tortured confessions and baseless charges that kept changing across the shifting grounds of Islamist factional politics. Similarly, Sarkuhi got a bitter taste of Ayatollah Yazdi's justice, leading to his exile. To question any of these anomalies in the justice system was to question the veracity of the *shari'ah*, a blasphemy punishable by death.

The fact that the clerics' attitudes toward those who were charged with political crimes had undergone little change was best shown in the indict-ments against the accused, marshaling an incredible mixture of offenses to throw the victim totally off balance. The cleric Rahbarpur, head of the Revo-lutionary Courts in Tehran, did not indict and convict; he demonized. In-dicative of the mind-set that controlled the Judiciary, this damning attitude presented itself even outside the court of law. Rahbarpur seemed to have always had a string of charges around his fingertips, tossing them around like his rosaries, not as mere accusations, but as already proven crimes. He was, it should be emphasized, the head of the most powerful court in the country. In that capacity, he functioned as both the prosecutor and the judge.

During the second period, as in the first ten years of their rule, the Islam-ist prosecutors have continued to add charges that had clear sexual dimen-sions. The prosecutors not only charged their victims with espionage but also denounced them as freaks, according to their notions of perversion. A sur-geon who was a leader of the Sunni community in Shiraz was charged with adultery and sodomy, and a well-known writer was accused of the crime of homosexuality. The Zendehdel group was not only charged with the crime of being in contact with the royal family abroad and conspiring to overthrow the regime, but also with all kinds of moral crimes, including encouraging prostitution. And the writer and editor Faraj Sarkuhi was imprisoned in 1996 and forced to confess to sexual relations with several women. He had not even met some of the women named by his tormentors. They even forced him "to speak about the sexual relations of other writers with each other's wives."[4] Hajji Rahmani, the infamous prison warden of the 1980s, was not unique after all.

Moreover, as the 1980s prison memoirs showed, interrogators, prosecutors, and judges were all enmeshed in a system in which torture was practiced in full view. It functioned on the assumption that the person in custody was guilty and that guilt had to be confirmed by inflicting pain. The religious state condoned torture as Islamic *t'azir*. A few steps separated the rooms where interrogators extracted confessions and the rooms where judges considered the confession as evidence of guilt. This physical proximity of the torture chamber and the judge's chamber was a feature of the Islamist system of justice for much of the 1980s. The Islamists did not consider the use of excessive force—torture—detrimental to the integrity of the judicial process. It was an integral part of it, signifying efficacy and competence in the interrogations. Under the Shah, security officials fashioned a separation between the legal and the illegal, or what a self-respecting modern state would designate as illegitimate. The regime decreased the discomfort of judges who passed the sentences that security officials demanded. The formality of the institutional setup did ostensibly conceal torture from the judges' mental view. In the Islamic Republic, however, it was all in common view. In the 1960 and 1970s, anti-Shah activists liked to report the dramatic gesture of a defiant defendant in court, revealing his back or legs and displaying the marks of torture. Prison memoirs of the Islamic Republic do not report such a gesture in a court of law; there was no need for it, since cries of pain reverberated through the Islamic court next door.

Of course, stoning to death, amputation of limbs, and flogging remain a particularly disturbing curse of the religious state. Stoning of convicts, although rooted in a defunct tradition, could not be defended by cultural explanations. It provided a graphic example of how the attempt to reimpose an old Islamic tradition was largely rejected by the practical ethics of today's urban society. Apparently instigated by the caliph in Arabia in the mid-seventh century as a punishment for adultery, stoning was a practice of a small, primitive community, protective of its cohesiveness and moral solidarity. The convict and the stone-throwers were cognizant of the communal dynamics that demanded the punishment. In Iran's complex society, the practice of stoning a man or a women accused of adultery, carried out by the authoritarian state, has appeared repulsive to people on the streets of large cities. The state executioners stood apart from the men on the street; no communal bond linked them in moral solidarity. Many people considered them the agents of a ruthless state. The Islamic Republic learned this lesson and modified this inhumane practice in Tehran by avoiding stoning in public squares. In the late 1990s, efforts were being made to prevent enforcement of the law; similarly, in the numerous court convictions between 1997 and 2000, the clerics no longer sentenced writers to flogging. This is indicative of the state's ability to abuse cultural elements, to arrange and rearrange them, to suit the changing political needs of men in power.

The Islamist judicial authorities in Tehran and their lay protégés in Geneva and New York were given ample opportunities, both in face-to-face discussions and by correspondence, to convince the UN representatives about the cultural appropriateness of Islamic punishments of stoning, amputation, and flogging. None of the UN human rights experts exhibited any antipathy to Islamic cultural tradition. Judging from their extensive reports, it sometimes appeared that they were appeasing the cultural sensitivities of Islamist rulers. In the 1990s, of all human rights violations, amputation and stoning seemed to have troubled the UN Representatives personally, as evidenced by a flicker of indignation shining through the otherwise prosaic diplomatic language. The Islamists failed to convince these international observers, and there is little possibility that they would ever succeed in convincing anyone except fellow Islamists in the region. International human rights NGOs have also consistently expressed their outrage.[5]

In Defense of State Secularism

Islamist activists in the Muslim world have considered the Islamization of society to be their movement's main goal—an eerie notion for societies that have been Muslim for centuries. The Iranian experience inspired little credence for such a goal. It was perhaps indicative of a profound sociopolitical crisis, a true measure of political underdevelopment. No matter what political tactics were used within the state to bring about Islamization, it ultimately required the use of force. Beyond the issues raised by the political struggle for power, the Islamists tried to alter the traditional definition of a "good Muslim." People refused to embrace Islamization precisely because it involved this disturbing redefinition. For example, before the twentieth century many Iranians probably did not include in the definition of a "good Muslim" an active commitment to an enforceable ban of alcoholic drinks. Nor did they imagine themselves any less than good Muslims if the Shah's state failed to punish infractions by flogging, amputation of limbs, and stoning to death. Most still do not, despite two decades of actions and propaganda by the political clerics. In Iran, the clerics' definition of a "good Muslim" has always clashed with the one held by many urban Muslims; Persian literature is replete with variations on that theme.

This is not to suggest that individual Muslims should refrain from redefining their understanding of Islam. Groups and associations around the world have tried to Christianize or Judaize their "lapsed" coreligionists. However, where the forces of the contemporary state are used for that purpose, the outcome will most likely be a failure.

In Iran's case, Islamization failed because what it entailed did not appear acceptable to the people of means and education. Islamization of Iranian urban society was not something that could be done to the middle classes; it would have to be done by them. The problem with Ayatollah Khomeini's Islamization was that the redefinition of Islam he offered was congenial largely to urban lower classes and to educated individuals from the traditional middle class or lower middle classes who were only one generation away from their rural background. Today, these educated groups who initially supported Islamization no longer feel excluded from power and wealth, as they did during the Shah's regime. In fact, for Muslim technobureaucrats running the state, the forced Islamization has become a major hindrance to effective utilization of newly conferred power and open enjoyment of new wealth. Their Islamic reformism might reflect self-interests.

For a human rights culture to emerge in Iran, people must take further steps to individualize and privatize their faith, rendering the religion less powerful as a feature in Iranian corporate identity. Generally, as Rhoda Howard argues, "This privatizing and individualizing of cultural characteristics make protection of human rights easier in the long run, because no state or institutional boundaries need to be placed on such choices and because the state is not obliged to protect collectivities. On the one hand, a citizen can adopt any religion or ethnicity he chooses. He can convert to Baha'i, pretend to be Jewish, or wear African-American costumes. On the other hand, as long as individual human rights are protected, the state has no obligation to ensure that his community survives."[6]

Howard's useful characterization is pertinent for a country like Iran. The process of privatizing and individualizing religious characteristics, well under way since the turn of the century, has been blocked by the establishment of the Islamic Republic in Iran.

Above all, cultural authenticity and relativism have become largely irrelevant in human rights discourse in Iran. In the late 1990s, Islamists who participated in the revolution of 1979 or grew up under its propaganda express opinions ranging from traditionalism to the most liberal Islamic reformism. The latter, though still Islamic in expression, strains the ears of the ulema to hear. Under the influence of Western secular thoughts, some liberal Muslim writers like Sorush and Ganji will always be willing to carry the arguments one step closer to modern secularism. The point of reference against which they ultimately measure the appropriateness or attractiveness of their positions is not Islam, as understood by generations of Muslims, but the secular normative paradigms of the late twentieth century. They are more at home with Karl Popper than Kulayni, the tenth-century writer of a Shiite compendium. Since they would not concede that they are somehow less authentic than their more conservative rivals, their claims to authenticity have become in essence relative. Relative authenticity sounds fantastic and incredible.

The existing elites may remain in power, or they may be replaced by counterelites using alternative discourses for political mobilization. The major concern of those in control of the state will continue to be the preservation of their own power and denial of legitimacy to their political opponents. During the current politically volatile transitional era, it is imperative that human rights standards and definitions closely model themselves on the rights provisions of the Universal Declaration, and not be left to the political vagaries of domestically constructed human rights schemes.

In his report on Iran in 1996, Abid Hussain, the UN thematic Special Rapporteur on Freedom of Opinion and Expression, pointed out the crux of the problem. He noted the problematic links between "the mosque and its clerical hierarchy" and the modern state and its institutions. He wrote that "the promotion and protection of the right to freedom of opinion and expression intimately relates to that of the right to freedom of thought, conscience and religion, as enunciated in Article 18 of the International Covenant on Civil and Political Rights." He seems to be saying, albeit discreetly, that the intrusion of the mosque into the state created problems for "the freedom to manifest one's religion or religious or non-religious belief." It has a deleterious "impact on the freedom of opinion and expression."[7] This was the closest that any UN Special Representative had come to identifying the root of the problem, by pointing out that the theocracy placed limits on the indivisible human rights. He did not complicate his report by needlessly resorting to the old debates over different interpretations of Islam, upholding a liberal interpretation against the more restrictive ones. Again, I venture to say that perhaps because of his own Islamic background, he showed no misplaced cultural sensitivity such as often inhibited the observations made by other UN Special Representatives with Western backgrounds.

I see no short-cut to a political culture that uses reason in making public policies, constructing sociopolitical institutions, and upholding the rule of law. Fred Halliday observes, "The central issue is not, therefore, one of finding some more liberal, or compatible, interpretation of Islamic thinking, but of removing the discussion of rights from the claims of religion itself. Unless this step is taken, the multiple levels of limitation identified here— text, culture, instrumentality and religious hegemony—will prevail."[8]

Islamic reformists and "feminists" have every right to argue that the Islamic precepts, as interpreted by them, are compatible with or superior to universal human rights. The interpretation itself is not a real issue. The problem begins whenever the reformists who seek political power intend to use such interpretation as state policy. When they try to support a state that bases the human rights of its citizens on their religious beliefs, they are bound to join the right-abusive conservatives (as the experience of the ratification of the Islamic Constitution showed). Their arguments may serve their competition with conservative rivals for power and influence, but they do not effectively serve the cause of human rights, especially for secular citizens. They both agree that Islam can provide the lens through which the modern state can view international human rights law and practice. They disagree on how it can.

Genuine progress in this direction, as historical evidence clearly shows, can only come from a separation of state and religion. If and when that separation occurs, then making appeals to the humanitarian ethics of the religion will have a positive effect on accelerating changes in discriminatory cultural practices. In politically developed societies where modern frames of references are well established and secular constitutional tradition is deeply rooted in the political culture, a humanistic reading of religious tradition may fulfill spiritual needs on the part of some human rights advocates. It may also reinforce the acceptance of the culture of human rights in the larger public, by countering the restrictive readings of the same tradition. In the absence of a religious state, human rights can benefit from religious teachings, as the alliance between religious groups and civil rights movements showed in the United States. Very few Islamic reformists with a political agenda would yet agree with a central premise in international human rights law: "that individuals are the best judges of their own interests, because individuals ultimately have greater insight into what they need to be happy than do any other persons or institutions."[9] If they did, they would have accepted the secular argument that religion should not be taken as a blueprint for public policies. In the post-*velayat-e faqih* period, secular Iranians watch the new generation of Islamist reformists with weary eyes. However, if they do impose such elasticity on Islam, the secularists would certainly experience a historic deliverance. In the meantime, they have no choice but to rely on the Universal Declaration of Human Rights.

Experience shows that the mixing of Islam and the modern state has trapped its citizens in concentric, hermeneutic mazes. Consider the case of Iran in 2000, where at least three official visions of Islam are locking horns within the regime over the future of the Islamic state, at the same time that they clash with equally authentic readings of Islam outside the ruling circles. The conservative rulers banned the Muslim feminists' interpretation of Islam, which fell outside the *shari'ah* framework. If the conservative Supreme Leader, Ali Khamenei, is somehow eased out of power, secular women would experience what moderate clerics like President Khatami would do, once they free themselves from the conservatives' dominance. There is no way to know how elastic their newly reinterpreted Islamic principles would be concerning freedom of choice for secular women, if and when the Islamic reformists were in a position to pass their own Islamic legislation.

All these Islamic (political) positions are capable of shifting, depending on who is in power and who is the main adversary in the struggle for power at any moment. What may remain fixed is religious rationalization for these positions. President Khatami is quite capable of saying one thing while struggling against the conservative Islamists and another thing when the reinvigorated secularists inevitably crowd the political landscape, offering him a credible resistance. This is why human rights of citizens of the modern state must be removed from the *shari'ah* paradigm altogether, unless the paradigm is redefined to such a degree that it ceases to be *shari'ah*. But Khatami seems unwilling or unable to advocate Islam as a private faith, since he still upholds one version of Islam as the "True Islam" and denounces the "diluted Islam" of the secularists as "one of the most dangerous pores for the West's cultural onslaught."[10] Even Akbar Ganji, who went further than any other popular writer in acknowledging that modernist sensitivities and concepts did not exist in Islam, wished to preserve "the religion's powerful presence in the public domain." To accomplish that task, "religious individuals have no way other than presenting a humanistic-rationalist portrait of the religion."[11]

Iranian secularists looked at Islamic reformers and "feminists" with weary eyes. The experienced secular journalist Changiz Pahlavan observed in 2000 that Islamic reformers did not care to cite the sources from which they borrowed their ideas. He criticized the former radical Islamists who, in the late 1990s, made a turnabout by selecting non-Islamic, secular concepts, attaching Islamic prefixes to them, and appropriating them as their own. Thus, they introduced into their Islamic discourses nongermane notions and ideas, without acknowledging the sources. Pahlavan worried that the phenomenon of borrowing ideas without giving due recognition to their secular origins had utilitarian purposes, serving political needs of those who compete for political power. What if political needs change? Having no deep roots in the Islamic paradigm, they may be discarded as easily as borrowed.[12]

Assured by secularism that diffuses the premodern religious intolerance sanctioned by the state, the future should belong to all political discourses. They will be further protected by pluralism, which supports the political diversity that is the inevitable product of an integrated world civilization in the grip of instantaneous communication and pervasive commercialization. One might reject secularism and pluralism as values in themselves. However, at this time, there is hardly any alternative that better permits a nation to deliberately reckon with its cultural heritage, select what is valuable in a climate that is free from xenophobia and reaction, and divest itself of the anachronisms of patriarchal values and practices.

As for Iranian intellectuals, the most liberating aspect of human rights culture is that it enables individuals to advance claims not only against the state but also against society. It curbs the tendency to privilege what are considered to be advantages to society; society's advantages cannot undermine an individual's claim to human rights. Using Steven Lukes's notion of a "protected space" for Iran, I argue that the new culture of rights reaches beyond the individual as a Muslim or an Iranian, whether these are self-identifying labels or socially conferred; it offers the individual a protected space within which she/he is free to choose a lifestyle in conformity with or deviating from the standards a society wishes to impose on its members.[13] This is a necessity in the world of nation-states, especially in non-Western parts, where many individuals are left politically exhausted and emotionally depleted by semimodern idealistic doctrines.

Thousands of women and men who have grown up in a Muslim society feel that there is nothing more liberating in the world today than the protection of human rights so that they can live their lives in dignity, within a space protected from the stultifying certitude of the Ayatollahs and the moral banalities of their mostly ignorant multitude. This is an existential reality in Iran, where all indications are that young secular men and woman long "to be themselves."[14] Protected by the relative security of their modern constitutional rights, our Western colleagues muse over postmodernism and grant deference to the Islamist claims to cultural *différance.* They have never been, nor could they ever imagine being, under political and cultural servitude to their own clerics. They will most likely never experience such humiliation. Having grown up in Islamic tradition, thousands of individuals are refusing to bear their culture as destiny, and they are rejecting some Western scholars' charges of "false universalism." One such eloquent voice of Iranian culture was Hushang Golshiri, the renowned novelist in Tehran and the recipient of Germany's Erich Maria Remarque Award, who died on June 5, 2000. "We have signed the Universal Declaration of Human Rights," said Golshiri, "which means we are entitled to rights merely because we are human."[15]

Notes

Preface

1. UN Doc. A/44/620.
2. In the 1980s, Afghanistan, Guatemala, Equatorial Guinea were also among the countries for which special representatives were appointed. Iraq, Cuba, Haiti, Myanmar, Yugoslavia, Somalia, Sudan, Rwanda, Burundi, and Zaire were added in the 1990s.
3. UN Doc. A/40/874, p. 2.
4. A. Paya, *Zendan-e Towhidi* (Prison of monotheism) (Germany, 1989); Parvaneh Alizadeh, *Khub Negah Konid, Rastagi Hast* (Look carefully, it is real) (Paris, 1997); M. Raha, *Haqiqat-e Sadeh: Khaterati as Zendanha-ye Zanan-e Jomhuri-ye Islami* (Plain truths: Memoirs from women's prisons in the Islamic Republic), 3 vols. (Germany, 1992–1994); F. Azad, *Yadha-ye Zendan* (Memories of prisons) (Paris, 1997); Hamid Azadi, *Dar-ha va Divar-ha, Khaterati az Zendan-e Evin* (Doors and walls: An Evin prisoner's memoir) (Seattle, 1997); Nima Parvaresh, *Nabardi Nabarabar, Gozareshi az Haft Sal Zendan, 1361–1368* (An unequal battle: A report of seven-year imprisonment, 1983–1990) (Paris, 1995); Reza Ghaffari, *Khaterat-e Yek Zendani az Zendanha-ye Jomhuri-ye Islami* (Memoirs of a prisoner of Islamic Republic's prisons) (Stockholm, 1998); Shahrnush Parsipur, *Khaterat-e Zendan* (The memoirs of prison) (Stockholm, 1996). I have also used the unpublished English version of Ghaffari's memoirs.
5. A few writers like Ali Shirazi and Akbar Sarduzami offer prison experiences as novellas. In addition, a novel presents itself as "a true story of an Iranian woman in Islamic Republic of Iran's prison." Masud Noqrehkar, *Panchereh-ye Kuchak Sellul-e Man* (My small prison's window) (Los Angeles, 1988).
6. Parsipur, p. 315.
7. UN Doc. E/CN.4/1985/20.

Chapter 1. Islamic Cultural Relativism in Human Rights Discourse

1. Abdullahi Ahmed An-Na'im, "Islamic Law, International Relations, and Human Rights: Challenges and Response," *Cornell International Law Journal* 20, no. 2 (1987): 319. Similar assertions are repeated throughout An-Na'im's works.
2. John L. Esposito, *Islam and Politics* (Syracuse, N.Y.: Syracuse University Press, 1984), p. 213.
3. Al-Sadiq Al-Mahdi, "Islam—Society and Change," in *Voices of Resurgent Islam*, ed. John L. Esposito (New York: Oxford University Press, 1983), pp. 231–232.

4. Abdullahi Ahmed An-Na'im, *Toward an Islamic Reformation: Civil Liberties, Human Rights, and International Law* (Syracuse, N.Y.: Syracuse University Press, 1990), p. 62. See also John L. Esposito, *The Islamic Threat: Myth or Reality?* (New York: Oxford University Press, 1992), pp. 9, 18.

5. Reza Afshari, "An Essay on Islamic Cultural Relativism in the Discourse of Human Rights," *Human Rights Quarterly* 16 (May 1994): 235–276. See also Tore Lindholm, "Response to Reza Afshari on Islamic Cultural Relativism in Human Rights Discourse," *Human Rights Quarterly* 16 (November 1994): 791–794.

6. Muhammad Mokhtari, *Tamrin-e Modara: Bist Maqaleh dar Baz-khani-ye Farhang* (Practicing tolerance: Twenty articles on rereading of culture) (Tehran, 1998), p. 164.

7. For a full discussion of communalism and cultural relativism see Rhoda E. Howard, *Human Rights and the Search for Community* (Boulder, Colo.: Westview Press, 1995).

8. UN Doc. A/43/705, p. 17.

9. *Kayhan,* July 25, 1995.

10. *Ettela'at,* May 30, 1990.

11. Interview with the editor of the conservative *Resalat,* published in *Iran,* August 17, 1998, p. 3.

12. For Ayatollah M. Motahhari's views on truthful opinions that deserve to be freely expressed and untruthful opinions that must be rejected, see Majid Muhammadi, "*Nowgarai-ye Dini va Tabu-ye Liberalism*" (Religious modernism and the taboo of liberalism) *Kiyan,* 9, no. 48 (August–September 1999): 15.

13. Hossein Mehrpur, *Hoquq-e Bashar dar Asnad-e Binalmellali and Muzeh-e Jomhuri-ye Islami-ye Iran* (Human rights in international instruments and the position of the Islamic Republic of Iran) (Tehran, 1995), pp. 37–38.

14. Ibid., p. 209.

15. Muhammadi, p. 16.

16. Mansour Farhang, "*Nazargah-e Do-sowyeh-ye* Khatami *dar Bareh-ye Azadi,*" (Khatami's contorted view about liberty), *Elm va Jame'eh,* 20 (September 1999): 10–11. For president Khatami's superficial understanding of the West see Muhammad Khatami, *Hope and Challenge: The Iranian President Speaks* (Binghamton. N.Y.: Institute of Global Cultural Studies, Binghamton University, 1997), p. 35.

17. Mehrpur, p. 39.

18. Ali Qaderi, "*Gozaresh-e Seminar-e Shenakht va Mabani-ye Hoquq-e Bashar*" (Report on the seminar on understanding the fundamentals of human rights), *Majaleh-ye Siasat-e Khareji* (Journal of Foreign Policy) (autumn 1991), 779. This is a publication of the Institute for Political and International Studies of the Foreign Ministry.

19. Ibid., p. 776.

20. In 1992 a cleric who considered himself an expert in human rights in Islam criticized the Universal Declaration for its formulation of the right to free speech. He considered it incomprehensible for a human society to provide no limits or boundaries for the freedom of expression that may lead to "insulting the prophets and the leaders of the community." Addressing the concept of dignity in Article 1, the cleric argued that the declaration does not give us what it means by dignity, and he seriously questioned the possibility of having dignity without God. "Hojjat al-Islam Muhammed Taqi J'afari's Speech," *Kayhan,* December 8, 1992, p. 15.

21. Paul Gordon Lauren, *The Evolution of International Human Rights: Vision Seen* (Philadelphia: University of Pennsylvania Press, 1998), p. 222.

22. Tore Lindholm, "Article 1, A New Beginning," in *The Universal Declaration of Human Rights,* ed. Asbjorn Eide et al. (Oxford: Oxford University Press, 1996), pp. 31–55.

23. Qaderi, pp. 777, 778.

24. Rhoda E. Howard, "Dignity, Community, and Human Rights," in *Human Rights in Cross-Cultural Perspectives*, ed. Abdullahi Ahmad An-Na'im (Philadelphia: University of Pennsylvania Press, 1992), pp. 87, 91.

25. Jack Donnelly, *Universal Human Rights in Theory and Practice* (Ithaca: Cornell University Press, 1989), p. 78.

26. David P. Forsythe, *The Internationalization of Human Rights* (Lexington, Mass.: Lexington Books, 1991), p. 1.

27. Adamantia Pollis. "Toward a New Universalism: Reconstruction and Dialogue," *Netherlands Quarterly of Human Rights*, 16 (1998), p. 7.

28. An interview with Nushin Ahmadi Khorassani, see <http://www.badjens. homepage.com> March 13, 2000.

Chapter 2. The Shiite Theocracy

1. Henry Munson Jr., *Islam and Revolution in the Middle East* (New Haven: Yale University Press, 1988), p. 24.

2. For a discussion of these versions see Mohsen Kadivar, *Nazariyyahha-ye Dowlat Dar Fiqh-e Shi'ah* (Theories of the state in Shiite jurisprudence), 3d ed. (Tehran, 1999). Kadivar argued, albeit discreetly, against Khomeini's understanding of the rule of the *faqih*. For his trial and sentence, see Chap. 14.

3. Quoted in Asghar Schirazi, *The Constitution of Iran: Politics and State in the Islamic Republic*, trans. John O'Kane (London: I.B. Tauris, 1997), p. 35.

4. Shaul Bakhash, *The Reign of the Ayatollahs: Iran and the Islamic Revolution* (New York: Basic Books, 1986), p. 86.

5. Abdolkarim Lahiji, *Poluralism-e Siasi dar Jomhuri-ye Islami-ye Iran* (Political pluralism in the Islamic Republic of Iran) (Paris, 2000), pp. 27–31.

6. Ann Elizabeth Mayer, *Islam and Human Rights, Tradition, and Politics*, 3d ed. (Boulder, Colo.: Westview Press, 1999), pp. 75, 96.

7. Schirazi, p. 162.

8. Ibid., pp. 64, 213.

9. Ibid., p. 165.

10. Ibid., p. 237.

11. Ibid., p. 168.

12. See Reza Afshari, "The Historians of the Constitutional Movement and the Making of the Iranian Populist Tradition," *International Journal of the Middle East Studies* 25 (1993): 477–494.

13. Parsipur, p. 109.

14. For its history see Ervand Abrahamian, *The Iranian Mojahedin* (New Haven: Yale University Press, 1989).

15. *Jomhuri-ye Islami*, December 23, 1994.

16. Muhammad Javad Larijani, before a gathering at Tehran University. *Iran Times*, June 30, 1995. Larijani was one of the most active members of the Majlis Foreign Relations Committee.

17. Marvin Zonis discussed a "second stratum" serving the Shah's state, "located structurally between the Shah and the non-elite." Marvin Zonis, "The Political Elite of Iran: A Second Stratum?" in *Political Elite and Political Development in the Middle East*, ed. Frank Tachau (New York: John Wiley, 1975), pp. 195–196.

18. Darius M. Rejali, *Torture and Modernity: Self, Society, and State in Modern Iran* (Boulder, Colo.: Westview Press, 1994), p. 5.

19. *Frankfurte Rundschau*'s interview with Bazargan, January 12, 1995. Reprinted in *Nashriyyah-ye Hoquq-e Bashar* 11, no. 34 (fall 1994):16–18. The latter is a publication of

the League for the Defense of Human Rights in Iran, based in Germany. The League is sometimes behind schedule; this is a backdated issue.

20. For full discussion of the Rafsanjani technobureaucrats see Reza Afshari, "An Essay on Scholarship, Human Rights, and State Legitimacy: The Case of the Islamic Republic of Iran," *Human Rights Quarterly* 18, no. 3 (August 1996): 544–593.

21. "Reflections of Events and News in Iranian Press," *Ettela'at*, International Edition, September 26, 1996, p. 2.

22. *Tehran Times*, December 12, 1999.

23. A summary of the interview was reprinted in *Kayhan* (London), February 22, 1996, p. 4.

24. UN Doc. A/44/620, November 2, 1989, p. 12.

25. Large-scale political executions and killings continued into the 1990s only in the areas of Kurdish resistance.

26. *Resalat*, October 29, 1997.

27. Quoted in *Iran Times*, October 31, 1997, p. 5.

28. *Ettela'at*, International Edition, November 13, 1997, p. 1.

Chapter 3. The Right to Life

1. See Ervand Abrahamian, *Tortured Confessions: Prisons and Public Recantations in Modern Iran* (Berkeley: University of California Press, 1999), p. 125.

2. Paya, p. 148.

3. Homa Omid, *Islam and the Post-Revolutionary State in Iran* (New York: St. Martin's Press, 1994), p. 103.

4. Parsipur, pp. 87–88.

5. Ibid., p. 158.

6. Alizadeh, p. 20.

7. Azadi, pp. 83–85; Raha, 1:31.

8. Ghaffari, pp. 81–82.

9. Parsipur, pp. 98, 100–101; Raha, 1:44; Azadi, p. 78.

10. Roger Cooper, *Death Plus Ten Years* (London: Harper Collins, 1993), p. 84.

11. Raha, 1:55.

12. Raha, 1:36, 38–39; Parvaresh, p. 39; Azadi, pp. 79–80.

13. One was Valiollah Rud-Geryan, a dedicated Marxist member of the Paykar Organization. After being tortured, Parvaresh was placed in a small cell where he met Rud-Geryan, who was also severely tortured. Rud-Geryan's brother had been executed in the provincial city of Amol three years earlier, followed by the execution of his fiancée a year later. Rud-Geryan refused to submit and walked defiantly to the execution ground on May 1983. Parvaresh, p. 17.

14. Abrahamian, 1999, p. 129.

15. Amnesty International, *Iran: Violations of Human Rights, 1987–1990* (New York, 1990).

16. Amnesty International, *Iran: Violations of Human Rights* (London, 1987), p. 43.

17. UN Doc. E/CN.4/1987/23, pp. 9, 19.

18. UN Doc. A/43/705, p. 15; UN Doc. E/CN.4/1989/26, pp. 8, 26.

19. Amnesty International, *World Report, 1995*, p. 165.

20. Amnesty International, *Iran: Violations of Human Rights, 1987–1990*, p. 5.

21. "Written Statement Submitted by Amnesty International to the Secretary-General," January 7, 1993. UN Doc. E/CN.4/1993/NGO/6, paras. 2–3. Amnesty International reported on the executions of Kurdish opponents of the regime. "In Baluchestan a clamp down on Baluchi nationalists appears to have coupled with the

continuing campaign against drug-trafficking, blurring distinctions between prisoners detained for political activities and those arrested for participation in illegal smuggling activities." UN Doc. E/CN.4/1991/NGO/5, para. 8. Galindo Pohl reported the case of two men who were sentenced to death by the Islamic Revolutionary Court in the city of Tabriz in March 1993. In response to his inquiry, the diplomats wrote that the two men were arrested "during a military altercation," and that they "confessed to the murders of several villagers and to terrorizing civilians from whom they demanded money to finance the activities of Komeleh." They also "confessed" to blowing up tractors and vehicles. The government also claimed that both men were represented in the court by defense attorneys. UN Doc. E/CN.4/1994/50, para. 29.

22. Human Rights Watch/Middle East, *Iran: Religious and Ethnic Minorities, Discrimination in Law and Practice* (September 1997), p. 25. See also UN Doc. E/CN.4/1988/24, p. 20.

23. "In earlier years it sufficed to read the Iranian press regularly in order to learn of most executions." UN Doc. E/CN.4/1994/50, p. 43.

24. UN Doc. E/CN.4/1991/NGO/5; UN DOC. E/CN.4/1993/41, para. 281; UN Doc. E/CN.4/1995/55, para. 78; UN Doc. A/51/479, para. 12. See also UN Doc. E/CN.4/1997/63, para. 27; UN Doc. A/52/472, para. 16.

25. UN Doc. E/CN.4/1994/50, para. 230. Galindo Pohl stated that in 1993 alone at least nineteen individuals were executed for political reasons, mostly those belonging to underground revolutionary organizations, especially those of the Kurdish resistance. UN Doc. E/CN.4/1994/50, para. 231.

26. Amnesty International, "Iran: Amnesty International Condemns Upsurge in Executions," January 6, 1997.

27. UN Doc. E/CN.4/1997/63, paras. 28, 29.

28. UN Doc. E/CN.4/1999/32, para. 63; UN Doc. A/54/365, para. 34.

29. UN Doc. E/CN.4/1989/26, pp. 10–12.

30. Amnesty International, *Iran: Violations of Human Rights, 1987–1990*, p. 8. Amnesty reported, "The measures to speed up the judicial process emerged as a result of political pressure, led by Ayatollah Khomeini. One hundred and ninety members of the Islamic Consultative Assembly supported a resolution criticizing the judiciary and calling on it to speed up its procedures in accordance with the leader's instructions on 18 January 1989" (p. 31).

31. UN Doc. A/44/620, November 2, 1989, p. 21; Amnesty International, *Iran: Violations of Human Rights, 1987–1990*, p. 8. The People's Republic of China has engaged in the same acts between 1995 and 1997. Seth Faison, "In Surge of Death Sentences, China Doomed 6,100 Last Year," *New York Times*, August 26, 1997, A4.

32. UN Doc. A/44/620, November 2, 1989, p. 31. For other examples of collective executions, see UN Doc. A/47/617, p. 10.

33. Ali Akbar Dareini, "Iran Acknowledges Prostitution," Associated Press, July 5, 2000.

34. For example, one military commander announced in 1994 that during a four-month military operation in Baluchestan "215 of the *ashrar* were captured and 64 of them were killed." *Kayhan*, August 10, 1994. In another case, the press reported that "the body of 8 *ashrar*, along with their various military hardware, were exhibited to the public in Sirjan." *Kayhan*, August 20, 1994.

35. Paya, p. 102.

36. Dareini, "Iran Acknowledges Prostitution," Associated Press, July 5, 2000.

37. UN Doc. A/44/620, p. 21.

38. See, e.g., *Jomhuri-ye Islami*, November 14, 1995 and June 9, 1996; UN Doc. E/CN.4/1999/32, p. 62.

39. *Iran Times*, August 22, 1997.

40. "Death Sentence Against Woman Charged with Adultery Lifted," press release from the World Organization Against Torture, May 20, 1998. <http://www.omct.org>.

41. Amnesty International, *Iran: Violations of Human Rights, 1987–1990*, pp. 19–20.

42. UN Doc. E/CN.4/1994/50, para. 232.

43. The number of 350 was ascertained by the Britain's parliamentary human Rights Group. *Kayhan* (London), July 4, 1996.

44. Thomas Sancton, *Time*, March 21, 1994.

45. UN Doc. E/CN.4/1994/50, para. 233.

46. Amnesty International, *Iran: Violations of Human Rights, 1987–1990*, p. 20.

47. UN Doc. E/CN.4/1994/50, para. 234.

48. UN Doc. A/ 52/472, para. 55.

49. UN Doc. E/CN.4/1995/55, para. 29. After the conclusion of the trial, Copithorne wrote that the oral findings of the court included the following statement: "The evidence has revealed the decision-making procedures within the Iranian leadership which in the final analysis have led to the liquidation of opposition politicians abroad." UN Doc. A/52/472, para. 55.

50. UN Doc. E/CN.4/1995/55, para. 60.

51. Amnesty International, press release, "Iran: Mykonos Trial Provides Further Evidence Of Iranian Policy of Unlawful State Killings," April 10, 1997.

52. UN Doc. A/51/479, para. 17.

53. Quoted by Muhammad Arasi, *Kayhan* (London), July 11, 1996. See also Amnesty International's report to the United Nations, UN Doc. E/CN.4/1993/NGO/6, para. 30.

54. *Iran Times*, September 13, 1996, p. 14.

55. *Tehran Times*, November 19, 1996, pp. 1–2.

56. *Jomhuri-ye Islami*, November 18, 1996, p. 3.

Chapter 4. The Right to Freedom from Torture

1. Paya, pp. 220–221.

2. Raha, 1:13–14; Azad, p. 4.

3. Alizadeh, p. 270.

4. Amnesty International, *Iran: Violations of Human Rights*, p. 81.

5. Akbar Sarduzami, *Gusha'ye az Rawayat-e Azam* (Azam's story) (Denmark, n.d.), p. 4.

6. Parsipur, pp. 83, 96.

7. Alizadeh, p. 270.

8. Raha, 1:32.

9. Azad, p. 16.

10. Parvaresh, p. 13.

11. Raha, 1:20, 22.

12. Parvaresh, p. 36; Ghaffari, p. 19.

13. For an example of whipping as punishment, with the victims randomly chosen by the warden, see Parsipur, p. 143.

14. Ibid., pp. 288–290, 297–299.

15. Parvaresh, pp. 54–55.

16. Ghaffari, unpublished English manuscript, chap. 8, p. 29.

17. Raha, 1:158.

18. Azadi, pp. 222–224.

19. Ghaffari, chap. 8, p. 22.

20. Hasan Darvish, "Didari Kutah" (A brief encounter) *Ketab-e Noqteh* 2 (autumn 1977): 219.

21. Alizadeh, pp. 40–41.

22. Raha, 1:30, 33; Azad, p. 73.

23. Azad, pp. 37, 43, 49–55, 67.

24. Ibid., pp. 67, 71, 83.

25. Ibid., p. 75.

26. Parvaresh, pp. 41–42.

27. Parsipur, pp. 233–234, 239; Parvaresh, p. 43.

28. Abbas Milani, *Tales of Two Cities: A Persian Memoir* (New York: Kodansha International, 1997), p. 164.

29. Raha, 2:73, 90–92, 94.

30. Azad, p. 168.

31. Azadi, p. 15.

32. Raha, 2:119.

33. Parsipur, pp. 211, 298–299, 308.

34. Amnesty International, *Iran: Violations of Human Rights*, p. 38.

35. UN Doc. E/CN.4/1987/23, p. 13.

36. UN Doc. A/42/648, p. 7.

37. Ibid., p. 7.

38. UN Doc. A/44/620, p. 15.

39. UN Doc. A/43/705, p. 9.

40. UN Doc. A/44/620, p. 28.

41. UN Doc. A/43/705, p. 9.

42. Amnesty International, *Iran: Violations of Human Rights*, p. 19.

43. Parsipur, p. 93.

44. UN Doc. E/CN.4/1990/24, p. 32.

45. Ibid., p. 42.

46. UN Doc. E/CN.4/1994/50, para. 88. See UN Doc. A/47/617, paras. 49–53 and UN Doc. E/CN.4/1993/41, para. 289.

47. See, e.g., UN Doc. A/47/617, paras. 46–47.

48. Amnesty International, *Iran: Human Rights Violations Against Shia Religious Leaders and Their Followers* (1997), pp. 18–19.

49. Amnesty International, *World Report, 1997*.

50. Amnesty International, "Shi'a Religious Leaders As Victims of Human Rights Violations," June 3, 1997.

51. The letter is addressed to the judicial authorities and dated March 23, 2000. Its English translation appeared at <http://www.iran-daneshjoo.org>, on June 29, 2000.

52. "The Open Letter of Gholam Reza Mohajeri Nezhad to Mr. Khatami," <http://www.iran-daneshjoo.org>, July 5, 2000.

53. UN Doc. A/43/705, p. 13.

54. UN Doc. E/CN.4/1987/23, p. 8.

55. Amnesty International, *Iran: Violations of Human Rights*, pp. 43–44.

56. Jan Goodwin, *Price of Honor: Muslim Women Lift the Veil of Silence on the Islamic World* (New York: Little, Brown, 1994), p. 111.

57. UN Doc. A/47/617, para. 55.

58. See for examples, UN Doc. A/47/617, para. 55; UN Doc. E/CN.4/1993/41, para. 291.

59. UN Doc. E/CN.4/1993/41, para. 290.

60. UN Doc. E/CN.4/1994/50, pp. 19, 90.

61. UN Doc. E/CN.4/1995/55, para. 92.

62. *Kayhan*, August 5, 1996; *Salam*, February 1, 1997; *Iran Times*, September 25, 1998, p. 15.

63. *Jomhuri-ye Islami*, November 21, 1995.

64. UN Doc. E/CN.4/1998/59, para. 21.

65. Amnesty International, *Iran: Violations of Human Rights*, p. 44; Amnesty International, *Iran: Violations of Human Rights, 1987–1990*, p. 11.

66. UN Doc. E/CN.4/1994/50, paras. 26–27.

67. UN Doc. E/CN.4/1993/41, para. 283. The Iranian press reported on at least eight executions by stoning between August and September 1994. "During the same period, at least 12 executions were carried out in public." UN Doc. E/CN.4/1995/55, para. 80. In the second half of 1994, the press reported eight executions by stoning for "moral crimes." UN Doc. E/CN.4/1995/55, paras. 13, 14, 16, and 80.

68. UN Doc. A/52/472, paras. 31, 34. This report dated October 15, 1997, in which he noted four individuals were stoned since mid-1996.

69. UN Doc. E/CN.4/1998/59, para. 21.

Chapter 5. The Right to Liberty and Security of Person and to Freedom from Arbitrary Arrest

1. Paya, p. 22.

2. Ibid., pp. 303, 304, 311.

3. Ibid., pp. 35, 36.

4. Ibid., p. 98.

5. Parsipur, pp. 114, 145.

6. Alizadeh, pp. 13, 15, 44.

7. Ghaffari, p. 29.

8. Parsipur, pp. 122–123.

9. Alizadeh, pp. 75–76.

10. Parsipur, pp. 122–123.

11. Azadi, pp. 132, 134.

12. Raha, 3:5.

13. UN Doc. E/CN.4/1987/23, p. 15.

14. Amnesty International, *Iran: Violations of Human Rights*, p. 14.

15. Ibid., p. 11.

16. UN Doc. E/CN.4/1989/26, p. 12.

17. UN Doc. A/43/705, p. 14.

18. *Iran Times*, October 15, 1999, p. 1.

19. For example, he reported on the arbitrary detention in the city of Khoramabad of a man who was arrested on the suspicion of being a collaborator of an "outlawed" political group (Fadai'ian-e Khalq). In the end, the clerical authorities became convinced of his innocence and set him free. However, the mistaken imprisonment cost his teaching job, as the office of education withdrew his teaching license, "thus preventing him from exercising his profession." UN Doc. A/47/617, para. 84.

20. Ibid., para. 77.

21. Ibid., paras. 37, 27, 28; UN Doc. E/CN.4/1993/NGO/6, para. 5.

22. UN Doc. E/CN.4/1994/50, para. 24.

23. *Iran Times*, April 7, 1995, p. 1.

24. *Salam*, April 5, 1995.

25. *Salam*, April 6, 1995.

26. *Resalat*, April 6, 1995.

27. *New York Times*, July 14, 1999, A1.

28. Amnesty International, *Iran: Violations of Human Rights, 1987–1990*.

29. *Khabar-Nama-ye Farhangi va Ejtema'i*, 80 (December 1990); this is a newsletter published by the Islamic Propagation Organization.

30. UN Doc. E/CN.4/1994/50, para. 109.

31. Ibid., para. 110.

32. UN Doc. E/CN.4/1995/55, para. 37.

33. *Kayhan*, August 24, 1996.

34. For a vivid description of a 1999 party visited by an extortionist morals police see Afshin Molavi, "Iran's Young Are Restless Under Islam," *Washington Post*, December 28, 1999, p. A17.

35. Judith Miller, *God Has Ninety-Nine Names: Reporting from a Militant Middle East* (New York: Simon & Schuster, 1996), p. 450.

36. *Iran Times*, September 8, 1995, p. 16.

37. *Jomhuri-ye Islami*, April 14 and 20, 1996.

38. Cherry Mosteshar, *Unveiled: One Woman's Nightmare in Iran* (New York: St. Martin's Press, 1997), pp. 175, 142.

39. Molavi, p. A17.

Chapter 6. The Right to a Fair Trial

1. Paya, p. 46.

2. Bakhash, p. 102.

3. Paya, pp. 48–50.

4. Ibid., p. 78.

5. *Kayhan*, February 6, 1979, p. 2.

6. Paya, p. 244.

7. Alizadeh, pp. 66–67.

8. Parsipur, p. 86.

9. Parvaresh, p. 27.

10. Raha, 1:86–87.

11. Ibid., 2:7.

12. Ibid., 2:45–46.

13. Ibid., 2:20.

14. Ibid., 2:45, 90–91, 99, 103, 123.

15. Ibid., 2:156, 157.

16. Ibid., 3:60, 69.

17. Azad, pp. 26–27. One ex-prisoner told Amnesty International that in Evin the authorities took pictures of prisoners, especially of those who were not yet accused of anything. They placed the photos in albums and showed "them to other prisoners, especially collaborators, in order to try and find out more information about them." Amnesty International, *Iran: Human Rights Violations*, p. 88. See also Alizadeh, p. 31.

18. Azad, pp. 33, 55.

19. Ibid., p. 41.

20. In 1995, Galindo Pohl wrote: "Mr. Entezam is said to have suffered various reprisals and to have been punished for speaking with the Special Representative, including refusal of medical treatment. . . . Mr. Entezam is reportedly asking to be tried with all the guarantees set out in the Constitution of the Islamic Republic of Iran . . . in the presence of a jury, in public, and with the assistance of legal counsel. Lastly, it has been reported that Mr. Entezam rejected a proposal by some officials to grant him his freedom in exchange for silence about what he has experienced and seen in prison since 1979." UN Doc. E/CN.4/1995/55, para. 36.

21. Ramin Ahmadi, "Violations of Human Rights in Iran: The Case of Abbas Amir-Entezam," master's thesis, Yale University, 1997, p. 10.

22. Galindo Pohl wrote: "According to the information collected, judges usually rely more on confessions than on testimony, and officers in charge of the investigation try to obtain the defendants' confessions, by whatever means they consider appropriate. Defendants are not permitted to call witnesses in their own defence or examine witnesses for the prosecution." UN Doc. E/CN.4/1989/26, p. 14.

23. Amnesty International, *Iran: Human Rights Violations*, pp. 17, 25.

24. Ibid., p. 5.

25. UN Doc. A/45/697, p. 13.

26. Abdollah Baqeri, a member of the Kurdish organization Kumaleh, was arrested in November 1992 in the Iranian Kurdestan and his taped confessions were broadcast on the state-run television at the beginning of 1993. Towfiq Aliasi was another Kumaleh member whose confessions were "broadcast on local television in Sanandaj in August 1992, some days before his execution." UN Doc. E/CN.4/1994/50, pp. 22, 104.

27. Ibid., pp. 23, 105.

28. See, e.g., UN Doc. A/49/514, paras. 44–56 and UN Doc. E/CN.4/1995/55, paras. 32–38.

29. UN Doc. E/CN.4/1994/50, para. 242. He seemed to be in agreement with Amnesty International's observation that the new regulations failed "to reflect fundamental safeguards provided under article 14 of the International Covenant on Civil and Political Rights." UN Doc. E/CN.4/1993/NGO/6, para. 6. Amnesty added that it "knew of no political trials before Islamic revolutionary Courts where prompt and full access to legal counsel had been permitted. . . . The proceedings are summary, often lasting only a few minutes." UN Doc. E/CN.4/1993/NGO/6, para. 6.

30. UN Doc. E/CN.4/1994/50, para. 242. UN Doc. A/47/617, paras. 57, 63.

31. Amnesty International, *Iran: Violations of Human Rights, 1987–1990*, p. 32.

32. UN Doc. E/CN.4/1994/50, pp. 20, 92, 93.

33. Ibid., p. 46.

34. UN Doc. E/CN.4/1995/55, para. 93.

35. The letter was signed by 90 individuals, some of whom were members of the Association for the Defense of Freedom and the Sovereignty of the Iranian Nation. The Association was formed largely by the members of Bazargan's Freedom Movement of Iran, although it included some individuals who belonged to the outlawed National Front. One such individual was Ali Ardalan, the chairman of the Association.

36. Human Rights Watch/Middle East, "Iran, Arrests of 'Loyal Opposition' Politicians," June 29, 1990, pp. 1, 2.

37. He named the prosecuted individuals. Subsequently, the Special Representative transmitted the names of nineteen other individuals arrested in relation to the open letter. UN Doc. A/45/697, p. 24.

38. Ibid., p. 54.

39. Elaine Sciolino, *Persian Mirrors: The Elusive Face of Iran* (New York: Free Press, 2000), pp. 244–247.

40. UN Doc. A/45/697, p. 15.

41. Ibid., pp. 64–65.

42. Ibid., p. 67.

43. UN Doc. E/CN.4/1992/34, para. 477.

44. The six were H. Zendehdel, F. Abuzia, A. Yazdanshenas, A. Sadeqian, A. Majd-Abkahi, and A. Sartipi.

45. *Jomhuri-ye Islami*, January 23, 1996, p. 2.

46. For example, in China the communist authorities usually drew "together several different charges to make a case appear more substantial." Jung Chang, *Wild Swans: Three Daughters of China* (New York: Anchor Books, 1991), p. 186.

47. *Jomhuri-ye Islami*, January 23, 1996, p. 2.

48. *Kayhan*, London, February 1, 1996, p. 2.

49. *Jomhuri-ye Islami*, January 30, 1996, p. 2.

50. *Kayhan*, London, February 1, 1996, p. 2.

51. Human Rights Watch/Middle East, *Iran: Religious and Ethnic Minorities, Discrimination in Law and Practice*, 1997, p. 20.

52. Amnesty International, "Iran: Amnesty International Condemns Upsurge in Executions," January 6, 1997.

53. UN Doc. E/CN.4/1996/59, para. 98.

54. Ibid., para. 29 c.

55. *Ettela'at*, June 28, 1995, p. 3.

56. Elaine Sciolino, "Iran's Alternative Voices Demand to Be Heard," *New York Times*, July 19, 1998.

57. *Iran Times*, October 27, 1995, p. 14.

58. *Jomhuri-ye Islami*, November 20, 1995, p. 3.

59. UN Doc. E/CN.4/1996/59, para. 56.

60. Quoted in *Iran Times*, September 8, 1995, p. 15.

61. Akbar Ganji, *Talaqi-ye Fashisti az Din va Hokumat* (The fascist interpretation of religion and government) (Tehran, 2000), p. 252.

62. Reprinted in *Kayhan*, London, September 10, 1998.

63. UN Doc. A/54/365, 21, para. 3.

Chapter 7. The Right to Freedom of Conscience, Thought, and Religion

1. UN Doc. E/CN.4/1985/20, p. 9.

2. Milani, p. 230.

3. Paya, p. 201.

4. Ibid., pp. 135–136.

5. Raha, 1:34, 56.

6. Amnesty International, *Iran: Violations of Human Rights*, p. 21.

7. The Islamic Prosecutor's Office of Tehran published a two-volume transcript of formal confessions and recantations by a group of Mojahedin, shown on national television. The Islamic Prosecutor's Office of Tehran, *Karnameh-ye Siah, Mavazeh va Amalkard-e Monafeqin Pas az Piruzi-ye Enqelab* (Black records, position, and practice of the *Monafeqin* [Mojahedin] after the victory of the revolution) (Tehran, 1983), 1:43.

8. Abrahamian, 1999.

9. Milani, p. 170.

10. Ghaffari, unpublished English manuscript, chap. 15, p. 152.

11. In 1989, the powerful clerics promoted Lajvardi as the chief of the entire prison system in Iran. In February 1998, newly elected President Khatami removed him from the post. On August 23, 1998, gunmen assassinated Lajvardi at his shop in Tehran's bazaar. The Mojahedin in exile claimed responsibility for the act.

12. Raha, 1:98, 106.

13. Ghaffari, unpublished English manuscript, chap. 9, p. 20.

14. Raha, 1:103.

15. Raha, 2:23.

16. Cooper, p. 77.

17. See, e.g., Parsipur, p. 204; Raha, 1:56.

18. Ghaffari, p. 185.

19. Raha, 1:57.

20. Parsipur, p. 185.

21. Raha, 1:56.

22. Marguerite Feitlowitz, *A Lexicon of Terror: Argentina and the Legacies of Torture* (New York: Oxford University Press, 1998), p. 78.

23. Raha, 1:77.

24. Raha, 1:79. Alizadeh also wrote about this process of identification by the *tawaban*. Alizadeh, pp. 50–51.

25. Azadi, p. 66.

26. Raha, 2:86.

27. Raha, 1:70. Hamid Azadi also witnessed this encounter and offered a slightly different version of what Hoda'i said to Ruhani. Azadi, pp. 246–247. Ghaffari's account of the encounter comes very close to what Raha related. Ghaffari, pp. 186–187.

28. Raha, 1:121.

29. Personal correspondence with a former professor of Tehran University who spent more than two years in prison in the early 1980s.

30. Raha, 1:57, 58, 78.

31. Azad, p. 22.

32. Ibid., pp. 99–100.

33. Ibid., p. 140.

34. Cooper, p. 82.

35. Parsipur, p. 86.

36. Ibid., p. 409.

37. Ghaffari, pp. 20–21.

38. Parsipur, pp. 139, 233.

39. Ibid., pp. 160–161.

40. Ibid., p. 203.

41. Ghaffari, p. 114.

42. Parsipur, p. 215.

43. Geraldine Brooks aptly used that expression for women in black chadors. Geraldine Brooks, *Nine Parts of Desire: The Hidden World of Islamic Women* (New York: Anchor Books, 1995), p. 25.

44. Parsipur, p. 215.

45. Ibid., p. 105.

46. Goodwin, p. 106.

47. Darvish, p. 219.

48. Parvaresh, p. 49.

49. Raha, 2:77.

50. Azad, p. 10.

51. Parvaresh, pp. 49–50.

52. Raha, 1:101.

53. Alizadeh, pp. 36–37.

54. Parsipur, p. 154.

55. Amnesty International, *Iran: Violations of Human Rights, 1987–1990*, p. 15.

56. Parsipur, p. 124.

57. Muhammad Javad Bahonar, whose tenure as Prime Minister was cut short by his assassination; Muhammad Ali Raja'i, president who replaced Bani Sadr; both were killed on August 30, 1981.

58. Muhammad Beheshti, the secretary general of the Islamic Republic Party, who was killed on June 28, 1981, by the devastating bomb attack on the central headquarters of the party.

59. Parsipur, pp. 128, 130.
60. Ibid., p. 128.
61. Ibid., p. 105.
62. Ibid., p. 358.
63. Azad, p. 182.
64. Raha, 2:25.
65. Ibid., 2:76.
66. Ghaffari, p. 259.
67. Parsipur, pp. 151, 137.
68. Ibid., p. 300.
69. Democratic Society of Iranians in France. *Dar Rahruha-ye Khun* (In the labyrinth of blood) (France, 1985), pp. 20, 24.
70. Azadi, pp. 96, 129.
71. Ibid., p. 243.
72. Ibid., pp. 130–131.
73. Ibid., pp. 143–147.
74. Ghaffari, pp. 86–87.
75. Azadi, pp. 145–146.
76. UN Doc. E/CN.4/1984/28, pp. 4–5.

Chapter 8. Renounce Your Conscience or Face Death

1. Parvaresh, pp. 97–98.
2. Ibid., p, 355; Azadi, p. 147; Ghaffari, p. 150.
3. The letter was printed for the first time in *Jomhuri-ye Islami*, November 27, 1997, p. 15. This newspaper was controlled by Montazeri's enemies.
4. Ghaffari, pp. 193–194; Parvaresh, p. 61.
5. Parsipur, p. 355.
6. Raha, 2:133; see also Azad, p. 137, and Parvaresh, p. 71.
7. Azad, pp. 129–130.
8. Parvaresh, p. 70.
9. Raha, 2:129.
10. Parsipur, p. 354.
11. Ibid., pp. 337–338.
12. Ibid., pp. 368–369.
13. Raha, 3:22.
14. Parvaresh, p. 85.
15. Raha, 2:155.
16. Raha, 2:166.
17. Raha, 3:61.
18. Ibid., 3:20.
19. Parvaresh, p. 77.
20. Abrahamian, 1999, pp. 162–167.
21. Raha, 3:27.
22. Ibid., 3:123.
23. Parvaresh, pp. 99–100, 102.
24. Ibid., p. 104.
25. Raha, 3:125–126; Parvaresh, pp. 106, 110.
26. Raha, 3:127. For the text of Ardabili's speech see *Ettela'at*, August 6, 1988.
27. Raha, 3:127. Amnesty International, *Iran: Violations of Human Rights, 1987–1990*, p. 16.

28. Parvaresh, p. 110.

29. Raha, 3:127.

30. Amnesty International, *Iran: Violations of Human Rights, 1987–1990*, p. 16.

31. Parvaresh, pp. 111–112, 115.

32. Ibid., p. 117.

33. Ibid., p. 119.

34. Raha, 3:130.

35. Raha, 3:135.

36. Parvaresh, p. 116.

37. Raha, 3:131, 132, 137–139.

38. Ghaffari, unpublished English manuscript, chap. 18, p. 217.

39. Ibid., pp. 127, 133.

40. Amnesty International, *Iran: Human Rights Violations, 1987–1990*, p. 6.

41. Mojahedin Organization, *Qatl-e Am-e Zendanian-e Siasi* (The massacre of political prisoners), 1999.

42. The information was provided by his wife in Germany. See Rushanak Tavassoli (a pseudonym), "In a Cage as Large as Iran," *Nashriyyah-ya Hoquq-e Bashar*, 12, no. 35 (Spring 1995): 19–23.

43. Raha, 3:190.

44. Amnesty, International, *Iran: Violations of Human Rights, 1987–1990*, p. 37.

45. Letters of Hossein Ali Montazeri to Khomeini, *Chashmandaz* 6 (Summer 1989): 35–37.

46. A summery of the statement was printed in *Iran Times*, August 20, 1999.

47. See *Ettela'at*, July 23–30, 1988.

48. *Ettela'at*, August 3, 1988.

49. Ayatollah Muhammad Yazdi, "Imam Khomeini and Judicial Problems," *Ettela'at*, May 30, 1990, p. 7.

50. Quoted in Amnesty International, *Iran: Human Rights Violation, 1987–1990*, p. 12.

51. For a collection of the regime's top officials' statements see Mojahedin Organization, pp. 219–224.

52. Published in *Ettela'at*, August 6, 1988; UN Doc. A/43/705, p. 16.

53. UN Doc. E/CN.4/1989/26, p. 5.

54. UN Doc. A/44/153, 28 February 1989, p. 4.

55. UN Doc. E/CN.4/1990/24, p. 27.

56. UN Doc. A/44/620, p. 30.

57. Parvaresh, p. 132; Raha, 3:147; UN Doc. A/44/620, p. 29.

58. For a different explanation of Khomeini's motives for the massacre, see Abrahamian, 1999, pp. 217–221.

59. Raha, 3:147.

60. Ibid., 3:167.

61. Ibid., 3:218.

62. Ibid., 3:220.

63. Ibid., 3:238.

64. Ibid., 3:242.

Chapter 9. The Right to Freedom of Thought, Conscience, and Religion: Iranian Religious Minorities

1. Olya Roohizadegan, *Olya's Story: A Survivor's Dramatic Account of the Persecution of Baha'is in Revolutionary Iran* (Oxford: Oneworld Publications, 1993).

2. "The Baha'is indicated that the accusations of espionage in favour of Zionism were based solely on the fact that the Baha'i World Centre was in Israel. They pointed out that this centre was established on Mount Carmel in the last century, before the establishment of the State of Israel." UN Doc. E/CN.4/1996/95/Add.2, para. 57.

3. UN Doc. E/CN. 4/1987/23, p. 16.

4. This study benefited from Mohamad Tavakoli-Targhi's excellent paper, "Iranian Subjectivity and the De-recognition of Baha'is," delivered at the 1999 annual meeting of the Middle East Studies Association.

5. UN Doc. A/51/479, para. 27.

6. *Khabar-Nama-ye Farhangi va Ejtema'i*, 52 (December 1988). This journal was published by the Central Office of the Organization for Islamic Propagation.

7. For example, see the advertisement placed by Mehrab Qasemnezhad, who converted to Shiism and requested that his "father and mother also convert to the *din mobin-e* Islam." *Kayhan*, July 2, 1994.

8. Roohizadegan, p. 133.

9. Ibid., p. 120.

10. UN Doc. A/42/648, p. 10.

11. Baha'i International Community, *Iran's Secret Blueprint for the Destruction of a Religious Community* (New York, 1999), p. 28.

12. *Resalat*, March 14, 1995.

13. UN Doc. E/CN.4/1996/95/Add.2, para. 56.

14. UN Doc. E/CN.4/1987/23, p. 17.

15. UN Doc. E/CN.4/1993/41, pp. 40, 221.

16. UN Doc. A/44/620, November 2, 1989, p. 23.

17. UN Doc. E/CN.4/1994/50, p. 29.

18. UN Doc. E/CN.4/1993/41, para. 222; UN Doc. A/51/479, para. 24; UN Doc. E/CN.4/1997/63, para. 52; UN Doc. A/51/479, para. 24 and UN Doc. A/52/472, para. 27.

19. UN Doc. A/52/472, para. 44.

20. Statement by American Baha'i Community, July 1998, <http://www.prnews wire.com/images/todayhed.gif>.

21. UN Doc. A/52/472, para. 23.

22. Human Rights Watch/Middle East, *Iran: Religious and Ethnic Minorities, Discrimination in Law and Practice*, p. 13.

23. UN Doc. A/52/472, para. 44.

24. UN Doc. E/CN.4/1996/95/Add.2, para. 60. In the 1980s, ten thousand lost their positions in administration and educational institutions. The government also denied their pensions: "Some who had been dismissed from their posts had been required to reimburse the salaries or pensions received. A circular from the Ministry of Labour and Social Affairs (no. 20361, dated 16/9/1360 A.H.) stipulated that: 'The penalty incurred by those who belong to any of the misguided sects . . . shall be permanent dismissal from public office . . . and also from organizations that can be classed as governmental associations or offices.'" UN Doc. E/CN.4/1996/95/Add.2, para. 640.

25. UN Doc. E/CN.4/1987/23, p. 17.

26. UN Doc. A/44/620, p. 23.

27. UN Doc. A/43/705, p. 15.

28. UN Doc. E/CN.4/1995/55, para. 53.

29. UN Doc. E/CN.4/1989/26, p. 9.

30. UN Doc. E/CN.4/1987/23, p. 17.

31. UN Doc. E/CN.4/1994/50, para. 162.

32. UN Doc. A/51/479, para. 25.

33. UN Doc. E/CN.4/1989/26, p. 9.

34. UN Doc. A/43/705, p. 14.

35. UN Doc. A/45/697.

36. Milani, p. 76.

37. UN Doc. E/CN.4/1988/24, p. 4.

38. UN Doc. E/CN.4/1990/24, p. 55.

39. At the end of 1992, Galindo Pohl offered a summary: "For the past 12 years, the Baha'i community has been denied the right of assembly and the right to elect and maintain its administrative institutions. These institutions constitute the core of religious community life, considering that there is no clergy in the Baha'i faith. Without administrative institutions the very existence of the Baha'is as a viable religious community is said to be seriously endangered. As individuals, Baha'is are officially considered 'unprotected infidels' and, therefore, their civil rights and liberties are often ignored. The non-recognition of their religion manifests itself in various ways, including the denial of the basic right to express their religious belief freely." UN Doc. A/47/617, para. 132.

40. UN Doc. A/51/479, para. 27.

41. UN Doc. E/CN.4/1999/NGO/12, p. 2. Written statement submitted by the Baha'i International Community, a nongovernmental organization in special consultative status.

42. UN Doc. E/CN.4/1999/32, para. 42.

43. UN Doc. A/47/617, para. 132; Mayer, p. 165.

44. UN Doc. A/44/620, 1989, p. 24.

45. U.S. Department of State, "Annual Report on International Religious Freedom for 1999: Iran," p. 4, <http://www.state.gov>.

46. UN Doc. A/45/697, p. 61.

47. UN Doc. A/47/617, para. 131.

48. UN Doc. E/CN.4/1995/55, para. 53.

49. UN Doc. E/CN.4/1996/95/Add.2, para. 63.

50. An accurate translation of the memorandum is provided in Baha'i International Community, 1999, pp. 50–51.

51. UN Doc. E/CN.4/1996/59, para. 69.

52. Ethan Bronner, "Iran Closes 'University' Run Covertly by the Bahais," *New York Times*, October, 29, 1998.

53. Reza Afshari, "Civil Society and Human Rights in Iran: A Review Essay," *Journal of Iranian Research and Analysis* 16 (April 2000): 61–72.

54. Morteza Rezvan, "*Mellati dar Tariki*" (A nation in darkness), *Par*, 15 (February 2000): 19.

55. *Iran Times*, November 12, 1999, p. 10.

56. UN Doc. E/CN.4/1999/NGO/12, p. 5.

57. Human Rights Watch/Middle East, *Iran: Religious and Ethnic Minorities, Discrimination in Law and Practice*, September 1997, pp. 20, 21. "In 1994 the Sunni community of Sanandaj raised more then 10 million toumans in order to enlarge the Dar al-Ehsan mosque. Despite the fact that all the necessary building permits were obtained from local authorities, the Ministry of Islamic Guidance stepped in to block the new extension and confiscated the funds raised to carry out the project" (21).

58. UN Doc. A/52/472, paras. 62, 63.

59. The Iranian authorities advised the Special Representative Copithorne that an autopsy had concluded the death of Molla Muhammad Rabi'i was the result of a heart attack. UN Doc. E/CN.4/1997/63, para. 62.

60. For example, following a demonstration in Zahedan, the regime arrested a

prominent Sunni religious leader, Molavi Abdolhamid. Amnesty International, *World Report, 1995*, p. 163.

61. Human Rights Watch/Middle East, *Iran: Religious and Ethnic Minorities, Discrimination in Law and Practice*, p. 22.

62. For example, on March 4, 1996, Molavi Abdolmalek, the son of the most prominent Sunni cleric in Iran, Molavi Abdolaziz, was gunned down outside his house in Karachi, Pakistan. Human Rights Watch/Middle East, *Iran: Religious and Ethnic Minorities, Discrimination in Law and Practice*, p. 23.

63. Since early 1990s he had experienced a number of detentions and interrogations with the government security forces, during which he was reportedly tortured. Amnesty International, *World Report, 1995*, p. 165.

64. Amnesty International, *World Report, 1995*, p. 165; Human Rights Watch/ Middle East, *Iran: Religious and Ethnic Minorities, Discrimination in Law and Practice*, p. 22.

65. Amnesty International, "Iran: Amnesty International Concerned About Possible Government Involvement in Deaths of Iranian National," February 28, 1996.

66. Human Rights Watch/Middle East, *Iran: Religious and Ethnic Minorities, Discrimination in Law and Practice*, p. 22.

67. UN Doc. E/CN.4/1999/32, para. 39.

68. Sa'id Towfiq, "*Ahl-e Sunant Chegowneh Mitawanand beh Hoquq-e Khud Dast Yaband?*" (How could the Sunnis gain their rights?), *Iran-e Farda*, December 29, 1999, p. 37.

69. Eliz Sanasarian, *Religious Minority in Iran* (New York: Cambridge University Press, 2000). This chapter was already completed and could not benefit from this excellent and concise study.

70. Howard, p. 67.

71. "Hossain Yusefi Eshkevari, an Islamic scholar . . . , points out that Iranians tend to consider Muslims more human (and more worthy of rights) than non-Muslims." Mahmood Monshipouri and Shadi Mokhtari, "Islamism, Cultural Relativism, and Universal Rights," *Journal of Iranian Research and Analysis* 16 (April 2000), p. 52.

72. Quoted in Lahiji, p. 48.

73. Michael M. J. Fischer and Mehdi Abedi, *Debating Muslims: Cultural Dialogues in Postmodernity and Tradition* (Madison: University of Wisconsin Press, 1990), p. 188.

74. Ahmad Razaqi, *Awamel-e Fesad va Bad-hijabi* (The causes of [moral] corruption and improper *hijab*) (Tehran: Islamic Cultural Propagation Organization, 1988), pp. 35–36.

75. See the organization's popular contest for 1998–99, question no. 41, *Kayhan*, August 23, 1998, p. 12.

76. Iranian Human Rights Working Group, " 'Baha'is Have Rights Too . . .'—President Khatami," November 1999, <www.ihrwg.org>.

77. Shirin Ebadi, *Trarikhcheh va Asnad-e Hoquq-e Bashar dar Iran* (History and documentation of human rights in Iran) (Tehran, 1994), p. 83.

78. "Interview with Shirin Ebadi," *Ruznameh-Zan*, August 23, 1998, p. 9.

79. Religious minorities receive lower awards in injury and death lawsuits. U.S. Department of State, "Iran Human Rights Practices, 1995," sec 5. The Islamic Civil Code (Article 881) prohibits transfer of property from a deceased Muslim to a non-Muslim relative. Conversely, if it happened that among the unfortunate beneficiaries of a religious minority was a Muslim relative, even a distant one, that lucky person will inherit the entire property of the deceased. Human Rights Watch observed, "Other lesser offenses also provide for differential sentences between Muslims and non-Muslims. For example, Article 88 of the Penal Code states that if a Muslim man

commits adultery with a Muslim woman, the penalty is 100 lashes for the man. However, if a non-Muslim man commits adultery with a Muslim woman, his penalty is death. No penalty is specified for the Muslim man who commits adultery with a non-Muslim woman. Similarly with homosexuality, under Article 121 of the Penal Code, non-penetrative sex between two Muslim men is punished by 100 lashes. However, if one of the partners is non-Muslim, the penalty for him is death. The crime of malicious accusation is punished . . . by eighty lashes if the victim is a Muslim. However, if the victim is non-Muslim, the maximum penalty is set at seventy-four lashes. In this article, non-Muslims are equated in their treatment with minors and those lacking their full mental capacities. Article 494 of the Penal Code provides penalties for violating the corpse of a Muslim; no penalties are stipulated for violating the corpse of a non-Muslim." Human Rights Watch/Middle East, *Iran: Religious and Ethnic Minorities, Discrimination in Law and Practice*, p. 9.

80. Janet Afary, *The Iranian Constitution Revolution, 1906–1911: Grassroots Democracy, Social Democracy, and the Origins of Feminism* (New York: Columbia University Press, 1996), 134.

81. John F. Burns, "In Islamic Mideast, Scant Place for Jews," *New York Times*, July 25, 1999.

82. Howard Schneider, "Spying Arrests Heighten Iranian Jews' Anxiety," *Washington Post*, November 22, 1999, A 17.

83. It was a case of political maneuvering marked by contradictory statements by different officials, promises of a fair trial for the "spies" and the surprising release of a few of them on bail. On September 12, 1999, the cleric Rahbarpur, the hardliner head of the Revolutionary Courts in Tehran, announced: "What I can say is that it is certain that these individuals are spies. There is no doubt about it, and there exist strong and sufficient documents and evidence to be presented to the court." Interview with *Jomhuri-ye Islami*, quoted in *Iran Times*, September 17, 1999, p. 1. This guilty verdict before trial, typical of Rahbarpur, did not apparently sit well with President Khatami, who most likely put pressure on the new Head of the Judiciary, who had replaced the hard-liner Yazdi. A week later, Hadi Marvi, the Deputy Head of the Judiciary, announced that the thirteen prisoners would be considered innocent until proven guilty. He added that the evidence was based on the confessions and statements of some of the accused. "Iranian Jews to Face Trial," September 20, 1999, <www.news.BBC.co.uk>. All indications were that like other politically motivated accusations, the fictitious "due process of law" was dependent on the resolution of unrelated factional-political issues. In May 2000, there began "a fair trial" that was closed to the public. The only evidence that was presented to international observers was the televised confession of eight of the accused, reminiscent of the regime's past practices of forced confessions. Their single court-appointed attorney stated that confession after fifteen months of incarceration lacked validity "because of the psychological pressure." <http://www.Iran-press-service.com>, May 25, 2000. Mansour Farhang observed: "The terror of being threatened with death or torture, particularly for members of religious minorities in a theocratic state, is sufficient to make the isolated victims willing to confess to whatever the authorities wished." Mansour Farhang, " 'Spies' Under the Persian Rug," *Nation*, June 26, 2000, p. 34. The trial ended and ten of the accused were sentenced to prison terms ranging from four to thirteen years. No evidence of espionage appeared other than the Jews' own confessions. The long statement issued by the judge, who also acted as the prosecutor and jury, showed that perhaps the only thing that he could prove was the Jews' "love for Israel," a sufficient cause for prosecution among the hard-line Islamists.

84. U.S. Department of State, "Annual Report on International Religious Freedom for 1999: Iran," p. 7, <http://www.state.gov>.

85. This is how a Jewish writer explained Elqaniyan's ordeal: "The show-trial was played out well. The judges sat with their backs toward the accused. It was a base, racist attack against a defenseless old Jew, the ancient blood libel thrown into his face. He was a spy for Israel, they contended. He had collected a fortune for the Zionists and transferred it to Israel to bomb the Palestinians. He fought against God and his messenger and all of the people of Iran." Aryeh Levin, "Habib Elghanayan: A Reflection of the Iranian Jewish Community," Center for Iranian Jewish Oral History, *The History of Contemporary Iranian Jews* (Beverly Hills, Calif.: Center for Iranian Jewish Oral History, 1999), 26 (English section).

Executions continued sporadically. For example, Amnesty International reported, "Feyzollah Mechubad, a 77-year-old member of the Jewish community, was executed on 25 February 1994. He had been imprisoned in Evin Prison since May 1992 and charged with espionage for the USA and Israel. These charges were reportedly based on telephone conversations he had with relatives and family members based in these two countries. It has been alleged that the real reason for his arrest, detention and subsequent execution is believed to have been his religious beliefs and activities within the Jewish community in Tehran. . . . According to reports received by Amnesty International, during the last six months of his imprisonment he had been flogged on his back, limbs and face and beaten repeatedly, resulting in the loss of some teeth and a bruised face." Amnesty International, *Iran: Official Secrecy Hides Continuing Repression* (New York, May 1995), 7.

86. UN Doc. E/CN.4/1996/95/Add.2, paras. 26, 29.

87. Following Khomeini's death in 1989, reporter Geraldine Brooks attended a press conference by President Rafsanjani. "That night a member of Iran's small Christian community called on me at my hotel, berating me for missing a chance to speak out against hijab on behalf of all the women who hated being forced to wear it." Brooks, p. 16.

88. Sorour Soroudi, "The Concept of Jewish Impurity and Its Reflection in Persian and Judeo-Persian Traditions," in *Irano-Judaica III: Studies Relating to Jewish Contact with Persian Culture Throughout the Ages*, eds. Shaul Shaked and Amnon Netzer (Jerusalem: Ben-Zvi Institute, 1994), pp. 143, 147.

89. UN Doc. E/CN.4/1996/95/Add.2, para. 97.

90. Ibid., paras. 42, 46.

91. Ibid., para. 45.

92. UN Doc. A/47/617, para. 124.

93. *Ettela'at*, February 21, 1994, pp. 1–2.

94. It is not that the Jewish leaders somehow failed to understand the Shiite clerics' anti-Semitism. As legal scholar Donna Arzt observed, traditional "Muslims picked up from European Christians some of the classic anti-Jewish caricatures of long-nosed money-bags and old canards, such as blood libels and plots to gain world domination." Donna E. Arzt, "Religious Human Rights in Muslim States of the Middle East and North Africa," *Emory International Law Review* 10 (1996): 157. The notorious *Protocols of the Elders of Zion* was translated and serially published in a semi-official newspaper. Throughout his anti-Shah activities, Ayatollah Khomeini closely associated the monarchy with the conspiratorial activities of disreputable Jews and Israelis. Menasheh Amir, an Iranian-born journalist in Israel, notes that before they established the Islamic Republic, the Shiite clerics routinely and openly directed their enmity against the Jews. After the revolution, perhaps out of consideration for adverse human rights publicity, they merely substituted terms like "Zionists" or "the occupying regime" for "the Jews." Menasheh Amir, "The Image of Jews in Contemporary Iranian Media," in *The History of Contemporary Iranian Jews* (Beverly Hills, Calif.: Center for Iranian Jewish Oral History, 1999), pp. 34, 37. For other similar

anti-Semitic statements, see Razaqi, p. 16; "Barasi-ye Naqsh-e Yahud dar Jahan az yek Negah-e Digar" (An alternative look at the role of Jews in the world), *Sobh*, no. 93 (May 1999). A *hezbollahi* organ, *Sobh* was often full of virulent anti-Semitism. It was not that only the conservative clerics exhibited anti-Semitism. The Islamic reformers sometimes shared their views. For example, Hesam ed-Din Imami, a senior columnist for the daily *Tous*, which became the most popular newspaper in 1998, considered President Clinton's episode with Monica Lewinsky to be the work of the American Jews. He concluded: "America's Zionists who have maintained a tight grip on most political and economic domains of that country had placed, from a few years ago, a Jewish woman in the White House." Then they used her when Clinton placed undue pressure on the Israeli government for implementing the derailed peace plan with the Palestinian Authority. They sent a message to Clinton: "Despite all the power at your disposal, we can tame you whenever we want, even in the hands of a Jewish girl." *Tous*, August 19, 1998, p. 3.

95. *Ettela'at*, February 24, 1993.

96. *Ettela'at*, March 7, 1993.

97. *Iran Times*, November 24, 1995, p. 5.

98. Statement by the Permanent Mission of the Islamic Republic of Iran to the United Nations, no. 179, June 14, 1999.

99. *Iran Times*, October 22, 1999, p. 2.

100. *Ettela'at*, March 1, 1993.

101. UN Doc. E/CN.4/1991/NGO/5, para. 12.

102. Special Rapporteur noted: "According to nongovernmental sources, the proportion of Muslim converts, amounting to at least 15,000 persons in the Protestant communities . . . is increasing, but in a clandestine way. As a general rule, in the light of their interpretation of Islam, the authorities prohibit all forms of proselytism and conversion of a Muslim to another religion, and this explains the limitations placed on the religious activities of the Protestant churches and the closure or restrictions to which some places of worship have been subjected." UN Doc. E/CN.4/1996/95/Add.2, para. 75.

103. Ibid., para. 21.

104. Human Rights Watch/Middle East, *Iran: Religious and Ethnic Minorities, Discrimination in Law and Practice*, p. 16.

105. UN Doc. E/CN.4/1996/95/Add.2, paras. 71–72.

106. Ibid., para. 74.

107. UN Doc. A/47/617, para. 123.

108. UN Doc. E/CN.4/1993/41, para. 248.

109. UN Doc. E/CN.4/1994/50, para. 14.

110. "The pastor of the Injili church (Presbyterian church) of Tabriz was arrested, imprisoned and tortured from December 1990 to August 1991. He suffers from long-term psychological and physical injuries sustained while in prison." UN Doc. E/CN.4/1993/41, p. 44, para. 245. "It was reported that the Iranian Bible Society, which was dissolved by the Government in 1990, is still closed. All Christian bookstores have been closed and all Christian books have been confiscated." UN Doc. E/CN.4/1993/41, para. 246. It was also reported that The Garden of Evangelism, a Christian training centre in northern Tehran, was closed after forty-five years of use for evangelism and pastoral training. UN Doc. E/CN.4/1993/41, para. 247. In his report for 1993, Galindo Pohl mentioned Muhammad Sepehr, a Muslim convert and a Christian leader in the city of Mashhad, who was imprisoned for several months in 1991. UN Doc. E/CN.4/1993/41, para. 244.

111. Human Rights Watch/ Middle East, *Iran: Religious and Ethnic Minorities, Discrimination in Law and Practice*, p. 16.

112. UN Doc. E/CN.4/1995/55, para. 82. See also Amnesty International, *Iran: Official Secrecy Hides Continuing Repression*, p. 10.

113. *Jomhuri-ye Islami*, February 26, 1994.

114. UN Doc. E/CN.4/1996/95/Add.2, para. 79.

115. UN Doc. E/CN.4/1995/55, para. 47.

116. UN Doc. E/CN.4/1996/95/Add.2, para. 80.

117. Human Rights Watch/ Middle East, *Iran: Religious and Ethnic Minorities, Discrimination in Law and Practice*, p. 18, footnote 37.

118. Ibid., p. 18.

119. *Ettela'at*, July 7, 1994.

120. *Kayhan*, July 6, 1994.

121. UN Doc. E/CN.4/1996/95/Add.2, para. 80.

122. Human Rights Watch/ Middle East, *Iran: Religious and Ethnic Minorities, Discrimination in Law and Practice*, p. 17.

123. UN Doc. E/CN.4/1996/95/Add.2, para. 80.

124. Human Rights Watch/ Middle East, *Iran: Religious and Ethnic Minorities, Discrimination in Law and Practice*, p. 17.

125. UN Doc. E/CN.4/1996/95/Add.2, paras. 83–85.

126. Human Rights Watch/ Middle East, *Iran: Religious and Ethnic Minorities, Discrimination in Law and Practice*, p. 18.

127. UN Doc. E/CN.4/1997/63, para. 63.

128. Ibid., para. 65.

129. Bijan Namvar, "*Beh Taraj Rafteha*" (The plundered) *Par*, November 1999, p. 10.

Chapter 10. Official Responses to the United Nations

1. UN Doc. E/CN.4/1984/28, pp. 4–5.

2. Ibid., pp. 5–6.

3. UN Doc. A/C.3/40/13, p. 5.

4. UN Doc. A/41/787, pp. 4–5.

5. UN Doc. A/42/648, p. 16.

6. UN Doc. A/44/620, p. 7.

7. For example, in mid-December 1985, the Prime Minister in Tehran blasted the negative resolution passed by the General Assembly as a huge conspiracy to mar the image of the revolution, adding that it would have no impact on the determination of the government to pursue its goal. The Speaker of the Majlis told reporters that the votes of fifty-five countries to condemn Iran on its human rights record would make no difference in how the government would behave. *Ettela'at*, December 14, 1985.

8. UN Doc. A/C.3/40/13, p. 2.

9. The regime's diplomat in New York noted with relish the report by the UN Special Rapporteur on the contemporary form of racism. The diplomat "stated that institutionalization, in the United States of America, of racism and racial discrimination is one of the abhorrent practices and an affront to the dignity of mankind." *Tehran Times*, December 2, 1995.

10. UN Doc. A/C.3/40/13, p. 2.

11. Presented to the same forty-first session of the Commission was a written statement submitted by Amnesty International, which has a consultative status with the Commission. The nine-paragraph statement offered a reasonably accurate picture of the human rights situation in Iran at that time. UN Doc. E/CN.4/1985/NGO/29.

12. William Korey, *NGOs and the Universal Declaration of Human Rights: "A Curious Grapevine"* (New York: St. Martin's Press, 1998), pp. 259, 263–264.

13. Louis Henkin, "International Law: Politics, Values and Functions," in *International Human Rights in Context*, ed. Henry J. Steiner and Philip Alston (Oxford: Oxford University Press, 1996), p. 353.

14. Human rights advocates could hardly complain about that part of the procedure which allows the record of a state to be scrutinized. They often express disappointment when politics allows a state to escape the Commission's censure. For example, the Commission failed to pass a very mild resolution on China's human rights violations, coming hard on the heels of the 1989 Tiananmen massacres. The resolution did not even mention the massacres; nevertheless, it was defeated. In 1996, China made direct appeals to the Third World members of the Commission. "What is happening to China today will happen to any other developing country tomorrow," the Chinese delegate said. Barbara Crossette, "China Outflanks U.S. to Avoid Scrutiny of Its Human Rights," *New York Times*, April 24, 1996, A12. The same outflanking occurred again in April 2000.

15. It should be noted that since enlargement of the Commission, it has often been the practice of the violating Third World states to prevent formal consideration of their fellow states. As human rights scholar Ramcharan noted in 1990, developing countries succeeded in increasing the number of state-members in the Commission on Human Rights from forty-four to fifty-five; this gave them the opportunity to have a voting control in the Commission. "All the new seats went to developing countries and will remain allocated to those countries in the future. The developing countries will therefore be able to have a decisive say over whether a country is investigated or not for alleged violations of human rights." B. G. Ramcharan, "Strategies for the International Protection of Human Rights in the 1990s," in *Human Rights in the World Community*, 2d ed., ed. Richard Pierre Claude and Burns H. Weston (Philadelphia: University of Pennsylvania Press, 1992), p. 271.

16. The report consisted of 262 paragraphs. The Committee considered the report in three sessions in November 1992 in Geneva, April 1993 in New York, and July 1993 in Geneva.

17. UN Doc. CCPR/C/28/Add.15, pp. 25–31.

18. Ibid., p. 4.

19. It quoted Article 32 of the Constitution: "In case of arrest, charges with the supporting grounds must be communicated and explained to the accused in writing without delay, and a provisional dossier must be forwarded to the competent judicial authorities within a maximum of 24 hours so that the preliminaries to the trial can be completed as swiftly as possible. Violation of this article will be liable to punishment in accordance with the law." UN Doc. CCPR/C/28/Add.15, p. 22.

20. UN Doc. A/C.3/40/13, p. 4.

21. "The Basic Principles on the Independence of the Judiciary," adopted by the Seventh United Nations Congress on the Prevention of Crime and the Treatment of Offenders and endorsed by the United Nations General Assembly in Resolution 40/32 of November 1985. Amnesty International, *Iran: Violations of Human Rights*, p. 25.

22. Ibid., p. 32.

23. UN Doc. E/CN.4/1989/26, p. 13.

24. UN Doc. A/42/648, p. 16.

25. Amnesty International, *Iran: Violations of Human Rights*, p. 3.

26. UN Doc. E/CN.4/1988/24, p. 18.

27. The UN Committee members posed a number of questions related to Article

167 of the Constitution of the Islamic Republic. The Article states: "The judge must attempt to find a basis for judgment for every case in the codified laws of the land. If he is unable to do so, he will issue a verdict based on reference to reputable Islamic sources or *fatvas*."

28. Mehrpur, p. 88.

29. Ibid.

30. Ibid., p. 89.

31. Ibid., p. 113.

32. UN Doc. A/C.3/40/13, p. 6.

33. The *New York Times* reported from Paris that "Rajavi's unexpected departure was seen here as part of the effort to restore normal ties between France and Iran and ultimately to help win the release of eight or nine Frenchmen being held hostage by pro-Iranian gunmen in Lebanon." *New York Times*, June 10, 1986.

34. UN Doc. A/42/648, p. 15. The same things were repeated for other militant groups: "The Tudeh Party is well known as a surrogate organization whose members are subjects of a foreign country. People's Fedaian Organization is a faction of the People's Fedai Guerrillas which split over some ideological disputes and choice of alliance with foreign Governments." UN Doc. A/42/648, p. 15.

35. UN Doc. A/44/620, p. 6, para. 8.

36. On 10 January 1990, the Special Representative met in Switzerland with Dr. Kazem Rajavi, brother of the Mojahedin leader. Rajavi presented a number of documents, which included: "(a) list of political prisoners executed as drug-traffickers; (b) political prisoners buried in secret common graves; (c) names and addresses of 410 relatives of persons who had been executed; (d) list of 643 prisons; (e) names and details of 4,725 political prisoners; (f) list of 1,786 persons accused of being torturers; (g) copies of official statements on human rights; (h) copies of reports in the international press on human rights in Iran." UN Doc. E/CN.4/1990/24, p. 13.

37. UN Doc. E/CN.4/1988/24, p. 15.

38. Peter H. Kooijmans, "The Role and Action of the UN Special Rapporteur on Torture," in *The International Fight Against Torture*, ed. Antonio Cassese (Baden-Baden: Nomos, 1991), pp. 60–61.

39. UN Doc. A/42/648, p. 22.

40. UN Doc. E/CN.4/1984/28, pp. 9–10.

41. UN Doc. E/CN./1988/24, p. 20.

42. UN Doc. A/43/705, pp. 5, 6.

43. UN Doc. A/43/705, p. 18.

44. The text of the statement is printed in *Jomhuri-ye Islami*, February 26, 1996.

45. UN Doc. A/42/648, p. 18.

46. UN Doc. A/C.3/40/13, p. 5.

47. UN Doc. E/CN.4/1989/26, pp. 9, 18.

48. UN Doc. A/44/620, 1989, p. 7.

49. John F. Burns, "New Rulers Won't Ease Restrictions," *New York Times*, October 9, 1996, A8.

50. UN Doc. E/CN.4/1988/24, p. 7.

51. UN Doc. E/CN.4/1987/23, pp. 7, 8.

52. UN Doc. E/CN.4/1988/24, p. 20.

53. UN Doc. E/CN.4/1987/23, p. 8.

54. UN Doc. E/CN.4/1990/24, p. 19.

55. UN Doc. E/CN.4/1987/23, p. 5. In its comprehensive report of 1990, Amnesty International offered the same argument rejecting the validity of the government's claim that applications of Islamic laws cannot be considered as human rights viola-

tions. Amnesty wrote "it is possible to observe that the way in which Islam is applied to questions of legal adjudication differs widely between various countries which claim Islamic Law as the basis of their legal systems, and that there are different interpretations on how Islamic Law should be applied within the Iranian Government itself." Amnesty International, *Iran: Violations of Human Rights, 1987–1990*, p. 56.

56. UN Doc. E/CN.4/1989/26, p. 10.
57. UN Doc. E/CN.4/1988/24, p. 17.
58. Mehrpur, p. 20.
59. UN Doc. E/CN.4/1988/24, p. 17.
60. Ibid.
61. UN Doc. A/43/705, p. 17.

Chapter 11. Changes of Tactics After Ayatollah Khomeini's Death

1. Alieh Arfaie et al., *Hoqug-e Bashar Az Didgah-e Majam'eh Binolmellali* (Human rights in the perspective of international organizations) (Tehran, 1993). See part 4.
2. Mehrpur, p. 19.
3. Mehrpur was perhaps chosen for his modern legal education. During his long career, he always exhibited Islamist tendencies, even when he served as a judge in the Shah's regime. He won the trust of the clerics, whom he served diligently after the revolution. He periodically wrote about his new experience as the Judiciary's point man in dealing with the United Nations and eventually published his articles in a book.
4. UN Doc. E/CN.4/1989/26, p. 5.
5. UN Doc. A/44/620, 1989, p. 29.
6. Galindo Pohl wrote about what the Foreign Minister told him: "He said he hoped that by now, at the end of his second visit to the country, the Special Representative was able to see that the allegations of human rights violations were false and that the situation of human rights in the Islamic Republic of Iran was comparatively better than in other countries of the so-called 'third world'. The Minister expressed surprise that the Commission on Human Rights should have decided to examine the situation of human rights in his country and not the situation in other countries where respect for those rights was known to be much worse." UN Doc. A/45/697, p. 49.
7. UN Doc. A/44/620, November 2, 1989, p. 5.
8. Mehrpur, pp. 50–51.
9. UN Doc. E/CN.44/1990/24, p. 22.
10. UN Doc. A/45/697, p. 38.
11. Ibid., p. 40.
12. Ibid., pp. 39–40.
13. UN Doc. E/CN.4/1990/24, p. 24.
14. Ibid., p. 34.
15. Ibid., p. 23.
16. Ibid., p. 28.
17. UN Doc. E/CN.4/1990/24, p. 24.
18. Ibid., p. 26.
19. UN Doc. A/44/620, p. 6.
20. Ibid.
21. UN Doc. A/44/153, 1989, p. 3.
22. UN Doc. A/44/620, p. 26.

23. Ibid., p. 17.

24. Ibid., p. 18.

25. Ibid.

26. Ibid.

27. For the text of these recantations see Abrahamian, *Tortured Confessions*, chap. 3. The testimonies of government witnesses closely followed the scripts of the prison confession-repentance. For further examples of such testimonies see UN Doc. E/CN.4/1990/24, p. 9.

28. For example, Parsipur described a broadcast episode that she watched in prison. An ex-member of the Mojahedin was confessing to the murder of a few Revolutionary Guards. The location where the confession was filmed was a desolate land where the confessor said he had buried his victims. Parsipur wrote that in the video the man stood in the hole in which he presumably buried his victims. Parsipur saw the marks of torture on the confessor's body, as he was denouncing his brethren, the Mojahedin, and expressing profound sympathy for the Revolutionary Guards. Parsipur wrote that the episode was so badly filmed that the prisoners watching it laughed (237).

29. Ghaffari, unpublished English manuscript, chap. 19, pp. 222–223.

30. UN Doc. A/44/620, p. 11.

31. UN Doc. E/CN.4/1990/24, pp. 37, 52. The official press reported the presence of "a group of families of the grouplets whose members are still in prison for their involvement in repeated terrorist attacks." The press then favorably reported the presence of two other groups: "the families of the martyrs of the terrorist actions" of the Mojahedin, and the repentant prisoners who came to testify to their own past armed attacks and to deny the presence of torture in prisons (*Kayhan*, January 24, 1990). The government even brought a group of Saudi Arabian citizens, most likely the Shiite activists who were harbored by Iran against the Saudi government, who wanted to testify to the human rights violations of their own government (*Kayhan*, January 24, 1990).

32. See Tavassoli, "In a Cage as Large as Iran," *Nashriyyah-ya Hoquq-e Bashar* 12, no. 35 (spring 1995):19–23.

33. For example, a man who called himself an "independent citizen" repeated faithfully the government's position "that human rights were fully respected in the Islamic Republic of Iran." Instead of Iran, a Special Representative should be appointed to other countries like Panama and Azerbaijan. He also protested what he considered to be the UN's favorable attitude toward the Mojahedin. Another group "felt that the United Nations should severely condemn the Mojahedin organization." Several men claimed they had been members of the Mojahedin and stated that their leaders told them "to show self-inflicted burns or other marks of torture in order to enhance the false propaganda spread by the organization." They said that the Iranian people would trust the United Nations more if it denounced the Mojahedin activities. UN Doc. E/CN.4/1990/24, p. 40.

34. Ibid., p. 42.

35. UN Doc. A/45/697, pp. 31–32.

36. Ibid., pp. 56, 57.

37. UN Doc. A/44/620, p. 32.

38. Ibid., p. 28.

39. Ibid., p. 32.

40. UN Doc. E/CN.4/1990/24, p. 52.

41. UN Doc. E/CN.4/1996/59, para. 2.

Chapter 12. The Special Representative's Meetings with the Judiciary and Security Officials

1. Raha, 3:204–207.
2. UN Doc. A/45/697, p. 52.
3. Ibid., p. 45.
4. Ibid., p. 63.
5. Cooper, p. 153.
6. UN Doc. A/45/697, p. 53.
7. UN Doc. E/CN.4/1992/34, paras. 302, 386.
8. Ibid., para. 303.
9. UN Doc. A/45/697, p. 46.
10. Ibid., p. 47.
11. Ibid., p. 39.
12. Ibid., pp. 39, 40.
13. UN Doc. E/CN.4/1990/24, pp. 24, 30. Amnesty reported on the same radio broadcast (BBC Summary of World Broadcasts, January 23, 1989): "The President of the Supreme Judicial Council, Ayatollah Ardebili, described a system whereby a representative of the leader of the Islamic Republic 'from outside the maze of the judicial system' could 'hold an immediate trial' and bring cases to an end 'in a matter of three, four or five days.'" Amnesty International, *Iran, Violations of Human Rights, 1987–1990*, p. 30.
14. UN Doc. E/CN.4/1990/24, p. 30.
15. Ibid., p. 31.
16. Ibid., p. 45.
17. Ibid., p. 48.
18. Ibid., p. 54.
19. In contrast to Galindo Pohl's lack of clarity in his conversation with the officials, Amnesty International's understanding in 1990 of the problems associated with the Islamic judiciary was clear and to the point. See Amnesty International, *Iran: Violations of Human Rights, 1987–1990*, p. 33.
20. UN Doc. E/CN.4/1990/24, p. 34.
21. Ibid., p. 25.
22. In his Persian writings for domestic consumption, Mehrpur expressed his wish that the judicial and security officials, especially judges, would read Galindo Pohl's reports (see Chapter 17).
23. UN Doc. E/CN.4/1990/24, p. 53.
24. UN Doc. A/45/697, p. 16.
25. UN Doc. E/CN.4/1990/24, p. 54.
26. Ibid., p. 53.
27. Ibid.
28. UN Doc. A/45/697, p. 10.
29. Ibid., p. 49.
30. Ibid., p. 51.
31. Ibid., pp. 64–65, quotation on p. 68.
32. UN Doc. E/CN.4/1991/35, p. 7.
33. Ibid., p. 3.
34. Ibid., p. 95.
35. UN Doc. E/CN.4/1991/35, p. 96.
36. See UN Doc. A/47/617, para. 7.
37. UN Doc. E/CN.4/1992/34, para. 328.
38. Ibid., para. 403.

39. UN Doc. E/CN.4/1993/41, para. 15.
40. UN Doc. A/47/617, para. 8.

Chapter 13. The Right to Freedom of Opinion, Expression, and the Press

1. UN Doc. A/47/617, para. 89.
2. Ibid., para. 20.
3. Ibid., para. 89.
4. "An Interview with Ayatollah Musavi Ardabili," *Ettela'at*, international edition, October 31, 1997, pp. 1–2.
5. Ibid.
6. *Ettela'at*, International Edition, November 14, 1997, p. 1.
7. Ali Hozuri's article was reprinted in *Kayhan* (London), November 5, 1998, p. 7.
8. *Iran Times*, July 21, 2000, p. 2.
9. Nateq Nuri, Speaker of the Majlis, in *Jomhuri-ye Islami*, December 1, 1992, p. 4.
10. Razaqi, p. 8.
11. For the forbidding rulings (*fatvas*) of the governmental ayatollahs, see *Resalat*, May 18 and 19, 1995.
12. *Iran Times*, February 24, 1995, p. 16.
13. UN Doc. E/CN.4/1995/55, para. 43.
14. Hojjat al-Islam Akhtari. "*Imam va Arzeshha-ye Islami*," (Imam and Islamic values) *Kayhan Farhangi*, June 20, 1990.
15. Interviewed by the German journalist Birgit Cerha, reprinted in *Nashriyyah-ye Hoquq-e Bashar*, no. 40 (spring 1997): 35.
16. *Resalat*, May 2, 1994. One newspaper wrote that "there are men and women among these pseudo intellectuals, who have [police] dossiers for illicit activities (*monkarati*), arrest records, and confessions to acts of prostitution and consumption of alcohol." *Jomhuri-ye Islami*, April 21, 1994.
17. UN Doc. A/51/479, para. 8.
18. *Iran Times*, December 10, 1999, p. 3.
19. For most systematic articulation of his ideas see Muhammad Mojtahed-e Shabestari, *Iman va Azadi* (Faith and freedom) (Tehran, 1997). Especially relevant is the chapter on faith, politics, and governance.
20. Abdolkarim Sorush, "*Raha'i az Yaqin va Yaqin beh Raha'i*" (Freedom from certainty and certainty of freedom), *Kiyan*, 9, no. 48 (August–September 1999): 9.
21. Ganji, *Talaqi-ye Fashisti az Din va Hokumat*.
22. *Iran Times*, October 20, 1995, p. 16.
23. From IRNA, March 26, 1999, <http://www.iranian.com/news/March99/ yazdi>.
24. Ganji, *Talaqi-ye Fashisti az Din va Hokumat*, p. 158.
25. Abbas Abdi, "*Hasteh-e Namar'i-ye Entekhabat-e Akhir*" (The hidden nucleus of the recent election), in *Entekhab-e Now: Tahlilha-ye Jame'eh Shenasaneh az Waq'a-ye Dovvom Khordad* (New choice: Sociological analysis of the event of *Khordad* the second), ed. Abdolali Reza'i and Abbas Abdi (Tehran, 1998), p. 103.
26. Christopher Dickey, "Iran Giving Voice to Freedom: Tehran's Intellectuals Won't Keep Quiet," *Newsweek International*, February 22, 1999.
27. *Sobh-e Emruz*, January 11, 1999.
28. Ibid., May 16, 1999.
29. Omid Farhang, "*Karnameh-ye Panjsaleh-ye Goshayesh-e Faza'-ye Matbu'ati* (A record of the five-year opening of the publication climate) *Goft-o-Gu* 4 (summer 1994): 9–26.

30. *Resalat* heaped insults on the editors of *Iran* for their "pleadings with the *digar andishan*." On one occasion where *Iran* quoted an experienced journalist, Mas'ud Behnud, who was a journalist during the Shah's time, *Resalat* called the act suspicious and regrettable. *Resalat*, June 15, 1994.

31. Ibid., July 29, 1995.

32. Mehrdad Farid, ed., *Khamushi-ye Darya* (Darkness at sea) (Tehran, 2000), p. 10. This book is a collection of articles on the banning of *Salam*.

33. *Kayhan*, April 10, 1997.

34. *Resalat*, May 3, 1997.

35. "A Conversation with Alireza Alavitabar," *Middle East Report*, fall 1999, p. 28.

36. UN Doc. E/CN.4/1995/55, para. 40.

37. In June 1995, 214 filmmakers issued an open letter, deploring governmental restrictions on filmmaking. They demanded the removal of "straightjacket regulations" and supervision. "In July 1995, 107 academics, in an open letter addressed to the president, requested the Government to respect the Constitution and the liberties granted therein and to take effective measures to prevent and counter the recurrent violent interference with the right to freedom of opinion and expression." UN Doc. E/CN.4/1996/39/Add.2, paras. 47, 55.

38. *Gardun* 5, no. 43 (December 1994): 43.

39. Robin Wright, "Testing the Limits of Cultural Freedom," *Civilization*, March/April 1995, p. 14.

40. Muhammad Mokhtari, *Tamrin-e Modara: Bist Maqaleh dar Baz-khani-ye Farhang* (Practicing tolerance: Twenty articles on rereading of culture) (Tehran, 1998), pp. 282–288.

41. *Khordad*, March 10, 1999.

42. *Jomhuri-ye Islami*, May 6, 1996.

43. Ahmad Shamlu, "In This Dead End," in Mahmud Kianush, ed., *Modern Persian Poetry* (Ware, U.K.: Rockingham Press, 1996), p. 93.

44. Hamid Dabashi, "Re-Reading Reality: Kiarostami's *Through the Olive Trees* and the Cultural Politics of a Postrevolutionary Aesthetics," *Critique: Journal for Critical Studies of the Middle East*, 7 (fall 1995): 79.

45. *Jomhuri-ye Islami*, December 21, 1995, p. 2.

46. Quoted in *Kayhan* (London), January 25, 1996, p. 2.

47. Parsipur, pp. 408, 443.

48. *Andishah-ye Jame'eh* 2 (January 1999): 35.

49. Mokhtari, pp. 287–288.

50. Ganji, *Talaqi-ye Fashisti az Din va Hokumat*, p. 11.

51. Mohsen Khalili, "*Mahdud Nemudan-e Azadi*" (Limiting freedom), in *Khat-e Qermez* (The Redline), ed. Nasser Fakuhi et al. (Tehran 1998), pp. 222–223.

52. Ibid., pp. 230–231.

53. Muhammad Reza Parishi, "*Parandeh-e Qap Gereftah*" (The framed bird), in *Khat-e Qermez* (The Redline), ed. Nasser Fakuhi et al. (Tehran, 1998), pp. 206–207.

54. See, e.g., Abdollah Amidi, "*Affat-ha-ye Rushanfekri dar Iran*" (Intellectual plagues in Iran), *Kayhan*, August 6, 1998; Mojtabah Ahmadi, "*Huzeh-ye Bidar-e Qom*" (Qom's alert seminaries), *Resalat*, September 2, 1998, p. 5.

55. An interview with Muhammad Kazem Anbarlu'i published in *Iran*, August 17, 1998, p. 3.

56. The President and his deputies, the Head of the Judiciary, the Majlis members, and the members of the Guardian Council and the Council of Experts. *Iran Times*, October 27, 1995, p. 14.

57. During the second visit, Galindo Pohl interviewed the Deputy Minister of Culture and Islamic Guidance, Aminzadeh, who explained the government's positions

on freedom of the press and publication of books: "The press enjoyed protection and freedom, but anything that was contrary to Islam and public order was inadmissible. The press promoted Islamic values, opposed colonialism, promoted morality and upheld the policy of 'neither East nor West.' " He further informed Galindo Pohl that any publication that insulted Islam, the Leader, or the government would be banned. UN Doc. A/45/697, p. 44. Distribution of paper was controlled by the Ministry. It was a well-known practice that those newspapers with the closest ties to the clerical factions were in a better position to procure the scarce paper. The Deputy Minister denied that "limitations had been placed on the amount of paper that the opposition press could receive." UN Doc. A/45/697, p. 44.

58. UN Doc. A/45/697, p. 67.

59. UN Doc. E/CN.4/1996/39/Add.2, para. 62.

60. Parsipur, p. 442.

61. UN Doc. E/CN.4/1994/50, para. 141.

62. Ibid., para. 129.

63. UN Doc. E/CN.4/1996/39/Add.2, para. 48. For the Iranian press report see *Kayhan*, August 24, 1995 and October 31, 1995; also *Resalat*, May 26, 1996.

64. *Kayhan*, April 13, 1996.

65. UN Doc. E/CN.4/1996/39/Add.2, para. 49.

66. *Zanan* 28 (March 1996): 2.

67. UN Doc. E/CN.4/1996/59, para. 76.

68. UN Doc. A/52/472, appendix 2, para. 5.

69. Babak Dad, *Akharin Salam* (The last *Salam*) (Tehran 2000), pp. 76–81. This book is based on an extensive interview with *Salam*'s publisher, Musavi Kho'iniha.

70. UN Doc. E/CN.4/1996/39/Add.2, paras. 39, 45.

71. *Iran Times*, October 20, 1995, p. 16.

72. UN Doc. A/51/479, para. 8.

73. Human Rights Watch/Middle East, *Power Versus Choice: Human Rights and Parliamentary Elections in the Islamic Republic of Iran*, March 1996, p. 10.

74. *Salam*, January 27, 1997.

75. In 1996, as the editor of the reformist *Bahman*, Mohajerani faced prosecution for creating public anxiety. The press jury found him guilty but, because of his previous services, recommended leniency in sentencing. The court imposed fines and prohibited him from engaging in journalistic activities for one year. Mohajerani's wife, Jamileh Kadivar, was also a strong advocate of a less constrained press.

76. During the confirmation hearing in the Majlis, Mohajerani was described by one hard-liner as "culturally tolerant and politically weak vis-à-vis the West." *Iran Times*, August 22, 1997, p. 14.

77. *Hamshahri*, August 22, 1998, p. 9.

78. For an excellent survey of the reformist press in this period see Zarir Merat, "Pushing Back the Limits of the Possible: The Press in Iran," *Middle East Report*, fall 1999, pp. 32–35.

79. Ibid., p. 34.

80. Elaine Sciolino, "Iran Alternative Voices Now Demand to Be Heard," *New York Times*, July 19, 1998.

81. Even high officials treated the two men differently. See Mohajerani's treatment of them in "Historic Defense," *Ettela'at*, International Edition, August 27, 1997, p. 9.

82. *Iran Times*, September 17, 1999, p. 4.

83. Amir-Hossein Alinaghi, *Nezarat bar Entekhabat va Tashkhis-e Salahiyyat-e Dawtalaban* (Supervision of elections, and determination of candidates' qualifications) (Tehran, 1999), p. 29.

84. *Khordad*, March 22, 1999.

85. Dad, p. 100.

86. Ganji, *Talaqi-ye Fashisti az Din va Hokumat*, pp. 245–253.

87. See, e.g., Muhammad Mahdi Reza'i, "*Jame'eh-ye Madani va Taghirat-e Ejtenab Napazir-e Eqtesadi*," *Ettela'at*, International Edition, October 16, 1997.

88. *Ettela'at*, International Edition, March 6, 1998, p. 1.

89. Excerpt of the article was reprinted in *Ettela'at*, International Edition, March 6, 1998, p. 1.

90. Abdolali Reza'i and Abbas Abdi, eds., p. 57.

91. Human Rights Watch, "Iran," in *World Report 1999* (New York, December 1998).

92. Quoted in *Iran Times*, March 12, 1999, p. 1.

93. *Iran Times*, March 13, 1998, p. 16.

94. *Resalat*, August 6, 1998.

95. Akbar Ganji, *Naqdi Baraye Tamam-e Fosul* (A critique for all seasons) (Tehran, 2000), p. 136. The entire Majlis proceeding in Nuri's impeachment is presented in this volume.

96. *Ettela'at*, International Edition, August 3, 1998, p. 2.

97. *Ettela'at*, International Edition, September 17, 1998, p. 2.

98. Amnesty International, "IRAN: Amnesty International Concerned by Arrest of Journalists and Former Prisoner of Conscience," September 24, 1998; *Ettela'at*, International Edition, October 26, 1998, p. 2.

99. "Against the Coup" was the title of the article, reprinted in *Ettela'at*, International edition, September 25, 1998, p. 1.

100. Ganji, *Talaqi-ye Fashisti az Din va Hokumat*, pp. 259, 287.

101. *Iran Times*, April 24, 1998, pp. 1, 12.

102. They launched *Tous* with a debut of 100,000 copies, which sold out within an hour on July 25, 1998. An editorial column stated that the paper "seeks to safeguard human rights and general freedoms." *New York Times*, July 26, 1998, p. 5. The same team launched *Neshat*, which was banned after publishing 149 editions; then they began *Asr-e Azadegan* in October 1999.

103. *Der Spiegel*, October 4, 1999. Quoted by A.W. Samii, "Iranian News Media, 1998–1999," *MERIA Journal* 3 (December 1999) <http:///www.biu.ac.il/soc/besa/meria>.

104. *Hoquq va Ejtema* (Law and society), special issue, August 1998.

105. *Iran Times*, January 14, 2000, p. 14. For a criticism of the current press law see Human Rights Watch, *"As Fragile as a Crystal Glass": Press Freedom in Iran* (New York, October 1999).

106. See his words in *Iran Times*, October 20, 1995, and *Hamshahri*, May 27, 1998.

107. Christopher Dickey, "Iran Giving Voice to Freedom: Tehran's Intellectuals Won't Keep Quiet," *Newsweek International*, February 22, 1999.

108. Copithorne wrote: "On 9 April 1997 the Special Representative requested to be informed of the results of the investigation into the death of Ibrahim Zalzadeh, a writer and journalist, aged 49, whose corpse was found on 29 March 1997 with multiple stab wounds to the chest." UN Doc. A/52/472, Appendix 1, para. 8.

109. For an interview with Ma'sumeh Mossadeq's former attorney in which he expressed suspicions about her killing, see the reformist daily *Arzesh*, January 16, 1999, p. 8.

110. UN Doc. E/CN.4/1999/32, paras. 8–9.

111. Dad, pp. 71–72.

112. Akbar Ganji, *Tarik-khaneh-ye Ashbah* (The dungeon of ghosts) (Tehran, 1999).

113. Ganji, *Talaqi-ye Fashisti az Din va Hokumat*.

114. *Khordad*, February 13, 1999, p. 2.

115. *Payam-e Emruz* 31 (June–July 1999): 14. This was a reformist magazine with

a deserved reputation of journalistic professionalism. See also *Iran-e Farda,* no. 62, November 17, 1999.

116. *Payam-e Emruz* 31 (June–July 1999): 30–31.

117. Quoted in ibid., p. 13.

118. *Payam-e Emruz* 34 (November 1999): 24.

119. Ibid., 28.

120. *Payam-e Emruz,* 32, August 1999, p. 71.

121. *Fath,* February 24, 2000.

122. *Hamshahri,* January 9 and 10. A summary of the interview with *Hamshahri* appeared in *Iran Times,* January 14, 2000, p. 1.

123. Mehrdad Balali, "Rafsanjani Links Reformers with Iran Abuses,' Reuters, January 26, 2000, <abcnews.com>.

124. *Salam,* July 6, 1999.

125. Farid, p. 21.

126. Dad, p. 67.

127. For the July events in the context of the larger student movement see Akbar Mahdi, "The Student Movement in the Islamic Republic of Iran," *Journal of Iranian Research and Analysis,* 15, no. 2 (November 1999): pp. 1–27.

128. *Iran Times,* July 30, 1999, p. 1.

129. Ibid., September 17, 1999, p. 1.

Chapter 14. The Most Revealing Cases of Violations of the Right to Freedom of Expression and the Press

1. *Jomhuri-ye Islami,* March 16, 1994.

2. *Payam-e Emruz,* 34, November 1999, pp. 23–24. After the extrajudicial killings of 1998–99, this reformist journal in Tehran published long reports in which many mysterious cases, including Sa'idi Sirjani, were discussed.

3. UN Doc. A/49/514, para. 59.

4. UN Doc. A/49/514/Add.2, p. 11.

5. UN Doc. E/CN.4/1995/55, para. 20; see also para. 99.

6. Ibid., para. 92.

7. Two of Sa'idi's letters addressed to the Supreme Leader of the Islamic Republic of Iran are translated and published in (no author) *Az* Sheikh San'an *ta Marg dar Zendan* (From *Sheikh San'an* to death in prison) (Washington, D.C., 1995). Quotation is from page 33. This book is a collection of articles on the occasion of the first anniversary of his death.

8. Ahmad Karimi-Hakkak, "A Storyteller and His Times: Ali-Akbar Sa'idi Sirjani of Iran," 3, *World Literature Today* (summer 1994): 522.

9. *Sobh,* November 1996.

10. From Sarkuhi's famous letter. An excerpt of the letter, with an excellent introduction by Shaul Bakhash, was published in the *New York Review of Books,* April 10, 1997.

11. Ibid., pp. 52–53.

12. It is remarkable that Sarkuhi developed a relatively clear understanding of what was happening to him at the time.

13. *Iran Times,* June 27, 1997, p. 16.

14. Sarkuhi's Open Letter, translated by PEN and posted on its website, <www. PEN.org>.

15. Ibid.

16. Ibid.

17. See Nora Boustany, "Keeping a Husband Alive," *Washington Post*, July 11, 1997.

18. *Salam*, December 22, 1996.

19. *Kayhan*, December 21, 1996.

20. Sarkuhi's open letter.

21. *Kayhan*, February 5, 1997.

22. All European and American human rights organizations reacted immediately. On July 2, 1997, the UN Special Representative on Iran, the Special Rapporteurs on Summary Executions, on Freedom of Expression and Opinion, and on the Independence of Judges made an urgent appeal for Sarkuhi to Iran's delegation to Geneva and to the Iranian representative to the United Nations. For Copithorne's report on Sarkuhi see UN Doc. A/52/472, para. 14.

23. Open letter from Sarkuhi's wife, June 27, 1997.

24. *Iran Times*, September 26, 1997, p. 16.

25. Ibid.

26. UN Doc. A/52/472, Appendix 4, para. 3.

27. In the second letter, the diplomat added: "He enjoys and will enjoy all legal rights in conformity with the due process of law, including the right to a fair trial and the right to a defence lawyer." UN Doc. A/52/472, Appendix 4, para. 4.

28. IRNA, "Sarkuhi's Brother Rejects Foreign Media Hype About His Brother," at <www.iranian.com>.

29. Interview with Farideh Sarkuhi [Zebarjad], *Mihan*, 20 (March 1997): 5. *Mihan* is a political magazine published by Iranian expatriates in Paris.

30. Ervand Abrahamian, *Iran Between Two Revolutions* (Princeton: Princeton University Press, 1982), p. 445.

31. Amnesty International, *Iran: Human Rights Violations Against Shia Religious Leaders and Their Followers*, p. 1.

32. UN Doc. E/CN.4/1997/63, para. 31.

33. For a well-written summary analysis of the regulations covering the conduct of the Court see Amnesty International, *Iran: Human Rights Violations Against Shia Religious Leaders and Their Followers*, pp. 3–6.

34. *Iran Times*, February 10, 1995, p. 16.

35. Ibid.

36. Ibid., p. 1.

37. Amnesty International, *Iran: Human Rights Violations Against Shia Religious Leaders and Their Followers*, p. 16.

38. Ibid., p. 17.

39. Ibid.

40. UN Doc. E/CN.4/1998/59, para. 36.

41. UN Doc. E/CN.4/1997/63, para. 33.

42. *Iran Times*, January 21, 2000, p. 3.

43. *Iran Times*, November 28, 1997, p. 1.

44. *Iran Times*, April 3, 1998, p. 2.

45. Amnesty International, *Iran: Human Rights Violations Against Shia Religious Leaders and Their Followers*, p. 11.

46. *Iran Times*, March 12, 1999, p. 1.

47. The letter was printed in *Kayhan* (London), September 10, 1998.

48. *Tehran Times*, January 28, 1999, p. 1.

49. *Tehran Times*, April 17, 1998, p. 11.

50. <www.ihrwg.org.ihrc1>.

51. Between May and October 1994, a number of clerics who were supporters of Ayatollah Shirazi were arrested in the city of Isfahan. Among them were Hojjat al-

Islam Makki Akhund, who "was reportedly subjected to two months of torture." He was arrested in May and by the end of the year was still not officially charged before a court. Amnesty International, *World Report, 1995*, pp. 164–165.

52. UN Doc. E/CN.4/1999/32, para. 52.

53. Zahra Rudi Kadivar, *Baha-ye Azadi: Defa'iyyat-e Mohsen Kadivar dar Dadgah-e Vizheh-ye Ruhaniyyat* (Price of freedom, Mohsen Kadivar's defense in Special Court for Clergy) (Tehran, 1999), p. 7.

54. Ibid., pp. 40–52.

55. Ibid., p. 59.

56. Ibid., p. 61.

57. Ibid., p. 143.

58. Ibid., p. 141.

59. Ibid., p. 143.

60. *Iran Times*, April 30, 1999.

61. John F. Burns, "Court Silences Iran Reformist with Jail Term," *New York Times*, November 28, 1999, p. A1.

62. Abdollah Nuri, *Shukaran-e Eslah* (Hemlock for advocate of reform) (Tehran, 1999). This volume covering Nuri's complete text of defense became a best-seller.

63. *Iran Times*, November 19, 1999, p. 1.

64. Geneive Abdo, "Jailing of Khatami Ally Provokes Outcry in Iran," *International Herald Tribune*, November 29, 1999.

65. *Tous*, August 19, 1998, p. 2.

66. Abdo.

67. "Iran Cleric Backs Jailed Reformer," Associated Press, December 2, 1999.

68. *Iran Times*, December 10, 1999, p. 1.

Chapter 15. The Rights to Participate in the Political Life of the Country and to Peaceful Assembly and Association

1. Bahman Bakhtiari, "Parliamentary Elections in Iran," *Iranian Studies* 26, nos. 3–4 (1993): 375.

2. Ayatollah Montazeri declined to be interviewed due to "other commitments," although it is easy to surmise the real reason. In the aftermath of the prison massacre of 1988, all the things he would have wanted to tell Galindo Pohl would have made life even more difficult for him.

3. UN Doc. E/CN.4/1990/24, p. 46.

4. UN Doc. E/CN.4/1995/55, para. 59.

5. UN Doc. E/CN.4/1990/24, p. 47.

6. UN Doc. A/45/697, p. 42.

7. *Salam*, March 9, 1992, as translated and quoted by Schirazi, 89.

8. UN Doc. A/47/617, para. 100.

9. Ibid., para. 101.

10. Once the anointed successor to Imam Khomeini, Ayatollah Montazeri, who was still under house arrest in early 2000, told a reporter: "But when they treat me like this, how must they be treating the others." Robert Fisk's interview with Montazeri, *Independent*, February 21, 2000.

11. UN Doc. A/47/617, p. 21, para. 102.

12. *Bayan*, June 25, 2000. In this issue Ali Akbar Mohtashemi wrote a strongly worded critique of the judicial system, after which the daily was banned by the Judiciary. *Bayan* had replaced *Salam*.

13. Democracy Network of Iran (DNI), <www.algonet.se/~farhad/dni/index>.

14. Human Rights Watch/Middle East, "Power Versus Choice: Human Rights and Parliamentary Elections in the Islamic Republic of Iran," pp. 6–7.

15. UN Doc. A/51/479, para. 5.

16. UN Doc. A/51/479/Add.1, para. 5.

17. UN Doc. A/51/475/Add.1, p. 4, para. 6.

18. Human Rights Watch/Middle East wrote: "Although Article 26 of the Constitution provides for the rights to form political parties, the rulers of the Islamic Republic have discouraged the formation of groups whose agendas it does not control. The official line has been that there should be no ideological division in the Islamic Republic, and that the country could be divided into those who support the concept of *velayat-e faqih* and those who do not. . . . But opponents of this concept have no place in the political contest. The decision as to who is for or against *velayat-e faqih* is not based on precepts established by law, rather it is a discretionary assessment of the leadership." Human Rights Watch/Middle East, "Power Versus Choice: Human Rights and Parliamentary Elections in the Islamic Republic of Iran," p. 3.

19. In October 1995, 160 political leaders in opposition, mainly from nationalist and Islamic liberal factions, formed an association, obviously without official permit, called the Searchers for Free Elections. They signed a declaration in which they set a number of conditions, guaranteeing freedom of elections for the Fifth Majlis, without which they would not participate in the elections. On January 2, 1996, the police prevented them from holding a press conference in Tehran. (The declaration was reprinted in *Enqelab-e Islami*, Paris, November 6–19, 1994.)

20. *Ettela'at*, International Edition, January 18, 1996.

21. UN Doc. A/52/472, para. 64.

22. *Tous*, August 19, 1998, p. 2.

23. Ganji, *Naqdi Baraye Tamam-e Fosul*, p. 71.

24. UN Doc. E/CN.4/1999/32, para. 67. See also *Iran Times*, October 30, 1998, p. 13.

25. *Iran Times*, October 30, 1998, p. 13.

26. Both letters were published in *Ettela'at*, International Edition, October 26, 1998, p. 3.

27. Ganji, *Naqdi Baraye Tamam-e Fosul*, p. 128. The entire Majlis proceeding for Nuri's impeachment is presented in this volume.

28. Ayatollah Montazeri's *fatva*, reprinted in *Washington Iranians*, June 18, 1999.

29. *Iran Times*, September 10, 1999, p. 2.

30. *Iran Times*, September 17, 1999, p. 4.

31. *Iran Times*, February 11, 2000, p. 4.

32. *Iran Times*, May 28, 1999, p. 1.

33. From a lecture by the President's advisor, Ali Akbar Mohtashemi, *Tous*, August 13, 1998, p. 9.

34. *Azadegan*, January 12, 2000, p. 2.

35. *Iran Times*, February 18, 2000, p. 4.

36. *Sobh-e Emruz*, January 10, 2000.

37. BBC World Service, January 28, 2000, <http://news.bbc.uk>.

38. John F. Burns, "Many Reformers Ruled off Iran Ballot," *New York Times*, January 24, 2000.

39. *Kayhan*, August 18, 1998, p. 3.

40. *Iran Times*, April 14, 2000, p. 4.

41. Susan Sachs, "Top Iranian Cleric Defends Closing of Reformist Publication," *New York Times*, April 29, 2000, A3.

Chapter 16. The Rights of Women

1. UN Doc. A/45/697, p. 27.

2. Parvin Darabi and Romin P. Thomson, *Rage Against the Veil: The Courageous Life and Death of an Islamic Dissident* (Amherst, N.Y.: Prometheus Books, 1999), pp. 171–173.

3. Ibid., p. 191.

4. Ibid., p. 201.

5. Ibid., p. 203.

6. For example, Article 76 of the law of punishment for adultery (*Qanun Mojazat Baraye Zina*); Article 119 for sodomy (*lavat*); Article 170 for drinking alcohol; Article 189 (B) for warring against God (*mohariba*); Article 199 (1) for robbery; Article 237(A) for a premeditated murder.

7. UN Doc. A/45/697, p. 27.

8. Mehrpur, p. 180.

9. UN Doc. A/45/697, p. 27.

10. UN Doc. A/47/617, p. 22.

11. UN Doc. E/CN.4/1992/34, para. 182 and A/47/617, para. 105.

12. UN Doc. A/45/697, p. 27.

13. UN Doc. A/47/617, para. 104.

14. UN Doc. A/54/365, para. 23.

15. "During the first half of the 1970's the number of girls attending elementary school rose from 80,020 to 1,508,387; the number of girls attending vocational training schools rose tenfold; the number of women candidates for the universities rose seven times." Mahnaz Afkhami, "Iran: A Future in the Past—The 'Prerevolutionary' Women's Movement," in *Sisterhood Is Global: The International Women's Movement Anthology*, ed. Robin Morgan (New York: Anchor Books, 1984), p. 335.

16. Regarding one such institution, Homa Omid observed, "What the Islamic University lacked in terms of intellectual rigour, was to be compensated by excess of Islamic zeal" (166).

17. Their names are listed by feminist scholar Haideh Moghissi, "*Zanan va Fa'aliyyat-ha-ye Siasi va Ejtema'i*" (Women and political and social activities), *Iran Times*, December 2, 1994, p. 9.

18. Haleh Esfandiari, "The Majlis and Women's Issues in the Islamic Republic of Iran," in *In the Eye of the Storm: Women in Post-revolutionary Iran*, ed. Mahnaz Afkhami and Erika Friedl (Syracuse, N.Y.: Syracuse University Press, 1994), p. 61.

19. "An Unrecorded Struggle, Interview with a Women Activist Inside Iran," September 1996, <www.tvs.se/womensvoice/enginter>.

20. *Zanan*, 17 (March–April 1994): 1.

21. UN Doc. E/CN.4/1996/59, para. 59.

22. I have offered a critical appraisal of these views. Reza Afshari, "Egalitarian Islam and Misogynist Islamic Tradition: A Critique of the Feminist Reinterpretation of Islamic History and Heritage," *Critique: Journal of Critical Studies of Iran and the Middle East* 4 (spring 1994): 13–34.

23. UN Doc. E/CN.4/1996/59, para. 62.

24. Interview with Fatemeh Ramazan-Zadeh, *Ruznameh-Zan*, August 22, 1998, p. 7.

25. Haleh Afshar, *Islam and Feminisms: An Iranian Case-Study* (London: Macmillan Press, 1998), p. 57.

26. Mehrangiz Kar, *Hoquq-e Siasi-ye Zan-e Iran* (Political rights of Iranian women) (Tehran, 1997), p. 45.

27. Mehrangiz Kar, "*Zanan dar Rah*" (Women on their way), *Zanan*, 28 (March 1996).

28. Kar, *Hoquq-e Siasi-ye Zan-e Iran*, p. 46.

29. *Hamshahri*, August 9, 1998, p. 12.

30. Schirazi, p. 142.

31. These intellectuals as well as intra-regime debates, especially in the Majlis by a few women representatives, have been the subject of many studies. See Afshar.

32. Schirazi, p. 218.

33. *Iran Times*, November 7, 1997, p. 1.

34. Schirazi, p. 219.

35. Parvin Paidar, *Women and the Political Process in Twentieth-Century Iran* (Cambridge: Cambridge University Press, 1995), p. 294.

36. Copithorne observed the problem of implementation in his report dealing with the second half of 1998. UN Doc. E/CN.4/1999/32, para. 29.

37. "Interview with Shirin Ebadi," *Ruznameh-Zan*, August 23, 1998, p. 9.

38. Nuri, p. 223.

39. Eliz Sanasarian, "The Politics of Gender and Development in the Islamic Republic of Iran," in *Women and Development in the Middle East and North Africa*, ed. Joseph G. Jabbra and Nancy W. Jabbra (Leiden: E. J. Brill, 1992), pp. 65–66.

40. UN Doc. E/CN.4/1996/59, para. 64.

41. UN Doc. E/CN.4/1997/63, paras. 22, 25.

42. From IRNA, March 26, 1999, <www.iranian.com/News/March99/yazdi>.

43. Human Rights Watch, *World Report, 1999* (New York, December 1998).

44. *Tous*, August 13, 1998, p. 9.

45. *Ruznameh-Zan*, August 16, 1998, p. 9.

46. Interview with Tahmineh Milani in *Ruzhameh-Zan*, August 12, 1998, p. 10.

47. Nushin Ahmadi Khorassani, ed., *Jens-e Dovvom, Majmu'ah-ye Maqalat* (The second sex, collection of articles) (Tehran, 1999), pp. 82–93.

48. Translated and quoted by feminist scholar Haideh Moghissi, *Populism and Feminism in Iran* (New York: St. Martin Press, 1996), p. 150.

49. Omid, p. 186.

50. Nayereh Tohidi, "Gender and Islamic Fundamentalism: Feminist Politics in Iran," in *Third World Women and the Politics of Feminism*, ed. Chandra Talpade Mohanty, Ann Russo, and Lourdes Torres (Bloomington and Indianapolis: Indiana University Press, 1991), p. 252.

51. Afshar, p. 18.

52. Maryam Poya, *Women, Work and Islamism: Ideology and Resistance in Iran* (London: Zed Books, 1999), pp. 136 and 148.

53. Goodwin, p. 112.

54. Esfandiari, p. 77.

55. The neofeminist analysis is characterized by its positive portrayal of Islamist "cultural renewal" and for its sympathy toward "Muslim feminists." Leila Ahmed, *Women and Gender in Islam: Historical Roots of a Modern Debate* (New Haven: Yale University Press, 1992), p. 223.

56. *Salam*, February 5, 1995.

57. Sousan Azadi (with Angela Ferrante), *Out of Iran: One Woman's Escape from the Ayatollahs* (London: Macdonald, 1987), p. 179.

58. Anouar Majid, "The Politics of Feminism in Islam," *Signs: Journal of Women in Culture and Society* 23, no. 2 (1998): 338.

59. Brooks, p. 26.

60. Goodwin, p. 105.

61. Brooks, p. 32.

62. Jack Donnelly, *International Human Rights*, 2d ed. (Boulder, Colo.: Westview Press, 1998), p. 35.

63. An internal judgment "asks whether the practice is defensible within the fundamental value framework of that society. An external judgment applies the standards of the evaluator." Donnelly, *International Human Rights*, p. 114.

64. The neofeminists will reject my line of argument as elitist. The Jordanian Lama Abu Odeh observes the following: "Unless I engaged in intellectual elitism by accusing these women of false consciousness and not knowing their own good, there was no way that I could point to instances of disempowerment of the veil." Lama Abu Odeh, "Post-colonial Feminism and the Veil: Thinking the Difference," *Feminist Review* 43 (spring 1993): 30. My argument is that one is not engaged in intellectual elitism if one places the adoption of the veil within its proper context, i.e., the modern nation-state and the ideologically sanctioned discourses of power. In the absence of such a perspective, the analyst sees no "instances of disempowerment" in the veil. Above all, the real human rights issue is not about its adoption but its imposition, a violation of the right of freedoms of conscience and expression.

65. Afshar, p. 6.

66. In an interview with the Japanese daily *Asahi Shimbun* on February 6, 1997, <www.zan.org/news>. Zan (woman) is an informative website.

67. "*Hijab, Habs, Ekhtelat, Ya . . . ?*" (Islamic dress, imprisonment, mixture, or . . . ?) *Ruznameh-Zan*, August 15, 1998, p. 8.

68. For full translation of this passage, see Omid, p. 181.

69. For this interesting interview with Ahmadi, see <www.badjens.homepage.com>.

70. In the first issue of the newspaper, Mrs. Hashemi Rafsanjani noted that one of the problems related to women themselves. "We still don't sufficiently believe in ourselves and think we have to accept all these things and get used to them. We think that we should not break the traditions. We think that traditions are the same as the *shari'ah* laws and standards (*mavazin*)." *Ruznameh-Zan*, August 8, 1998, pp. 1–2.

71. Translated and quoted by Afshar, p. 205.

72. *Ettela'at*, May 10, 1990, p. 2.

73. *Joumhuri-ye Islami*, February 26, 1994.

74. *Joumhuri-ye Islami*, April 11, 1994.

75. *Iran Times*, October 13, 1995, p. 1.

76. UN Doc. E/CN.4/1992/34, paras. 185, 186.

77. He wrote that "arrests of Iranian women for non-observance of full Islamic code or wearing make-up, colourful garments or adornments have continued." UN Doc. A/47/617, para. 108. On May 16, 1992, several women were arrested "during a search-and-control operation carried out in private companies, clinics and public places, including the Tehran suburbs, by the forces of the greater Tehran Security District." UN Doc. A/47/617, para. 109.

78. The following two examples revealed the nature of the conflict:

"On 26 July 1991, in downtown Isfahan, a group of women were allegedly harassed, beaten and arrested by revolutionary guards on the charge of being improperly veiled. Various groups of people attempted to free the arrested women from the guards, and were allegedly shot and wounded by the Guards who opened fire in an attempt to disperse them; 355 persons were allegedly arrested. According to *Salaam* of 29 July 1991, the clash began after police and members of the 'Headquarters to combat social vices' organization stopped women in central Isfahan square." UN Doc. E/CN.4/1992/34, para. 190.

"It was reported that on 24 April 1991 Ms. Parivash Ameri, aged 19, was arrested at Vali-Ahd Square, Tehran, by Guards of the Islamic Revolution because she was not dressed in accordance with Islamic regulations. She was allegedly tortured while in detention. On 5 June 1991, while in a coma, she was handed to her parents who took her to Pahlavi hospital. Dr. Houshang Oveissi and Dr. Mohammad Sadeghi reported to the police at station No. 8 Ms. Ameri's state as a result of torture. The authorities allegedly suspended the doctors from their jobs, imprisoned them and later proclaimed that Dr. Oveissi and Dr. Sadeghi were responsible for the death of Ms. Ameri." UN Doc. E/CN.4/1992/34, para. 133.

79. UN Doc. E/CN.4/1994/50, para. 119.
80. Ibid., para. 177.
81. Ibid., para. 178.
82. Ibid., para. 181.
83. Ibid., para. 182.
84. Ibid., para. 181.
85. Ibid., para. 182.
86. UN Doc. E/CN.4/1995/55, para. 55.
87. Goodwin, pp. 111–112.
88. UN Doc. A/52/472.
89. UN Doc. E/CN.4/1996/39/Add.2, para. 63.
90. UN Doc. E/CN.4/1997/63, para. 24.
91. In an interview with a French reporter, translated and reprinted in *Kayhan* (London), May 20, 1999.
92. *Iran Times*, November 19, 1999, p. 1.
93. "A Conversation with Alireza Alavitabar," *Middle East Report*, fall 1999, 30.

Chapter 17. UN Monitoring, 1984–2000

1. UN Doc. E/CN.4/1987/23, p. 18.
2. UN Doc. A/42/648, p. 7.
3. UN Doc. E/CN.4/1988/24, p. 19.
4. UN Doc. E/CN.4/1996/59, para. 78.
5. *Kayhan*, February 5, 1996.
6. He published a number of articles about his experiences. His depictions of the problems that the Islamic Republic faced were more complex than what the diplomats and the semiofficial press presented in their propaganda.
7. Mehrpur, pp. 107–108, 175.
8. Ibid., pp. 78–79.
9. Ibid., p. 106.
10. Ibid., p. 176.
11. Amnesty International, *Iran: Violations of Human Rights, 1987–1990*, p. 57.
12. Mehrpur, p. 176.
13. Ibid., pp. 107–108.
14. Ibid., p. 177.
15. Ibid., pp. 177–178.
16. Ibid., p. 178.
17. Ibid., pp. 178–179.
18. UN Doc. E/CN.4/1994/50, p. 19, para. 85.
19. Mohsen Armin and Hojjat Razzaqi, eds., *Bim va Omid* (Fears and expectations) (Tehran, 1999), pp. 235–236.
20. UN Doc. E/CN.4/1996/39/Add.2, para. 37.
21. Human Rights Watch/ Middle East, "Power Versus Choice, Human Rights and Parliamentary Elections in the Islamic Republic of Iran," March 1996, p. 6.

22. See Chapter 10. UN Doc. A/C.3/40/13, p. 2. In 1984, he proudly stated that the "Universal Declaration of Human Rights, which represented secular understanding of the Judaeo-Christian tradition, could not be implemented by Muslims and did not accord with the system of values recognized by the Islamic Republic of Iran." He went on to assert that his state would "not hesitate to violate its provisions." Quoted in Mayer, p. 8.

23. These activities included presenting the interest of minorities in education, property rights and granting of passports; responding and processing over 1,000 complaints; providing human rights education for officials; public human rights education through the media.

24. UN Doc. E/CN.4/1997/63, para. 59.

25. UN Doc. A/52/472, para. 48.

26. Copithorne added: "The Special Representative would note that the President and several members of the Islamic Human Rights Commission itself and its subcommittees are current or former senior figures or officials in the Government. Whether the Commission has significant freedom of action remains to be seen. In that regard, the Special Representative recommends that the Commission move quickly to begin publishing a detailed description of the types of complaints it is receiving, of the interventions it is making and of the success it is having in reversing the conduct that give rise to the complaints." UN Doc. A/52/472, para. 52.

27. UN Doc. E/CN.4/1996/59, annex VII.

28. The following separate charges were listed for each man: "Disseminating lies and rumours against the sovereignty of the country in meeting with foreign residents." "Disseminating lies and rumours against the sovereignty of the Islamic Republic of Iran and its official." "Dispatching false publications and illegal consignments for the members of the organization." "Fabricating and disseminating lies and rumours and provoking people abroad against the Islamic Republic of Iran." "Disseminating lies and rumours . . . in foreign countries with the aim of confronting the Islamic Republic of Iran." "Sending false information to foreign countries with the aim of creating a psychological war and damaging the reputation of the State."

29. UN Doc. E/CN.4/1996/95/Add.2, para. 60.

30. *Ettela'at*, International Edition, December 2, 1997, p. 10.

31. This interview took place in September 1997. Iran News Political Desk, <www.seraj.org>.

32. *Ettela'at*, International Edition, December 2, 1997, p. 1.

33. Ganji, *Talaqi-ye Fashisti az Din va Hokumat*, pp. 395–398.

34. <www.ihrwg.org/ihrc1>.

35. *Iran Times*, August 1998, p. 14.

36. *Iran Times*, March 12, 1999, p. 1.

37. *Iran Times*, April 28, 2000, p. 10.

38. UN Doc. E/CN.4/1997/63, para. 9.

39. *Salam*, December 1, 1996.

40. UN Doc. E/CN.4/1994/50, para. 127.

41. Ibid., para. 128.

42. Ibid., para. 130.

43. Ibid., para. 133.

44. *Salam*, August 28, 1995.

45. Agence France-Presse, reporting from Tehran, March 1, 1998.

46. "Kharrazi: Kinkel's Words Are Very Strange," *Ettela'at*, September 12, 1997, p. 1.

47. John F. Burns, "Arrests Shake Ancient Roots of Iran's Jews," *New York Times*, October 17, 1999, p. 1.

48. *Ettela'at*, September 2, 1997, p. 13 and "Iranian Jews to Face Trial," September 20, 1999, <http:news.BBC.co.uk>.

49. Permanent Mission of the Islamic Republic of Iran to the United Nations, no. 179, June 14, 1999.

50. *Iran Times*, July 2, 1999, p. 1.

51. Susan Sachs, "Spy Trial of 13 Leaves the Jews of Iran Shaken," *New York Times*, June 30, 2000, pp. 1, 4.

52. Iran's UN Mission, "Text of the Statement by H. E. Dr. Kamal Kharrazi," New York, September 22, 1997, pp. 6–7.

53. *Salam*, August 23, 1994.

54. Farid, pp. 67, 165–168.

55. Ibid., p. 165.

56. For example, see the daily *Fath*'s editorial in its inaugural issue, December 11, 1999, p. 2. Upon the banning of *Khordad*, Nuri's supporters launched *Fath*.

57. Lauren, p. 281.

58. Robert Fisk's interview with Montazeri, *Independent*, February 21, 2000.

59. Quoted by Associated Press, December 20, 1999.

Conclusion

1. Edwin E. Moise, *Modern China: A History* (New York: Longman, 1994), p. 182.

2. Feitlowitz, p. 29.

3. *Bahar*, July 25, 2000, p. 1.

4. Sarkuhi's open letter, translated by PEN, and was posted on its website, <www. PEN.org>.

5. "Amnesty International believes that cruel punishments such as flogging violate Iran's international obligations under the International Covenant of Civil and Political Rights ratified by Iran, which prohibit the use of torture or ill-treatment." Amnesty International, "Magazine Editor Sentenced to Prison Term and Lashes," January 29, 1996.

6. Howard, p. 38.

7. UN Doc. E/CN.4/1996/39/ADD.2, para. 61.

8. Fred Halliday, *Islam and the Myth of Confrontation: Religion and Politics in the Middle East* (London: I.B. Tauris, 1996), p. 157.

9. Mayer, p. 160.

10. Khatami writes: "Alongside the regressive version of Islam, we have the camp that believes in a diluted Islam, a fabricated, inauthentic form of the faith that merely goes through the motions of piety without any real knowledge of Islam or real belief in its teachings. Their Islam has so many foreign, imported elements that it cannot be called Islam at all. Diluted Islam represents one of the most dangerous pores for the West's cultural onslaught" (Khatami, p. 55).

11. Akbar Ganji, *Naqdi Baraye Tamam-e Fosul*, p. 59.

12. Pahlavan, Changiz, "*Bohran-e Goftar dar Iran-e Emruz*" (Crisis of discourse in today's Iran), reprinted in *Washington Iranians*, May 19, 2000, p. 14.

13. Steven Lukes, "Five Fables about Human Rights," in the Oxford Amnesty Lectures, 1993, *On Human Rights* (New York: Basic Books, 1993), p. 29.

14. This was also the sense conveyed by the three participants from Iran on a panel chaired by the secular scholar Azar Nafisi at the Third Biennial Conference on Iranian Studies in Bethesda, Maryland, May 25–28, 2000. Naghmeh Zarbafian, "The Domain of Dead Dialogues: Youth and Art in Post-Revolution Iran"; Reza Ha'eri,

"Dangerous Liaisons: Being Young and a Filmmaker in Iran"; Goli Imami, "Iran's Martians: Iranian Youth Twenty Years After the Revolution."

15. Golshiri made that simple but poignant remark in the context of his argument rejecting the clerics' binary vision of the insiders and outsiders that demonizes the secularists. *Iran Times*, August 6, 1999, p. 5.

Selected Bibliography

Abrahamian, Ervand. *Iran Between Two Revolutions*. Princeton: Princeton University Press, 1982.

———. *The Iranian Mojahedin*. New Haven: Yale University Press, 1989.

———. *Tortured Confessions: Prisons and Public Recantations in Modern Iran*. Berkeley: University of California Press, 1999.

Abu Odeh, Lama. "Post-colonial Feminism and the Veil: Thinking the Difference." *Feminist Review* 43 (spring 1993): 26–37.

Afary, Janet. *The Iranian Constitution Revolution, 1906–1911: Grassroots Democracy, Social Democracy, and the Origins of Feminism*. New York: Columbia University Press, 1996.

Afkhami, Mahnaz, and Erika Friedl, eds. *In the Eye of the Storm: Women in Post-Revolutionary Iran*. Syracuse, N.Y.: Syracuse University Press, 1994.

Afshar, Haleh. *Islam and Feminisms: An Iranian Case-Study*. London: Macmillan Press, 1998.

Afshari, Reza. "The Historians of the Constitutional Movement and the Making of the Iranian Populist Tradition." *International Journal of the Middle East Studies* 25 (1993): 477–94.

———. "Egalitarian Islam and Misogynist Islamic Tradition: A Critique of the Feminist Reinterpretation of Islamic History and Heritage." *Critique: Journal of Critical Studies of Iran and the Middle East* 4 (spring 1994): 13–33.

———. "An Essay on Islamic Cultural Relativism in the Discourse of Human Rights." *Human Rights Quarterly* 16 (May 1994): 235–76.

———. "An Essay on Scholarship, Human Rights, and State Legitimacy: The Case of the Islamic Republic of Iran." *Human Rights Quarterly* 18 (August 1996): 544–93.

———. "Civil Society and Human Rights in Iran: A Review Essay." *Journal of Iranian Research and Analysis* 16 (April 2000): 61–72.

Ahmadi Khorassani, Nushin, ed. *Jens-e Dowwm, Majmu'ah-ye Maqalat* (The second sex: Collection of articles). Tehran, 1999.

Ahmadi, Ramin. "Violations of Human Rights in Iran: The Case of Abbas Amir-Entezam." Master's thesis, Yale University, 1997.

Ahmed, Leila. *Women and Gender in Islam: Historical Roots of a Modern Debate*. New Haven: Yale University Press, 1992.

Alinaghi, Amir-Hossein. *Nezarat bar Entekhabat va Tashkhis-e Salahiyyat-e Dawtalaban* (Supervision of elections and determination of candidates' qualifications). Tehran, 1999.

Alizadeh, Parvaneh. *Khub Negah Konid, Rastagi Hast* (Look carefully, it is real). Paris, 1997.

Amir, Menasheh. "The Image of Jews in Contemporary Iranian Media." In *The History of Contemporary Iranian Jews*. Beverly Hills, Calif.: Center for Iranian Jewish Oral History, 1999.

An-Na'im, Abdullahi Ahmed. "Islamic Law, International Relations, and Human Rights: Challenges and Response." *Cornell International Law Journal* 20, no. 2 (1987).

———. *Toward an Islamic Reformation: Civil Liberties, Human Rights, and International Law.* Syracuse, N.Y.: Syracuse University Press, 1990.

An-Na'im, Abdullahi Ahmed, ed. *Human Rights in Cross-Cultural Perspectives.* Philadelphia: University of Pennsylvania Press, 1992.

Amnesty International. *Iran: Violations of Human Rights.* London, 1987.

———. *Iran: Violations of Human Rights, 1987–1990.* New York, 1990.

———. *Iran: Official Secrecy Hides Continuing Repression.* New York, 1995.

———. *World Report 1995.* London, 1995.

———. "Iran: Amnesty International Concerned About Possible Government Involvement in Deaths of Iranian National." February 28, 1996.

———. "Iran: Amnesty International Condemns Upsurge in Executions." January 6, 1997.

———. *Iran: Human Rights Violations Against Shia Religious Leaders and Their Followers.* New York. 1997.

———. "Iran: Mykonos Trial Provides Further Evidence of Iranian Policy of Unlawful State Killings." April 10, 1997.

———. "Shi'a Religious Leaders as Victims of Human Rights Violations." June 3, 1997.

———. *World Report 1997.*

Arfaie, Alieh, et al. *Hoqug-e Bashar Az Didgah-e Majam'eh Binolmellali* (Human rights in the perspective of international organizations). Tehran, 1993.

Armin, Mohsen, and Hojjat Razzaqi, eds. *Bim va Omid* (Fears and expectations). Tehran, 1999.

Arzt, Donna E. "Religious Human Rights in Muslim States of the Middle East and North Africa." *Emory International Law Review* 10 (1996): 139–61.

Azad, F. *Yadha-ye Zendan* (Memories of prisons). Paris, 1997.

Azadi, Hamid. *Dar-ha va Divar-ha, Khaterati az Zendan-e Evin* (Doors and walls: An Evin prisoner's memoir). Seattle, 1997.

Azadi, Sousan (with Angela Ferrante). *Out of Iran: One Woman's Escape from the Ayatollas.* London: Macdonald, 1987.

Baha'i International Community. *Iran's Secret Blueprint for the Destruction of a Religious Community.* New York, 1999.

Bakhash, Shaul. *The Reign of the Ayatollahs: Iran and the Islamic Revolution.* New York: Basic Books, 1986.

Bakhtiari, Bahman. "Parliamentary Elections in Iran." *Iranian Studies* 26, nos. 3–4 (1993): 375–88.

Brooks, Geraldine. *Nine Parts of Desire: The Hidden World of Islamic Women.* New York: Anchor Books, 1995.

Cassese, Antonio, ed. *The International Fight Against Torture.* Baden-Baden: Nomos, 1991.

Chang, Jung. *Wild Swans: Three Daughters of China.* New York: Anchor Books, 1991.

Claude, Richard Pierre, and Burns H. Weston, eds. *Human Rights in the World Community.* 2d ed. Philadelphia: University of Pennsylvania Press, 1992.

Cooper, Roger. *Death Plus Ten Years.* London: HarperCollins, 1993.

Dabashi, Hamid. "Re-Reading Reality: Kiarostami's *Through the Olive Trees* and the

Cultural Politics of a Post-Revolutionary Aesthetics." *Critique: Journal of Critical Studies of the Middle East* 79 (fall 1995): 63–89.

Dad, Babak. *Akharin Salam* (The last *Salam*). Tehran, 2000.

Darabi, Parvin, and Romin P. Thomson. *Rage Against the Veil: The Courageous Life and Death of an Islamic Dissident.* Amherst, N.Y.: Prometheus Books, 1999.

Darvish, Hasan. "Didari Kotah" (A brief encounter). *Ketab-e Noqteh* 2 (autumn 1977).

Democratic Society of Iranians in France. *Dar Rahruha-ye Khun* (In the labyrinth of blood). France, 1985.

Donnelly, Jack. *Universal Human Rights in Theory and Practice.* Ithaca: Cornell University Press, 1989.

———. *International Human Rights.* 2d ed. Boulder, Colo.: Westview Press, 1998.

Ebadi, Shirin. *Trarikhcheh va Asnad-e Hoquq-e Bashar dar Iran* (History and documentation of human rights in Iran). Tehran, 1994.

Eide, Asbjorn, et al., eds. *The Universal Declaration of Human Rights.* Oxford: Oxford University Press, 1996.

Esposito, John L. *Islam and Politics.* Syracuse, N.Y.: Syracuse University Press, 1984.

———. *The Islamic Threat: Myth or Reality?* New York: Oxford University Press, 1992.

Esposito, John L., ed. *Voices of Resurgent Islam.* New York: Oxford University Press, 1983.

Fakuhi, Nasser, et al. *Khat-e Qermez* (The Redline). Tehran, 1998.

Farhang, Mansour. "*Nazargah-e Do-sowyeh-ye* Khatami *dar Bareh-ye Azadi*" (Khatami's contorted view about liberty). *Elm va Jame'eh* 20 (September 1999).

———. " 'Spies' Under the Persian Rug." *Nation,* June 26, 2000

Farid, Mehrdad, ed. *Khamushi-ye Darya* (Darkness at sea). Tehran, 2000.

Feitlowitz, Marguerite. *A Lexicon of Terror: Argentina and the Legacies of Torture.* New York: Oxford University Press, 1998.

Fischer, Michael M. J., and Mehdi Abedi. *Debating Muslims: Cultural Dialogues in Postmodernity and Tradition.* Madison: University of Wisconsin Press, 1990.

Forsythe, David P. *The Internationalization of Human Rights.* Lexington: Lexington Books, 1991.

Ganji, Akbar. *Tarik-khaneh-ye Ashbah* (The dungeon of ghosts). Tehran, 1999.

———. *Naqdi Baraye Tamam-e Fosul* (A critique for all seasons). Tehran, 2000.

———. *Talaqi-ye Fashisti az Din va Hokumat* (The fascist interpretation of religion and government). Tehran, 2000.

Ghaffari, Reza. *Khaterat-e Yek Zendani az Zendanha-ye Jomhuri-e Islami* (Memoirs of a prisoner of Islamic Republic's prisons). Stockholm, 1998.

Goodwin, Jan. *Price of Honor: Muslim Women Lift the Veil of Silence on the Islamic World.* New York: Little, Brown, 1994.

Halliday, Fred. *Islam and the Myth of Confrontation: Religion and Politics in the Middle East.* London: I. B. Tauris, 1996.

Howard, Rhoda E. *Human Rights and the Search for Community.* Boulder, Colo.: Westview Press, 1995.

Human Rights Watch/Middle East. "Iran: Arrests of 'Loyal Opposition' Politicians." June 29, 1990.

———. *Power Versus Choice: Human Rights and Parliamentary Elections in the Islamic Republic of Iran.* New York, 1996.

———. *Iran: Religious and Ethnic Minorities, Discrimination in Law and Practice.* New York, 1997.

———. "*As Fragile as a Crystal Glass*": Press Freedom in Iran. New York, October 1999.

Iranian Human Rights Working Group. " 'Baha'is Have Rights Too . . .'—President Khatami." November 1999. <www.ihrwg.org>.

Islamic Prosecutor's Office of Tehran. *Karnameh-ye Siyah, Mavazeh va Amalkard-e Mo-nafeqin Pas Az Piruzi-ye Enqelab* (Black records: Position and practice of the *Mona-feqin* [Mojahedin] after the victory of the revolution), vol. 1. Tehran, 1983.

Jabbra, Joseph G., and Nancy W. Jabbra, eds. *Women and Development in the Middle East and North Africa.* Leiden: E. J. Brill, 1992.

Kadivar, Mohsen. *Nazariyyahha-ye Dowlat Dar Fiqh-e Shi'ah* (Theories of the state in Shiite jurisprudence). 3d ed. Tehran, 1999.

Kadivar, Zahra Rudi. *Baha-ye Azadi: Defa'iyyat-e Mohsen Kadivar dar Dadgah-e Vizhe-ye Ruhaniyyat* (Price of freedom: Mohsen Kadivar's defense in Special Court for Clergy). Tehran, 1999.

Karawan, Ibrahim A. " 'Re-Islamization Movement' According to Kepel: On Striking Back and Striking Out." *Contention* 2 (fall 1992).

Karimi-Hakkak, Ahmad. "A Storyteller and His Times: Ali-Akbar Sai'di Sirjani of Iran." *World Literature Today* 3 (summer 1994): 516–22.

Kar, Mehrangiz. *Hoquq-e Siasi-ye Zan-e Iran* (Political rights of Iranian women). Teh-ran, 1997.

Khatami, Muhammad. *Hope and Challenge: The Iranian President Speaks.* Binghamton, N.Y.: Institute of Global Cultural Studies, Binghamton University, 1997.

Kianush, Mahmud. ed., *Modern Persian Poetry.* Ware, Herts., U.K.: Rockingham Press, 1996.

Korey, William. *NGOs and the Universal Declaration of Human Rights: "A Curious Grape-vine."* New York: St. Martin's Press, 1998.

Lahiji, Abdolkarim. *Poluralism-e Siasi dar Jomhuri-ye Islami-ye Iran* (Political pluralism in the Islamic Republic of Iran). Paris, 2000.

Lauren, Paul Gordon. *The Evolution of International Human Rights: Visions Seen.* Phila-delphia: University of Pennsylvania Press, 1998.

Levin, Aryeh. "Habib Elghanayan: A Reflection of the Iranian Jewish Community." In *The History of Contemporary Iranian Jews.* Beverly Hills, Calif.: Center for Iranian Jewish Oral History, 1999.

Lindholm, Tore. "Response to Reza Afshari on Islamic Cultural Relativism in Human Rights Discourse." *Human Rights Quarterly* 16 (November 1994): 791–94.

Mahdi, Ali Akbar. *Farhang-e Irani, Jame'eh-ye Madani, va Daghdaghe-ye Demokr'asi* (Ira-nian culture, civil society, and concern for democracy). Toronto, 1998.

———. "The Student Movement in the Islamic Republic of Iran." *Journal of Iranian Research and Analysis* 15 (November 1999): 1–27.

Majid, Anouar. "The Politics of Feminism in Islam." *Signs: Journal of Women in Culture and Society* 23, no. 2 (1998): 321–61.

Mayer, Ann Elizabeth. *Islam and Human Rights, Tradition, and Politics.* 3d ed. Boulder, Colo.: Westview Press, 1999.

Mehrpur, Hossein. *Hoquq-e Bashar dar Asnad-e Binalmellali and Muzeh-e Jomhuri-ye Islami-ye Iran* (Human rights in international instruments and the position of the Islamic Republic of Iran). Tehran, 1995.

Merat, Zarir. "Pushing Back the Limits of the Possible: The Press in Iran." *Middle East Report,* fall 1999, 32–35.

Milani, Abbas. *Tales of Two Cities: A Persian Memoir.* New York: Kodansha Interna-tional, 1997.

Miller, Judith. *God Has Ninety-nine Names: Reporting from a Militant Middle East.* New York: Simon and Schuster, 1996.

Moghissi, Haideh. *Populism and Feminism in Iran.* New York: St. Martin Press, 1996.

Mohanty, Chandra Talpade, Ann Russo, and Lourdes Torres, eds. *Third World Women and the Politics of Feminism.* Bloomington and Indianapolis: Indiana University Press, 1991.

Moise, Edwin E. *Modern China: A History*. New York: Longman, 1994.

Mojahedin Organization. *Qatl-e Am-e Zendanian-e Siasi* (The massacre of political prisoners). 1999.

Mojtahed-e Shabestari, Muhammad. *Iman va Azadi* (Faith and freedom). Tehran, 1997.

Mokhtari, Muhammad. *Tamrin-e Modara: Bist Maqaleh dar Baz-khani-ye Farhang* (Practicing tolerance: Twenty articles on rereading of culture). Tehran, 1998.

Monshipouri, Mahmood, and Mokhtari, Shadi. "Islamism, Cultural Relativism, and Universal Rights." *Journal Of Iranian Research and Analysis* 16 (April 2000): 37–60.

Morgan, Robin, ed. *Sisterhood Is Global: The International Women's Movement Anthology*. New York: Anchor Books, 1984.

Mosteshar, Cherry. *Unveiled: One Woman's Nightmare in Iran*. New York: St. Martin's Press, 1997.

Muhammadi, Majid. *"Nowgarai-ye Dini va Tabu-ye Liberalism"* (Religious modernism and the taboo of liberalism). *Kiyan* 9 (August-September 1999).

Munson, Henry, Jr. *Islam and Revolution in the Middle East*. New Haven: Yale University Press, 1988.

Namvar, Bijan. *"Beh Taraj Rafteha"* (The plundered). *Par*, November 1999.

Noqrehkar, Masud. *Panchereh-ye Kuchak Sellul-e Man* (My small prison's window). Los Angeles, 1988.

Nuri, Abdollah. *Shukaran-e Eslah* (Hemlock for advocate of reform). Tehran, 1999.

Omid, Homa. *Islam and the Post-Revolutionary State in Iran*. New York: St. Martin's Press, 1994.

Oxford Amnesty Lectures 1993. *On Human Rights*. New York: Basic Books, 1993.

Paidar, Parvin. *Women and the Political Process in Twentieth-century Iran*. Cambridge: Cambridge University Press, 1995.

Parsipour, Shahrnush. *Khaterat-e Zendan* (The memoirs of prison). Stockholm, 1996.

Parvaresh, Nima. *Nabardi Nabarabar, Gozareshi az Haft Sal Zendan, 1361–1368* (An unequal battle: A report of seven-year imprisonment, 1983–1990). Paris, 1995.

Paya, A. *Zendan-e Towhidi* (Prison of monotheism). Germany, 1989.

Pollis, Adamantia. "Toward a New Universalism: Reconstruction and Dialogue," *Netherlands Quarterly of Human Rights*, 16 (1998).

Poya, Maryam. *Women, Work and Islamism: Ideology and Resistance in Iran*. London: Zed Books, 1999.

Qaderi, Ali. "Gozaresh-e Seminar-e Shenakht va Mabani-ye Hoquq-e Bashar" (Report on the seminar on understanding the fundamentals of human rights). *Majaleh-ye Siasat-e Khareji* (autumn 1991).

Raha, M. *Haqiqat-e Sadeh: Khaterati as Zendanha-ye Zanan-e Jomhuri-ye Islami* (Plain truths: Memoirs from women's prisons in the Islamic Republic). 3 vols. Germany, 1992–94.

Razaqi, Ahmad. *Awamel-e Fesad va Bad-hijabi* (The causes of [moral] corruption and improper *hijab*). Tehran: Islamic Cultural Propagation Organization, 1988.

Rejali, Darius M. *Torture and Modernity: Self, Society, and State in Modern Iran*. Boulder, Colo.: Westview Press, 1994.

Reza'i, Abdolali, and Abbas Abdi, eds. *Entekhab-e Now: Tahlilha-ye Jame'eh Shenasaneh az Waq'a-ye Dovvom Khordad* (New choice: Sociological analysis of the event of *Khordad* the second). Tehran, 1998.

Roohizadegan, Olya. *Olya's Story: A Survivor's Dramatic Account of the Persecution of Baha'is in Revolutionary Iran*. Oxford: Oneworld Publications, 1993.

Sarduzami, Akbar. *Gusha'ye az Rawayat-e Azam* (Azam's story). Denmark, n.d.

Schirazi, Asghar. *The Constitution of Iran: Politics and State in the Islamic Republic*. Translated by John O'Kane. London: I. B. Tauris, 1997.

Sciolino, Elaine. *Persian Mirrors: The Elusive Face of Iran.* New York: Free Press, 2000.

Shahidian, Hammed. "National and International Aspect of Feminist Movement: The Example of Iranian Revolution of 1978–79." *Critique: Journal of Critical Studies of Iran and the Middle East* 1 (spring 1993).

Soroudi, Sorour. "The Concept of Jewish Impurity and Its Reflection in Persian and Judeo-Persian Traditions," in *Irano-Judaica III: Studies Relating to Jewish Contact with Persian Culture Throughout the Ages,* ed. Shaul Shaked and Amnon Netzer. Jerusalem: Ben-Zvi Institute, 1994.

Steiner, Henry J., and Philip Alston, eds. *International Human Rights in Context.* Oxford: Oxford University Press, 1996.

Tachau, Frank, ed. *Political Elite and Political Development in the Middle East.* New York: John Wiley, 1975.

Tavakoli-Targhi, Mohamad. "Iranian Subjectivity and the De-recognition of Baha'is." Paper presented at the 1999 meeting of the Middle East Studies Association.

Tavassoli, Rushanak. "In a Cage as Large as Iran." *Nashriyyah-ya Hoquq-e Bashar,* 12, no. 35 (spring 1995): 19–23.

United Nations. Document E/CN.4/1984/28: "Report of the Secretary-General prepared pursuant to paragraph 4 of Commission on Human Rights resolution 1983/34 of 8 March 1983." February 29, 1984.

———. Document E/CN.4/1985/20: "Preliminary report by the Special Representative of the Commission, Mr. Andrés Aguilar, appointed pursuant to resolution 1984/54, on the human rights situation in the Islamic Republic of Iran." February 1, 1985.

———. Document E/CN.4/1985/NGO/29: "Written statement submitted by Amnesty International." February 20, 1985.

———. Document A/40/874: "Situation of human rights in the Islamic Republic of Iran, note by the Secretary-General." November 13, 1985.

———. Document A/C.3/40/13: "Statement of the Islamic Republic of Iran with regard to the recent proceedings of the 3rd Committee." December 4, 1985.

———. Document A/41/787: "Report on the situation of human rights in the Islamic Republic of Iran, prepared by the Special Rapporteur of the Commission on Human Rights." November 3, 1986.

———. Document E/CN.4/1987/23: "Report on the situation of human rights in the Islamic Republic of Iran by the Special Representative of the Commission on Human Rights." January 28, 1987.

———. Document A/42/648: "Interim report on the situation of human rights in the Islamic Republic of Iran, prepared by the Special Representative of the Commission on Human Rights." October 12, 1987.

———. Document E/CN.4/1988/24: "Report on the situation of human rights in the Islamic Republic of Iran by the Special Representative of the Commission on Human Rights." January 25, 1988.

———. Document A/43/705: "Interim report on the situation of human rights in the Islamic Republic of Iran, prepared by the Special Representative of the Commission on Human Rights." October 13, 1988.

———. Document E/CN.4/1989/26: "Report on the situation of human rights in the Islamic Republic of Iran, prepared by the Special Representative of the Commission on Human Rights." January 26, 1989.

———. Document A/44/153: "Letter dated 28 February 1989 from the Permanent Representative of the Islamic republic of Iran to the United Nations addressed to the Secretary-General." February 28, 1989.

———. Document A/44/620: "Interim report on the situation of human rights in the Islamic Republic of Iran, prepared by the Special Representative of the Commission on Human Rights." November 2, 1989.

———. Document E/CN.4/1990/24: "Report on the human rights situation in the Islamic Republic of Iran by the Special Representative of the Commission on Human Rights." February 12, 1990.

———. Document A/45/697: "Interim report on the situation of human rights in the Islamic Republic of Iran, prepared by the Special Representative of the Commission on Human Rights." November 6, 1990.

———. Document E/CN.4/1991/NGO/5: "Written statement, submitted by Amnesty International: Concerns human rights situation in the Islamic Republic of Iran." January 15, 1991.

———. Document E/CN.4/1991/35: "Report on human rights situation in the Islamic Republic of Iran by the Special Representative of the Commission on Human Rights." February 13, 1991.

———. Document E/CN.4/1992/34: "Excerpts from the UN Special Representative's report on human rights violations in Iran." January 2, 1992.

———. Document CCPR/C/28/add. 15: "Consideration of reports submitted by states parties under article 40 of the Covenant, Islamic Republic of Iran." May 22, 1992.

———. Document A/47/617: "Interim report on the situation of human rights in the Islamic Republic of Iran, prepared by the Special Representative of the Commission on Human Rights." November 13, 1992.

———. Document E/CN.4/1993/NGO/6: "Written Statement Submitted by Amnesty International to the Secretary-General." January 7, 1993.

———. Document E/CN.4/1993/41: "Final report on the situation of human rights in the Islamic Republic of Iran by the Special Representative of the Commission on Human Rights." January 28, 1993.

———. Document E/CN.4/1994/50: "Final report on the situation of human rights in the Islamic Republic of Iran prepared by the Special Representative of the Commission on Human Rights." February 2, 1994.

———. Document A/49/514: "Report of the Special Representative on the situation of human rights in the Islamic Republic of Iran." October 14, 1994.

———. Document A/49/514/add. 2: "Letter from the Permanent Representative of the Islamic Republic of Iran addressed to the Special Representative on the situation of human rights in the Islamic Republic of Iran." November 4, 1994.

———. Document E/CN.4/1995/55: "Report on the situation of human rights in the Islamic Republic of Iran, prepared by the Special Representative of the Commission on Human Rights." January 16, 1995.

———. Document E/CN.4/1996/95/add. 2: "Report submitted by Mr. Abdelfattah Amor, Special Rapporteur, in accordance with Commission on Human Rights resolution 1995/23." February 9, 1996.

———. Document E/CN.4/1996/39/add. 2: "Report of the Special Rapporteur on the promotion and protection of the right to freedom of opinion and expression, Mr. Abid Hussain." March 11, 1996.

———. Document E/CN.4/1996/59: "Report on the situation of human rights in the Islamic Republic of Iran, prepared by the Special Representative of the Commission on Human Rights." March 21, 1996.

———. Document A/51/479: "Interim report of the Special Representative on the situation of human rights in the Islamic Republic of Iran." October 11, 1996.

———. Document A/51/479/add. 1: "Situation of human rights in the Islamic republic of Iran, note by the Secretary-General." November 27, 1996.

———. Document E/CN.4/1997/63: "Report of the Special Representative on the Islamic Republic of Iran." April 9, 1997.

———. Document A/52/472: "Interim report on the situation of human rights in the Islamic Republic of Iran, prepared by the Special Representative of the Commission on Human Rights." October 15, 1997.

———. Document E/CN.4/1998/59: "Report on the situation of human rights in the Islamic Republic of Iran, prepared by the Special Representative of the Commission on Human Rights." January 28, 1998.

———. Document E/CN.4/1999/32: "Report on the situation of human rights in the Islamic Republic of Iran, submitted by the Special Representative of the Commission on Human Rights." December 28, 1998.

———. Document E/CN.4/1999/NGO/12: "Written statement submitted by the Bahaa'ii International Community, a non-governmental organization in special consultative status." January 29, 1999.

———. Document A/54/365: "Interim report on the situation of human rights in the Islamic Republic of Iran, prepared by the Special Representative of the Commission on Human Rights." September 21, 1999.

Iranian Newspapers and Journals

Andishah-ye Jame'eh, Arzesh, Azadegan, Bahar, Bayan, Chashmandaz, Elm va Jame'eh, Enqilab-e Islami, Ettela'at, Ettela'at (international), *Fath, Gardun, Goft-o-Gu, Iran, Iran-e Farda, Iran Times, Hamshahri, Hoquq va Ejtima, Jomhuri-ye Islami, Kayhan, Kayhan* (London), *Kayhan Farhangi, Ketab-e Noqteh, Khabar-Nama-ye Farhangi va Ejtema'i, Khordad, Kiyan, Majaleh-ye Siyasat-e Khareji, Mihan, Nashriyyah-ye Hoquq-e Bashar, Par, Payam-e Emruz, Resalat, Ruznameh-Zan, Sobh, Sobh-e Emruz, Tehran Times, Tous, Washington Iranians, Zanan.*

Index

Abdi, Abbas, 191
Abrahamian, Ervand, 87, 225
Adel Abad prison (Shiraz), 99
Afary, Janet, 134
Afkhami, Mahnaz, 250
Afshar, Haleh, 256, 261, 265
Agha-Jeri, Hashim, 245
Aguilar, Andrés, xxi; upholding universality, 84; denounced, 147
Ahmadi Khorassani, Nushin, 261, 266–67
Alizadeh, Parvaneh, xviii; on exhibitions of bodies, 36; on torture, 49; on prison officials and guards, 59; on religious rituals, 96
Allah-Karam, Hossein, 27, 213. See also *hizbollahis*
Amir-Entezam, Abbas, 53, 74, 81
Amnesty International: on right to life, 38–40; on torture, 55; on security of person, 61–64; on fair trial, 75; on dissident clerics, 224
Amor, Abdelfattah (UN Rapporteur), 83, 121, 126, 136, 137, 142, 144, 273
Ardabili, Abdolkarim Musavi (Ayatollah), 109, 115, 177, 186
Armenians: as protected minority (*dhimmis*), 130–34; political price of protection, 135–38; Islamic criteria limiting rights, 131; inequality and legal discriminations, 132–34; self-preservation, 134–35; considered *najes* (unclean), 136
Ash'ari, Ali Akbar, 274
Askaroladi, Habibollah, 238
Assembly of Leadership Experts (Majlis-e Khobregan-e Rahbari), 16, 17, 241–42
Assessment Council (Expediency Council), 20

Association of Combatant Clerics (Jame'eh-ye Ruhaniyyat-e Mobarez), 27, 237–38
Assyrians and Chaldeans: as protected minority (*dhimmis*), 130–34; political price of protection, 135–37; Islamic criteria limiting rights, 131; inequality and legal discriminations, 132–34; self-preservation, 134–35; considered *najes* (unclean), 136
Ayala Lasso, José, 272
Azad, F., xviii, on torture, 47–48; on babies in prison, 50; on religious rituals, 95–96
Azadi, Hamid, xviii; on torture as *ta'zir* (Islamic punishment), 49; views on reeducation in prison, 101–3

Badamchian, Assadollah, 238
Baha'is: considered *najes* (unclean) in prison, 51; Considered apostates, 119–20; religious reasons for persecution, 121; killing of leaders, 121–23; desecration of holy places and cemeteries, 124; denied legal protection, 124–25; condemned to civil death, 126; blamed for their own plight, 127; denied education, 127; Muslim Iranians' hostilities and indifference, 127–28; denied status of a religious minority, 156–58; demonized, 157–58. See also Roohizadegan
Bakhash, Shaul, 16
Bakhtiar, Shahpur, 42–43
Baluchis, 39. See also Sunni Muslims
Barazandeh, Hossein, 212
Basiji paramilitary forces, 26–28, 29, 63, 201
Bazargan, Mahdi, 16, 25–26, 70, 74, 77, 185, 235; See also Freedom Movement of Iran
Behbahani, Farhad, 78

Beheshti, Muhammad Hossein (Ayatollah), 16

Behruzi, Maryam, 262

Besharati, Ali Muhammad, 235, 270

Britain: Parliamentary Human Rights Group, 42

Brooks, Geraldine, 263

Burns, John, 135, 246

Burqani, Ahmad, 204, 209

China, 149, 292

Constitution of the Islamic Republic: Islamic qualifications, 16–17; amendments, 17. See also Guardian Council, Schirazi, velayat-e faqih

Cooper, Roger, 37, 61, 88, 93, 176–77

Copithorne, Maurice, xviii; on executions, 39–40; on assassinations abroad, 43; on torture, 55; on Islamic courts, 80; on "independent" judiciary, 82; on Baha'is, 126; on religious minorities, 144; on freedom of expression, 202, 211, 274; on dissident clerics, 227, 229; on political participation, 239, 241; on women, 254–55, 258, 270; on Islamic Human Rights Commission, 279

cultural authenticity, 8, 12, 292

cultural relativism, 3–4; its irrelevance, 10–11, 240, 290, 293–97

Darabi, Dr. Homa, 251, 271

digar andishan. See right to freedom of expression

Donnelly, Jack, 10, 264

drug traffickers: campaign against, 41, 179, 181

Ebadi, Shirin, 133–34, 257

Eliassi, Manuchehr, 135

Elqaniyan, Habib, 136

Esfandiari, Haleh, 254

Eshraqi, Morteza (Ayatollah), 109–10

Evin prison, 34, 73, 87, 101; massacre of 1988, 108; Galindo Pohl's visits, 175–77. See also Lajvardi

Executives of Constructions (Kargozaran-e Sazandegi), 243–44

extrajudicial killings. See right to freedom of expression, right to life

Fallahian, Ali, 26–27, 140, 213–14, 220; German warrant for his arrest, 44; discus-sion with Galindo Pohl, 166, 178. See also Intelligence Ministry

Feitlowitz, Marguerite, 292

Fisk, Robert, 286

Foruhar, Daryush, 211

Freedom Movement of Iran (Nehzat-e Azadi Iran), 235, 245. See also Bazargan

Galindo Pohl, Reynaldo, xviii; reports' structure, xxi–xxii; on right to life and executions, 38–40; on executions of drug traffickers, 41; on stoning, 42; on assassinations abroad, 43–44; on tor-ture, 52–53, 55; on fair trial, 74–78; on prison massacre, 116; on Baha'is, 125; on recognized religious minorities, 137; responding to Iranian charges, 155–56; on Islamic reformism, 159–61; visits to Tehran, 165; listening to official narrative, 166–67; receiving governmental "human rights" delegations, 169–71; frustration and resignation, 173, 183–84; on free-dom of expression, 186, 200–201; on freedom of association, 235; on elections, 237; on women, 84, 250, 253, 269; on UN monitoring, 273–74

Ganji, Akbar, 82, 191–92, 203, 206, 209, 212–14, 241, 281, 298

Ghaffari, Reza, xviii, on torture, 48, 112; on prison officials and guards, 59; on Hajji Rahmani, 94; on Islamic rituals in prisons, 100; on reeducation in prison, 103

Ghassemlu, Abdul Rahman, 39, 42. See also Kurds

Gohar Dasht prison, 109, 111

Golshiri, Hushang, 189, 302

Goodwin, Jan, 270

Guardian Council (Showra-ye Negahban), 19, 31, 206, 233, 236–37, 239–43, 245–46

Gust, Jens, 220. See also Sarkuhi

Hajjarian, Sa'id, 208

Halliday, Fred, 299

Haqani religious school, 213, 238

Hashimi, Fa'ezeh (Rafsanjani), 247, 265–66

Hashimi, Hadi, 228

Hashimi, Mahdi, 108

Henkin, Louis, 149

Hezbollahis (Ansar-e Hezbollah), 27–29, 63, 186, 194, 200–202, 209, 215, 241

Hicks, Elahé, 143. See also Human Rights Watch

hijab (Islamic dress code). *See* rights of women
Hoda'i, Manizheh, 90. See also *tawaban*
Hofer, Helmut, 61–62
Hosseini, Ghafar, 212
Hosseinian, Ruhollah, 213
Howard, Rhoda, 3, 10, 132, 298
Hozuri, Ali, 187
Human Rights Department of Foreign Ministry, 278–79
human rights discourse, xvi
human rights scholars, xvii, xviii
Human Rights Watch: on destruction of Kurdish villages, 39; on Islamic judiciary, 82; on Baha'is, 123; on Sunni Muslims, 130; on a visit to prison, 143; on *hezbollahi* vigilantes, 202; quoted by officials, 208; on Majlis elections, 239–40; on women, 264. *See also* Hicks, Megally
Hussain, Abid (UN Rapporteur), 200, 270, 273, 299

Imami, Sa'id, 189, 212, 215
Intelligence Ministry, 26, 211–13, 215–17, 246. *See also* Fallahian, Imami, Reyshahri
Iran-Iraq War: UN Resolution 598, 109
Islamic Cultural Propagation Organization, 132, 187
Islamic Human Rights Commission, 279–81
Islamic incantations and rituals in prison, 95–100. See also *tawaban*
Islamic Iran Partnership Front (Jebheh-ye Mosharekat-e Iran-e Islami), 243–44
Islamic Party of Labor (Hezb-e Islami-ye Kar), 244
Islamic punishments, 54–56, 178–80, 277; *hodud, qesas, ta'zir, diyat,* 68–69. *See also mofsed fel arz, mohareb,* right to a fair trial
Islamic radicals (Old Left), 190, 192–93
Islamic reformism (and reformists), 15, 190–91, 193, 203–4, 207–8, 215, 289, 294, 298–99. *See also* rights of women
Islamic Republic Party: assassination of leaders, 49
Islamic technobureaucrats, 24, 195
Islamization, 1, 3; injecting metaphysics into human rights, 4; creating the perfect human, 5, 192; imposing a binary vision, 9, 12, 19–20; views on women, 21; moral cleansing, 21; in prison, 83–86, 95–100; reeducation in prison's Amuzeshgah, 100–103; violating freedom of thought, 103;

violating women's rights, 253–61; failure, 298. *See also* Milani, prisons, *tawaban*

Jala'eipur, Hamid Reza, 210, 245
Jannati, Ayatollah Ahmad: discussion with Galindo Pohl, 166–80; defending *hezbollahi* vigilantes, 201; defending Guardian Council's exclusionary power, 242
Jewish Iranians: anti-Semitism, 45; as protected minority (*dhimmis*), 130–34; political price of protection, 135–38; Islamic criteria limiting rights, 131; inequality and legal discriminations, 132–34; self-preservation, 134–35; the case of the thirteen, 135, 137, 284; considered *najes* (unclean), 136

Kadivar, Mohsen, 229–31, 281
Kar, Mehrangiz, 256
Karbaschi, Gholam-Hossein, 243–44
Karrubi, Mahdi (Hojjat al-Islam), 238–39, 242
Khalili, Mohsen, 198
Khalkhali, Sadeq, 237
Khamenei, Ayatollah Ali: rejecting the Western notion of rights, 4; becoming the Supreme Leader, 17–18; supporting conservative candidates, 31, 240, 247; defining the Islamic Redline, 195–96, 208; lacking charisma, 205–6; not acceptable as a *marja-e taqlid,* 225; on elections, 240–41, 245–47
Kharrazi, Kamal, 283–85
Khatami, Muhammad (Hojjat al-Islam), 4, 6; becoming president, 29–31; disturbing the security apparatus, 31; on Baha'is, 128; the Do-e Khordad Movement, 203, 243; on extrajudicial killings, 212–13; attacking liberal Muslims, 301
Khatami, Muhammad Reza, 243, 246
Kho'iniha, Muhammad Musavi, 192–93, 202, 206, 212, 247
Khomeini, Ayatollah Ruhollah, 15, 17, 35; *fatva* on Islamic ordinances, 19–20; his adulation, 21; *fatvas* as laws, 76; *fatva* for the massacre of 1988, 115. See also *velayat-e faqih*
Kiarostami, Abbas, 196
Kooijmans, Peter H., 155
Kumaleh Organization, 39. *See also* Kurds
Kurds, 75, 156; Democratic Party of Ira-

Kurds (*continued*)
  nian Kurdestan (KDPI), 39. *See also* Sunni
  Muslims

Lahiji, Abdolkarim, 16, 81
Lajvardi, Assadollah, 36, 50; forcing recanta-
  tion, 87–90
Lashgari, Davoud, 110
Lauren, Paul Gordon, 7, 286
Lavasani, Muhammad Hossein, 154, 159, 170
Lukes, Steven, 301

Mahallati, Muhammad Ja'far, 115–16, 168
Mahrami, Zabihollah, 122–23. *See also*
  Baha'is
Majlis (parliament), 18; women deputies,
  256. *See also* right to political participation
Maleki, Muhammad Ali, 103
Manukian, Archbishop Ardak, 139
Ma'rufi, Abbas, 197, 201–2
Masjed-Jam'i, Ahmad, 202
Mayer, Ann Elizabeth, 16, 125–26
Megally, Hanny, 208. *See also* Human Rights
  Watch
Mehr, Haik Hovsepian, 133
Mehrpur, Hossein, 5, 6, 152, 164, 166, 180,
  253; an embarrassed cultural relativist,
  275–77; confirming past violations, 278
Mesbah Yazdi, Ayatollah, 248
Milani, Abbas, 84, 88, 125
Miller, Judith, 65
Mir'ala'i, Ahmad, 194, 212
Mir-Salim, Mostafa, 202
mofsed fel arz (one who corrupts the earth),
  33–34, 188
Moghiseh-ye, Shaikh Muhammad, 110–11
Mohajerani, Attaollah, 204, 209–10, 285
mohareb (warring against God), 32
Moise, Edwin, 292
Mojahedin Organization: armed resistance,
  23, 29, 96; in Iraq, 106, 109; massacred
  in prison, 109–13; a precondition for UN
  Special Representatives, 153–56; being
  portrayed as principal violators of human
  rights, 168–71. *See also* Rajavi
Mokhtari, Muhammad, 2, 195, 197, 211
Mola'i, Mehrdad, 286
monafeq (hypocrite), 9
Montazeri, Ashraf, 228
Montazeri, Hossein Ali (Ayatollah), 32, 108;
  improving prisons, 105; criticizing the
  massacre, 114; harassed, 227–29; on Nuri's

trial, 232; on *velayat-e faqih*, 241; criticizing
  the Guardian Council, 243; on human
  rights, 286
mortadd (apostate), 9, 140
Mossadeq, Ma'sumeh, 212
Mosteshar, Cherry, 66
Motahhari, Morteza (Ayatollah), 5, 6, 101,
  265
Mota'llefeh (amalgamation) Group, 238
Mottaki, Manuchehr, 166, 183
Movahedi Savuji, Ali, 260
Mykonos restaurant: assassinations in, 43–
  44, 212, 214, 220; official reactions to the
  German court, 44–45

Nabavi, Behzad, 193, 237
Nabavi, Sayyid Ibrahim, 207
Namvar, Bizhan, 144–45
Nateq, Homa, 261
Nateq-Nuri, Ali Akbar (Hojjat al-Islam), 31,
  197, 237
Nasseri, Syrous, 157, 162, 182
Nayeri, Ja'afar (Hojjat al-Islam): Inquisitor
  in prison massacre, 109
Nuri, Abdollah (Hojjat al-Islam), 116, 167,
  203, 208, 231–32, 241, 243–44, 258, 271,
  287

Office for Strengthening Solidarity (Daftar-e
  Tahkim-e Vahdad), 244
Organization of the Mojahedin of Islamic
  Revolution, 239

Pahlavan, Ghangiz, 301
Paidar, Parvin, 257
Parsipur, Shahrnush, xviii, 23; memoirs'
  significance, xix–xx; on executions, 36–
  37; witnessing torture, 47; tortured and
  pronounced *najes* (unclean), 51–52, 106;
  on prison officials and guards, 59–60; in
  the Islamic Court, 71; on *tawaban*, 89; on
  hijab, 93; on Islamists' fascination with
  sexuality, 93–94; on religious rituals, 97,
  99–100
Parvaresh, Nima, xviii; tortured, 48; in the
  Islamic Court, 71; on religious rituals, 96;
  on Mojahedin in prison, 106; on prison
  massacre, 108–11
Paya, A. (Parviz Ousiya), xviii, xix; description of prisons early in revolution, 33–34;
  on torture, 46; on prison guards, 57–

58; on due process of law, 69–70; on prisoners' religiosity, 85–86

Paykar Organization, 90

Pollis, Adamantia, 11

Poya, Maryam, 261

prisons: general description, 34–35, 104–5; Islamic *hijab* forced on women, 92–95, 106; improved conditions, 105–7. *See also* Evin, Gohar Dasht, Montazeri, Qezel Hesar, women

prison massacre: end of Montazeri's influence, 108; extended to the leftists, 110; sparing female leftists, 111; estimates, 113; Khomeini's *fatva*, 115; Khamenei's justification, 115. *See also* Mojahedin, Parvaresh, Raha

Protestants: unrecognized recent converts, 139; discrimination and prosecution, 140; targets of Intelligence Ministry, 140–41; murder of Dibaj, Mehr, Mikhaelian, 141–43

Puyandeh, Muhammad Ja'far, 197–98, 211

Qaderi, Ali, 7–8

Qezel Hesar prison, 87–88, 92, 96, 99, 105, 107. *See also* Rahmani

Qomi, Sayyad Hasan (Grand Ayatollah), 226

Rafsanjani, Ali Akbar Hashimi, xxi, 24, 31–32, 189, 192, 199, 214, 244, 247, 249, 276; protecting the two faces of the states, 24–25, 27–28, 202

Raha, M. (Monireh Baradaran), xviii, xix; tortured, 47–48; describing the *najes* category, 51; on prison officials and guards, 60; in Islamic Court, 71–73; on *tawaban*, 91–92; on religious rituals, 95, 99, 106–7; on preconditions for freedom, 107; road to freedom, 117–18

Rahbarpur, Gholam Hossein, 79–81, 216, 295

Rah-e Kargar Organization, xix, 92

Rahmani, Hajji Davoud, 48; forcing recantation, 87–90; forcing the black chador, 92–95; removed as warden, 105. *See also* Ghaffari, Parsipur

Rahnavard, Zahra, 261–62

Raja'i Khorassani, Sa'id: quoting Richard Falk, 148; criticizing the past, 278

Rajavi, Kazem, 42

Rajavi, Mas'ud, 153

Razini, Ali, 213

Rejali, Darius, 25

repentance. See *tawaban*

Revolutionary Guards, xx, 26, 28–29; arresting political activists, 34–35, 37, 59, 61; beating prisoners, 50

Reyshahri, Muhammad, 26, 108, 113, 116

Reza'i, Mohsen, 27–28, 63

Rezvan, Morteza, 128

rights of women: imposition of Islamic Family Law, 252–53; Islamic "feminists" fighting back, 254–60, 262; secularists, 21, 260–61; imposition of *hijab*, 251, 261–64; *hijab* as an enabling outfit, 262–63; *hijab* as a violation of freedom of conscience, 265; demonizing those who refuse to submit, 265–66; attacks on *bad-hijabi*, 268–71. *See also* Schirazi

right to a fair trial, 74–77; lack of due process of law, 69; the *mashkuk* category, 73; the case of Bazargan's associates, 77; the case of Zendehdel group, 79–80; the case of Amir-Entezam, 80–81; trials without defense lawyer, 179–80; the press cases, 209, 215. *See also* Parsipur, Parvaresh, and Raha, Yazdi, Rahbarpur, Galindo Pohl

right to freedom from torture: extracting confession, 47; lashing as *ta'zir* (Islamic punishment) 47, 49, 55, 296; stoning, 42, 55, 296–97; the *qapan* position, 48, 102; *dastgah*, 48; *najes* (unclean), 51; whipping in lieu of prayers, 112; during Khatami's presidency, 54; amputations, 54–55; official admission, 105; exposure in press, 208. See also Amnesty International, Copithorne, Galindo Pohl, Islamic punishment, Parsipur, *tawaban*

right to freedom of assembly and association, 235–36; the Article 10 Commission, 235, 243. *See also* Executives of Constructions, Islamic Iran Partnership Front, Islamic Party of Labor

right to freedom of expression and the press, 163; struggle of *digar andishan*, 9, 188, 193–95, 199, 211–15; Islamic Redline, 195–96, 199, 208; Press Law (and Court), 197–98, 200, 210, 215, 229, 248. *See also* Khamenei

right to freedom of thought, conscience, and religion. See Armenians, Assyrians, Baha'is, Chaldeans, Islamization, Jewish Iranians, Protestants, rights of women (*hijab*), *tawaban* right to life, 34–38; executions for moral crimes, 41; extrajudicial killings, 42–45. *See also* Baluchis, drug traffickers, Galindo Pohl, Kurds, *mofsed fel arz*, *mohareb*, prison massacre

right to political participation: extralegal exclusion, 233; formal exclusion, 235–37, 239; the 1992 Majlis elections, 237; the 1996 Majlis elections, 239; the 1997 presidential election, 31, 237, 241; the 1998 Assembly of Experts elections, 241–42; the 2000 Majlis elections, 244–49. *See also* Guardian Council; right to freedom of assembly and association

right to security of person: harassment in public and private houses, 64–65, 67; Ali Reza Farzaneh-Far's death, 66; harassment of secular women, 64–65

Robinson, Mary, 283

Roohizadegan, Olya, 120–21. *See also* Baha'is

Ruhani, Hossein Ahmadi. See *tawaban*

Ruhani, Muhammad Sadeq (Grand Ayatollah), 226

Safa'i, Yahya Rahim, 28

Sa'idi Sirjani, Ali Akbar, 217–19

Sane'i, Yusof (Ayatollah), 232

Sari'ol Qalam, Vahid, 90, 92. See also *tawaban*

Sarkuhi, Faraj, 219–24

Schirazi, Asghar, 19–20, 257

Sciolino, Elaine, 63, 205

secularism: praxis of life, 2, 253–54, 257–59; in defense of, 297–302

secularists, 13, 189, 194–98, 199. *See also* rights of women

Shabestari, Muhammad Mojtahid-e, 191

Shamlu, Ahmad, 22, 196

Shams ol-Va'ezin, Mashallah, 204–6, 210

shari'ah, 19, 255. *See also* Shiism, Schirazi

Shari'ati, Ali, 265–66

Shari'atmadari, Hossein, 27

Shari'atmadari, Muhammad Kazem (Grand Ayatollah), 225

Sherkat, Shahla, 255, 270

Shiism: its Imams, 14; its *marja-e taqlid* (source of emulation), 14, 206, 225; its *mojtahid* (Islamic jurists), 14, 275–77; its Imam Hossein, 15; its religious verbiage, 21; See also *velayat-e faqih*

Shirazi, Sayyad Muhammad (Grand Ayatollah), 226–27

Shuja'i, Zahra, 256

Society of Combatant Clerics (Majma-e Ruhaniyyun-e Mobarez), 238, 244–45

Soroudi, Sorour, 136

Sorush, Abdolkarim, 190–91, 298

Special Court of Clergy, 108, 209, 225–26, 228–32. *See also* Kadivar, Nuri

Special Representative of the Commission on Human Rights on Iran. *See* Aguilar, Copithorne, Galindo Pohl

stoning. *See* right to freedom from torture

Sunni Muslims: the case of Ali Mozaffarian, 76; the double jeopardy, 129; discrimination and persecution, 129–30. *See also* Baluchis, Kurds, Towfiq

Tafazzoli, Ahmad, 212

tahajom-e farhangi (cultural invasion), 187, 255

Taheri, Jalaledin (Ayatollah), 232

Talaqani, Azam, 245–46, 261

Talaqani, Mahmud (Ayatollah), 133

taqiyyah (dissimulation), 260

tawaban (repentant prisoners), 86; confession and recantation, 87–90; unrepentant leftists' view of, 91–92. *See also* Hoda'i, Islamization, Ruhani, H., Sari'ol Qalam

Towfiq, Sa'id, 130

Union of Journalists, 204

United Nations Commission on Human Rights, xvi, 4, 5, 148–49, 182, 273, 282

United Nations Human Rights Committee: receiving Iran's report, 150–51, 165

United Nations Special Procedure, xvii, 28–29

Universal Declaration of Human Rights, 4, 7, 288–89, 300–301

Urban disturbances: Islamabad, 62–63. *See also* right to security of person

velayat-e faqih, 15–16; in crises, 17–18; failure, 24–25, 30–32; under attack, 193, 199, 203, 206–7, 225, 227, 231, 239, 241, 248–49

Velayati, Ali Akbar, 29, 181–82

Writers' Association, 194

Yazdi, Ibrahim, 53, 245

Yazdi, Muhammad (Ayatollah), 151; on Islamic reformists, 31; on the Mykonos trial in Germany, 44; on Islamic judiciary,

76, 79–80, 115; on religious minorities, 137; discussion with Galindo Pohl, 177–78; denouncing liberal Muslims, 191, 208–9, 258. *See also* Sa'idi Sirjani, Sarkuhi, right to a fair trial

Zalzadeh, Ibrahim, 211
Zarif, Muhammad Javad, 142
Zebarjad, Farideh. *See* Sarkuhi

Zendehdel, H. *See* right to a fair trial
Zoroastrians: as protected minority (*dhimmis*), 130–34; objecting to being considered *dhimmis*, 132; political price of protection, 135–38; Islamic criteria limiting rights, 131; inequality and legal discriminations, 132–34; self-preservation, 134–35; considered *najes*, 136

Acknowledgments

Many friends and colleagues helped and encouraged me during the past four years writing this book. My affection and appreciation for Augustina Traver, Haleh Vaziri, Janet Afary, Mahmud Rafi, Mohammad F. Saidi, Howard Feingold, Gevork Haratoonian, Shaowen Wang, and Xiaohong Hu. I would like to acknowledge all those who have assisted in the publication of the book, in particular Patricia Reynolds Smith, Noreen O'Connor, Laurel Frydenborg, and the anonymous referees who provided constructive criticism. Bill Doorman read the entire manuscript and offered useful suggestions and much encouragement. I would like to pay special thanks to Mansour Farhang, who enthusiastically volunteered to read a much longer version when I did not feel it was ready for his critical eyes. For the next eighteen months, he read a few more drafts and offered valuable suggestions. I am also indebted to Ellen Skinner, friend and colleague at Pace University, who for the past fifteen years encouraged me in all of my research projects. I have been encouraged by Bert B. Lockwood, who unhesitantly published my articles in *Human Rights Quarterly*.

Above all, this book would not have been possible without Heideh Afshar, whose serene and delightful presence makes everything easy.